THE GRANDEST
MADISON
SQUARE
GARDEN

Art, Scandal, and Architecture
in Gilded Age New York

SUZANNE HINMAN

Syracuse University Press

The generous assistance of the following is gratefully acknowledged:

Furthermore:
a program of the J. M. Kaplan Fund

First Edition 2019
19 20 21 22 23 24   6 5 4 3 2 1

∞ The paper used in this publication meets the minimum requirements of the
American National Standard for Information Sciences—Permanence of Paper for
Printed Library Materials, ANSI Z39.48-1992.

For a listing of books published and distributed by Syracuse University Press,
visit www.press.syr.edu.

ISBN: 978-0-8156-1110-3 (hardcover)   978-0-8156-5485-8 (e-book)

Library of Congress Cataloging-in-Publication Control Number: 2019004384

Manufactured in the United States of America

In memory of those we lost that spring
Jean, Joe, and Kitty

Contents

List of Illustrations   ix

Acknowledgments   xiii

Prologue: *November 2, 1891*   1

Part One. On Madison Square: *July 1887*

1. The "Red-Haired Trial"   13
2. On Madison Square   27
3. A Practical Education   42
4. Enter Augustus Saint-Gaudens   50
5. Women, Horses, and a Curse?   66

Part Two. Building a Palace of Pleasure: *August 1889*

6. The Walls Come Down   89
7. Continental Influences   97
8. Laying Plans   104
9. In the Office and Out   113
10. The Walls Go Up   126
11. *Diana* Defrocked   136
12. Baked Earth   147
13. An Irksome Spring   157
14. Opening Night   169
15. More of the Pieces   179

Part Three. The Virgin and the Tower: *March 1891*

16. On the Model Stand   195

17. The Tower Rises   205

18. *Diana*, Doing and Making   212

19. Oriental Fantasies   219

20. The Virgin Installed   230

21. *Diana* Reigns   237

22. Up under the Stars   246

23. A Home in the White City   254

24. A Second *Diana*   267

25. Within the Tower   281

Part Four. Epilogue: *The Last of the Story*

26. *Diana* Redux   291

27. A Murder at the Garden   305

28. The Tower Falls   316

29. The Last of the Story   329

Notes   345

Selected Bibliography   427

Index   431

Illustrations

1. Madison Square, 1893 — 2
2. Madison Square Garden — 2
3. Map showing Madison Square, 1885 — 4
4. Broadway and Fifth Avenue, 1903 — 11
5. Stanford White — 14
6. Interior view of the Hoffman House Bar, 1890 — 40
7. Preliminary plan for Madison Square Garden, 1887 — 48
8. Augustus Saint-Gaudens, engagement portrait, 1875 — 51
9. Augusta Homer Saint-Gaudens, engagement portrait, 1875 — 57
10. *David Glasgow Farragut Monument*, 1877–80 — 65
11. Union Depot, Madison Square, 1857–71 — 69
12. *P. T. Barnum's Grand Roman Hippodrome*, ca. 1874 — 71
13. First Madison Square Garden, ca. 1880 — 77
14. Madison Square Garden arcade, ca. 1910 — 87
15. *Faith*, Giralda Tower, Cathedral of Seville — 93
16. *Diana*, Frederick MacMonnies, 1890 — 102
17. Preliminary sketch for Madison Square Garden tower figure — 108
18. *Mercury*, eighteenth century, after sixteenth-century model — 109
19. Floor plan, Madison Square Garden, 1891 — 110
20. Century Association Clubhouse front elevation, 1889 — 116
21. William Mead and Royal Cortissoz, ca. 1885 — 117
22. *Building Construction Details*, Madison Square Garden, 1891 — 131
23. Interior, Madison Square Garden Amphitheatre, 1890 — 133
24. *Diana the Huntress*, Jean-Antoine Houdon, 1790 — 139
25. *Diana Smiling*, Augustus Saint-Gaudens — 142
26. Davida Johnson Clark — 143

27. Madison Square Garden, Madison Avenue entrance, 1925 — 152

28. Madison Square Garden roofline belvederes, 1890 — 154

29. Madison Square Garden, Fourth Avenue entrance, ca. 1890 — 155

30. Augustus Saint-Gaudens with his life sculpture class — 161

31. *Proscenium Arch of the New Garden Theatre*, 1890 — 180

32. *At the Horse Show*, 1894 — 183

33. Madison Square Garden arcade — 189

34. Scene under the Madison Square Garden arcade, 1891 — 190

35. *Diana* on the tower of Madison Square Garden, ca. 1915 — 193

36. *With the Art Students*, 1895 — 199

37. *Davida Johnson Clark, Study for the Head of Diana*, ca. 1886 — 201

38. Model of *Diana*, Augustus Saint-Gaudens, ca. 1891 — 203

39. *Circe Drinking*, Ugo da Capri, sixteenth century — 204

40. Drawing of the Madison Square Garden Tower, 1891 — 208

41. First *Diana* at the W. H. Mullins foundry, 1891 — 217

42. Madison Square Garden Tower, ca. 1905 — 220

43. *Street Scene in Seville under the Shadow of the Giralda*, 1906 — 221

44. Sarah Bernhardt as "Cleopatra," 1891 — 225

45. *The Madison Square Garden's Weather Vane, the Huntress Diana*, 1891 — 233

46. *Created by St. Gaudens. Purified by St. Anthony Comstock*, 1906 — 240

47. *The Madison Square Roof Garden*, 1892 — 251

48. *World's Columbian Exposition: Court of Honor*, Chicago, 1893 — 263

49. *Reclining Nude Figure of a Girl*, Thomas Wilmer Dewing — 269

50. Model of the second *Diana*, 1891 — 273

51. Second *Diana* at the W. H. Mullins foundry, 1893 — 275

52. *Diana* on the Madison Square Garden tower, ca. 1912 — 279

53. *Chicago Fire-Burning of Cold Storage Warehouse—Worlds Fair*, 1893 — 285

54. *Diana Moves*, 1925 — 289

55. *Diana*, Augustus Saint-Gaudens, bronze reduction, 1889 — 292

56. *Diana*, Augustus Saint-Gaudens, bronze reduction, ca. 1894 — 295

57. *Diana of the Tower*, bronze reduction, cast 1899 — 298

58. *Diana of the Tower*, plaster bust, ca. 1907 — 302

59. Half-size *Diana* in Saint-Gaudens's Cornish studio — 303

60. *Scene of the Stanford White Murder Drama and the Chief Actors*, 1906   306

61. *Diana*, in the form of Stanford White shooting virgins, 1906   312

62. George Lewis "Tex" Rickard   319

63. *Demolition of Old Madison Square Garden*, 1925   328

64. *Progress Lighting the Way for Commerce*, 1900   331

65. Upper half of the first *Diana*, 1909   332

66. Head of *Progress Lighting the Way for Commerce*, 1900   333

67. *Diana Goes to Philadelphia*, 1932   337

68. The second *Diana* installed at the Philadelphia Museum of Art   339

Acknowledgments

WHEN RESEARCHING and writing over the course of twelve years, it is inevitable that names scribbled on scraps of paper or lost emails will vanish with time; staff at libraries, museums, and research institutions will change; and countless acts of kindness will go unremembered. It is my hope that those I have failed to acknowledge will forgive the oversight and will attribute it more to poor memory and the toll of time rather than a willful ignoring or ingratitude.

Among those who must be thanked are the many colleagues who generously shared their knowledge, including Curator Henry Duffy and retired Chief of Interpretation & Visitor Service Gregory Schwarz at the Saint-Gaudens National Historical Park, who first introduced me in 2007 to the wealth of nineteenth-century newspaper resources online; Thayer Tolles, Marica F. Vilcek Curator of American Paintings and Sculpture at the Metropolitan Museum of Art; John A. Ochsendorf, Professor of Architecture and Civil and Environmental Engineering at MIT and Director of the American Academy in Rome; Frederick MacMonnies biographer Mary Smart; Curator Michael O'Connor at the Enfield Shaker Museum for his steadfast early support; Elizabeth Wyckoff, Assistant Director for Curatorial and Education at the Davis Museum, Wellesley College; Kenneth Rower and the late sculptor Lawrence "Doobie" Nowlan Jr. for their technical expertise; Stanford White researcher Ron Rice; and Doug Richards for his supply of wonderful vintage postcards.

Also of primary importance and deserving of much gratitude are the dedicated staffs at a variety of additional research institutions, including Peter Carini, Dartmouth College Archivist; Morgan Swan and the staffs of Rauner Special Collections Library and Baker Library, Dartmouth College;

Janet Parks, Curator of Drawings and Archives at the Avery Architectural and Fine Arts Library, Columbia University; Susan K. Anderson, the Martha Hamilton Morris Archivist at the Philadelphia Museum of Art; New York Public Library; Patricia D. Klingenstein Library, New-York Historical Society; Metropolitan Museum of Art Archives; Archives of American Art, Smithsonian Institution; the Library of Congress, Manuscript Division; the New York Life Insurance Archives; and the Penrose Library, University of Denver.

My dauntless literary agent, Charlotte Raymond, deserves everlasting thanks for her continuing faith and support, while eagle-eyed editor Elizabeth B. Myers made the book so much better. At Syracuse University Press, the angelic acquisitions editor Alison Maura Shay, assistant editor Kelly Balenske, design specialist Lynn Wilcox, and marketing analyst Mona Hamlin have earned my gratitude for their knowledge, enthusiasm, and endless patience.

And never to be overlooked, sincerest thanks go to Barney Levitt and Tom Wilhelm, for their much valued advice and consent; son-in-law Michael Maher for technical assistance; Ben Chentnik, visual wizard and Creative Director of Lucid Prints; Eric J. Nordstrom of Building 51 / Urban Remains Chicago; Janet Stewart at Newsbank and Meghan Brown at Art Resource; Mark Coen, President of Page Belting Co. in Boscawen, New Hampshire, for information on Saint-Gaudens's Columbian medal; Jim from Carbonite who found my missing files and photos when my computer was mysteriously wiped clean; Char because I said I would; and the kind and caring staff at Dartmouth-Hitchcock Medical Center, who pulled me through two rounds of cancer during the course of the book and patiently let me blather on when I needed to.

And finally, but certainly not last, the home team, for their love and support, including dear sister Judith, brother Robert, and Jake and Laurel, Jessie and Mike, Claire and Seth, Ali and Nick, and all their bambini. And of course, my beloved husband Jeffrey, who made notes on every chapter, always had just the right idea, ever knew the right person to contact at Dartmouth, and endured twelve years of this.

THE GRANDEST
MADISON SQUARE GARDEN

Prologue

November 2, 1891

NEW YORK CITY, "the diamond stickpin on the shirtfront of America."[1] Thousands were beginning to fill Madison Square and the streets surrounding it, standing out in the crisp evening air on Fifth Avenue, on Broadway, and on Madison, crowding in front of Manhattan's finest hotels, celebrated restaurants, and exclusive shops, fingers pointing, mouths agape. Male and female, young and old, greenhorns off the boat and old Fifth Avenoodles—on that night New Yorkers of all sorts had come from all over the city and from the now-nearby suburbs as well, brought in by ferry and bridge, railroad, horse car, cable car, and elevated railway.

At seven o'clock a sharp flood of light illuminated the graceful arcade of roofed arches on Madison Avenue that had been built in the Italian Renaissance style. It was a new sort of walkway, the first in the city—one meant to welcome and to shelter. It was constructed, finally, after a year of wrangling with the city fathers, who feared such a place would surely become a haven for loose women and thieves.[2] Above the arches rose walls of shimmering buff-yellow brick, their lavish terra-cotta ornament visible in the reflected light. Let churches claim the sharp and unforgiving Gothic style, and financial institutions the staid and solid Greek and Roman columns. This Renaissance style—with its richly decorated loggias, niches, colonnades, balustrades, belvederes, and magnificent tower—was for pleasure, for sport, for the arts, for merrymaking and make-believe. The crowd waited, and then, suddenly, one hundred electric arc lights, eight thousand incandescent lights, and two of the world's most powerful searchlights bathed the new Madison Square Garden in a

1

1. Madison Square, New York, J. S. Johnston, 1893. The New York Public Library / Art Resource, NY.

2. Madison Square Garden, *The Arts* (Dec. 1928). Wikimedia Commons.

veritable pyramid of light. It was unlike anything ever seen in New York City—ever seen anywhere.[3]

"Nobly planned and admirably constructed,"[4] it was simply the largest building in the world devoted solely to extravagance, elegance, sawdust, and splendor, all whipped up and tossed together in the heart of America's Gilded Age and its golden city. Nowhere were the fruits of American expansion and industrialization more gleefully gathered or more lavishly celebrated than here in Manhattan. And how welcome was this night's celebration, a momentary break from the nearly crushing issues and worries of the day: a flood of immigration, labor union demands, domestic terrorism, political corruption, the overt display of wealth, recession, and a coming war half a world away.

•

The Garden claimed the northeast corner of Madison Square, taking up the full block between Madison and Fourth Avenues, East Twenty-Sixth and Twenty-Seventh Streets.[5] Over the previous year and a half, New Yorkers had flocked here to the horse show, the dog show, the flower show, the prizefights, the circus, and a hundred other events held in the Garden's vast oval arena. Finished the previous June, the Madison Square Garden Amphitheatre's gala 1890 opening was attended by Vanderbilts, Roosevelts, Belmonts, and all the rest of society. Three months later the lavishly decorated, 1,200-seat Garden Theatre premiered for light opera and romantic comedies, as did a gold-and-white Louis XVI–style concert hall that cleverly converted to an elegant ballroom to host the most lavish affair.

It was said that Gilded Age New Yorkers never did anything by half, and, at 93,000 square feet, the Garden could justifiably proclaim itself the largest and most magnificent interior space in the world, its facilities unequaled for colossal events of every type: national celebrations, athletic games, political conventions, musical performances, expositions, religious crusades, and trade fairs. But that night in November the crowds were there for a different reason, to dedicate and celebrate the Garden's soaring tower. Completed just weeks before, it was a fanciful creation in the style of Seville's Giralda, the Hispano-Moorish twelfth-century minaret that had been converted four hundred years later to a cathedral bell tower by the addition of 100 feet of Renaissance columned folderol.

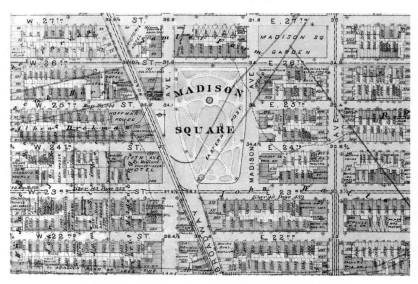

3. Madison Square, detail from the *Atlas of the City of New York*, 1885, E. Robinson. Lionel Pincus and Princess Firyal Map Division, The New York Public Library Digital Collections, image 1512161.

At 319 feet,[6] the Garden tower was the tallest spot in the tallest city, the loftiest tower in the United States, the second highest manmade structure in the country, second only to the Washington Monument. Madison Square Garden's fanciful, almost fairytale complex was nearly complete, and with the addition the next spring of its festive roof garden, it would quite simply be the most magnificent playland in the world.

Madison Square itself was quite the perfect location for this new palace of pleasure. For most of its life, the square had been known for its show of spectacle, its fast horses, a handful of mysterious murders, plenty of beautiful women, and some quite scandalous art. Formerly a drill field, a playing field, a suburban resort, and then a society enclave, Madison Square served as the city's premier shopping and amusement center, and New Yorkers had long been accustomed to coming to this part of town for their entertainment. Just up Broadway, from West Twenty-Third to Forty-Second Street, stood the best new theaters brightly lit by electric lamps— a Gay White Way,[7] as it was known. But just another block west of the square was Sixth Avenue, known as the wildest, wickedest street in the city for its concert saloons, all-night dance halls, French peep shows, high kickers, and various other forms of depravity, or so it was reported. The patch between Sixth and Seventh Avenues, from West Twenty-Fourth up to Thirtieth Street and beyond, was known to reformers as Satan's Circus, with some fifty-seven brothels within a matter of blocks.

•

This grand new Madison Square Garden, actually the second to stand on the spot, was very much the creation of Stanford White, soon to become America's most celebrated architect. He and his partners at McKim, Mead & White had solidified the Beaux-Arts style, borrowing from the past to combine the classical orders and monumental scale with richly colored marbles and carved fifteenth-century Italian ornament, murals and mosaics, light and air to create a grand new eclectic Renaissance Revival style. It was also very much an American style, sparking what some were calling an American renaissance that they believed would surely certify the country's role in the world as heir to the greatest of Western civilizations.

With nearly a thousand commissions eventually on the books, McKim, Mead & White would continue to shape the New York landscape, from the Washington Square Arch just nearing completion to the magnificent Pennsylvania Station, still more than a decade away. And far beyond the city, the firm would leave its mark across the country, designing countless fine homes, commercial buildings, libraries, museums, post offices, city halls, and state capitols, all culminating in a remodel of the White House and the National Mall in Washington, DC.

But on that night, all eyes were focused on the south side of the Garden. At exactly ten o'clock, the arc and incandescent lights on the amphitheater went out except for a few on the arcade, and then the Garden's new tower was lit with incendiary red fire. Boom, crash, boom again in a shower of color as bombs and rockets were set off over and over for a full hour.[8]

There among the smoke stood a tall redheaded man—hot, grimy, his bristling mustache singed black[9]—running among the installations, making certain every flare, bomb, skyrocket, and Roman candle was fired in its proper order. Stanford White had to fight hard for the Garden, even harder for this tower. Faced with ever-rising costs, more than $4 million for the project, the Madison Square Garden Company Building Committee had been ready to write off the tower, but White would not let that happen.[10]

Stanford White had always had a fondness for towers. He had built some fine ones, dating back to the 1876 Trinity Church in Boston. There had to be a tower—*that* he knew—and he begged, pleaded, harangued, and hounded until the money was raised. For nearly two years masons had been at work setting its two million creamy yellow bricks as the tower slowly reared its head over the roofs of the city. With all the cost cuts, it was not quite the fantastical tower he planned, but still, it was d-mned impressive.

No doubt prominent that evening were members of the Madison Square Garden Company Board of Directors. Led by its president, legendary banker and financier J. Pierpont Morgan, the board was composed of old and new money, railway presidents, industrialists, bankers, men from the California gold fields, financiers, and speculators—all among the richest men in the country and leading figures of what White's old friend Mark Twain had dubbed the "Gilded Age."[11]

Men whose money and power allowed them to live like princes had paid for this palace, for the boxes and promenades to show off their wives, daughters, and horses. But the pleasures of the Garden were not strictly for the rich. Anyone with the price of a ticket was admitted—the new middle class, the office and factory managers, the engineers, the salesmen and clerks, typewriters and seamstresses, in fact, any soul searching for some amusement when the day's work was done. It was they and their families who would have to fill the thousands of seats. The Garden was not just for a few—it would belong to all New Yorkers, and beyond—for it would capture the imagination of the entire country.

•

Finally, the smoke cleared away and the tower was lit up again as it would be every night there was a concert, play, performance, prizefight, or extravaganza of some sort. One after another each set of lights came on until all of the 1,300 were ablaze. The second Edison searchlight, mounted on a trolley at the highest set of open arches, ran around on rails at nearly

300 feet, shining out for a distance of three miles, picking out the Statue of Liberty and ships in the harbor.

Dark again at eleven o'clock, just the red lights on the tower illuminating its seven upper floors of private apartments and five columned loggias, cupolas, and lanterns, one set on top of the other and each serving as an outlook over the city. The bombs and rockets started up again, seen from as far away as Staten Island. Then all the lights went dark except for those on the tower, which would burn until midnight.

Twenty-five cents would buy a thirty-second elevator ride nearly to the tower's top for a stunning view never before seen by the human eye. Earlier on that opening day, some ten thousand visitors had paid their quarter for that view across the great expanse of the city. To the north lay Central Park, the Harlem River, and the Palisades above Yonkers; to the east, the silvery East River, Queens, and the great sandy stretch of Long Island; south was Brooklyn and its great bridge, Staten Island, and the New Jersey shore; then finally to the west, the Hudson River and the rolling green of the Jersey hills.[12]

The next evening, election night, the tower's great searchlight would be put to a unique purpose by arrangement with the *New York Herald*, signaling the results of the election for governor of New York State to homes in the city and beyond. Stanford White was so pleased with the idea that in the midst of the opening festivities he climbed to the searchlight's platform to make certain that the mechanics were well prepared to handle the telegraphic returns. If the Democratic candidate were in the lead, they were set to pedal the light around to the east, to the west if it were the Republican, and to the south toward the offices of the *Herald* if the results were unclear. The newspaper suggested that its readers cut out this information and paste it in their hats for handy reference, and the next night, when the great magnesium light swung around the tower to flash out news of the Democratic victory, there would be a roar of applause in the city like the roar of the sea.[13]

•

On the afternoon of November 1, 1891, another crowd had gathered in the streets, more gentlemen than ladies and many well equipped with field glasses. The newspapers had made it known that the huge sculpture topping the tower's bullet-headed arched lantern of steel and iron would finally be unveiled, that it would be a figure of the Roman goddess Diana, and that her costume might be skimpier than imagined.[14]

After her very dramatic unveiling, to be discussed further in greater detail, came a murmur and then a gasp from the crowd. There, standing on one tiptoe was a gilded copper statue of Diana, Virgin Goddess of the Chase, Goddess of the Moon, and sister to Apollo of the Sun, reigning nude except for a flying drape wound under her breasts and over one shoulder. Not tucked away in a gallery or museum, but "stepping out freely and fearlessly into the grey air"[15] for all to see, her golden limbs shining against the darkening sky—the first sculpture to ever be so illuminated by electricity.

This astounding yet very elegant figure had been created by the man who was quite likely America's finest sculptor, Augustus Saint-Gaudens. He had studied the great figural works of Greece, Rome, and the Renaissance and then transformed them through his own modern eye, setting a new standard and a new direction for American sculpture. His *Farragut Monument*, dedicated ten years earlier, stood nearby in Madison Square. There followed some of his greatest public pieces—the *Standing Lincoln* in Chicago, *The Puritan* in Springfield, Massachusetts, the *Adams Memorial* in Washington, DC—all, like the *Farragut*, done in collaboration with Saint-Gaudens's dearest friend, Stanford White, who helped pick the sites and designed the settings and the bases. It had been fifteen years since their first job together working on the Trinity Church in Boston, and now, once more, here on Madison Square.

How did Saint-Gaudens come to choose this particular goddess in this state of undress? There had been some very recent rumors that the figure would be something quite different and far more modest. But this decidedly unclothed *Diana* stood poised on her left foot, her right leg bent back, her bow drawn, arrow held in place. *Diana of the Crosswinds* she had been named, her arrow pointing directly into the wind. She was a wind vane, but one "before which all other weathercocks pale and dwindle" gushed the *New York Times*.[16] Achingly beautiful, her slim, almost boyish young body—18 feet tall of gilded, hammered copper—turned readily in the light breeze. Yet she would soon come to be replaced on the tower by an even lovelier version and then reign over the glorious Chicago World's Fair—until quite mysteriously disappearing!

•

But on the night of the tower's dedication, while a shower of fire whirled about her head and red and blue fires burned at her feet, *Diana's* sculptor likely stood with the members of the board and city officials, watching the ceremonies with perhaps some pride and yet a good bit of unease. It was said that there was not a man in the city with warmer friends than Augustus Saint-Gaudens,[17] with his honesty and utter lack of affectation. But there was nothing he liked less than attention. And he was still recovering from the terrible error made at the foundry in Ohio where *Diana* was cast, where they had run the mounting pole through the heel of her foot instead of the toe.[18]

Perhaps off to one side stood a cluster of men and women dressed with a certain Bohemian flair. They might have been the chums and colleagues of the sculptor and the architect from their days in Paris, or Saint-Gaudens's studio in Rome, or from one of their private clubs that kept their membership secret, reserving special apartments for their "physiological explorations," as one member described them.[19] It was mostly painters who made up Saint-Gaudens's and White's circle of friends—men like Thomas Wilmer Dewing, Louis Comfort Tiffany, William Merritt Chase, and John Singer Sargent. Madison Square had always been friendly to artists—just two blocks away stood the National Academy of Design—and there were art dealers, galleries, and art supply stores scattered around the square and the neighborhood.

This artistic group might have also included some of the best-known female models of the day, of which more than a few would later claim *Diana's* lithe figure as their own. Although there were rumors, there was little chance that the sculptor's wife, Augusta Homer Saint-Gaudens, then in her forties, would have been the inspiration for the sculpture.

Perhaps a rather striking young woman stood just a little farther off, one who spoke with a Swedish accent. Davida, as she was called, claimed the sculptor's heart and his second son as her own. Most definitely absent was Evelyn Nesbit, Stanford White's famed lover, who would one day be blamed as the cause of his death here at the Garden. Years later some would suggest she surely was Saint-Gaudens's model, but on that night, she was just a six-year-old in Tarentum, Pennsylvania, still at her mother's knee.

No doubt out in the streets, clasping thin wraps against the chill, stood hundreds if not thousands of other young women, immigrant or native, from foreign lands or farms and mill towns around the country. Some dreamed desperately of fame on the stage; of love, marriage, wealth, security, or any reasonable combination thereof, while others more independent of spirit—bachelor girls they called them—sought respectable occupations or perhaps even professions to support themselves. But there must have been more than a few among them who wondered, perhaps with some fear mixed with a bit of delight, whether someday they too might find themselves standing in a sculptor's studio or in a classroom full of art students, dropping a robe to pose in the toot-and-scramble.[20]

•

While Stanford White's reputation with the female sex was well known, it was not just young, slim, innocent women who appealed to him. Life is often more complicated than that, as was his relationship with Augustus Saint-Gaudens. Stan and Gus loved their work, their wives, their sons, their mistresses, their assorted friends, and each other. Some may have known the more hidden details of Stanford White's life, the things that went on in his various hideaways, like the special apartment within *Diana*'s tower, draped in leopard skin and golden damask and filled with fresh orchids.[21] But it was not until America's most famous architect was brutally murdered in an act of passion—here in the shadow of *Diana*'s tower—that the more shocking allegations were screamed out in newspaper headlines worldwide, although the full nature of the crime of the century would remain hidden.

It had been quite the journey to this golden virgin goddess twirling about the tallest tower. The story of *Diana* and the grandest Madison Square Garden has remained a tale largely untold, and on that November night in 1891 the story was still far from over.

PART ONE
On Madison Square

July 1887

*The brightest, prettiest, and
liveliest spot in the great city.*[1]

4. Broadway and Fifth Avenue north from Twenty-Third Street, George P. Hall &
Son, 1903. The New York Public Library / Art Resource, NY.

1

The "Red-Haired Trial"

A JULY MORNING, 1887. Reform Democrat Grover Cleveland was in the White House, while monopolies and trusts controlled the treasure that rolled in from the Pennsylvania oil fields and the California gold fields, the steel mills that forged the track and the railroads that hauled it east, the financiers who kept the wheels rolling and the banks that were stuffed full. Princes of capitalism preached a Gospel of Wealth that dictated the right to be rich, and labor struck for an unlikely eight-hour day. Bombs were thrown in American cities and anarchists were hung, while Pinkerton men slyly stroked their mustaches in the shadows.

Earmuffs and fire escapes were patented that year, Sherlock Holmes first appeared in print, Thomas Edison invented the motor-driven phonograph, Verdi's "Othello" premiered, the first New York social register was printed, gambler-gunman "Doc" Holiday died of tuberculosis, and the Wild West passed into myth.

And at nine o'clock in the morning it was already steaming in Manhattan. There, at the very southern tip of the island where the city first began, where a Wickquasgeck trail became a Dutch cow path, became Broad Wagon Way, became the Broad Way, became the greatest thoroughfare in America. Where an old wooden stockade became a Wall Street where the moneymaking heart of the city would remain. There were more than one million people on the island of Manhattan in 1887, where millionaires were now too numerous to be counted. New York, the gilded city, was not quite yet the financial and cultural center of the world but near to it.

On the third block of Broadway up from Battery Park, a tall, strongly built man in a white summer suit might have just hopped off one of those

5. Stanford White.
Aline and Eero Saa-
rinen Papers, 1906–77,
Archives of Ameri-
can Art, Smithsonian
Institution.

rail-run horse cars. Thirty-three years old, with long legs and broad shoulders, he was built more like a heavyweight fighter than the city's view of
an aesthete. With arms swinging, steps short and quick, body bent forward, he was all energy in an almost childlike way. "Fuzz-Buzz" some
called him, for his cropped tawny red hair that bristled up almost straight
and for the fire in his tail.[1] The "red-haired trial" was another soubriquet
well-earned in some circles.[2]

His palest-of-pale skin was covered with freckles, and he was not
quite what was called handsome—but that fiercely thick red mustache
and a certain look in his light eyes drew others right in. Over 6 feet tall
in his boot heels when most men were slighter, Stanford White was hard
to miss, barreling along at his usual sixty miles an hour with those short,
girlish steps,[3] laughing, talking, waving his hands, rushing somewhere

to meet some fellows, catch a show, design a building, or plan a parade. As Paul R. Baker, White's principal biographer, has described him, he was "a man of enormous appetites, hungry for excitement, delighting in the unconventional and in shocking others."[4]

Down Broadway he would charge, along the row of narrow old stone and cast-iron-front buildings crowded in from the boom of the 1850s when the rush to build commercial demanded height and speed. There at the corner of Broadway and Tin Pot Alley, just a block south of Wall Street and Trinity Church's towering steeple, at number 57, on the top floor just above the Pinkerton Detective Agency, sat the offices of McKim, Mead & White, architects.

Stanford White had no time for the creaky metal-cage elevator added for the ease of the firm's more decorous clients. Up the five flights of treadbare stairs he would race, bursting through the book-filled reception room. Swish, bang. He would shoot through the outer double swing doors into the main drafting room, past the dozen or so drafting tables and the seventy-some men intent over their pencils and T squares, past the plaster casts of classical ornament, Venetian wrought iron, the odds, ends, rough sketches, and finished drawings that covered the walls. Swish, bang. Through the leather-covered swinging doors that connected to the "holy of holies," the drafting rooms reserved for White, his two partners, and their assistants. And woe to anyone foolish enough to stand behind those swinging doors when White was on the premises.[5]

•

Reinvention could have been Stanford White's middle name if he had time to bother with one. A life of privilege might have been claimed for him, but in truth he was born November 9, 1853, in a rented house on East Thirteenth Street and grew up in a middle-class neighborhood of brick and brownstone houses that perched precariously just east of the Irish and just north of Little Germany and the Bowery's dance halls and cheap saloons.

White told most people that he attended private schools and was taught by tutors, but it was actually public Grammar School 35 on West Thirteenth Street where he seemed to have ignored penmanship and spelling—barely managing a rushed scrawl and spelling words as he pleased.

At home, however, there were plenty of books and copies of famous paintings, great ideas and the names of important men his father surely knew.

White's late father, Richard Grant White, was as tall and redheaded as his son. Polished and literate, vain and obstinate, and always short of cash, "big Papa" roiled bitter over his reduced circumstances and the life that should have been his had his father not lost the family's modest fortune when he failed to replace his clipper ships with steamers. Although a well-known if not notoriously critical reviewer of music, art, and drama for the *Morning Courier* and the *New-York Enquirer* and the author of some 750 articles and books, including twelve annotated volumes of Shakespeare's plays, Richard White also moonlighted as a clerk in the New York City Customs House, "ever weary of the grind."[6]

The elder White had possessed a fine library, including a collection of illustrated erotica, until financial woes forced him to sell at public auction in 1870. There was talk that Richard had kept a secret, second family, or perhaps just a lover of uncertain gender,[7] which may have explained his constant shortness of funds. With a particular irony, Stanford White may well have been certain that his own life would be quite different from his father's social striving, endless debts, long-suffering wife, yet ever-continuing pursuit of pleasure.

White's "darling Mommie," Alexina Black Mease White but better known as Nina, came from a Charleston, South Carolina, family, although she was born in New York City. She too felt the slight of fortune and the stain of a middle-class life after losing a plantation promised to her by a family friend, or perhaps it was a bachelor cousin. The stories differed. In later years when her hair stayed dark, she wore a gray wig so that people would not suppose she was common enough to dye her hair.[8]

Nina and Richard married in 1850. Their first child, Richard Mansfield White, known as Richie, was born in 1851, a querulous, troublesome disappointment. Stanford was the second son, born three years later and named for a piano dealer friend of his parents, or possibly a great uncle. Nina always indulged him, always forgave him, and they were exceedingly close, exchanging intimate and affectionate letters. She called him Stannie; as a grown man, his wife and a few friends and lovers would spell it with a *y*.

•

It was an excellent partnership—Stanford White, Charles Follen McKim, and William Rutherford Mead—and an exceedingly successful one. After only seven years together, they had more than two hundred projects finished or on the boards, racking up a total of $4.5 million in commissions. They were acknowledged not only as the preeminent firm in American architecture but as the most stylish. No other firm in New York could keep up among the great wave of public monuments, mansions, office buildings, country cottages, churches, seaside casinos, yachts, and a parlor car or two that needed to be designed.

Most of their clients were rich, looking to demonstrate not only their wealth and power but their exceedingly good taste. The men at McKim, Mead & White knew how to cherry-pick two thousand years of architectural history to create what was needed and more. White had had a weakness for French Gothic and Romanesque, McKim for Roman Empire and American colonial; both were fascinated by the Renaissance—Italian, Spanish, and French. But while they may have spoken classical and Renaissance, their technology was up-to-the-minute, their materials—including colored marbles and terra cotta—were often new and innovative, the work of their carefully chosen craftsmen and vendors was very fine, and their attention to interior design was unmatched.

Aside from his drawing skills, Stanford White possessed the imagination, style, and hot-headed energy that had quickly made McKim, Mead & White so successful. Clients looked to White for rich materials and vibrant color, along with gorgeous detail, often supplied by the antique bits and bibelots he had bought up in Europe to finish off the most brilliantly decorated clubroom or drawing room.

Deliberate and reserved yet genial, blandy, baldy, blarney[9] Charles "Charley" McKim was born outside Philadelphia, in Chester County, Pennsylvania. There his father, James Miller McKim, a Presbyterian minister and abolitionist organizer, and his Quaker mother, Sarah Speakman McKim, were devoted to the antislavery movement, with his sister married to a son of William Lloyd Garrison, the prominent and radical abolitionist. He had the École des Beaux-Arts training, historical knowledge, faultless taste, and patience to organize and create some of McKim, Mead

& White's greatest public projects. While White produced a multitude of buildings that were graceful, charming, and filled with exuberant detail, McKim built a few in the grand manner—logical, austere, and sober, but with a truly noble quality.

William Rutherford "Dummy" Mead,[10] handsome, good-humored, frank, level-headed, and tight-lipped around his ever-present cigar, was born to an artistic and intellectual family in Brattleboro, Vermont. His father, Larkin Goldsmith Mead, was a lawyer, while his mother, Mary Jane Noyes, was the sister of utopian socialist and free love advocate John H. Noyes and first cousin to President Rutherford Hayes. His older brother, Larkin Jr., was a well-known sculptor, and an older sister was married to influential writer William Dean Howells. It was his knowledge of scientific construction, obtained during a year in an engineer's office, that the partners claimed helped to keep their buildings standing upright.

Mead also had the needed business sense to keep the firm running smoothly. Lumbering around rather like a friendly bear, he oversaw the mechanics of the office, the bankbooks, the writing of checks, and the handing out of pay envelopes on Saturday afternoons, while claiming to spend most of his time keeping his two partners from making fools of themselves, rather like the cartoon their friend Augustus Saint-Gaudens had drawn showing Mead struggling mightily to control two contrary kites labeled "McKim" and "White."[11]

•

There was a great deal of building going on in the late 1880s as fashionable New York continued to move uptown, with many of McKim, Mead & White's projects in a revival of the classically derived Italian Renaissance. The firm had been working in the style for the previous five years, ever since their reputation-making Villard Houses on Madison between East Fiftieth and Fifty-First, and on through to the Boston Public Library currently on McKim's drawing board.

The office itself was part schoolroom, part salon, part circus. Almost anyone might drop by—artists, critics, editors, and an opera star or two. In the midst of the chaos, Stanford White would work quickly with pencil and pastels on colored paper, sketching out his ideas as they came to him, rubbing in or scrubbing out with his silk handkerchief, whistling bits of *Don Giovanni*, calling out for something or someone, or just adding an opinion to the chatter in the office. White always had an opinion. Whether the subject was pictures, jewelry, rugs, lamps, book covers, the draft-gear of a freight train, fishing or canoeing, he would soon take the lead, his strong voice rising over all like the wail of a bagpipe.[12] To friends and colleagues he seemed "a prophet of taste, gorgeously endowed with an appreciation of beautiful things, with a priest-like enthusiasm for them, he could not let others rest until they had shared his enjoyment."[13]

McKim, Mead & White's clients were not typically members of old New York society—the "Knickerbockers" of the Schuyler, Van Rensselaer, Stuyvesant, De Peyster, and Beekman ilk were passing from the scene like the triceratops. They clung to their 1830s Greek Revivals, 1850s Italianates, 1860s Gothic Revivals, and the mansarded 1870s Second Empire row and townhouses in now-dull and dingy brick and brownstone that lined the streets around Washington Square and up Fifth Avenue to Gramercy Park and even as far as Madison Square. Nor was it likely that their clients were the very social Vanderbilts, Oelrichses, or the Fishes. These families tended to prefer the designs of Richard Morris Hunt, America's first graduate of the Paris École des Beaux-Arts, or his protégé, George B. Post, who built them sixteenth-century-style chateaux in the manner of French nobility. Clients were more likely to be Villards or Tiffanys or Goelets—the more newly *riche* entrepreneurs and socially ambitious whose fathers had known rough work or stood behind mercantile counters but now ran railroads or ruled as merchant princes. It would not be until after McKim, Mead & White's success with Madison Square Garden and other high-profile projects in the 1890s that more of the society crowd would find their way to the firm.

•

It was in July 1887 that McKim, Mead & White received the news of a tremendous commission for a new Madison Square Garden,[14] intended to become the most magnificent amusement place in the world. After due consideration, William R. Ware,[15] founder of America's first program in architecture in 1868 at the fledgling Massachusetts Institute of Technology and eminent professor at Columbia University, had selected the firm's design for a new Garden to be erected at the site of the current hall, at the northeast corner of Madison Square.

There had been a very real need in the city for a suitably grand structure to serve a panoply of purposes, including conventions, exhibitions, meetings, and revivals. The city had lost its bid to host the 1888 Democratic National Convention to St. Louis simply because there had been no suitable venue. An equally grand center for amusement and entertainment was also desired by many for concerts, theater, and athletic competitions, not solely for the rich but a palace of pleasure for everyone.

The new Garden complex, expected to cost $1 million, was planned to include a vast amphitheater able to seat up to eighteen thousand for sporting events, exhibitions, and conventions along with a wonderful and "almost fearful"[16] agglomeration of attractions, as the *Brooklyn Eagle* observed, including a concert hall, an opera house, the largest ballroom in New York, a summer and winter roof garden, restaurant, studios, art gallery, supper rooms, beer saloon, flower market, an arcade with thirty shops, street stalls, a basement exhibition hall for livestock, stables for 450 horses, Turkish baths, an aquarium, bowling alleys, billiard parlor, shooting galleries, and bachelor apartments.

The newspapers had been very quiet as to which firms had been in the running to build the new Madison Square Garden, a project that came with a hefty architect's commission of $75,000. According to a story widely published in June 1887, six different architects had submitted designs in a supposedly blind competition, but none were rumored to have been up to the mark.[17] Planning the Garden was an exceedingly complex problem, as the *New York Times* had pointed out. With such a grand array of requirements and logistics, the paper rather boldly suggested that ordinary New Yorkers should have a say in the plan, for it was certain that if the selected architect carried it out to public satisfaction, "he will likely be famous for all time."[18]

What the *Times* did not know was that McKim, Mead & White had already been judged the victor. Apparently the Madison Square Garden Company had asked all involved parties to keep mum, for there was no official mention of the award until mid-September, and the plans would not be published until the first of November 1887 in *Harper's Weekly*.[19]

•

Was there a great whoop from Stanford White's small office, a shout of "bully, just bully," as was his habit when something especially pleased him, and the popping of champagne corks? Although the firm had never built an amphitheater, nor even a large-scale theater, the award of this grand commission had likely not come as much of a surprise to White. He had been involved almost from the beginning, when the idea of a new Garden was first floated, and he had been working night and day on the firm's proposal.[20]

Despite its name, the original and present Madison Square Garden, owned by the New York and Harlem Railroad Company and hence the Vanderbilt family, was a firetrap—a grimy, drafty, patched-up old shell that had long been sliding into disrepair and had been condemned after a dreadful disaster there in 1880. Boxing "demonstrations" by "Professor" John L. Sullivan were the major attraction, except in November when the Garden was taken over by a very different crowd. The National Horse Show began there in 1883 and had quickly become the first significant event of the social season, held about a week before the opening of the opera at the new Metropolitan House.

With most of the town overtaken by equine fever, officers of the National Horse Show Association of America realized the need to secure their venue. Several attempts to purchase the old Garden were made but without success. Finally, in December 1886 the Garden and the thirty-four city lots it covered were provisionally sold to one of their own, James E. Woodward, president of the Hanover Bank, for $1 million, while Vanderbilt's Harlem Railroad took a mortgage of $600,000.[21]

In the spring of 1887, the newly formed Madison Square Garden Company floated a capital stock issue to purchase the site for $1.5 million, promising the public to build a new and splendid structure forever dedicated to public amusement and exhibition. Woodward, a founding member of the board, transferred the deed to the property. J. P. Morgan bought three thousand shares of the $1.5 million capital stock offering and was named president of the company. Wall Street broker William F. Wharton bought an even larger number of shares and was soon made managing vice president.[22]

The remainder of the appointed directors of the board were a mixture of longtime members of the horsey set and new money millionaires, including Alfred P. Darling, proprietor of the stylish Fifth Avenue Hotel on the west side of Madison Square; the aforementioned banker and horse breeder James T. Woodward, who inherited a fortune made selling textiles to the Confederate army; Darius Ogden Mills, a former bank clerk who went west and opened his own bank among the California gold fields; Charles Crocker, an upstate dry goods clerk who also made good out west and became president of the Southern Pacific Railroad; bankers Charles Lanier and George S. Bowdoin; attorney for the company and well-known judge of fine horseflesh, W. C. Gulliver; Adrien Iselin, banker, railroad and mining magnate, and head of one of New York's most socially prominent families; Cornelius Fellowes, broker and president of the National Horse Show; and Edward Dean Adams, president of the Niagara Falls Power Company, for whom Stanford White designed an estate on the New Jersey shore.

Others who would soon become involved in the Madison Square Garden project included William Waldorf Astor, great-grandson of founding patriarch John Jacob Astor and manager of the family's immense fortune; Scottish-born steel magnate Andrew Carnegie; Hiram Hitchcock, Darling's partner in the Fifth Avenue Hotel; Herman Oelrichs, shipping heir and widely known as one of the handsomest men in New York; James Stillman, Texas land and railroad owner whose two daughters both married Rockefellers; James T. Hyde, founding father of the National Horse Show; yachtsman and wine merchant Francis P. Osborn; C. C. Baldwin, president of the Louisville and Nashville Railroad Company; T. W. Pearsall, vice president of the International and Great Northern Railway; horse breeder Joseph Agostini; and Wall Street broker H. I. Nicholas.

•

Around five o'clock in the evening, Stanford White would usually summon one of the office boys to take his private correspondence, quickly dictating notes in reply to invitations to dinner, the theater, and more personal affairs. "You got that?" he would bark at the office boy around seven, finishing his last letter but still shouting instructions as he stepped through the front door and clattered down the stairs.[23]

From the office, White would typically run for the Sixth Avenue elevated train that would carry him some three miles uptown to a small rented brownstone at 56 West Twentieth Street. In 1887, he and Elizabeth "Bessie" Smith White had been married just three years. They were first introduced in 1880 by partner Charles McKim, who brought White fifty miles east to Smithtown, on the north shore of Long Island, to meet Judge John Lawrence Smith and Sarah Nicoll Clinch Smith's prodigious clan. McKim's old roommate from Harvard, Prescott Hall Butler, had married the eldest sister among the thirteen siblings, and McKim, who was designing a house for the newlyweds, came out often.

There had been something of a flirtation between Bessie and Kimmie, as she called him, and they remained devoted friends for life. But in those days McKim was a rather melancholy divorced man of thirty-three with a young daughter his ex-wife kept from him, hardly the appropriate partner for an energetic seventeen-year-old who loved clam-digging and baking ginger cookies. So he talked up his younger partner, and eventually Stanford White was invited to call.[24]

In 1880 White was an attractive man in his late twenties with good prospects, but he had not made much progress finding a suitable wife. He had briefly paid court to the wealthy Sara Delano, whose family had an estate near his aunt in upstate New York. The attentions of the "red-haired trial," decidedly not of their sort, caused Sara's family to have her shipped off to China. A Roosevelt cousin named James was a far more welcome suitor and suitable mate for Miss Delano, whose son Franklin would become the thirty-second president of the United States. But a relative recalled many years later that Sara loved only one man, and that was Stanford White.[25]

Upon hearing of Charles McKim's marital troubles, White had written to his friend the sculptor Augustus Saint-Gaudens, "Damn strong-minded women, say I. I tell you. You no catchee me marry!"[26] But on his first visit to the Smith family home, White was impressed by Bessie's remarkable ability to both sing and whistle at the same time.[27] Bessie had spied him through a keyhole and longed to run her hand over his stand-up red hair.[28] In spite of her placid, forthright ways, and her talent for milking cows and shearing sheep, Bessie's tall, full figure, strong features, expressive dark eyes, and exceedingly impressive inheritance turned a few heads.[29]

Following a lengthy, long-distance, on-and-off courtship, they were secretly engaged in the spring of 1883 after White wrote his "puss" from an adventurous trip with Gus Saint-Gaudens to New Mexico, assuring Bessie that she would surely be along on his next trip out west.[30] It was on the train to New Mexico that White explained the reason for his idiotic smiles, finally confessing to Saint-Gaudens that he had been courting Bessie Smith for the past three years and was now relieved that his troubles were all over, to which Saint-Gaudens answered after a preliminary dance around the car that "au contraire, they have just begun."[31] White showed Saint-Gaudens a picture of Bessie, whom he had pronounced very, very lovely. White was pleased with the thought that Bessie was so different from Saint-Gaudens's "cross-grained clothes rack of a frau."[32] In truth, however, the Saint thought Bessie cold and tight-lipped.[33]

Six months later the engagement was formally announced by the happy parents, and Stanford White and Bessie Smith were married with all due solemnity on February 7, 1884, at the Episcopal Church of the Heavenly Rest uptown on Fifth Avenue.

Augustus Saint-Gaudens presented the wedding couple with a very fine white-marble low relief of Bessie White with a bouquet of roses in her left hand, her right lifting her wedding veil away from her face. He had dropped all paying commissions to work on it as a gift to the groom and as a way to pay back loans White had made during the trip west.[34] But there had been a bit of a rift over it. It was Saint-Gaudens's habit to create bas-reliefs in stone or bronze of good friends and family, but perhaps not so surprisingly he had some difficulty rendering Bessie. One day after studying the clay model in the studio, White cried out, "Oh, Gus, that's rotten!" Saint-Gaudens retorted by smashing it to the floor.[35] White was always quick and certain in his judgments, and Saint-Gaudens, with his temper, was equally swift to deal with an affront. Later, however, Saint-Gaudens redid the piece, and White designed an elaborate Renaissance-style gilt-wood frame for it.

After a brief trip to Saint Augustine, Florida, came a six-month honeymoon trip to Europe that White spent scooping up art and antiques for himself and for his clients. When they returned in September 1884, Saint-Gaudens and McKim were waiting at the dock, and Saint-Gaudens noted—perhaps due to an expectant, prematernal glow—that Bessie looked quite pretty and less hard than he had recalled. And having White back in town "was like champagne" to him.[36]

The newlyweds soon rented the small brownstone on Twentieth Street, and in December 1884 they welcomed Richard Grant White, named for his paternal grandfather. White was the proud possessor of a son and "hair . . . certainly the most beautiful baby ever born, but o Lord how he can holler!"[37] But the next summer, during a visit to Smithtown, the baby—only seven months and seventeen days old—died suddenly of cholera and was buried in the Smith family plot.

•

Bessie White's promised inheritance came not from her blue-blooded ancestors, including two mayors of New York City,[38] but from a great-uncle by marriage, Alexander Turney Stewart, better known as A. T. Stewart and everywhere known as one of the richest men in America. A Protestant from the north of Ireland, he first came to New York in 1818, where he met Cornelia Mitchell Clinch—Bessie White's grandmother's sister—while attending church. He returned to Ireland for five years, but in 1823 came back with a respectable inheritance and a stock of Belfast laces and linens that he used to open a store across from city hall and to marry Cornelia.

With the novelty of set and uniform prices, special reduction sales, handsome salesmen, and a general catering to the ladies, his business flourished. In 1848 he opened the city's first luxury dry goods establishment and the nation's first department store on Broadway, a block from city hall. The seemingly aristocratic façade reflected the century's first wave of Italian Renaissance Revival style that had arrived by way of London's elegant new men's clubs.[39] Stewart eventually moved uptown in 1862, opening the immense Palace of Trade at Broadway and Ninth that filled a full city block and in its day was the largest iron-frame commercial building in the world.[40] After his passing, and then that of his widow—the richest single woman in America—as well as a series of endless lawsuits, Bessie White inherited $100,000 and the promise of additional funds and properties after the passing of her mother, who was the recipient of $250,000 outright and an estimated near $5 million of the residual of the estate.[41]

If the summer of 1887 were an ordinary one, Bessie White would have been out in the country, while Stanford White, like most other husbands of the upper-middle class, would try to manage weekend visits. But in July 1887 Bessie White was seven months pregnant and, despite the crushing heat of the city, had chosen to remain in town.

•

Perhaps that evening Stanford White decided the commission award called for a night out, some "bumming 'round town,"[42] as he put it. White always tried to dress like a gentleman, in a well-cut coat, high stand-up collar, and bright-colored silk shirt and tie. As soon as he was able he began spending enormous sums on his wardrobe, ordering suits from Hill Brothers in London, gloves and cravats from the best boutique in Paris, and silk shirts from Kaskel & Kaskel haberdashers just off Madison Square.[43] But he dressed as quickly as he did everything else, and his fine suits were always rumpled and wrinkled. Once he famously appeared very late for a dinner party at Mrs. Hermann Oelrichs's magnificent Fifth Avenue home and slipped into his seat while everyone else was halfway through the meal, wearing a dinner jacket thrown over his morning trousers and shirt. "It never takes me more than five minutes to dress," he boasted. "So I should imagine," Mrs. Oelrichs replied, rather coldly.[44]

2

On Madison Square

PERHAPS THAT EVENING IN JULY 1887, Stanford White would have stridden from his home down on West Twentieth Street to the corner, turned left at Fifth Avenue—the most fashionable promenade in town— and joined the throngs up another three blocks and beyond, past stylish clubs, galleries, hotels, haberdashery, and some of the grandest homes in America.

Not even the most jaded New Yorker could help but be impressed by these mansions built to match the bank accounts and social aspirations of a new American nobility of bankers, industrialists, merchants, inventors, and entrepreneurs who emerged unscathed from the Civil War. Even before the war, the newly *riche* from the California gold fields, the Pennsylvania oil fields, the steel mills, and the railroads had joined some of the older money and begun moving up Fifth Avenue. By the late 1880s those grand chateauesque mansions extended up to "Vanderbilt Row" at Central Park and beyond, with the avenue still the city's most stylish address.

•

At Fifth Avenue and Twenty-First Street stood the Union Club, oldest in the city and probably the richest, most exclusive men's club in the world. It was here on its palatial steps that White's friend and client James Gordon Bennett Jr., *New York Herald* editor and publisher, was once horsewhipped by his fiancée's brother after drunkenly urinating in the parlor fireplace, or perhaps it was the grand piano at the family's New Year's party.[1]

After another blow-up at the most exclusive club in Newport, Rhode Island, Bennett resigned his membership and vowed to build a rival clubhouse. His awarding of the commission in 1879 to the newly formed McKim, Mead & White partnership for the Newport Casino—with its café, restaurant, ballroom theater, piazza for music and dancing, shops, offices, and newly fashionable tennis courts—did much to associate the firm with money, style, and pleasure from the first, as well as provide bona fides for the Madison Square Garden project.

Two more blocks up, at the corner of Fifth Avenue and Twenty-Third and almost to the square, the edge of which was visible a block to the east, remained one of the last old private mansions—William C. Schermerhorn's old Parisian-style home at number 49—which suffered to find itself adjoining on Twenty-Third the tourist-favored Eden Musée Waxworks and Chamber of Horrors.[2] Once the height of fashionable living, the fine old Madison Square mansions now continued to give way to shops, theaters, stables, churches, and various establishments of lesser repute.

A little further west down Twenty-Third and just across Sixth Avenue stood Koster & Bial's Music Hall, a popular "concert saloon," which simply described a place where patrons heard music while drinking beer. The music hall had also been in trouble and closed since February 1887 due to numerous violations of the excise and amusement laws, along with complaints about lewd women from the priest at the nearby St. Vincent de Paul Church. Another troublesome issue was the music hall's desecration of the Sabbath by remaining open for business on Sundays. Following a series of police raids, other concert halls had also been charged, including the old Madison Square Garden, and Sunday entertainments not fully sacred in nature would not be judged fully legal for decades.[3]

Koster & Bial's rather novel layout—a row of exclusive boxes, and then above them a promenade level with tables and chairs where beer, champagne, and food were served—may well have been an important influence on White's plan for the new Garden, along with the discovery that food and liquid refreshments were far more profitable than admission tickets. Koster & Bial's had tried to evade city laws forbidding the sale of food and drink in theaters by tearing out the proscenium stage and its curtain in favor of a simple platform with a backdrop,[4] another feature that would be adopted in the Garden Amphitheatre.

Between East Twenty-Third and Twenty-Fourth Streets, Fifth Avenue collides with Broadway, which in the 1880s was the main business artery of the city and the most crowded thoroughfare in America, jammed from sunrise to sunset with more than twenty thousand vehicles a day. Horse-drawn streetcars and double-decker omnibuses brought workers and shoppers in from the outskirts, and two-wheeled carts and lumbering four-wheeled express wagons hauled goods up from the warehouses downtown, while smart carriages paraded past more of the city's finest mercantile establishments, hotels, theaters, and restaurants.

•

A lush six-plus acre urban park, Madison Square ran then, as now, south to north from East Twenty-Third Street to Twenty-Sixth, from Fifth Avenue on the west to Madison Avenue on the east. Noble old oaks, elms, and sycamores shaded its curving walkways, and flowers bloomed thickly in their beds, creating a woodsy oasis amid a haze of late nineteenth-century wooden poles with their telegraph, telephone, and electrical wires.

Old Glory flew from the tops of the buildings, their sides covered with painted ads for mustard plasters and patent medicines. Those horsecars and omnibuses, delivery wagons, hansom cabs, hackney coaches, traps, four-wheelers, four-in-hand carriages, and coupés for hire jockeyed with private landaus, victorias, phaetons, broughams, tandems, and dog carts that clattered around the park with horns, gongs, and whistles blaring. The crush of traffic, both horse-drawn and on foot, was under the direction of a tall policeman, a member of the dandy "Broadway Squad," each well over 6 feet and giant in build, who would direct traffic with a rattan stick like a bandmaster conducting a symphony. As for the thousands of pounds of manure, estimated at ten pounds per day per horse, and the gallons of horse urine in the streets, they were more or less the facts of life.[5]

It was said that all of New York came together at Madison Square, and if one stood there long enough, they just might meet everybody in the world: sober bankers and solid clubmen in top hats, jaded members of the artsy crowd and gawking out-of-towners, politicos and princes, sporting gents and sharpies, shopkeepers and salesmen, cyclists and boxers, messenger boys and maids with baby carriages, peddlers with puppies and schoolboys on roller skates, streetwalkers and Johnnies, young dudes and society doyennes all on parade. While fashionable hotels, restaurants, and theaters lined the west side, on the other three sides the elegant old townhouses and mansions were still interspersed with tasteful commercial establishments. All in all, Madison Square was widely known as the brightest, prettiest, and liveliest spot in the great city.[6]

•

Madison Square had always had a certain sporting air to it, back to the very beginning when it was still a swampy hunting ground far north of the town, fed by a meandering Cedar Creek that filled a pond and then ran all the way to the East River. Apparently of little value, 30 acres just to the west of what was to become the square was granted in 1670 to Solomon Peters, a "free Negro" and perhaps servant to the English Governor Francis Lovelace, Nieu Amsterdam having been seized from the Dutch six years before and renamed in honor of the future King James II, Duke of York.

The spot also seems to have early had the calling of a public space and was so designated in 1686 by the first city charter. In 1703 the square's western boundary was set when a road that became known as Blooming-dale, and eventually upper Broadway, was cut through to the countryside of Bloemendael, the "Vale of Flowers" as the Dutch called it, with its tidy hamlets, pretty farms, and country residences. In 1803 most of the land was converted to the Parade, a 244-acre drilling field devoted to training the New York State Militia.

Five years later an imposing stone and brick arsenal was constructed adjoining the field to the southwest as protection from the British who threatened to invade the city during the War of 1812. After the American victory in 1814, the Parade's size was reduced to 89 acres, and in 1824 the arsenal barracks were converted to the New York House of Refuge of the Society for the Reformation of Juvenile Delinquents, the first such institution in America devoted solely to the care of youthful miscreants, including six wretched girls and three ragged boys.[7] In the spring of 1839 a fire broke out in a nearby workshop and spread to the House of Refuge, destroying it in the midst of a riotous battle between volunteer firemen and visiting gang members from the notorious Five Points district as they fought for cherries off the trees behind the building.

•

In 1716 Solomon Peters's widow sold her land to the Horn family, who established wagon-building and wheel-making shops where the Bloomingdale Road joined Love Lane and the Eastern Post Road that ran up to the village of East Harlem and then by ferry to what became the post road to Boston.[8] On the spot where the very exclusive Union Club would later be ensconced sat John Horn's Buck Horn Tavern, marked by a pair of huge antlers hung over its entrance. In 1783 Horn's tavern hosted General George Washington and later served as a stagecoach stop on the post road, although its large horse shed and its broad oak and elm–sheltered verandas attracted horse-trotting enthusiasts from the city as well as inbound travelers.

But the city plan devised in 1811 by the Commission on Streets and Roads was based on cost and use rather than the aesthetic, and it decreed that the downtown's northern environs would be divided up into a regular grid of twelve north-south avenues and 155 east-west streets from Fourteenth Street up. When Twenty-Second Street was cut through in 1826, the militia moved south to Washington Square, the old tavern was torn down, and the farmhouse of Horn's granddaughter Margaret Mildeberger was moved to the newly formed corner of Fifth and Twenty-Third. When Fifth Avenue was cut through in 1839, Corporal William Thompson of the militia acquired the farmhouse and renamed it Thompson's Roadhouse at the Sign of the Buck-Horn. Under the corporal's genial management, the little yellow tavern became a special favorite among the horsey crowd, who would end a ride in the country with a visit to the corporal's barroom and a sip of his special reserve under the long, low slanting roof, "always trim as a lady's boudoir."[9]

The windows of the roadhouse faced the park, where some of the fashionable young sportsmen and outdoor enthusiasts played a kind of rounders, a children's version of English cricket but with more batting, running, and tossing. In 1844 the post road that traversed the square was closed off, and the following year some of the young men organized the Knickerbocker Base Ball and Social Club to encourage open-air exercise. On a vacant sandlot at Twenty-Seventh and Madison, or perhaps it was an open spot at Broadway and Twenty-Second, they refined what came to be known as the "New York game." One member, volunteer fireman Alexander J. Cartwright, worked out new rules, with flat stone bases set out in the shape of a diamond, three strikes allotted per player, and three outs to each side.[10]

As the city grew around it, the now-drained open acreage was gradually reduced, with the gamers moving to Hoboken, New Jersey. In 1847 the land was set aside as a park by the city's Common Council in memory of James Madison, fourth president of United States, who—in his eighties—had faded away that summer and was found dead sitting in front of his uneaten breakfast tray. The city also contributed $2,000 for leveling and seeding what had become a rocky cow pasture. Corporal Thompson renamed his tavern the Madison Cottage, and Madison Street, which had been cut through in the 1820s, was rechristened an avenue and extended north beyond the square to Forty-Second Street.

Greened and enclosed by a low black iron fence, the park formally opened as Madison Square on May 10, 1847, within its present four blocks. As the population of New York reached more than half a million, the city continued to creep northward, lapping around its edges, and in the name of continuing progress the Madison Cottage was razed in 1852.

•

Sporting fellows looking for something novel found it the following spring when Franconi's Hippodrome rose on the very same spot in only twenty-five days. It was erected by a partnership of circus and equestrian showmen in the style of the Cirque des Champs-Élysées in Paris, a huge arena and track that showcased daring equestrian display and grand military pageants.[11]

The New York version of a hippodrome (*hippo* as in Greek for "horse," *drome* as in "track") was the idea of grocer-turned-impresario Avery Smith and equestrian star Seth B. Howe.[12] Forming a syndicate of fellow performers and investors, they engaged Henri Franconi, who had the year before managed the London Hippodrome, to once more stage spectacular re-creations of the great Egyptian, Greek and Roman games, gladiatorial combats, and chariot races, this time in New York City.

Franconi's Hippodrome, built at an astounding cost of $200,000, was a 20-foot-high, two-story red-brick-walled building 350 by 200 feet, with a tent-like roof of 90,000 square feet of canvas spread over a vast arena. There was seating for about six thousand spectators and room for another three thousand standees. Inside, races took place on a 40-foot-wide, 1/6 of a mile track, with circus acts performing in the infield amid fountains and huge vases of flowers brilliantly lit by one thousand gaslights.[13]

The "Hip" lasted just two spring-and-summer seasons, 1853 and 1854. While some argued it had always been intended merely as a temporary amusement, there were troubles from opening day when a wild stampede for seats ensued and many were knocked down in the crush. The site continued to advertise sensational and heart-stopping exhibitions of derring-do twice daily, designed to excite rather than delight, scolded the *Times*, which decried the liberal supply of groggeries inside and out and declared the whole place injurious to public morals. A chastened management tried to go higher-toned with grand pageants, a historical spectacle in the style of Louis XIV "as performed before three queens," a grand fete procession in honor of the goddess Ceres, and the addition of 150 ladies in the corps de ballet.

But on June 24, 1853, one of the ballet girls was fatally burned when her thin gauze dress caught fire from a lighted candle as she climbed up from an underground passage during a performance of "The Fêtes at Versailles."[14] Then on July 3 one of the young women riding the hurdle race had her saddle slip and was whirled around the entire course at breakneck speed, still clinging to the reins and saddle.[15] "What imaginable pleasure could possibly be extracted from unnatural contortions and useless risks?" asked the newspapers.[16] But still, Madison Square had been marked as the place where beauty and pleasure might be celebrated, with danger and death just a step away.

•

Despite the shocking events at the Hippodrome, 1850s Madison Square was on the verge of becoming not merely respectable but a desirable place to live, an island of calm and elegance between urban chaos and rural disarray. South of the square, New York City was bustling, busy, crime-ridden, and full of immigrants—Germans, Irish, and newly urban American bumpkins who had fled failing farms and now crowded into rooming houses and tenements. Hardly better, to the north of Madison Square still lay open pasture, and amid the stagnant pools and garbage-strewn shanty towns stood livestock pens and slaughterhouses, while wild bullocks knocked down and maimed citizens in the streets. The Common Council was finally forced to forbid cattle drives south of Thirty-Fourth Street during daylight hours, and it bumped the horse and cattle market traditionally held on the grounds of the Madison Cottage far uptown to the wilds of Forty-Second Street.[17]

Society's drive northward in the 1850s could not be stopped, and Madison Square's horsemen and livery stables would soon make way as rows of solid, Italianate brick and brownstones began crowding them out. They rose four and five stories high, complete with the city's first indoor water closets—although this convenience was widely attacked as both unsanitary and immoral.[18] Following their society congregants came the churches, most notably the 1853 Madison Square Presbyterian Church in highly respectable English Gothic style on the east side of the square at Twenty-Fourth, and shortly after the Gothic Trinity Chapel on West Twenty-Fifth, an uptown satellite of Trinity Church. Among the well-known residents of the square were the Roosevelts and their son Teddy at 28 East Twentieth and the Joneses at 14 West Twenty-Third—the very ones with whom one must have kept up— and parents of Edith Jones, who married Teddy Wharton of Boston in 1886 at that Trinity Chapel.

•

Just across Twenty-Third Street at Fifth Avenue stood the Fifth Avenue Hotel, one of Stanford White's favorite watering holes and the building that rose on the very lot that once housed Franconi's Hippodrome. When it became clear that the Hippodrome would not last, the site was purchased by Amos F. Eno. A dry goods heir with a talent for acquiring real estate, he had the arena razed in 1856. A luxury hotel may not have been Eno's original intention (a great marble dry goods store was also considered), but a hotel was what it became. The site was so far uptown that few could imagine wanting to stay up there among the goats, and it boded ill when excavators turned up bones from an old Potter's Field. Doubters dubbed it "Eno's folly."[19]

Constructed in 1859 during that early revival of interest in the Italian Renaissance, the classically detailed, palazzo-style, white marble–faced monster of a hotel six stories high—fronting both Fifth Avenue and Broadway—consumed a full acre. As the center of town and fashionable life continued to move toward Madison Square, the Fifth Avenue Hotel become known as New York's finest hostelry, renting out among its 600 rooms 125 parlor suites with attached dressing rooms, baths with hot and cold water, and private water closets that in 1887 cost an astounding $30 a night.[20] The hotel's deluxe cachet had been assured after a widely publicized stay in 1860 by the Prince of Wales, Britain's future King Edward VII, when crowds 250,000 strong mobbed Madison Square calling for the handsome nineteen-year-old prince to appear and then followed along to each of his official stops.

According to legend, a ladder was provided for the prince's secret egress from the hotel each evening, and under the guidance of certain New Yorkers he managed to see the town far more privately after midnight.[21] Augustus Saint-Gaudens vividly recalled seeing the prince, "a comely youth," riding down Broadway, the crowd doffing their hats as he passed.[22] In the following years, every American president made the hotel his residence when visiting New York City.

The hotel boasted one of the grandest bars in town, guarded by several porters who stood watch at the door for those less than gentlemen and the obviously intoxicated.[23] Stanford White was known to sprint about the room with a brandy cocktail, hallooing and pumping hands. Have you seen this or that he would ask, raising his two fists, "It's lovely! It's bully, wonderful, gorgeous!" And then if there were something else he could not abide, so too he insisted on informing the crowd before moving on, leaving those who remained a little breathless, as if a foam-crested wave had just swept through, recalled his friends.[24]

Apart from its size and elegance, the Fifth Avenue Hotel boasted something else quite remarkable, the very first fully enclosed hotel passenger elevator, installed at the tremendous cost of $25,000. Its inventor, the brilliant Otis Tufts of Boston, called his elevator a "vertical screw railway" because it was powered up by a gigantic 2-foot-thick spiral-grooved iron shaft that ran from basement to attic right through the elevator car, and when rotated by a steam-powered belt it "screwed" the car up to the top of the building and back down.[25]

Only two screw elevators were ever sold by Tufts, however, due to their great expense and slow and clumsy operation—but still, a Rubicon had been crossed. The city began to move upward as well as out. Using wrought- or cast-iron columns and wrought-iron beams for support, more iron-framed buildings began to rise to an impressive six stories. And even after "cloud-pressers" of ten and eleven stories popped up around town, for the next half-century the buildings around Madison Square would keep to a more modest scale, retaining its open and refined air until the proposed new Madison Square Garden tower came into the picture.

•

Madison Square remained the social center of the city through the 1860s, despite the hardships of the Civil War. During those long years beginning in 1861, Madison Square was crowded with canvas tents housing new recruits and stables for the cavalry squadrons. Cheering thousands lined in front of the Fifth Avenue Hotel to wave off the gallant Seventh Regiment of the New York State Militia on its way to war. It was said that President Lincoln was a frequent visitor to the hotel, attending secret conferences to save the Union but always late in the evening to escape attention.[26]

The worst of it for the city and for Madison Square were the terrible Draft Riots of 1863, begun on the hottest day of July just two days after the first Conscription Act draft slips were pulled by lottery wheel. A mob of nearly 70,000 men, mostly working class and many Irish gang members, lashed out against the draft that had just taken place. Their first target was the rich, who were able to buy their way out of military service for $300 apiece, and then the city's African Americans, who surely seemed to blame for all their troubles.

William O. Stoddard, President Lincoln's secretary, reported a "surging, swaying crowd coming up Broadway, whooping, yelling, blaspheming and howling, demoniacs such as no man imagined the city of New York to contain." Carrying guns, pistols, axes, hatchets, crowbars, pitchforks, knives, bludgeons, paving stones, and brickbats, they cried "Down with the rich men! Down with property! Down with the police!"[27] The Fifth Avenue Hotel's iron shutters swung shut, and a stack of firearms was piled in the hallway as guests remained in a state of siege. Howitzers were fired in the streets, and ten thousand federal troops were bivouacked in Madison and Washington Squares to finally restore order.

By the time it was over, three days later, more than two thousand New Yorkers were dead and another eight thousand injured. Countless African-American homes had been destroyed by fire, businesses looted, the innocent lynched, and the Colored Orphan Asylum on Fifth Avenue destroyed. On Madison Square, men lay dead in the gutters of Twenty-Third Street, and whole blocks of storefronts had been looted and burned on the west side.[28] Yet as soon as the rubble could be cleared away, a line of new luxury hotels was constructed and speculation in real estate ran wild, with lot prices rising up to $1 million.[29]

In April 1865 mourners lined Fifth Avenue on Madison Square to watch President Lincoln's funeral procession, the glass hearse pulled up from city hall by a team of sixteen horses, the church bells tolling, and all the buildings draped in black crepe.[30] Eight months later came a delirious victory parade down Broadway for General Ulysses S. Grant and his Union forces, with a tumultuous reception at the Fifth Avenue Hotel and a supper room riot over the insufficient quantity of oysters and champagne to feed the overflow crowd of thousands.[31] A year later, from another room in the hotel, came the Republican Party's decision to run Grant for president.[32]

Madison Square Park had taken quite a beating during the Civil War years, and afterward some tidying up was called for. In 1870, the Common Council voted to fully fund the square's refurbishment. Ignaz Pilat, the Austrian landscape architect who had played a major role in the planting design for Central Park in the late 1850s, undertook the re-landscaping project. Although terribly ill with tuberculosis, Pilat worked until his death in September that year to replace the park's blocky design and right-angled paths with more pastoral open lawns, flowerbeds, and curving walkways enclosed by an iron rail fence.[33] Unfortunately, the following year's widening of Broadway at its juncture with Fifth Avenue to accommodate both traffic and parked hansom cabs caused the southwest corner of the park to be sheared off.

Despite these efforts, or perhaps because of the work on the park, the rich and the upwardly mobile began to abandon the square, moving farther and farther up Fifth Avenue. Certainly the display of the soon-to-be Statue of Liberty's arm and torch from 1874 to 1876—and the fifty-cent ride to the top to raise money for its pedestal—were enough to drive out most of what was left of society. It was the hotels, clubs, theaters, and restaurants that were left behind as Madison Square became increasingly devoted to the commercial rather than the residential, replacing Union Square six blocks to the south as the center of New York's urban and urbane civilization.

•

The corner of the Fifth Avenue Hotel was cleverly angled along the intersection where Fifth Avenue and Broadway cross paths. According to a 1902 account, it was said that all the "nice" people (i.e., the ladies) would bear to the right up Fifth, continuing past Madison Square and then on to its elegant homes and stately churches, while all the rest (i.e., the gentlemen) would lean left up the street known simply as "the boulevard" toward familiar and festive haunts up Broadway.[34]

Just down Twenty-Fourth Street to the west—where in 1897 Stanford White would rent a brownstone hideaway with the infamous red velvet swing—stood the Madison Square Theatre. Originally built during the Civil War as an adjunct to the Fifth Avenue Hotel, it had served as an evening gold and stock exchange. Known after the war as the Fifth Avenue Hall, it was turned into a sort of theater and run under a series of names, companies, and disasters until it was renovated and reopened in 1880 under the genius of actor-director-inventor Steele MacKaye, a cousin of Bessie White. As a devoted theatergoer, Stanford White was surely familiar with MacKaye's many innovations, such as the mechanical double-decker stage for quick scene changes and fifty-five second intermissions, mood-setting indirect stage lighting, rows of raised and raked seating for a perfect view of the stage, and the removal of house musicians from the pit to a balcony over the proscenium.[35]

Even more remarkably, it was the only theater in the city "cooled by iced air," and in the summer the most comfortable place in all of New York. Even during the hottest dog days, the air was as cool and refreshing "as if it had been blown over a bank of spring violets." This miracle was due to the huge cakes of ice delivered each day to the basement and a steam-run fan wheel on the roof that drew fresh air in, down over the ice (in winter over a steam radiator), and up through the floor heating grates and the 4-inch pipes set under each seat.[36] Due to this bit of engineering, the Madison Square was one of the few legitimate theaters in New York to remain open during the heat of summer, traditionally the season when most venues failed to make a sufficient gate to cover their expenses.

•

On Broadway just across Twenty-Fourth stood the Albemarle Hotel, an 1860s marble palace with a definite aura of refinement and considered the most decorous of all the Madison Square hotels. While it boasted a French Second Empire–style mansard roof and a chateauesque corner tower, the interior bore an English-style elegance, with many suites taken on a permanent basis by wealthy local bachelors.[37]

Adjacent to the Albemarle sat another marble palace, the celebrated Hoffman House, named for the family estate of former New York City mayor and state governor John T. Hoffman on which it was erected in 1864 and then enlarged in 1885. While both hotels shared an uninterrupted view onto the square, the Hoffman House catered to a faster crowd than the Albemarle, from the nabobs of railroading, finance, industry, and mining, to sporting men and familiar faces from politics and the stage. Just as the Fifth Avenue Hotel served as unofficial headquarters for the Republicans, Democrats had found a home at the Hoffman House.[38]

However, the hotel's fame was primarily due to its collection of paintings installed throughout the four-hundred-room establishment, a collection so fine that one day a week any lady calling at the hotel was offered a tour and a printed catalogue describing the works of art. While the collection included a fair number of nudes, the hotel was known worldwide for one particular piece installed in its equally famous bar, French painter William Bouguereau's quite scandalous 1873 *Nymphs and Satyr*. The painting had originally been owned by hardware heir John Wolfe, a former resident of the square, who had paid 30,000 francs for it after it hung in the Paris Salon of 1873. In 1882 it was purchased from Wolfe's estate for $10,010 by the hotel's owner, convicted murderer and Sing-Sing alumnus Edward S. "Ned" Stokes.[39]

Stokes came from a socially prominent family, the first to build on Madison Square, and fell into business with financier, stockbroker, and generally infamous railroad magnate James Fisk Jr. After Stokes stole

6. H. A. Thomas & Wylie's interior view of the Hoffman House Bar, 1890, chromolithograph. Chronicling America, Library of Congress.

away Fisk's mistress, the two men traded charges of blackmail, libel, and embezzlement until Stokes, frustrated by their endless legal tangles, shot Big Jim point blank on the staircase of the downtown Grand Central Hotel. After serving a four-year term for manslaughter, Stokes decided to pursue the hotel business himself, and his success as a partner in the Hoffman House earned him a spot in planning the new Madison Square Garden, an enterprise that was enthusiastically supported by all the neighborhood hoteliers.

The hotel's notorious painting was housed in the famed downstairs bar, mobbed every day for its sumptuous buffet lunches, served free except for the price of a drink and a twenty-five-cent tip. The bar itself was a magnificent 75 feet of carved mahogany serviced by twenty bartenders mixing up the latest cocktails and slings, including a dollar-a-glass antique Hennessy brandy, the highest priced drink in America. A running mirror behind the bar kept the *Nymphs and Satyr* in view under a swagged red velvet canopy illuminated by an electrified crystal chandelier hanging from the lofty ceiling.[40]

The painting narrowly escaped destruction just the year before in 1886 when one of the electric lights exploded and set its velvet canopy ablaze, but the quick-thinking bar bouncer emptied a bottle of seltzer water on the fire, and no nymphs were lost.[41] Executed in a rather florid style, the 9-by-6-foot painting depicted four laughing nymphs dragging a reluctant satyr into a pool of water. In the foreground, one of the nymphs, her back to the viewer, displayed an immensely large and fleshy pair of bare buttocks. It was the obvious focus of the painting, although a few bare breasts were also visible, more discreetly projected and obviously of lesser interest. It was acknowledged among patrons that after enough drinks the nymphs would begin to stir and adjust their veils and garlands.[42] Unclad beauties were another longstanding tradition on Madison Square.

3

A Practical Education

STANFORD WHITE never set out to be an architect. A clever, outgoing boy with a head for solving problems, he clearly had creative ability from the very first. Young Stannie painted in watercolors before he could spell his name, and by the time he was twelve he was sketching imaginary buildings on bits of paper. He wanted to be a painter and tried his hand at landscapes, but there was no money for a Paris education, by then considered de rigueur for any serious artist.[1]

In 1870 Stanford White was sixteen, and his father was in need of some guidance as to his son's future. The elder White arranged a visit with a neighbor, the painter John La Farge. At the age of thirty-seven, La Farge was not only a versatile artist, having worked in oil, watercolor, engraving, and illustration, but a poet with a tendency to mystical thought. He himself had been disappointed by a struggling career, was deeply in debt, and was only just recovering, he claimed, from a bout of paint-induced lead poisoning. La Farge bent his strangely large head over young White's drawings and watercolors, his deep-set, heavy-lidded eyes popping open for emphasis as he noted White's talent for rendering buildings and decoration. With some pleasure, La Farge often repeated the story in later life as to how *he* had been the one to tell Stanford White to forget painting and its meager rewards and to consider architecture instead.[2]

The elder White wanted a second opinion on his son's likely future, and so they visited another old acquaintance, one with whom he had shared a commitment to the abolitionist movement before the war and a continuing interest in transcendental thought. Frederick Law Olmstead, already famed for his designs of the city's Central Park and Prospect Park in Brooklyn, concurred on the choice of architecture for young White and arranged an introduction to Henry Hobson Richardson, an up-and-coming architect.[3] So his future was decided, a path that on some days he would still question and perhaps even regret.

An apprenticeship was arranged, and most likely late in the summer of 1870 Stanford White came to join Richardson's small office on Hanover Street in Lower Manhattan.[4] Architecture was still barely considered a profession in the early 1870s, perhaps only slightly more elevated than a trade. The most practical way to learn was on the job, as assistant and general errand boy in the office of an established architect. There was little formal training available in the States, and few Americans could manage a year or two of study in Paris at the newly reformed and reorganized school of the Académie des Beaux-Arts, the famed École des Beaux-Arts. Richardson was only the second American who had studied there, and he had been back in New York and in practice for just four years when White arrived with absolutely no training.

Mr. R., as White called him to his face—the "great mogul"[5] behind his back—was southern-born on a plantation near New Orleans, Harvard-educated, genial, confident, enthusiastic, and witty, with a brilliant smile and a bright yellow waistcoat. He was a big man with the build and driving force of a bison,[6] and hands so huge that he had his pencils specially made. He also had a particular fondness for the dining table and often suffered for it.

In the offices Richardson shared with his partner, Charles Gambrill, or more often from his chronic sickbed, Richardson would come up with a small, rough sketch and leave it to the draftsmen to make scale and presentation drawings, and then more drawings after he had made his revisions. "Do what you can with it,"[7] he would say. He taught by suggestion, and his draftsmen learned to think and design for themselves. White soon attached himself to Richardson's head draftsman, Charles Follen McKim, for some practical instruction.[8]

•

Charley McKim was just twenty-three that year, a quiet, shy, and gentle man of medium height, with blue eyes, a drooping mustache, and reddish hair already fleeing his prominent forehead. McKim held firm but idealistic convictions about art and most other matters but was never pompous or pushy. Neither terribly sober or somber but quietly persuasive, by all accounts he possessed a generous spirit with a merry good humor when not struggling with episodes of depression. "Charley the Charmer" was the name by which he was often known.[9]

After a year of engineering at Harvard, McKim abandoned the college's Lawrence Scientific School for Paris and three years' study of architecture at the École. A grand tour of Europe introduced him to the city of Rome, and he would repeatedly return to Italy and its architecture for inspiration. The growth of cities and the possibilities of great urban design intrigued him, so in the spring of 1870 McKim traveled to New York, where he quickly found a job with Gambrill & Richardson just a few months before Stanford White arrived.

McKim had much to teach his young assistant, and he and White got on well from the first. Soon it became clear that while McKim excelled in drafting systemized drawings of exterior facades, executed equally well with either hand, White had a talent for rendering handsome room interiors with a certain impressionistic flair, and thus he was charged with most of the interior detailing on residential projects.[10]

There were a fair number of major projects in the works when White joined Gambrill & Richardson, but the most important was the commission the firm had won that summer of 1870 on the strength of McKim's drawings, the Congregationalist church on Brattle Square in Boston's newly opened Back Bay. It was very different than anything the firm had designed before, and when it was done a new style had been born. With its medieval roots and a vocabulary that looked back to Roman times, Richardsonian Romanesque was characterized by heavy, rough-faced stone walls and trim often set in contrasting bands, rounded windows, and prominent arches and arcades. In general, Richardson had been inspired by the eleventh- and twelfth-century medieval Romanesque architecture of Italy, Spain, and most particularly the Auvergne region of France, re-envisioned in a way that was strong, fresh, solid, secure, and somehow very American.

As for the Brattle Square Church, most impressive of all and most significant for the future Madison Square Garden was its tower, 176 feet tall with four carved angels at the corners blowing trumpets. Soon the inhabitants of Beantown had given it a nickname, the Church of the Holy Bean Blowers.[11] However, the grandeur of the finished product proved the ruination of the congregation, driven into bankruptcy by cost overruns that resulted in the sale of the property to the Baptist Church.

Richardson said that for the sake of work he would plan anything a customer wanted, "from a cathedral to a chicken coop,"[12] but in the spring of 1872—again based on McKim's drawings—the firm won another commission that would ensure Richardson's place among the immortals of American architecture. It was for a second church in Back Bay Boston, Trinity Church for the more fashionable High Church Episcopalians.

But within a few weeks of winning the competition, McKim announced his resignation to set up his own firm down the hall from Gambrill & Richardson's new office at 57 Broadway. Relations remained friendly between McKim and the firm, but suddenly all the responsibility for the Trinity Church drawings, as well as the firm's other projects, rested in Stanford White's eighteen-year-old hands.[13]

The work was exhausting, but White fared well under Mr. R's wing, diving into enormous platters of the great mogul's favorite boiled tripe, downing magnums of champagne, and smoking thick cigars. Richardson worked in his studio dressed in a monk's robe, cowled and roped across his immense belly and looking for the world like one of his own great, brown buildings. Stanford White would remain with Gambrill & Richardson while continuing his friendship with McKim and then accompanying McKim and his two new partners, his brother-in-law William Bigelow and William Mead, on what became a legendary tour of New England's colonial architecture. In 1879 White joined the firm after McKim's acrid divorce and Bigelow's departure. McKim talked Mead into taking on White as a junior partner, assuring him that although he had not had much training in architecture, White could draw like a house afire.[14]

•

If Stanford White were still circling Madison Square that night in July 1887, he would have continued up Broadway and crossed Twenty-Fifth Street where stood the old Worth House, wedged rather uncomfortably on an oddly shaped spot of land tucked behind the obelisk monument and grave marker for Major General William Jenkins Worth, namesake of Fort Worth and hero of a handful of domestic wars.[15] The building was occupied at the time by the New York Club, transformed into another one of those paneled, leather-filled retreats for a certain class of men in business, finance, various professions, and the arts who banded together primarily to smoke cigars, drink, and play bridge. These clubs served men like Stanford White as a second home, a quiet respite from the cares of work, the ever-increasing crush of the city, and domestic obligations. White would eventually find himself the architect-designer of some of the most elegant clubhouses in Manhattan, including the Players' and the Century in 1888, the Metropolitan in 1894, and the Lambs, the Colony, the Harmonie, and the Brook in 1904 and 1905—and with his typical tendency to excess, would himself be a member of more than fifty clubs, societies, and organizations.[16]

Just beyond the Worth House, on the corner of Fifth Avenue and Twenty-Sixth Street, stood the legendary Delmonico's, the most elegant dining spot in the city and the most celebrated meeting spot for celebrities—from Oscar Wilde to Diamond Jim Brady—in the entire United States, if not the western hemisphere. White was well known here by the fourth-generation-proprietor, Charles C. Delmonico, but doubtless had to wait in line, for no reservations were taken except for the private supper rooms upstairs.

A typical menu served that summer of 1887 in the grand dining room or the outdoor Parisian-style café on Fifth Avenue might have begun with lucines orangée clams in the half shell or pickled oysters accompanied by a glass of Chablis from the restaurant's exceedingly well-stocked cellar of imported wines; then a consommé Andalouse with caviar on toast; then a specialty of the house, lobster à la Newberg, as prepared by New York's first celebrity chef, Charles Ranhofer, and his staff of forty-two. The main course might have been pigeon cutlet, roast duck with cherries, or even the seasonally special roast ptarmigan or calf ears in tomato sauce.[17] A suitable dessert and coffee might then be served in the dining room or in the gentlemen's cafe on the Broadway side.

The del Monico family had emigrated to the United States from the southernmost, Italian-speaking section of Switzerland, and there was a definite palazzo style to the establishment, with splendidly refined mahogany furniture, mirrored walls, frescoed ceilings, silver chandeliers, and a flower-banked fountain. Opened in 1876 at the former site of the Dodworth dance studio—where little Teddy Roosevelt once stumbled through dance class[18]—it was a far cry from the original wine and confectionary store established downtown in 1827 by wine merchant Giovanni Delmonico, later called John, and his pastry chef brother Pietro, later called Peter. In its day, the original Delmonico's was the first to offer French pastries, and in the 1830s, following the arrival of third brother Francesco, later François, they transformed it into a restaurant Français, and soon "French" and "fine cuisine" had become synonymous in the States.[19]

Delmonico's was also known for its sometimes scandalous private supper parties held in the upstairs dining rooms, for the civic and business dinners in the third-floor banquet hall, and for the grand nights in the elegant red-and-gold ballroom for the city's exclusive Patriarchs' Ball, where young girls made their debuts and old New York society reigned. One theory suggests that it was in this ballroom, which held about four hundred comfortably, that New York's social elite were narrowed down to that near legendary number. And it would be in this very spot on Madison Square, nineteen years later, after Delmonico's had been taken over and remade into Café Martin, that Stanford White would enjoy his last meal on earth.

●

The *Times* had just proclaimed on July 18, 1887, that when the Madison Square Garden's architect was chosen, he would be famous for all time, or perhaps infamous if things were to go awry. "If the building is fine the city will gain very much in splendor," the editorial read rather pessimistically, but "if it is the usual failure it will be another cause for hanging the head."[20] There would be no ducking, for few sites in the city would be more visible or more frequently visited. The commission would, in fact, make Stanford White the best-known architect in America.

Perhaps here in the dining room Stanford White would have reviewed his proposed plans for the new Madison Square Garden, taking notes and making sketches, as was his habit, on stamped and self-addressed penny postcards pulled from his pocket.[21] His preliminary plan included a vast number of facilities, from an amphitheater to an aquarium to a shooting

7. Preliminary plan for Madison Square Garden, McKim, Mead & White, *Harper's Weekly* 31 (Nov. 5, 1887).

gallery to Turkish baths, all demanding light and air, comfortable temperatures, ease of access, safety for spectators, and the elimination of offensive odors.[22]

The design McKim, Mead & White had submitted to the competition was nothing if not eclectic. There was a strong Byzantine flavor to the main building, in the style of the old Roman emperors who ruled from Constantinople from the fourth century AD and had built Hagia Sophia, the Church of the Holy Wisdom, in the mid-sixth century. The broad, low dome that was intended to cover the summer and winter gardens and the wide arched central window on the façade were something new in White's stylistic repertoire, inspired quite likely by his honeymoon travels to Istanbul. The ground level arcade, however, with its restrained, full arches, was very Northern Italian Renaissance. The decorative material chosen for the structure was a long, flat, speckled brick like that found in the ancient walls of Rome and further adorned with terra-cotta ornament.[23]

But certainly the most dramatic feature of the plan was the tower sited at the southwest corner of the building at Madison and Twenty-Sixth. It was to be a fantasy of Spanish flavor with more than a certain similarity to the Giralda, the bell tower of Santa Maria de la Sede, the cathedral of Seville. It was a miraculous joining of a twelfth-century Islamic minaret—in its day the second tallest tower in the world—with a multistoried sixteenth-century Renaissance belfry, topped by a huge weathercock in the form of a nearly nude classical goddess in the guise of *Christian Faith.*

A representation of the Giralda had appeared in an August 1882 *Harper's Magazine* article authored by the brother of artist Francis Lathrop, a friend and associate of both Stanford White and Augustus Saint-Gaudens dating back to the Trinity Church project.[24] A second illustration of the Giralda, as viewed down one of Seville's laundry-draped alleyways, was published in the December 26, 1885, issue of *American Architect and Building News.*[25] Both were no doubt included among the volumes in McKim, Mead & White's well-stocked architectural library. But White's own vision was far more elaborate than the Spanish model, with three arcaded stages instead of just one on top of the solid bricked base. Replacing the Giralda's rather slight, elongated belfry top, his new version was more substantial yet smoothly tapering, crowned by a circular, peripteral temple with a domed cupola and a ball at its pinnacle. And it would soon be announced, in October 1887, that White's new tower, like the Giralda, would be topped by a sculptural figure, but that this one would carry a powerful electric light.[26]

4

Enter Augustus Saint-Gaudens

IT WAS ANOTHER SUMMER—in the year 1875—that Stanford White and Augustus Saint-Gaudens first met.[1] One afternoon White found himself on an errand at the new German Savings Bank, a triangular sort of building on the corner of Fourteenth Street and Fourth Avenue. From up on the second floor he heard someone bawl what sounded like the andante of what was later recalled as Beethoven's Seventh Symphony[2] and then sing out the "Serenade" from Mozart's opera *Don Giovanni* but with strangely raucous words in French. Curiosity pulled him up the iron stairs and down a long, dim corridor to what turned out to be a sculptor's studio. And there stood another young man, nearly as red-bearded as White.[3] They were friends at first sight. "We came together like two sticking plasters," Saint-Gaudens said. "Every time I see Saint-Gaudens, I hug him like a bear," White wrote to his mother.[4]

After a quick introduction, the sculptor explained that he had learned the serenade while in art school in Paris from a howling Frenchman who could shout it even louder. Saint-Gaudens would continue to sing or "whistle to split your ears" whenever his work was going well. He too was light-eyed[5] with a piercing look under his heavy, almost demonic brows, his nose long, straight, and broad in a catlike way. Unlike White's, his reddish-brown mane was thick and almost wiry.[6] In those days, he sported a trim auburn mustache and French-style patch on his long chin—as "hard and sharp as a sculptor's chisel."[7] Saint-Gaudens was shorter than White and a bit stockier, and his legs were a little bowed. He was streetwise with a quick temper and an almost furious energy but loved whooping it up with friends. He feared himself too shy and bashful, but friends enjoyed his lively turn of phrase and his jokes when in one of his sunnier moods.

8. Augustus Saint-Gaudens, engagement portrait, 1875. Courtesy of the US Department of the Interior, National Park Service, Saint-Gaudens National Historical Park, Cornish, NH.

He cared little for formal society but was very fond of people. And when he felt something strongly, it seemed he could see it so clearly that he had a way of making others share his vision as well.[8]

Although Stanford White was five years Saint-Gaudens's junior, he was far more familiar with the ways of genteel society and from their first meeting had been happy to add a little polish to the shoemaker's son. Aside from their coloring and great talent, the two men had much in common: both radiated a tremendous energy, they had tempers to match but were ever kind to their many devoted friends, and most important, they were both passionate about their work, for which they lived, and about beauty—whether to be found in art, music, or a comely face.

•

The son of a bluff and lively French father and a sad-faced, sweet Irish mother, Augustus Saint-Gaudens was born in Dublin on March 1, 1848. Described as "an erect old Frenchman with a fine leonine head, an aristocratic bearing, and good blood in his veins,"[9] Bernard Saint Gaudens had traveled from the village of Aspet at the foot of the French Pyrenees as a journeyman shoemaker, first to London and then on to Dublin. There he met Mary McGuinness of County Longford, who came from a family of plasterers but worked binding slippers in a shoe factory where they were both employed.[10]

Within a few months of Saint-Gaudens's birth, the family had emigrated to Boston and then New York, where Bernard opened a shop selling "French Ladies' Boots and Shoes" two blocks from city hall and just one block over from A. T. Stewart's new Marble Palace. Two more sons were born, Andrew and Louis, and a few years later Bernard moved the shop and family near Union Square, then Madison Square, where Mary sewed the fasteners while the family lived over a grocery store. Although Bernard Saint Gaudens's shoes were described as damnably uncomfortable—due to his singular belief in the need to squeeze the foot so that the toes might spread—they remained in great demand among New York society, perhaps owing to the persistent fashion for all things French or his charming Irish brogue spoken with a fierce Gallic accent.[11]

Meanwhile, young Augustus fought in the street, stole food from vendors, and knocked the helmets off policemen. He was often lined up against the wall with the other bad boys for the whack of a rod on his outstretched hands or even a full caning, and school to him was "one long misery, one long imprisonment."[12] So when his father told him at the age of thirteen that he must leave school and find work, Saint-Gaudens said he did not care what he did but asked if it could be something that would help him be an artist.[13] In 1861 he was apprenticed to Louis Avet, a cameo cutter of amethyst and malachite scarf-pins sold at Tiffany & Co. Avet was a hard master with a raging temper, yet oddly enough amid fits of rage he dragged Saint-Gaudens along on snipe hunting trips out on the Weehawken Flats. Saint-Gaudens tried "not to dwell on the ugly side of things."[14]

For three years of what he could only call "miserable slavery,"[15] Saint-Gaudens worked at a pedal-driven lathe, learning to carve life from the stone until he was fired one day for failing to sweep up his lunch crumbs. He soon found far pleasanter employment at Jules Le Brethon's engraved gem and shell-cameo workshop a block down Broadway. There the master sang from morning until night and taught Saint-Gaudens Beethoven's "Andante" while he carved gods and goddesses, as well as New York bankers and merchants, out of small, flat pieces of stone and shell. Although Le Brethon had a reputation for indulging in drink and thereafter chasing apprentices around the studio,[16] he also took time to teach Saint-Gaudens three-dimensional modeling in clay—a medium Gus would prefer throughout his life. In the evenings, Saint-Gaudens took advantage of the drawing classes at the Cooper Institute that were offered free to all children of immigrants and the working class, remaining in the studio classroom until nearly midnight every night.

In 1866 Saint-Gaudens transferred to the just-built National Academy of Design that adjoined his father's new shop on Fourth Avenue at East Twenty-Third Street, a block beyond Madison Square. In the academy's handsome Italian Gothic–style building that recalled the Doge's Palace in Venice, Saint-Gaudens first came to appreciate the art of Greece and Rome, drawing in charcoal, crayon, and pencil from plaster casts of classical masterworks, then from live, undraped models.[17]

All the talk in the classroom in 1866 was of the upcoming Exposition Universelle in Paris that the emperor Napoleon III promised would be the greatest spectacle the world had ever seen. Surely Saint-Gaudens realized there would be little chance of his traveling abroad until one day in early 1867 when Bernard Saint Gaudens handed over steerage passage to Paris and one hundred dollars he had saved out of his son's wages. Apparently an old friend, an art buyer at Tiffany's, had convinced the elder Saint Gaudens that if Gus hoped to become an artist, he must visit Paris. At a festive going-away dinner, Master Le Brethon added another one hundred francs in gold to the wallet.[18]

Europe had called to American artists since Benjamin West first ventured to Italy in 1760. For years London, Munich, Antwerp, Dresden, and Düsseldorf attracted a fair number of American painters, while well-established sculptors usually ventured to Rome or Florence in mid-career to both display their work and gain new inspiration. But in the second half of the nineteenth century, as travel became cheaper and quicker, it was the younger, more outward-looking artists who were eager to soak up all the Old World had to offer, seeking inspiration not only from Greek and Roman sculpture and paintings by the old masters in the galleries and museums of Europe but through formal training as well.[19]

Saint-Gaudens knew that he wanted to be a sculptor and that most of the eminent American sculptors—such as William Wetmore Story, Henry Rinehart, and Harriet Hosmer—lived and worked in Italy, with its millennia of magnificent sculpture from the Roman to the Renaissance, the Baroque, and the Romantic; its famed supply of Carrara marble; and its abundance of well-trained cutters. But France had its own sculptors of note studying and teaching at the École des Beaux-Arts. Aside from its training, the school's government-sponsored annual Salon was the place where the best work was hung in more than a hundred galleries, medals awarded in countless competitions, reputations made in the press, and collectors and contacts cultivated among well-to-do Americans on the grand tour.[20]

•

It was on a cold afternoon in February 1867 when, at the age of nineteen, Augustus Saint-Gaudens first arrived in the City of Light for what had been presumed to be a short visit.[21] But within a day or two of his arrival, Saint-Gaudens suddenly applied for admission to the École des Beaux-Arts.[22] Two months later, while waiting for his application to be accepted, he entered one of the many nearby private schools for classes in drawing and sculpture. Nicknamed the "Petite École," the École Gratuite de Dessin had been founded in the mid-eighteenth century to teach poor boys the applied arts. It now served as a training ground for the grand École, claiming Auguste Rodin among its alumni, and specialized in teaching anatomy by drawing from plaster casts and from life. Here, in the back row with the other "mud-slinging" sculpture students, Saint-Gaudens modeled his first full nude in clay and won two first-prize medals for his work.[23]

In late fall of 1867, Saint-Gaudens was finally allowed to join one of the three sculpture ateliers attached to the École des Beaux-Arts.[24] Home to more than a thousand art students—both French and foreign-born—the École offered free tuition in its classrooms and studios sprawled across the grounds of a seventeenth-century convent on the Seine's Left Bank. On the advice of a friend, Saint-Gaudens applied to the atelier of François Jouffroy, whose students regularly captured most of the school's prizes. He presented his drawings, was accepted within two days, and immediately began work.[25] According to his friends, Saint-Gaudens was one of the wildest in the studio, but he lived frugally, barely supporting himself by carving tombstones and cameos in the afternoons while attending class mornings and evenings. Yet still Saint-Gaudens managed to attend Sunday afternoon concerts, join a gym for exercise and cold baths, and travel the French countryside and through Germany and much of Switzerland.[26]

But then in the summer of 1870, after the Spanish crown had been offered to a Hohenzollern prince, the Second French Empire of Napoleon III felt threatened by nearby German presence and declared war on the North German Confederation led by the Kingdom of Prussia. Within months the emperor and the entire French army had been captured, the Second Empire was over, and the Third Republic had begun. Meanwhile, the lives of all the students at the École were thrown into chaos. Many of the French students enlisted, and Saint-Gaudens intended to join the French army as well—but the sight of regiments departing, women weeping for their loved ones at the front, and other such scenes of misery weakened his resolve.[27]

On borrowed funds Saint-Gaudens fled to his brother Andrew, now running a porcelain factory in Limoges,[28] then to Marseilles, and finally by boat to the Italian port of Civitavecchia, bringing along only his stone-cameo lathe. After the cold, gray weather of France, the misery of war, and two terrible days of mal de mer across the Mediterranean, the journey by train that finally brought him to Rome seemed like the entrance into paradise.[29]

•

Saint-Gaudens spent five happy years in Rome enjoying all its "blessed charms, as if a door had been thrown wide open to the eternal beauty of the classical."[30] He rented a small but delightful studio in the gardens of the Palazzo Barberini that he shared with a fellow refugee. Now it was time to begin work on his first great figure, one he was certain would astonish the world. Saint-Gaudens decided it would be an Indian warrior,[31] one of the few nude male subjects considered appropriate for an American sculptor. He modeled in clay a seated *Hiawatha* of Longfellow fame in the coolly restrained neoclassical style then in vogue, his chin resting on hand while musing on the fate of the Iroquois people, quiver of arrows at his side, and a fringed cloth across his lap to ensure a bit of modesty.

Soon enough there were wealthy American visitors who found their way to the Barberini garden studio, attracted by the presence in the main palazzo of William Wetmore Story, one of America's most prominent sculptors of that neoclassical style, turning out exotic yet untouchable females from *Cleopatra* to *Salome*. One of those Americans, New York lawyer Montgomery Gibbs, financed *Hiawatha*'s casting in plaster but for the future advised Saint-Gaudens to follow Story's example and model "some good looking women, for they always sell."[32]

In 1873 Saint-Gaudens was joined in Rome by his rather melancholic younger brother Louis, who helped cut the cameos Saint-Gaudens still sold for ready cash. Despite bouts of Roman fever that his doctor blamed on moonlight strolls about the Coliseum in the evening *mal'aria*,[33] Saint-Gaudens managed a trip to see the grand eruption of Vesuvius in 1872, was briefly arrested as a brigand in Calabria, dropped a great forkful of asparagus on the dining room floor of the American Consul in Livorno, was overcome by the beauty of Venice, and danced with the local girls on the Isle of Capri.[34]

•

Saint-Gaudens may have had a few flirtations back in New York—later he remembered being in love four times—but due to his shyness it was likely they came to little.[35] Then at a holiday reception for visiting Americans in December 1873, Saint-Gaudens met the tall, reserved, rather shy, and partially deaf Miss Augusta Homer. An artist as well, like her cousin Winslow, she had quite impressed her teachers in Boston before leaving home to further her study of painting and consult with doctors on the Continent regarding her delicate health. Dr. Gruber in Vienna diagnosed throat trouble that had spread to the nerves of the ear. If the condition's progress were not arrested, she was told, she would soon be totally deaf. While in Rome, she spent her days in the galleries around town, skillfully copying old master paintings to sell to tourists or family friends back home.[36]

Saint-Gaudens managed to obtain her name and address and soon called on her at her lodgings, followed by walks in the Medici Gardens, excursions to various artist studios, and a New Year's Eve visit to the Coliseum by moonlight.[37] One month later they were engaged, and Saint-Gaudens happily cut his last cameo, an oddly chosen *Mary Queen of Scots* that he had set for Augusta Homer's engagement ring.[38] The gossips said that she was an heiress, but in truth her parents' circumstances were

9. Augusta Homer Saint-Gaudens, engagement portrait, 1875. Courtesy of the US Department of the Interior, National Park Service, Saint-Gaudens National Historical Park, Cornish, NH.

quite reduced—although later Saint-Gaudens would credit his success to his fancy French name and his wife's rich relatives. In any case, Saint-Gaudens thought it only honorable that marriage be postponed until he had scored a commission large enough to ensure their financial future.

In June 1874 Augusta Homer left for the States to look after her health, while Saint-Gaudens remained behind to complete commissions to reproduce Greek and Roman busts as well as model the heads of several New York lawyers in the same neoclassical style. As prices rose for marble as well as wages for his assistants, Saint-Gaudens ran out of funds. In early 1875 he returned to New York in search of work, offering private drawing lessons and taking that studio upstairs of the German Savings Bank where he sang out while running water from the faucet to remind himself of the fountain in the Roman garden where he once had his studio.[39]

•

The first professional association between Stanford White and Augustus Saint-Gaudens occurred in 1876, when Saint-Gaudens came to work on

Trinity Church in Boston's Back Bay and White was still in the employ of H. H. Richardson and supervising the project. It was all a little murky as to who introduced whom, but when John La Farge was given the commission to conceive and paint the church's decoration and only five months to finish it, he tapped every artist he knew—including Saint-Gaudens the sculptor.

La Farge assembled his team and began developing a waterproof paint of wax melted with turpentine and alcohol and a scheme to cover the vast church interior with angels, saints, prophets, symbols of the evangelists, scrolls of scripture, and bands of geometric stenciling in a style that borrowed from the Byzantine to the Italian Renaissance in shades of Pompeian red with turquoise moldings and luminous blue-green gilt. Neither La Farge nor any of his young team of artists—Francis Lathrop, Francis Millet, George Maynard, and Augustus Saint-Gaudens—had ever attempted a mural, used the type of encaustic paint La Farge devised, or worked on this scale before. When finished, it would be the first decoration of a church by fine art painters and the first large-scale mural project in the United States.[40]

White's part of the Trinity project continued with the interior furnishings, including the design for the pews, and he came by as often as he could to coordinate details and watch the progress, and just because he liked being around painters. Calling upon his Beaux-Arts training, Saint-Gaudens completed a green-robed Saint Paul for the chancel's horseshoe arch and then a seated Saint James in a lunette above the transept, glad for the pay and glad for a reason to stay in Boston near his "darling Dimply," "darling girl."[41] La Farge was demanding and hard to please, but they got along well. Saint-Gaudens later said that, in terms of his art, he owed more to La Farge than anyone he ever met.[42]

Both White and Saint-Gaudens made close and enduring ties among the painters of the Trinity project, as evidenced by their membership in the elite and rather esoteric artistic brotherhood of the Tile Club. Founded in 1887, the club's older members included Winslow Homer, William Merritt Chase, and Elihu Vedder along with younger artists like J. Alden Weir, George Maynard, Francis Millet, and John Twachtman, who became lasting friends and enjoyed its secret location and rituals that included dancing around the clubhouse dinner table three times before every Wednesday evening meal, as well as their soubriquets including "the Beaver" or "Builder" for White and "the Saint" for Saint-Gaudens.[43]

•

While painting away on his saints in late 1876, Saint-Gaudens received some remarkable news. An entry he had submitted among a string of sculpture competitions had won an important commission.[44] It was to be a bronze statue of Admiral David Glasgow Farragut, hero of the Civil War Battle of Mobile Bay who had lashed himself to the rigging at the head of the fleet to exclaim, "Damn the torpedoes. Full speed ahead!" And it was to be installed on Madison Square.

An eager Stanford White quickly volunteered to draw its pedestal, for both men knew that there would be much public notice for the sculpture that just might make their names. "I shall go down to fame (even if it is bad), reviled for making a poor base to a good statue,"[45] added White. It was the first time ever that an architect and sculptor would work together so closely and from the very inception of a piece of public art. And it would be only the first of their twenty-some remarkable collaborations.

With the award of the *Farragut Monument*, Saint-Gaudens now had the wherewithal to marry, and he and Augusta, known to friends and family as Gus and Gussie, were joined in a Unitarian ceremony in the Homers' Roxbury parlor in June 1877. Within days they had left for the Continent, where Saint-Gaudens would be able to afford a studio in Paris large enough to model the 8-foot figure of Admiral Farragut upon its tall base and then step back to view it as if it were out on-site.[46] France had the finest bronze foundries in the world, where it would also be easier to find trained assistants to help with the work. Saint-Gaudens and White kept in close touch by mail on the details for this project, as well as others as they came along.

•

Until the following spring of 1878. After eight years with Richardson, Stanford White was restless and anxious to explore what Europe had to offer, to see Saint-Gaudens once more, and to continue their work on the design for the base of the *Farragut*. During his time with the great mogul, White had not only overseen that Trinity Church project in Boston and the renovation of the New York State Capitol in Albany but had played a major role in creating the first of the grand Shingle-style Queen Anne "cottages" in Newport and other elite enclaves, as well as designing their handsome and often novel interiors. He saved up some money for travel from his wages and borrowed some more, and resigned his position in Richardson's firm. Letters were exchanged, along with an invitation to visit the Saint-Gaudenses in Paris. Then, at the last minute, Charles McKim decided to make the trip as well.

It seems that McKim's marriage had fallen apart in a most unpleasant way. In May 1878, after just three and a half years of marriage, Annie McKim obtained a legal separation and departed with their young daughter for her family home in Newport. She would later charge him with neglect, cruelty, and "unnatural acts against the bounds of Christian behavior" that were "repugnant to and in violation of the marriage contract." What exactly that meant was never explicitly detailed, but homosexual acts were suspected. McKim claimed desertion and countercharged that it was the baby nurse, an old friend of his wife's, who had alienated her affections, and rumors of a lesbian liaison were widely whispered.[47]

While the divorce was not yet final, for all purposes Charles McKim was a single man and more than ready to leave behind New York and the whole affair's public humiliation. He and Saint-Gaudens were old friends, having met three years earlier in an ice cream saloon over a big plate of chocolate, strawberry, and vanilla, which they discovered they both adored. They had both studied at the École des Beaux-Arts in Paris the exact same three years, although in different ateliers so they had never met. Saint-Gaudens called him "Blarney Charles" for his smooth style, and they got along fine.[48]

•

It is not hard to imagine the kind of treasure chest France opened that summer of 1878, not only to Saint-Gaudens, White, and McKim but to wave upon wave of aspiring young American artists and architects. White and McKim tried to talk Saint-Gaudens into making a tour to the South of France, but he insisted he was far too busy working on the all-important *Farragut* commission. Then some artist friends dropped by the studio and joked that Saint-Gaudens had obviously given the *Farragut* his own bowed legs. In response, Saint-Gaudens carefully lifted off the admiral's head to save it, then smashed the plaster model to the floor saying, "Come on, I'll go to hell with you fellows now!"[49]

They traveled by garlic-scented riverboat down the Rhône, bumped over the Montes de la Margeride atop a stagecoach, and tramped among the chateaux of the Loire Valley, White sketching and scribbling all the while. Saint-Gaudens commemorated the trip by casting a bronze medallion complete with caricatures of the three redheads, with captions that alluded to humorous incidents, the façade of Saint-Gilles (the best piece of architecture in France, according to White), a T square, and the letters KMA for "kiss my ass." "Damvs Solvm" writ next to a quickly rendered image of White's beard and stand-up hair referred to an incident in which White hopped on a train just as it was starting up and rushed into the compartment reserved for ladies only, which resulted in a grand altercation as the French guards dragged him away, while "Ticlevm fvrio" alluded to a vigorous tickling episode. Saint-Gaudens treasured his medallion, as White surely did, and McKim's remained forever on his mantelpiece back home.[50]

•

Charles McKim abandoned his traveling mates and returned to New York after six weeks in France, apparently exhausted by White and Saint-Gaudens's drinking, joking, and associated ribaldry.[51] So in the late summer of 1878 White moved his few belongings into Saint-Gaudens's Paris apartment to camp out between his own excursions into the countryside. Saint-Gaudens's younger brother Louis lodged there as well, and it is likely that he and White shared the servant's room on the topmost floor.

Now it was time for work to begin in earnest on the design for the statue of Admiral Farragut. Although he kept Greek and Roman casts about, Saint-Gaudens no longer cared to render toga-clad contemporaries in the neoclassical style that had been in favor at the École des Beaux-Arts. Nor was he much influenced by the maudlin fallen queens, playful fauns, bound slaves, and blind Pompeian beggar girls created in marble by his fellow American sculptors in Italy. Instead, he was turning to the Neo-Florentine style popular with younger sculptors in Paris who rejected those cold and lifeless copies of Greek and Roman figures. These artists

took their inspiration from the courtly subject matter and refined naturalism of the fifteenth-century Italian Renaissance, creating sculpture cast in
warm bronze in which the spirit of Michelangelo, Ghiberti, Donatello, and
Verrocchio seemed to live again.[52]

While living in Italy Saint-Gaudens had come to know firsthand the
great works of those masters of the Renaissance, and on the walls of his
studio also hung relief casts by della Robbia and Donatello. It was something of that spirit—of realism, movement, and beauty of line—that had
inspired his proposed design for Admiral Farragut and would mark the
work that would follow—all the way to the Madison Square Garden.

•

After largely completing the design for the *Farragut* base at the end of
February 1879, White, who was mad for French Gothic architecture,
began to travel on his own to visit some of the old cathedral towns like
Amiens and Laon. On a tour of Rheims, the Gothic figures on the face
of the cathedral so excited him that he sent a telegram to Saint-Gaudens
insisting that he come at once. Saint-Gaudens complied, but Augusta
sent her sister Genie Homer along, perhaps as chaperon, and the three of
them stayed at a little hotel in Rheims, drinking champagne and roasting
apples before the fire.[53]

Every few weeks White happily returned to Paris and Saint-Gaudens's
apartment. He always had a bear hug for Saint-Gaudens and would have
hugged Augusta as well, "if she was pretty—but she ain't—so I don't . . .
She is an animated clothes-rack, slightly deaf—a double-barreled Yankee." White railed on about Saint-Gaudens's choice of mate, declaring,
"Why fate should have ordained that such a man should be harnessed to
such a woman, Heaven only knows."[54]

In the summer of 1879, White and Saint-Gaudens traveled all over
Italy, both together and apart, searching out relief panels as inspiration for
the allegorical figures they planned for the *Farragut*'s base. At some point
a real disagreement arose, although the cause is not known—it may have
been something as mundane as the height of the monument or something
more personal.

Although the pedestal design for the *Farragut* had not yet been final-
ized, Stanford White left Europe in August 1879 (following a misadventure

of some sort in London and a threatened legal action of an unknown sort).[55] Saint-Gaudens had previously sent him an apology from Rome for "things in Italy and what not, I am more sorry than I can express, etc. etc. . . . Of course I ought to be punched—knocked against a wall, thrown off the N. Y. Post Office flagstaff." White replied some time later, "Good God man, hell and the devil, what do you mean. If ever a man acted well, you did, and I ought to have been kicked for many reasons, kicked in the behind. Thunder and guns. Nuff said."[56] Letters would continue to be exchanged on their various projects, addressed to "My Beloved Snooks" and "Doubly Beloved" from White, "Darling and Beauty" from Saint-Gaudens.

•

In the fall of 1879, with a thousand details yet to be settled on for the *Farragut Monument* and Saint-Gaudens still in Paris, White continued to dash off letters scribbled in pencil on pieces of tracing paper. The *Farragut* contract called for a granite base, but he had seen a stunning piece of Hudson River bluestone that would recall the color of the sea. Finally they both settled on a design for the base that was all very new and modern. Instead of a typically vertical stone, the base would be a broad ellipse in the shape of a bench with a high back to allow for two low-relief allegorical figures of Loyalty and Courage and a long inscription recalling Admiral Farragut's brave deeds, rewritten by Stanford White's ever-finicky father.[57]

After the figure of Admiral Farragut had been successfully cast in bronze at the Paris foundry of Adolphe Gruet and a plaster cast of the figure shown with success at the 1880 Paris Salon,[58] Saint-Gaudens and brother Louis sailed home in June 1880. Gussie, seven months pregnant, retired at once to her parents' home in the Boston suburbs to be fussed over, while Gus and Louis returned to work in New York. Writing to his wife, Saint-Gaudens teased, "Did I ever tell you what a lot of handsome female models there are here? A great many more than in Paris and all of them have that rare thing—fine breasts."[59]

Paris had been and would remain a great source of inspiration for White, Saint-Gaudens, and so many other American artists and architects, even if they may have moved past specifics of the French Romanesque and Gothic styles for their aesthetic sources. For many Americans, Paris would also be a continuing source and touchstone for not only what was stylish and beautiful but what was considered sensual, exotic, and even dangerous. And, surprisingly enough, when it came time to design a tower for Madison Square Garden, Stanford White may well have thought back to Paris as much as to Moorish Spain.

•

Perhaps after sipping the last of his Delmonico's coffee, Stanford White may have made a quick detour past the statue of Admiral Farragut in Madison Square Park just across the avenue. How he had stewed over the exact placement of the sculpture, deciding finally on a fine site at the Twenty-Sixth Street corner of the park facing Fifth Avenue. On a beautifully sunny Memorial Day, 1881, the *Farragut Monument* was finally dedicated. Military bands played, flags waved, artillery discharged, and orators delivered. When the covering was finally pulled back by John H. Knowles, the sailor who had lashed Farragut to the mast so that he might have a better view of the battle, the illustrious guests and crowd of ten thousand viewers were in for a surprise.[60]

This was no coolly noble, neoclassic hero clad in toga. And while Farragut's pose may have been inspired by Donatello's *Saint George* on the Orsanmichele in Florence, of which Saint-Gaudens kept a cast in his studio, neither was this some otherworldly saint. This hero, remarkable in its naturalism, was rendered astride the deck, swaying with the sea and wearing his fatigues, wrinkled and weather-beaten, his coat blown aside to reveal a stout figure, his head turned slightly to the side, his eyes fierce upon the horizon.[61]

On the base, the low-relief carved figures of Loyalty and Courage appeared as two beautiful, strong-featured women, one seminude and one in breastplate, realistically rendered with a nod to Michelangelo yet romanticized rather in the Pre-Raphaelite style so popular in English painting.[62]

The *Farragut Monument* was tremendously well received, and it was clear to the critics that a new era had begun in American sculpture. Even the style of lettering in the inscription was considered revolutionary in its beauty and organic line, encouraging other sculptors to devise similar fonts of "equal charm and refinement." Not only did the monument

10. *David Glasgow Farragut Monument*, Augustus Saint-Gaudens, 1877–80, bronze on stone exedra. The New York Public Library / Art Resource, NY.

represent the union of architecture and sculpture, but by White's careful planning it took into consideration its place in the landscape as well as its visual effect on the viewer.[63]

While Delmonico's whipped up salmon à la Farragut, a whole poached fish decorated with truffles, crawfish tails, anchovies, and tarragon leaves, surrounded by crawfish, oyster, and clam tartlets,[64] a *New York Times* editorial declared it the handsomest monument in the city, and the *Herald* acknowledged the monument as one of the most noble and thoroughly artistic productions in America. Augustus Saint-Gaudens's and Stanford White's reputations had indeed been made.[65]

5

Women, Horses, and a Curse?

PERHAPS WITH A TIP OF HIS HAT to Admiral Farragut, Stanford White may have set off along the Madison Square Park's curving pathway back to Twenty-Sixth Street, passing in front of the brownstone-and-brick Hotel Brunswick set at the northwest corner facing Fifth Avenue. Commissioned in 1870 by the former co-owner of the Hoffman House, the firm of Gambrill & Richardson was tasked with cobbling together three adjoining homes and remodeling them into a rival first-class hotel. Following a design by Charles McKim while he was still at the firm,[1] the three sections were united under a slated French mansard roof, still in style and still redolent of a certain Continental elegance. It was one of the firm's first architectural commissions, executed before Richardson fixated upon the Romanesque, and would be one of just a handful of alteration projects the firm completed in New York City.

While the Albemarle Hotel catered to actresses and bachelors and the Hoffman House to a more sporting crowd, the Brunswick was known as the official watering hole of the wealthy and socially prominent horsey set.[2] Each spring crowds flooded Fifth Avenue to watch the annual outing of the New York Coaching Club, founded in 1875 when patricians like Colonel William Jay and Colonel DeLancey Astor Kane chose to revive the romance of ye olde English coaching days and encourage four-in-hand driving in America, still a popular pastime among the English upper classes. Joined by other society "whips" August Belmont II, J. Roosevelt Roosevelt, Leonard Jerome, James Gordon Bennett, and a sprinkling of the Vanderbilts, Astors, Iselins, and Havemeyers,[3] they somehow found tooling along in one's best morning clothes on a four-horse-drawn copy of an English mail coach a preeminently fashionable sport.

The coaching club's parade on the last Saturday in May not only reflected Madison Square's appreciation of fine horseflesh but served as a rare aesthetic treat for even the most jaundiced eye. The club's dozen or so painted and decorated four-in-hand drags would assemble in front of the hotel, the horses' coats shining like satin, their necks festooned with flowers. The gentlemen all wore bottle-green cutaway coats with gilt buttons and huge nosegay boutonnières, yellow-striped waistcoats, light trousers, and gray top hats (at least until 1888, when black top hats were adopted). The brightly colored coaches in red, yellow, and blue seemed more like giant baskets of flowers on wheels, while perched on top like butterflies reigned the most beautiful women in society. The coaches dashed up the avenue, around Central Park, and back down to the square, hooves clattering, horns blaring. And it was this group of sporting and socialite lovers of horseflesh that would be the first and very devoted supporters of a new Madison Square Garden.[4]

•

Just past the Brunswick stood a block of old brownstone-front row houses from the 1860s, their high-ceiling rooms still home to a variety of Wall Street bankers, brokers, and industrialists, including horseman and stock speculator Frank Work at number 13; philanthropist and president of the New-York Historical Society Benjamin H. Field at number 21; and devoted horseman and founding member of the Madison Square Garden Company Adrian Iselin at number 23.

The first high-toned residence on Madison Square had been built on the east side in 1851 by businessman and banker James Stokes. More beautiful homes of brick and brownstone in the Italianate palazzo style were soon constructed, and Madison Square was written up in local guidebooks as the central point of life in uptown Manhattan. On Saturdays and Sundays, residents strolled among the flowerbeds and fountains on 6,600 feet of straight-angle walkways on a rigid, diamond-like grid that cut through the park to connect with the streets and avenues.[5]

Continuing on just across Madison Avenue to the corner at Twenty-Sixth Street, Stanford White would have finally reached the first and original Madison Square Garden. Not much of a garden anymore, the smells were more of sweat and excrement, blood, sawdust, and soured champagne. Perhaps it occurred to White that unlike the already-crumbling bluestone base of another man's sculpture, the new Madison Square Garden would be his own grand monument on the square, his own mark on the city.

That evening in 1887 carpenters and painters were doubtless working late to transform the old place into the semblance of a concert hall and restore its garden-like charms. A last hurrah was in the works—a series of festive August concerts were about to be tried in an effort to still make a profit, as few places in town offered good music during the summer months.[6] A new bandstand was rising in the center of the arena surrounded by tables where food and drink would be served, while a line of workmen hauled in tubs of evergreen and flowering shrubs to enclose the tables and border a wooden promenade, 25 feet wide and nearly half a mile long, that wound around the floor. Fountains would be scattered throughout the building, and a new cooling apparatus installed in the cellar to be powered by winged disks that would send the air rushing out into the arena through rubber tubing.[7]

But the nonsense of it all was that this Madison Square Garden would soon be just a memory, although most certainly an oddly diverse one for New Yorkers. In just the first six months of 1887 the Garden had hosted Barnum's Greatest Show on Earth, political rallies for a free Ireland, Buffalo Bill Cody's Wild West Show, the trials of the Westminster Kennel Club, cross-country athletic games, and the world's largest dairy and cattle show. Perhaps the most ambitious undertaking was a revival of Gilbert & Sullivan's *H.M.S. Pinafore*, complete with a replica of Her Majesty's ship floating in a huge tank of water. Several thousand attended opening night, and a long run was expected, but *Pinafore* folded after just six nights. It was always a gamble to put on a show in the old building during the summer months, and with a weekly rental of $1,250, the producers barely managed to break even.[8] High costs, poor acoustics, and low-ticket sales had long been the refrain. But the dour financials did not deter Stanford White from his grand plans for a new Garden. Nor would the continuing northward movement of society beyond Madison Square and toward Central Park deter the new Garden directors from its old site. That was where the Garden had always been and where they vowed it would remain.

•

As the largest public venue in the city, the old Madison Square Garden had been the center for sport, amusement, and general edification for the past nearly fifteen years. But this spot's history on Madison Square went back a great deal further. That northeast corner of the square had first been claimed by the New York and Harlem Railroad as a milk and produce depot in 1832, and in 1845 the railroad erected a multitowered passenger station with freight shed and car barn in the new Italianate style. Three years later the New York and New Haven line that connected the city to Connecticut via Long Island Sound reached an agreement to use the station as well.

In 1857 the new Union Depot was erected on the spot, servicing the trains that brought in shoppers and diners from the hinterlands and whose first-class passengers filled the rooms at the Fifth Avenue Hotel and its neighboring hostelries. This new depot was composed of castellated, medieval-inspired accommodations for the New York and New Haven line at Twenty-Seventh Street, while a station in the more elegant Renaissance Italian palazzo style was constructed for the New York and Harlem Railroad at Twenty-Sixth Street, with the two stations separated by a rail yard.[9]

11. Union Depot, Madison Square, 1857–71, *American Architect* (Dec. 20, 1925).

Under the far-reaching control of railroad king Cornelius Vanderbilt—forever known as "the Commodore" for his early steamboat shipping ventures—the New York and Harlem line joined with the New Haven and New York Central and Hudson River Railroads, and in 1871 Vanderbilt opened the immense Grand Central Depot sixteen blocks north at East Forty-Second Street. The old Union Depot on Madison Square—by then deteriorated into a bleak and grimy spot—was abandoned, but Vanderbilt hung on to the property.[10]

The Union Depot sat vacant for two years until it came to the attention of Phineas T. Barnum. A onetime grocery clerk, blackface singer, and sometimes magician from Danbury, Connecticut, he was by then well known and well established as proprietor of Barnum's American Museum on Broadway. His long career of displaying curiosities, human oddities, humbugs, wild animals, and entertainments of all types included popular sensations like the diminutive General Tom Thumb, Swedish nightingale Jenny Lind, and Siamese twins Chang and Eng.

Although officially in retirement after the museum's destruction by fire in 1865 and then its replacement in 1868, Barnum was restless and ready for something new, and so it would be a circus. A show was soon assembled, "P. T. Barnum's Grand Traveling Museum, Menagerie, Caravan & Hippodrome," which opened in 1871 and played at various venues around the city. Buoyed by its success, Barnum bought the Hippotheatron at Broadway and Fourteenth Street, enlarging and remodeling it as winter quarters and exhibition hall to contain his circus, menagerie, and museum. But a Christmas Eve fire in 1872 destroyed everything except for two elephants and a camel.

In the fall of 1873—while about-to-be-widower Barnum was in Europe courting his about-to-be-second wife—his general manager, W. C. Coup, obtained a lease on the abandoned Vanderbilt railroad property. He quartered the elephants in the old horse barn and next to the passenger station erected a gigantic double tent—the largest ever seen in the city—to house a two-ring circus and menagerie.

Eventually most of the old depot was torn down, the tracks torn up, and a new building quickly and crudely built upon the old 28-foot-high brick wall that had enclosed the huge open rail yard. Within the yard, an oval arena was constructed under a partially enclosed roof, with boxes and rows of wooden seats to accommodate 12,000 paying customers.[11] A particularly striking feature of the building was the entranceway at Fourth and East Twenty-Sixth Street, a tall tower in the mansarded French Second Empire style.

Christened Barnum's "Great Roman Hippodrome" in the spring of 1874 (but also known as the "Grand Roman Hippodrome" and "Barnum's Monster Classical and Zoological Hippodrome"), it was the largest amusement center ever constructed. And the largest crowd ever assembled in one building was treated to Roman chariot races with female drivers, wirewalkers, a twice-weekly hot-air balloon ascension, Japanese tumblers, waltzing elephants, racing giraffes, Civil War reenactments, a Comanche chief roping cattle, and an English stag hunt complete with hounds. Every performance was grandly opened by the "Congress of Nations," an extravagant one-thousand-actor parade of splendidly garbed historic rulers and their courts that ranged from the emperor of China

12. *P. T. Barnum's Grand Roman Hippodrome, Madison Square*, ca. 1874. Irma and Paul Milstein Division of United States History, Local History and Genealogy, The New York Public Library Digital Collections, image 1691042.

to Napoleon to the pasha of Egypt. President Grant and his cabinet were among the duly impressed audience.[12]

During the summer, while Barnum traveled the circus around the country by train, the Roman Hippodrome was let to a variety of privately run events, a tradition that would continue in succeeding years. But after a female rider fell from her horse during a hurdle race and died, the *Times* bemoaned the public's depraved taste and warned that "this was just one more added to a long list of fatal casualties reported from this popular place of amusement." When an agent of the Hippodrome contradicted the long list, the *Times* agreed that perhaps there were only several fatal accidents that they could document, but "even one death was one too many."[13] Death in the pursuit of pleasure would be another theme played often here.

While most of the Hippodrome seats were covered by a pine roof, a giant canvas canopy had to be erected over the arena in wet weather. Despite the installation of base-burner stoves when the show reopened that November, the climate in the amphitheater remained what the *Herald* described as "Alaskan."[14] Mr. Coup had a breakdown due to overwork, the country was suffering from recession, and Barnum was overextended and taxed by various disasters that had plagued the traveling circus over the summer. So Barnum bowed out after one year, and in 1875 the lease was auctioned off.[15] Barnum's Hippodrome had not lasted long, but it continued the habit of New Yorkers heading to Madison Square for a good and thrilling time.

It was bandleader Patrick Sarsfield Gilmore, famed composer of the Civil War anthem "When Johnny Comes Marching Home," who took over the lease in partnership with theater manager Sheridan Shook and promptly reopened the Hippodrome at the end of May 1875 as Gilmore's Concert Garden, a venue for Gilmore's brass band, the largest and best trained in the country.

The "garden" appellation derived from the so-called pleasure garden as an open-air spot for concerts, an old New York tradition originating no doubt with the biergartens of Little Germany south of Union Square, where Americans first learned to drink lager *bier*. A pleasure garden was more casual in style than a concert hall, not as threatening to the God-fearing as a theater, and definitely not highbrow—no symphonies or grand opera were offered. Instead, the city's "gardens" presented summertime concerts for the whole family at reasonable prices, five-cent beer, and perhaps a chance to take the floor for a Bohemian waltz or glide mazurka.[16]

Under Gilmore and Shook's management, the rather shoddy Hippodrome was transformed into a lovely spot, raved the *Times*,[17] where one could stand or sit amid green grass, fragrant shrubs, or a forest of thick pines. They turned the old circus track into a graveled promenade and built an immense 60-foot-high cascade of water that tumbled down over huge moss-covered rocks and ferns into a wide pool filled with goldfish. To the old arena floor, they added grand gaslit chandeliers, multicolored spraying fountains, statuary, and beds of flowers in preparation for the gala reopening in 1875 to a crowd of twenty thousand.[18]

During the fall and winter of 1876 the management ventured far afield once again from the jolly summer concert to sublet the garden to a long and varied list that included Dwight L. Moody and Ira D. Sankey's evangelical revivals sponsored by J. P. Morgan, who led the hymns every night from a seat on the stage,[19] the first Westminster Kennel Bench Show of Dogs, horticultural exhibits, temperance meetings, the Policemen's Ball, beauty contests, and gloved boxing "demonstrations" and "illustrated lectures" conducted by pugilistic "professors" in tights, as 1856 state law forbade bare-knuckled prizefighting.

Expenses once again triumphed over income, however, and when the lease on Gilmore's Garden expired in December 1878, Gilmore and Shook could not meet Vanderbilt's demand for the $40,000 annual rent.[20] Instead, Gilmore joined the crowds enjoying the surf and cooling breezes of the newly transformed Coney Island—now made accessible by six railway lines, steamboat, and a concourse that led directly from Brooklyn to the sea—establishing Gilmore's Pavilion at the now stylish Manhattan Beach.[21] In 1888 Gilmore and his band would begin the tradition of celebrating New Year's Eve in what would eventually be called Times Square, but he just could not make a go of that Garden on Madison Square.

•

Thus, in 1878 the building returned to the Vanderbilt railroad empire and the management of its new president, William Henry "Billy" Vanderbilt, who had assumed control the year after the death of the family patriarch.

Of the Commodore's twelve children, Billy was the chief heir, and despite his being a "blockhead" according to his father, he was the only one deemed fit enough to carry on the family's interests.[22]

It was clear that under Vanderbilt's leadership Gilmore's Garden—as it was still known—would now follow a rather different plan, abandoning the concert program in favor of solely athletic events. A devoted horseman with a stable of fast trotters, Vanderbilt hired well-known sportsman William M. Tileston to manage the place and run a riding school on the track. An archery range and lawn tennis courts were installed within its central grassy space in summer, and in winter an 18,000-square-foot skating rink. Tileston again sublet out the arena, continuing the Westminster Dog Show—of which he had been a founder—as well as hosting lacrosse tournaments, the games of the Knickerbocker Athletic Club, wrestling matches, and fancy shooting exhibitions.[23]

Undoubtedly the most popular events at Gilmore's Garden were part of the new craze for long-distance walking. The fad, like so many others, had begun in England but spread to the States shortly after the end of the Civil War when Edward Payson Weston walked a distance of 1,227 miles from Portland, Maine, to Chicago in twenty-six days dressed in a ruffled shirt and black velvet knee britches. Lecturing on the benefits of exercise and clean living, Weston became a symbol of health and strength, not just individually but for the whole country newly emerged from the terrible war.

In September 1878, Gilmore's Garden hosted the first six-day pedestrian race in America, and a second the following March. By the early 1870s, virtually everyone was walking—even the once-dissolute James Gordon Bennett Jr., editor and publisher of the *New York Herald*, walked from Fifth Avenue and Thirty-Eighth Street to the Bronx and won a $6,000 prize. Many businesses had walking teams, with Lord & Taylor holding the championship of the Department Store League. Women walked as well as men, with Bertie Le Franc of the New York Ladies Walking Club the first woman to cover one hundred miles in less than twenty-eight hours.[24] By then, walking races had become so popular that a riot ensued when an overflow mob demanded entrance into Gilmore's Garden until a squad of policemen—their long clubs swinging—beat the crowd back with a rain of bone-crushing blows.[25]

On the third day of the race in March 1879, while ten thousand watched inside the Garden, there suddenly came a terrible rumbling, a sharp crack, and then a deafening crash. A 40-foot wooden gallery at the corner of the building nearest Madison Avenue and Twenty-Sixth Street, just to the right of the main entrance, had collapsed. Crashing timbers, boards, and one hundred shrieking human bodies fell from the tier boxes onto spectators seated below. Half of the crowd stayed in their seats, continuing to cheer the walkers as the band struck up a lively tune. The other five thousand rushed for the Madison Avenue side, some to rescue the slashed and maimed, others to flee what appeared to be the complete collapse of the building, trampling survivors and smashing every window in the process.

Upon hearing the cries and seeing some about to leap from the windows, the crowd outside the Garden believed the building was on fire and "fought almost like wild beasts" to press their way to the front. Then the mobs rushing to escape and those pushing in met head-on, completely blocking the way for the rescuers. News of the disaster spread like a flash around the square to the hotels and bars, and the streets were once again filled with thousands. Yet the mayhem did nothing to dampen the enthusiasm of newcomers still trying to enter the Garden. They discovered, after rather casually stepping over the victims lying in front of the box office, that the price of general admission had been suddenly raised from fifty cents to one dollar. And an hour later, after the debris on the track had been cleared away, the walk continued to the cheers of the indefatigable crowd.[26]

Apparently, over the winter an addition to the Garden had been quickly made to accommodate the anticipated audience. Twenty-four new gallery boxes had been built out over the main floor, and eight of these boxes and all the spectators in them had collapsed on those sitting below. Despite the mayhem, amazingly no one in the Garden was killed and only nine were injured. Real disaster, however, had only been postponed and not completely averted.[27]

The next month the *Times* noted that "if Gilmore's Garden had a tongue it would be pretty sure to ask to be given a rest."[28] It was clear that some changes needed to be made to cleanse the place, to erase the memory of recent events, and to restore the Garden to its proper place in the city's life. Many hoped that the walking craze had died out in New York, as landlord Vanderbilt considered several very different schemes for the spot, including a grand shopping arcade.[29]

An army of men working night and day transformed the place into a true garden, with winding gravel walks amid flowerbeds, shrubbery, and palm trees. An even larger waterfall was installed along with hanging baskets of twittering songbirds. More gas jets gave way to cooler carbon arc lights that would make the Garden the first real test of electric light for popular use, and admission was reduced to twenty-five cents.[30]

Then came the big announcement. On May 22, 1879, the New York newspapers let it be known that, according to Mr. Vanderbilt's wishes, Gilmore's Garden would hereafter be known as the "Madison-Square Garden," officially reopening under its new name on Memorial Day with a gala concert attended by thousands. Light summer concerts were reinstated and offered nightly, while lager beer was sold at the Garden's ever-busy long bar, even on Sundays, when the police dared not interfere. Once again the Garden was the place of all places for amusement-loving New Yorkers.[31]

•

During the winter of 1879–80, more extensive repairs and improvements were made. The exterior of the building was made more attractive by raising the height of the Madison Avenue wall by 8 feet and replacing a pair of rather hideous sphinxes at the main entrance with an ornamental iron portico. It is likely that at this point the old tower was renovated, its Gothic details eliminated, the French mansard roof removed, and the top flattened to give it that more Italianate look. Completing the modernization, the interior was repainted, polished hardwood wainscoting added around the galleries, and the cascade removed. A newly constructed upper story under the raised roof was handsomely decorated with more wainscoting and frescoed walls in the Italian style, and thirteen new hot-air furnaces were installed to keep it comfortable all winter, along with arches of colored lights, new fountains, and singing birds.[32]

The Madison Square Garden continued to be rented out not just for sporting events but for a run of musical comedies, plays, dog shows, balls,

13. First Madison Square Garden, ca. 1880. The Museum of the City of New York / Art Resource, NY.

and benefit fairs. In mid-April, the Garden was set up for the gala Hahnemann Homeopathic-Hospital Fair to benefit their free-bed fund. The fair itself would be held on the Garden floor, while the new second-story would be divided into a restaurant, dancing hall, and a picture gallery— with $150,000 worth of paintings by artists such as George Inness, Thomas Cole, Eastman Johnson, John La Farge, Elihu Vedder, and Albert Bierstadt on display, along with assorted bronze sculpture and antiquities.

On that terrible evening of April 21, 1880, a brilliant crowd of more than three thousand filled the arena ablaze with electric and gaslit chandeliers and strolled among flower stands and rows of booths decorated with Japanese fans and parasols. The Ninth Regiment Band played from the balcony just above the Madison Square entrance. But around five o'clock in the evening the art gallery manager, watchman, and an on-duty police detective began to hear ominous cracking noises and noticed pieces of plaster falling from the ceiling. Not wanting to cause undue panic, they informed the fifty or so art lovers in the gallery that the room was dangerously overheated and must be evacuated. Even dimming the lights had little effect on the crowd who had paid their twenty-five-cent admission to see Bierstadt's monumental painting of *King's River Canyon with Mount Brewer in the Distance* and the 150 other objets d'art. Finally, at nine thirty as the last few reluctantly departed, the walls began to bulge and the chandelier to sway. Then a huge piece of plaster 6 feet long fell from the ceiling, which then fell open and slid toward the avenue while the west wall tottered and fell outward. Or did the wall give way and *then* the ceiling crashed down in a great mass of rubble? Later testimony was uncertain.[33]

In a room south of the art gallery, sixty couples were happily dancing. By some oversight, they had not been informed of the falling plaster and were unaware of the gallery's impending collapse until the appearance of what seemed to be a cloud of smoke. A dull explosive sound was heard, then a crackling and groaning of wood and brickwork as the ceiling split apart, the chandelier fell, and debris rained down. Despite total darkness and a door jammed shut, most of those in the dancing hall were able to escape, although some were nearly trampled before the wall fell out, and twenty or so were hit by falling masonry. It seemed as if a tornado had swept through the dance hall.

Meanwhile, the attendees on the main floor of the arena heard odd noises from the second floor that grew louder until it seemed like a succession of explosions. Suddenly the upstairs throng came rushing down the stairs, men carrying collapsed women in their arms, their faces pale with fright and made more ghastly by the lime dust that covered them from head to toe. Ladies in the arena began to shriek and fall fainting at the sight.

When the final thundering crash occurred and a white cloud of dust rolled through the arena, some on the main floor cried "fire," and many began to rush wildly for the stairs. The throng surged toward the Madison Avenue exit, over which bricks, plaster, and timbers were still falling. In the midst of the panic a young man picked up a pair of cymbals and struck them together, crying out "No danger!" Others took up the cry, then a few musicians struck up "Yankee Doodle," and the crowd fell back toward the middle of the Garden. After a janitor with the key was finally located, the back exit doors onto Fourth Avenue were unlocked and the crowd freed at last. Many ladies, some hysterical according to the newspapers, sought refuge in the parlors of the Union League Club, waiting for news of friends and relatives still unaccounted for.

The police and firemen who had been on regular duty at the Garden rushed into action to clear the great piles of brick, masses of asphalt roofing, shattered boards, broken beams and trusses, and lath and mortar to search for bodies by lantern light. The call of fire had summoned four hook-and-ladder companies, and ambulances and fire engines filled the streets. Members of the Seventh Regiment, who happened to be holding a moonlight march down Fifth Avenue and had just passed the Garden, rushed back to join in the rescue efforts, as did dozens of fashionably dressed fair guests—all no doubt grateful that the collapse had not occurred fifteen minutes earlier when the sidewalk in front of the Garden had been packed with spectators.

One of the most terribly injured was William M. Tileston, the Garden's former manager. He was found mortally injured in the street beneath a pile of bricks and broken timber, his head badly cut, both legs, one hip, and one arm broken. Taken away by ambulance, he was heard to say that he would not want to live with such a maimed body and died soon thereafter. In addition to Tileston, three fairgoers were found dead at the Madison Avenue entrance, their bodies crushed into a shapeless mass. There were many victims with cuts and bruises and ten or twelve injured severely, while two hack cabs parked in front of the building were smashed and their horses killed.[34] And lastly, perhaps as many as ten bronze sculptures and forty paintings were ruined, although Bierstadt's great landscape, the largest in the show, survived with only damage to the frame.[35]

A coroner's inquest was immediately called, and in the next few weeks it was learned through expert testimony and much theorizing that new trusses supporting the roof were of improper material and construction to support its weight. When they gave way, the roof collapsed on the new Madison Avenue wall, which was not as thick as it should have been nor sufficiently anchored, nor were the bricks sufficiently mortared or cured.[36]

The Garden's much-touted two-story addition had been designed not by an architect but by F. S. Curtis, the Harlem Railroad's chief engineer, who confessed no knowledge of the building laws and whose original plans had in fact been turned down by the city's Department of Buildings. The construction firm of Smith & Prodgers admitted violating the law, yet all inspections had been approved by the department's Superintendent Henry J. Dudley, who, to no one's surprise, had previously been employed by several railroad companies.

It was clear that the whole Madison-Square Garden addition had been run up too quickly, in an improper manner, and with the cheapest possible materials. The old railroad depot was in no condition to be roofed over in the first place. Barnum had only intended his hippodrome to be temporary, but the rotten timbers and the brittle wall had remained, year after year, built and rebuilt upon. Just the year before, after the first collapse, the *Times* had warned that the gallery was just waiting to be crushed down to the floor below.[37] "Does cheapness of construction and low wages justify the sacrifice of public safety, comfort, and happiness for the sake of a few dollars more of already inordinate gain?"[38] demanded the *New York Sun*.

The coroner's inquiry closed with a strong verdict of censure upon the Harlem Railroad Company and the Department of Buildings. The *Times* recommended that the "old rattle-trap that disfigures one of the finest blocks of land in the City" should be wiped out until "it shall exist only as a hateful memory."[39] Many recalled the long history of disasters at the Garden, dating back to Barnum's time when circus riders were thrown from their horses, performers on the trapeze fell headlong to the ground, and broken limbs and cracked heads were the rule rather than the exception. And once again an exorcism of sorts was called for.[40] On May 15, 1880, the Department of Buildings served the Vanderbilts a formal notice condemning the Madison Square Garden and in accordance with the coroner's jury ordered the entire structure be razed to the ground.[41]

Meanwhile, P. T. Barnum jumped back in to announce that the new Barnum Museum Company, in which Billy Vanderbilt was a major investor, intended to purchase the spot from the railroad for the sum of $800,000 and erect a mammoth new five-story amusement center, including—aside from his museum—a huge arena for chariot races, fairs, and balls in the basement; the largest opera house in America on the ground floor; a dramatic theater, concert halls, aquarium, skating rink, zoological garden, and tropical winter garden; and at the southwest corner of the building adjoining Madison Square, a brick and iron tower or observatory 250 feet high that would be illuminated with a coronet of electric lights.[42] But five months later, the grand if somewhat impractical (illiterate and awkward, according to some) scheme had been abandoned due to lack of financing and Mr. Barnum's declining health.[43] Although, perhaps, it was not entirely forgotten.

Despite the order of condemnation, the Vanderbilts refused to accept liability for damages during the Hahnemann Fair—"the public be damned," Billy Vanderbilt would famously declare three years later—and presented expert testimony that the building was safe and sturdy.[44] Money talked, and the crisis passed.

•

High-stepping horses had clearly been a part of Madison Square's history since the very beginning, but in the fall of 1883 a whole new era began. In June that year, at a formal dinner at Delmonico's, the National Horse Show Association was founded. While pigs and chickens had their own annual exhibitions at the Garden, there was no comparable meeting to display the beauty, breeding, and formation of the horse. Now, finally, trotters, runners, high jumpers, saddle horses, coach horses, and driving, working, and breeding horses of every type would be on view in the city and at the Garden, which the association furthermore proposed to transform into its own permanent exhibition building.

It was feared that there might be limited interest in the project among the horsey set until the organizers of that first show were so swamped with entries that one hundred additional stalls had to be constructed in a temporary annex. Major alterations to the building were called for and made under the supervision of architect Henry Hardenbergh—when he was not distracted by his design for a new luxury apartment building on the Upper West Side, which seemed as impossibly far away from Madison Square, wits ventured, as the Dakota Territory.[45]

Thus, the old Garden was spruced up with fresh timber for floors and stalls, disinfectant, and a great deal of whitewash, while the center of the arena was converted to a tanbark show ring encircling a water jump and banked with flowers. Flags, streamers, bunting, and coats of arms neatly covered a variety of old sins as they hung from the rafters, swagged the balconies, and decorated the columns. The four hundred equine entries were housed in newly built and gaily beribboned stalls, were led about by grooms in elegant livery, and were said to sleep on linen sheets embroidered with their owners' crests.[46]

Over the following years the horse show at the Garden became a New York institution, usually held the week preceding the opening of the Metropolitan Opera and ushering in the fall and winter social season. Stanford White escorted his wife, Bessie, to the horse show, for whether one cared or not, horseflesh was the topic of the day, with a certain amount of enthusiasm required.[47] But to many in the crowd that swarmed the arena, horses were truly of secondary importance to the styles sported in the boxes and on the promenade, where fashion reigned supreme, and even the newspapers gave greater coverage to the gowns than to the equine entries.

•

In 1884, backed-up smoke from a bad chimney in one of Madison Square Garden's offices—or perhaps it was rubbish in a second-floor kitchen—was quietly extinguished to prevent panic among the audience. But red flags had been waved, and by the next afternoon the fire department's chief inspector had reported on various issues of safety in the arena, including wooden seats, cluttered aisles, no clear exit from the balcony, and the only two exits to the street unmarked. Management cooperated, and many of the problems were corrected by that evening, but the fear that the place might be a firetrap was very real.[48] Within days the *Times* reported that the old Madison Square Garden would soon become a thing of the past. A syndicate of National Horse Show Association members had come up with the idea of buying the Garden and constructing a new, luxurious, million-dollar hippodrome on the site. Soon organized as the Madison Square Garden Company, they began the search for an architectural firm able to take on their grandiose plans.[49]

In that summer of 1887 the old Madison Square Garden still hung on, a grimy, drafty, patched up old shell "halfway between a stable and a dive,"[50] but there were some New Yorkers who just could not stay away.

To circumvent various city laws that remained on the books against prizefighting, pugilistic "demonstrations" were presented by "Professor" John L. Sullivan, holder of the bare-knuckle heavyweight championship, who offered any student $1,000 and half the gate receipts if he could last through four rounds of "instruction."[51] By the grace of police and Tammany Hall payoffs, opera hats and white shirtfronts jostled caps and checked shirts for the best view, joining together to shake the Garden with "a storm of strong-lunged cheers" when the fighters appeared.[52] But as reformers and public opinion raged against the cruel, barefisted boxing matches—some lasting as long as seventy-five rounds—the barely paid-off police more frequently interrupted and even canceled the prizefights still technically banned by law. Fights were thrown as sales dwindled, and a new Madison Square Garden dedicated to equestrian events seemed like an appealing solution.[53]

•

Continuing around Madison Square from the old Garden, just across East Twenty-Sixth Street and down Madison Avenue, stood the grandest home on the square, the five-story, red-brick and white-marble mansarded mansion that once belonged to Leonard Jerome. A Wall Street broker, partner in Vanderbilt railroad interests, part owner of the *New York Times*, cofounder of the New York Coaching Club and the American Jockey Club, and builder of Jerome Park Racetrack in Westchester County, Jerome was known all around as the "Father of American Turf."

Along with his three-storied, crimson-carpeted, black walnut-paneled stables, said to be the finest in America, stood a six-hundred-seat ballroom theater where Jerome would present the charms of his favorite young singers and actresses in public and in very private concerts. Leonard Jerome's generous devotion to the arts and artistes apparently failed to impress his wife, who in 1873 removed herself and her three daughters to Europe, where the captivating Jennie would marry Lord Randolph Churchill and become mother to young Winston eight months after the wedding.[54] Beautiful women had long reigned on Madison Square along with the horses.

After the once-crowned king of Wall Street found himself in need of cash, Jerome was forced to lease out his mansion to a series of private men's clubs, and since 1884 it had been home to the University Club[55] for college-bred men—of which Stanford White was not one, despite honorary degrees from Columbia and the City University of New York that his father managed to wrangle for him. There were certain odiferous drawbacks to the club's location just across from Madison Square Garden, and the clubmen had hoped that the old Garden would be replaced by a music school or opera house—either being more likely to attract more "lovely young things" to the neighborhood. The members had bought up a fair number of shares in the Madison Square Garden Company in hopes of exerting some influence on the decision, but to no avail. The University Club was, however, promised a device on the Garden's new planned tower to indicate wind direction so that appropriate windows might be opened or shut.[56]

Further south beyond the Jerome House, as Madison Avenue continued down the east side of the square, lay a length of old, ivy-covered brownstones and their last remaining denizens. At the south end of the square, just one block to the east down Twenty-Third Street stood the National Academy of Design, where young Augustus Saint-Gaudens first studied the art of Greece and Rome. And adjacent to it on Park Avenue was theatrical genius Steele MacKaye's Lyceum Theatre, newly erected on the former site of Bernard Saint Gaudens's shoe shop, which had been razed in 1884 for the theater's construction. The theater was first in the city to offer folding seats, and all its electric light fixtures had been personally installed by Thomas Edison. Again these innovative features were undoubtedly noted by Stanford White for the Madison Square Garden's new theater.[57]

•

Perhaps there was a rumble of thunder that evening, one of those quick and violent July storms that drove strollers under the awning of Dorlon's famed oyster house at the corner of Twenty-Third and Broadway. On the top floor of the building the American Art Association held its exhibitions. It was in these skylit galleries in 1878 that Augustus Saint-Gaudens organized the first show of the newly founded Society of American Artists, composed of fellow young Turks reacting against the conservatism of the National Academy of Art,[58] and in 1907 that Stanford White's own astounding collection of art and antiques would be auctioned off after his murder to settle his many outstanding debts.[59]

In Madison Square Park, the only females to be found that late in the evening would have been the flashily dressed streetwalkers who plied their trade under the harsh glare of the 160-foot sun towers' electric arc lights.[60] There were said to be some five thousand "fallen sisters" working between Madison Square and the theater district. "Only a dollar, dearie, and I got the room,"[61] one might call, grabbing a passerby's arm. And then there were the even younger girls—children really—selling flowers. One might hail a gentleman with the usual cry, "Give me a penny, mister?" to let him know it was more than flowers she was vending.[62] And it would not be for another two years until the age of consent in New York was raised from ten years to sixteen.

Stanford White may have been tempted by the square's "lost sisterhood" some evenings; later he would carry a bag of twenty-dollar gold pieces for a quick encounter in a convenient alleyway.[63] But it was just as likely that he might shoot back to the offices of McKim, Mead & White, where he often turned up any hour of the night to throw off his coat and pounce on a lone draftsman, ready to work out a new project or an old problem, for according to his staff, White routinely found sleep unnecessary and night nonexistent.[64]

PART TWO
Building a Palace of Pleasure
August 1889

A temple of the Muses;
The mighty pile that is to be erected.[1]

14. Madison Square Garden arcade, ca. 1910. The Museum of the City of New York / Art Resource, NY.

6

The Walls Come Down

THERE WAS ANOTHER CRASH and a boom on Madison Square. Dishes rattled in the Hotel Brunswick's five dining rooms and whiskey bottles in its bar. A grimy workman, face white with plaster dust, sledgehammer slipping in sweaty hands, pounded a whitewashed brick wall as it crumbled about him while a hundred others and nearly as many horses joined the chorus.[1] It was another steaming day in the city, the seventh of August, 1889, the day the old Madison Square Garden came down.

According to newspaper reports, gangs of men perched on top of the old walls drove in wedges until they began to topple and then leapt off like cats in the opposite direction. They were at it with jack, jimmy, crowbar, picks, and spades, careful that not a brick landed on the sidewalk, not a hack's horse was startled, not a man watching from a clubhouse window was routed from his chair. This army of men and horses were at work around the clock, knocking down walls during the day and hauling away rubble through the night, except for the old bricks that would be reused to construct the walls of the new Garden.[2] But nowhere to be seen among the rubble and the dust was the man who had planned for this day for three years, the whirlwind who reveled in noise and flash.

Stanford White was, in fact, on a three-month trip to Europe accompanied by wife Bessie, their two-year-old son Larry, and his "darling Mommie," Nina. After "hollering after the hounds for three years"[3] to get something done on the Garden, to move the plans along, to revise and redo, his absence as the walls came down did "seem a little hard," he wrote to William Mead, sorry that he "should not be up at that 'death'" at Madison Square. He admitted that "I really just didn't think it would go

89

through this summer,"[4] and then nearly rushed back from London when the news came through by cable.

•

After winning the commission for McKim, Mead & White in 1887 and completing the preliminary plans and renditions, which were made public a few months later with the very optimistic completion date of Christmas 1888, came the endless meetings of the Madison Square Garden Company Building Committee, composed of Messrs. Hitchcock, Oelrichs, and Hollister, as well as the full board of directors, with and without the stockholders.[5]

Meetings dragged on, the stock market fell, and the project continued to hang fire. In March 1888, a new prospectus issued by the board revealed that the more modest 1,500-seat theater had been abandoned in favor of a huge 3,000-seat concert hall.[6] Yet the newspapers also reported rumors that the whole project had been abandoned and the site was to be given over to a less costly glass-and-iron shopping arcade in the style of the new Galleria in Milan, Italy, or perhaps a swimming bath, ice rink, or industrial museum.[7]

Later in the month, while the towering white drifts of the deadly Great Blizzard—the worst in the city's history—still lined the square, and poles and wires snapped by the ice lay in the street,[8] a reporter from the *New York Times* cornered Stanford White. "Is there any truth to the rumors of a serious split among the stockholders?" he queried. That all the schemes would likely be given up and the site cut up into building lots? A clearly discouraged White admitted that there had been many meetings, many schemes floated as to modifying the original plan.[9]

"And the lofty tower to crown it all? Haven't there been objections to this structure in particular?" Again, "Yes," White responded, "some of the directors are opposed to the outlay of money needed to build it," with little likely return. However, White assured the reporter that "there would be a superb view from the top" and that, with a charge for the ride up, the elevators up "would soon become a source of profit."[10]

A month later Stanford White had still not been able to demonstrate to the shareholders how the tower, estimated to cost $450,000, could possibly pay for itself. That it would be an object of beauty and grandeur, and an ornament to the city seemed to make little difference. Inspired by France's efforts to construct Gustave Eiffel's design for the world's tallest iron tower to crown the 1889 Exposition Universelle, some had hoped even to surpass it. "For a while, New York was hugging herself with the belief that she was to have a tower, too," but that dream seemed shattered. The *Times* further warned that if the Garden's architecture was dictated purely by economics, "if the scale be mean or ordinary," then the public would take little interest in the new Garden, "but if New York is proud of it as a work of art, everything connected with it will succeed."[11]

In June 1888 a new board of directors was elected, essentially remaining as it had been but with Hiram Hitchcock of the Fifth Avenue Hotel and chairman of the building committee named president. Still somewhat uncertain, a committee was appointed to investigate further the feasibility of the new building. In September, the press reported that the Madison Square Garden project seemed to have come to naught, with no prospects to lease the concert hall or theaters, and that this lack of interest would likely sink the entire plan.[12] Meanwhile, the old Garden lumbered on, managing to host in more-or-less respectable fashion its usual attractions: the six-day walking matches, the Westminster Kennel Club show, Barnum & Bailey's Circus, a variety of amateur athletics, and of course the annual horse show. The most novel attraction was doubtless the six-day ladies' bicycle race for the world championship that mesmerized the city in February 1889, the competitors shockingly clad in bright-colored tights and jackets.

•

According to the building scheme first announced in 1887, plans for the Garden's tower called for a sculpted figure at its top, perhaps one carrying some sort of powerful electric light.[13] The obvious sculptor to produce such a figure would certainly have been Stanford White's old friend and longtime collaborator, Augustus Saint-Gaudens, at work in his studio at 148 West Thirty-Sixth Street, some ten blocks north of Madison Square.

The studio came about after Stanford White's old boss, architect H. H. Richardson, set up an interview for Saint-Gaudens in 1881 with a committee awarding another Civil War monument, this time in Boston, this time honoring the young Colonel Robert Gould Shaw, who had died leading his brave regiment of African American soldiers. Saint-Gaudens was hired on Richardson's suggestion, delighted by the opportunity to devise what he assumed would be his first equestrian statue. He drew in pen-and-ink an officer, sword in hand, poised on top of a pawing stallion, but he was sorely disappointed when the Shaw family quickly rejected the design as far too grand and pretentious. After considering other possibilities, Saint-Gaudens fell upon the more successful plan of depicting a freestanding Colonel Shaw leading his troops against a panel in exceedingly high relief.[14]

With the *Farragut* pedestal being carved in stone and the *Shaw Memorial* and several other large commissions in the works, Saint-Gaudens needed sufficient space, so he took what had once been a painter's supply shed and before that a stable, set just off Broadway. He partitioned off two smaller rooms from the studio, using one as a reception room for the display of his work and the other as sleeping quarters for brother Louis. He added a toilet and new floor, cut out a skylight, and built a bench around the walls of the big room, which he had painted white. This "great white studio" or "long white studio," as it came to be known, would be his headquarters for the next fifteen years and a familiar meeting place for almost everyone in the literary or artistic world, but on Augustus Saint-Gaudens's own terms and timetable.[15]

Bits and pieces of his previous collaborations with Stanford White were scattered throughout the barn-like studio—drawings, photographs, and sketches in clay and plaster of past projects, including the 1883 Mausoleum in the Green-Wood Cemetery in Brooklyn dedicated to David Stewart (father to Boston art collector and patron Isabella Stewart Gardner), the *Robert R. Randall Monument* of 1884 for the Sailors' Snug Harbor on Staten Island, and the so-called *Standing Lincoln* in Chicago's Lincoln Park and *The Puritan* in Springfield, Massachusetts, both unveiled in the fall of 1887.

Their current project was a memorial to Marian "Clover" Hooper Adams, a photographer who had taken her own life in 1885 by drinking darkroom chemicals, that was destined for Rock Creek Cemetery in Washington, DC. Saint-Gaudens had been playing endlessly with a "simple and mysterious" seated, hooded figure, not even permitting White a real look at it.[16] As in all these projects, Saint-Gaudens designed

15. *Faith*, Giralda Tower, Cathedral of Seville, 2015, cropped color photograph. By Carlos Teixidor Cadenas [CC BY-SA 4.0 (https://creativecommons.org/licenses /by-sa/4.0)], Wikimedia Commons.

the central sculptural figural, while White executed the setting, bases, platforms, and steps.

There was no real figure indicated for the tower in the first drawing that won the competition for McKim, Mead & White. However, the Madison Square Garden Company prospectus of 1888 did show a weather vane very much in the style of the figure of *Faith* on the Giralda in Seville, still in service.[17] Weighing more than 2,000 pounds, that hollow bronze figure had been mounted upon an iron rod run through a great bronze globe set beneath her feet and rotated with the wind. Holding a palm frond in one hand and the Roman standard of Constantine, the first Christian emperor, in the other, the figure also functions as a weather vane, a *giradillo*. Thus, over the centuries the tower had become secondary to the figure who gave her nickname to the structure—an irony apparently overlooked by Stanford White to his later regret.

There were no funds allotted by the Madison Square Garden Company for a tower sculpture, but White offered that if Augustus Saint-Gaudens would contribute his time and expenses and those of his studio toward modeling a small figure and enlarging it to the necessary size, he would pay the cost of erecting it. Saint-Gaudens quickly agreed, delighted for the opportunity to create this monumental figure. Among the Civil War heroes, mausoleum pieces, deceased presidents, and portraits of friends and family, he had had little chance to create a fully three-dimensional female figure that represented no particular individual but just an abstract ideal that was simply beautiful[18]—and perhaps barely dressed at that.

•

By March 1889, only $900,000 of the necessary $1.5 million Madison Square Garden capital stock had been subscribed. Meanwhile, a renegade group of music-loving investors, frustrated with the board's slow pace on the project, had taken an option on another piece of property. The president of the Symphony Society, industrialist Andrew Carnegie, withdrew his subscription of $75,000 in Garden stock with the intention of teaching the Garden board how to carry out a grand scheme with much less fuss. It was a terrible shock for Stanford White and the board when the music lovers withdrew, intending to build for themselves a more "serious" music hall that would serve as a permanent home for a symphony orchestra just uptown at West Fifty-Seventh Street and Seventh Avenue. Begun in 1890, it would be renamed Carnegie Hall in 1893 after its founding patron.[19]

After boldly announcing to the press that the loss of the symphony faction would make no difference, the board scrapped Stanford White's original plans. White then quickly submitted sixteen additional and alternative designs, eliminating the Turkish bath, shops, multiple bachelor apartments, basement exhibition hall, and tower art gallery, and stripping it down to a complex focused more purely on public entertainment.[20] J. P. Morgan, holder of a $300,000 investment in a majority three thousand shares of common stock, finally swung the vote to proceed. The future course for the Garden was at last resolved, with three-fifths of the capital guaranteed by a broad group of investors, now including the commercial interests of Barnum & Bailey and Tiffany & Co.[21] The Madison Square Garden Company was confident enough to announce in March 1889 that demolition and then construction were expected to begin within a month, and that the building would be ready for dedication in the fall of 1889.[22]

But then the work was postponed for two months while the directors—led by Morgan and John Jacob Astor—decided to peddle the remaining two-fifths shares of stock to the public at the ground-floor price of $75 a share, realizing that they were unable to keep the stock corralled among the usual gentlemen of means within their own select circle. To their great surprise, the public failed to snap it up, and no more of the stock was sold. As a result, Stanford White and his draftsmen were forced to scramble together yet another series of three alternative plans, for a complex that could be built at a cost of $800,000, $1 million, or $1.25 million in place of the original $1.5 million.[23] In the meantime and on the sly, the directors listed the property for sale, leading to widespread rumors that an English syndicate was after the lot, that the city planned to bid on it for a new post office, or that other investors had plans afoot for a grand hotel.[24] These delays and frustrations may well explain why Stanford White chose to leave New York for a tour of the Continent rather than spend another summer in the city.

•

But then, in mid-July 1889, the Garden board announced with high spirits that all the stock of the Madison Square Garden Company had been taken—mostly by J. P. Morgan and his Wall Street firm of Drexel, Morgan & Co., and the money needed to begin construction was at hand.[25] On the morning of August 7, the building committee issued the order to demolisher and dealer in secondhand building materials Francis W. Seagrist Jr. that as of "one o'clock this afternoon, one hundred men with the requisite number of horses and carts were to begin the work of tearing down the old Madison Square Garden."[26] Fixtures would go first, then furniture and trappings were to be removed, and then the floors ripped out. The occupants of various offices, who had no idea their eviction was imminent, were only given till the end of the day to vacate the premises.

It took just three weeks for the old Madison Square Garden to come down under the direction of Seagrist's demolishing crew, whose progress was of unending interest to Madison Square strollers. More than two thousand wagonloads of brick, iron, timber, and nails were carted away, and a small frame house was erected on the site for use as a superintendent's office.[27]

7

Continental Influences

IN JULY 1889 Stanford White and his family set out across the Pond on a trip that would be a combination of business and pleasure and the first back to Europe for the Whites since their honeymoon. It would also serve as an opportunity to explore new advances in architecture, building materials, and related technologies on the Continent that might well have some relevance for the Madison Square Garden project. Apart from White's stated intention of visiting every theater in Europe,[1] there was much to be observed and noted at the 1889 Paris Exposition Universelle International that formally celebrated the one-hundredth anniversary of the storming of the Bastille and the start of the French Revolution.

Visitors to the exposition streamed in through the now-completed arched base of Gustave Eiffel's puddled iron-work tower,[2] at 984 feet the tallest structure in the world. Aside from serving as the first transmitter of radio waves, the tower was illuminated by ten thousand gas lamps mounted on the steeple and platforms. In addition, a rotating tricolor light at its apex illuminated the night sky while the world's two most powerful mobile light projectors rotated on a circular rail to light the city below. French-built, piston-driven elevators brought visitors to the first platform for observation, while hydraulic elevators built by the Otis firm brought them to the second—features that would all appear in one form or another on the Madison Square Garden tower.

Doubtless of particular interest to Stanford White and his plans for the Garden was the remarkable Palais des Machines—an enormous and very modern building of glass, wrought iron, and steel that enclosed the world's largest interior space. Modeled after the glorious 1860s St. Pancras Train Shed in north London, the enormous transverse-trussed pointed

97

barrel vault, at 143 feet high, covered four acres of exhibition space to showcase mechanical innovation, including 493 of Thomas Edison's remarkable inventions.

The trusses that supported the vault were hinged at both the base and crown to compensate for environmental expansion and contraction and thus needed no weighty stone or concrete buttresses to support them. Nor were they politely hidden away under a layer of plaster but fully exposed to display the strength of their material and the boldness of their design.[3] In general, the 1889 exposition clearly demonstrated the triumph of a variety of technological inventions, as fountains swathed in electric lights changed color in time to music and opera was transmitted via telephone in stereophonic sound while dirigible balloons circled above.

•

Stanford White had also convinced Augustus Saint-Gaudens to join him in Paris to visit the exposition.[4] Among the fine arts on view at the Palais des Beaux-Arts was a bust Saint-Gaudens had created of a battle-weary General Sherman that would later serve as a study for his 1903 monument in New York City. But it was doubtless another figure that was the focus of Saint-Gaudens's attention—a life-sized plaster model of Diana, Roman goddess of the moon and the hunt. Winner of an honorable mention at the spring Salon de la Société Nationale des Artistes Français, this spritely nude was the work of an old friend and former protégé, Frederick William MacMonnies.

At the age of sixteen, Brooklyn-born Willie MacMonnies had been Augustus Saint-Gaudens's studio boy, sweeping the floor, tending the fire, and running errands while the master labored on the *Farragut Monument*. Saint-Gaudens noticed that the tall, red-haired young man was "pale, delicate, and attractive looking"[5] but otherwise paid him little attention. Until MacMonnies showed him some very charming little terra-cotta animals he had modeled, and Saint-Gaudens realized his promise.[6] "This angel boy," Augustus Saint-Gaudens said, was clearly "a gentle, tender bird that needed caressing out of its egg"[7] and so took him on at the studio for five years, coming to feel as if he were his own. On his many visits to the studio, Stanford White also noticed MacMonnies, with his droll smile, his hair always a tumble.[8] The young man was eventually promoted to mixing clay and keeping the account books, all the while taking night classes at the Cooper Union, the National Academy of Design, and then the Art Students League.[9]

In 1884, after having completed his apprenticeship, MacMonnies was ready to leave for study at the École des Beaux-Arts in Paris. When cash-strapped Saint-Gaudens could not come up with his back pay or a promised loan for expenses, Charles McKim kindly lent him fifty dollars. The talented and ambitious MacMonnies quickly established himself in Paris as a student of promise and at the urging of Saint-Gaudens applied for and was accepted into the atelier of Jean-Alexandre-Joseph Falguière, a former student of Saint-Gaudens's old teacher François Jouffroy. In short order, MacMonnies, who now called himself a more cosmopolitan Max or Mac, was hired as Falguière's assistant, had work accepted into the 1887 Salon, and won the École des Beaux-Arts' annual *prix d'atelier* in 1887 and 1888 for best work.[10]

Master Falguière, known in France as the great sculptor of flesh,[11] had himself already completed two well-known depictions of the goddess Diana. The first was a life-sized plaster for the Salon of 1882. Instead of the chaste young virgin of myth, it presented a rather coarse-faced, heavy-footed, stoutly middle-aged figure who seemed to critics to have just removed her corset.[12] This *Diana* in all her very lifelike modernity garnered much notice and was popularly reproduced for parlor decoration as both a marble bust and as a full-figure bronze reduction just 18 inches high, while cheap plaster copies were sold to passersby in the boulevards.[13]

Falguière's second figure was titled *Hunting Nymph*—a grinning *grisette* off the streets of Paris in pursuit of her prey, balanced on one foot, her left leg flung back a bit too high, her arrow just let fly. Distractingly realistic and quite theatrical in execution, it too was shown to titillated acclaim in plaster at the Salons of 1884, then in bronze and marble in the years following.

•

Augustus Saint-Gaudens had actually been quite aware of MacMonnies's own *Diana* for several years prior to the 1889 exposition. Mac-Monnies had written to him about his efforts, and various friends kept

Saint-Gaudens posted on its progress.[14] Known to the early Romans as Diana and conflated with Artemis of the Greeks, the goddess of the hunt had become quite the fashionable subject among the Beaux-Arts-trained sculptors. Although in classical times she was usually depicted draped, since the Renaissance French sculptors had chosen to represent her in the nude. Toting her bow for identification, Diana provided sculptors like MacMonnies the perfectly respectable and even erudite opportunity to create a nude female figure, and not simply nude but one in active motion.

A female figure in athletic endeavor was quite in keeping with the contemporary interest in female exercise and sport in Europe and even more so in the United States. Not just a few grandstanding competitors at the Madison Square Garden, but more and more middle- and upper-class American women were riding bicycles, playing lawn tennis, golf, and baseball, rowing, and competing in archery, which was rapidly becoming one of the most popular pastimes. Unlike some other sports "filled with rush and hurry," archery demanded the use of both brain and body, calling into play all of the muscles, particularly those of the chest and arms, while developing "an upright carriage and graceful movement."[15] Within a year, Charles Dana Gibson, Saint-Gaudens's onetime errand boy hired in the early 1880s but soon fired amid a rain of curses for carelessness, would immortalize this new goddesslike girl in print—tall, straight, strong, and unassailable, her gaze fearlessly direct.[16]

•

Frederick MacMonnies had corresponded with Saint-Gaudens about the *Diana* as he struggled with the figure, trying to match the grace of Greek and Roman examples while simultaneously imbuing it, as Saint-Gaudens had reminded him, with the natural beauty of a living, breathing creature.[17] In September 1888, he encouraged MacMonnies by letting him know he had "heard that the piece was passing good and entering very good."[18]

Friends traveling through Paris not only reported back on the *Diana* but provided details on the soon-to-be Mrs. Mac, Mary Fairchild, an American painter five years his senior. The struggling couple was finally able to marry when Stanford White heard of their penniless condition and arranged for MacMonnies's first paying commission, three hovering bronze angels above White's renovated Renaissance high altar for New York's Saint Paul the Apostle Catholic Church on Columbus at West Fifty-Ninth.[19]

Augusta Saint-Gaudens was warmly received by the newlyweds on a summer trip to Europe in 1888 and reported favorably to her husband on both the *Diana* and the bride. But MacMonnies was still far from pleased with his efforts, working and reworking the clay figure in a hundred ways, trying his wife's head on the model's shoulders and making casts of his wife's arms, until he was nearly suicidal. With barely a week to go before the deadline for the 1889 Salon, MacMonnies finally had the figure cast in plaster and long-requested 8-by-10-inch photographs made for Saint-Gaudens.[20] Saint-Gaudens wrote back a largely congratulatory letter, praising *Diana*'s elegance and unusual grace. Although he added rather backhandedly that when he first saw the photo, he "was not bowled over by it, having heard so much and knowing Mac so well" that he "had expected greater things, but perhaps it was all the fault of the damned photo."[21]

As finally revealed to Saint-Gaudens at the Paris Expo, MacMonnies's *Diana* was depicted as caught running, left shoulder forward with unstrung bow in hand, left leg bent behind. It was a spontaneous, realistic figure, clearly inspired by Falguière with its certain ungainly quality, her legs spread a bit too wide apart.

Although there were plans for MacMonnies to one day reproduce her in marble, a full-sized *Diana* was soon abandoned, the plaster cast lost. Within months, however, MacMonnies had produced a more practical run of small "parlor bronze" reproductions,[22] far lighter in feel and in flesh than the life-sized original, the knees now nearer together. Stanford White quickly acquired one of these reduced *Diana*s, and when Saint-Gaudens saw the reproduction among the captured treasures in the Whites' lavishly decorated Gramercy Park home, he wrote to Mac-Monnies praising it as "very beautiful and high in style with a tang to it."[23] Yet, as time passed and Saint-Gaudens came to develop his own

16. *Diana*, Frederick MacMonnies, 1890, bronze reduction, 30¾ in. Metropolitan Museum of Art, Gift of Edward D. Adams, 1927.

version of the goddess, he would warn friends of MacMonnies and of those who would come to steal your ideas.

•

Aside from visiting various theaters and the exposition in the summer of 1889, Stanford White was also scouring the antique shops of Paris and making side trips to London, Rome, and Florence in search of treasures for himself and his Fifth Avenue clients. This was the first of many such trips to scoop up doorframes and church altar tops, fireplaces and ceilings, carpets and tapestries, panels and pilasters, baubles and bric-a-brac, gilded columns and ivory doorknockers. These treasures had been left behind after Napoleon III's redesign of Paris in the 1850s and 1860s, the general impoverishment of European aristocracy after the Franco-Prussian War, and the political turmoil of the 1870s.[24] America's old and newly rich still preferred Old World art and manufactures as a means of demonstrating their good taste, and Stanford White's clients were happy to fund accounts for his treasure-seeking on foreign shores.[25] Defending the craze he had begun for decorating with antiquities, White explained that "dominant nations have always plundered works of art from the past. America is taking a leading place among nations and surely has the right to obtain art wherever she can."[26]

The cachet of winning the Madison Square Garden commission in 1887 and the continuing boom in business and building had brought in additional and substantial city projects to McKim, Mead & White in the succeeding two years, all executed in the Italian style. A temporary Roman-style arch just north of Washington Square that Stanford White designed to commemorate the April 1889 centennial of President Washington's inauguration would prove so popular that funds would be raised to re-create in marble the assemblage of plaster, wood, papier-mâché, stuffed bald eagles, flags, and a brightly painted statue of George Washington that he had found in an old junk shop. Aside from its Roman origin, reinforced perhaps by Paris's Arc de Triomphe, what was significant about this jury-rigged pile of bits and pieces was the way Stanford White had played with its lighting. At night, the arch was illuminated by hundreds of small incandescent electric lights powered by a dynamo in an adjacent yard, probably the first such occurrence in the United States.[27]

It would take another six years, however, for a permanent marble arch to become a reality, its decoration sculpted by MacMonnies, who modeled high up on a north-facing spandrel—on Stanford White's suggestion—Bessie White as the face of *War*.

8

Laying Plans

AMID SEEING THE SIGHTS and shopping extravagantly in Paris, Stanford White had learned the good news that all the capital stock had been subscribed, the full $1.5 million had been raised, and the construction of the Madison Square Garden would now be pushed as quickly as possible.[1]

Back at the offices of McKim, Mead & White there was a scramble as working plans were now urgently needed. Charles McKim offered to have a go at it, imagining classical columns and pediments in a sort of Temple of Sport, but soon abandoned the effort, realizing that White's original concept was far more engaging.[2]

William Mead then stepped in during the summer of 1889, just prior to demolition of the old Garden, to temporarily supervise the project. Writing to White for help in clarifying the details, he admitted that there was much about the plans—particularly the cost estimates and bids—of which he knew little.[3] Perhaps taking advantage of White's absence, constructor David H. King Jr., always the sharp businessman, continued to press on expenses and promised cost allowances. His bid on the project had not necessarily been the lowest, but McKim, Mead & White preferred to use the most reputable and responsible builders, and much would be left to King's on-site judgment.[4] No doubt there would be a thousand more questions to come, and Mead promised "Dear Stanny" to do his best, but if the result varied from what White had in mind, surely he would not be blamed.

White replied that it was too bad Mead had all the bother and extra responsibility on his shoulders. "Fire away and fix things as you best can—but leave everything you can—at least the arcade and tower—until I return."[5] White's heart was very much in the job, and he offered to cut

short his time in Paris if needed, while in the meantime he was busy studying the French brick and terra cotta used at the Exposition Universelle and
"having a hell of a time."[6] But still he complained that "the French are
the damnedest people to get information out of!" It took a letter from the
American minister to convince them he was not out to steal their ideas,
although White did find a splendid tile for the water closets, writing that
it could easily be shipped back to New York. "Cut the terra cotta bid in half
if necessary," White advised, but keep the tower and Madison Avenue end
rich in detail. And how about a copy of the bronze horses from the front
of St. Mark's in Venice? White could have them made cheap in terra cotta.[7]

Mead and McKim both sent off copies of working plans the draftsmen
had developed,[8] and White sent them right back, covered with scribbled
notes and instructions to make the skylight wider and reminding them
not to leave off the basement. With his taste for the spectacular, White
instructed them to add to the plans a sunken tank in the middle of the
arena for aquatic shows with girls in tights dropping from trapezes and
tightropes. And an open-air promenade around the upper level, whereby
box-holders might stroll about and chitchat during intermission. While
he also enclosed a sketch of what he had in mind for the lower part of the
tower, with alternating courses of white and yellow brick, he added most
emphatically, "and be sure and have Wells make the tower."[9]

That would have been Joseph Morrill Wells, the firm's leading draftsman and head man. Wells was the first staff they hired in September 1879
as the firm of McKim, Mead & White was about to be officially established. Hailing from Winchester, Massachusetts, and a claimed descen-
dant of Samuel Adams, Wells had studied architecture on the job with
several firms in Boston and briefly with Richard Morris Hunt in New
York. Known to his friends as Joe—except for White who insisted on calling him Wellzey—he was a brilliant if short-tempered designer. Augustus
Saint-Gaudens described him as "a man of infinite taste and judgment,
great learning, and delightful conversation," although most others, especially clients, found his prickly ways rather hard to tolerate.[10]

After a tour of Europe in 1881, Wells fell in love with the Italian
Renaissance, and with his rendered drawings of the Palazzo Farnese
and the Cancelleria in Rome hanging on the office walls, he was likely

the one who helped wean White and McKim away from the picturesque, the Romanesque, the Queen Anne, the French Gothic, and the American Colonial, and toward the Italian and the classical monumental.[11]

One of the first such projects was the Villard Houses on Madison Avenue, a block behind Saint Patrick's Cathedral. These were six contiguous homes around a courtyard the firm designed in 1882 for Henry Villard, president of the Northern Pacific Railroad and married to McKim's sister's sister-in-law.[12] It was the largest commission yet awarded the firm in those early days, and although White had made some preliminary designs, he was off traveling with Saint-Gaudens to New Mexico when the working drawings were needed.[13] Wells agreed to take over as job captain on the project, the story goes, but only if he could discard virtually everything already designed, making over the facades in the style of late fifteenth-century Italian palazzi.

Already quite enamored of the Italian architectural style, White and McKim were immediately won over when they returned from their various travels and saw what Wells had wrought in the finished elevations for the Villard Houses—their balance, proportion, and perfection of line.[14] And New York's second Italian revival,[15] following that first, simple, round-arched style of the 1840s and 1850s, had begun. White brought in friends like Augustus Saint-Gaudens, John La Farge, and Louis Comfort Tiffany for interior decoration, and with a gathering of the best artists doing superb work, creating princely palaces in the Italian style, it was little wonder that the New York culturati were writing about an American Renaissance.[16]

•

Now it was also time for Augustus Saint-Gaudens to begin to work out the figure for the top of the proposed Madison Square Garden tower, certainly a great sculpture that would also serve as a weather vane. Figures of this sort that would catch the wind, most typically in a bit of drape, were to be found all over Europe—including not only the sixteenth-century *Faith* atop the Giralda in Seville, but a seventeenth-century *Fortuna* on the Dogana da Mar customs house in Venice and an eighteenth-century *Fortuna* on Charlottenburg Palace in Berlin[17]—but they were generally of a stout, heavy-footed sort. The figure for the Garden needed to be something light, playful, sporting, bully, and beautiful, as Stanford White would put it, something that would set New York on its ear.

As Saint-Gaudens was no doubt aware, to function properly, any weather vane must be positioned on the highest point of a structure, must be perfectly balanced on its rotating axis, and must possess a pointer device on one side of the axis with a larger mass on the other against which the wind can blow. As a vane spins to reduce the force of the wind on its surface, the end with the greater mass is pushed away from the wind, while the pointer heads directly into the wind. Thus a vane is able to forecast by indicating the approach of a particular sort of weather that may habitually come from a certain cardinal point.[18]

The history of weather vanes reaches far back into antiquity, with the earliest recorded in metal—a bronze figure of the Greek god Triton atop the Tower of the Wind in ancient Athens. The idea spread across the known world, reaching England at the time of William the Conqueror and then extending to churches and barns of its far-flung colonies in the seventeenth century. Since that time, cast-iron or copper-sheet angels blowing horns and proclaiming God's message had twirled on top of innumerable American churches.[19]

•

"I will start the figure for the tower today, something in this character," Saint-Gaudens scribbled in brown ink on an undated piece of paper and sent to White with a sketch of an allegorical Greek figure of Fame.[20] A female figure in a classical Doric Greek chiton balanced on a sphere, drapery floating behind her, a great banner or oriflamme, as Saint-Gaudens described it, billowing high above her head and perhaps caught over her arm, while she blew a long Greek salpinx horn of good repute.

There were many contemporary examples of this type by French sculptors, including a colossal gilt-bronze *Fame* by Marius-Jean-Antonin Mercié—one of Saint-Gaudens's fellow students and an alumnus of both Jouffroy and Falguière's ateliers in Paris—hoisted atop the dome of the Palais du Trocadéro for the 1878 Exposition Universelle. The single-footed pose in motion, leaning forward into space with one arm raised and the opposing leg bent behind, was likely inspired by the French Renaissance *Fame* (1597) by Pierre I. Biard, who is said to have in turn

17. Preliminary sketch for Madison Square Garden tower figure, undated, brown ink on paper. Stanford White correspondence and architectural drawings, 1887–1922, Avery Architectural and Fine Arts Library, Columbia University.

drawn upon Giambologna's 1580 *Flying Mercury*, an Italian Renaissance image filled with movement that was frequently reproduced in bronze into the nineteenth century and would certainly be recalled in Saint-Gaudens's final design.

•

During Stanford White's 1889 European sojourn, the draftsmen at Mc-Kim, Mead & White continued to arrange and rearrange pieces of the Madison Square Garden project as White and Mead exchanged letters across the Atlantic. Finally, in mid-August as demolition continued, the firm was able to make public their revised and corrected plans. The main, quadrangular building—now estimated at a cost of $1.25 million in addition to the $1 million paid for the land—would be designed essentially in the style of the Italian Renaissance, absolutely fireproof, and constructed of glass, iron, and masonry faced with buff brick and white terra cotta.

18. *Mercury*, eighteenth century, after a sixteenth-century model by Giambologna, bronze, 13¾ in. Metropolitan Museum of Art, bequest of Irwin Untermyer, 1973.

The main entrance would be on Madison Avenue with a second, parallel entrance on Fourth Avenue. The amphitheater, 315 by 200 feet, would have a track 1/10 of a mile in length that enclosed a large arena. Six thousand spectators could be seated around the track in 150 private boxes, but the arena could also be floored over for conventions, fairs, revivals, and expositions to accommodate up to twelve thousand without crowding—double the number that could be seated in the old Garden. A hall 6 feet below ground and 35 feet wide would circle the amphitheater for stabling various creatures during shows and circuses. A section of the glass-domed roof, 112 by 200 feet, was designed so that it could be opened in fair weather, much like the Paris Hippodrome, with a covering that could be secured within fifteen minutes in the case of rain.

A restaurant and café would front on Madison Avenue at Twenty-Sixth Street, to the right of the main entrance. On the opposite corner, at

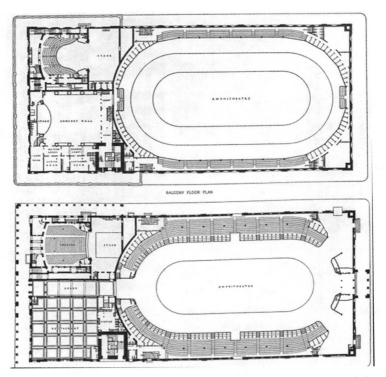

19. Floor plan, Madison Square Garden, 1891. *A Monograph of the Work of McKim, Mead & White 1879–1915* (1915; repr., New York: Dover Publications, 1990).

Madison and Twenty-Seventh, would be a hall for fairs and exhibitions. Just above, on the second floor, would be a theater devoted to drama and light comedy accommodating an audience of 1,200, and nearby, on the Twenty-Sixth Street side, a vastly reduced concert hall would seat only half as many as the three thousand originally planned but would have a small adjoining hall for supper parties. On the third floor would be located two dining rooms and a kitchen, lavatories, and dressing rooms, while in the basement the boiler, engine, and dynamo rooms would run the building's heating, cooling, ventilation, and incandescent electric light systems. A summer roof garden overlooking Madison Avenue was still being contemplated.

Further eliminations from the preliminary and quite grandiose plan were the street stalls, aquarium, shooting gallery, bowling alley, and artist studios. The sidewalk arcade was reduced to covering only Madison Avenue and 112 feet along its two adjoining sides. But the tower remained in the plan, looking rather like London's Big Ben with its huge dial and equipped with elevators and staircases to bring visitors to an observation lookout 250 feet above the sidewalk.[21]

William Mead met with constructor David King on-site nearly every day, but the firm had not yet delivered final working plans. Still, King promised that in accordance with his contract the amphitheater would be completed the following year, in March 1890; the concert hall in June of that year, "God willing," he added; and the remainder of the complex, including the tower, by August.[22] In response, the newspapers crowed that New York would finally have its own grand facility capable of holding great audiences. There were few sites left on the island of Manhattan that might accommodate such a project, and with the location for this temple of amusement so central and so accessible, how could it ever fail?[23]

•

In September 1889 the relatively final set of plans was filed at city hall,[24] while William Mead reassured Stanford White—now back in Paris after those buying trips to Florence and Rome—that in addition to Joseph Wells he would have a bully force of men at the office when White returned, ready to complete all the final details.[25]

Teunis van der Bent, a young Dutch architect and trained engineer who had joined the firm two years earlier ("and is a treasure,"[26] said Mead), was supervising the project from the office. Working drawings, elevations, specifications, and designs for the terra-cotta ornamentation were all laid on the table, as were plans for drainage, heating, electricity, structural iron, masonry, and carpentry. It had not been so very long ago that all an architect needed was a basic knowledge of wooden posts, beams, lintels, and trusses, along with an idea for a pretty facade. But by the late 1880s, it had become clear that a modern New York architect needed also to be something of a civil, mechanical, and sanitary engineer, with more than a passing familiarity with the science of electricity, hydrostatics, heating, ventilation, and plumbing.[27]

•

Finally, the Madison Square Garden project was handed over to constructor David King. There were thousands of tons of dirt and rock left over from the demolition that still needed to be smashed, plowed up, picked through, shoveled, and carried away,[28] but excavation began at once, and King rushed it for all he was worth. On the Fourth Avenue side, steam drills and pounds of dynamite were employed to blow the bedrock to pieces as they excavated the basement for the steam power plant that would heat and light the Garden and run its elevators.

Handling explosives was a dangerous job, and the nitroglycerine, the blasting cap, and the fuse were an unstable combination even in the hands of the experienced. Accidental explosions rocked the city on a regular basis, throwing up masses of earth and stone, injuring workmen, shaking up neighborhoods, and knocking down houses. Just months earlier, a very experienced handler working at an excavation site on West Seventy-Seventh managed to atomize himself into nearly three hundred separate pieces—including a toe driven into the bark of a tree—as well as cause other injuries, send ladies in the neighborhood into "hysteria," and wreck houses within twenty-four square blocks from Riverside Drive to Ninth Avenue.[29] But the Madison Square project was in undeniably good hands, for constructor King was the man who had laid the masonry on the concrete foundation base and erected the Statue of Liberty on Bedloe's Island, and on budget no less.[30]

9

In the Office and Out

IT HAD BEEN AWFULLY QUIET in the offices of McKim, Mead & White during the summer of 1889 with both Stanford White and Charles McKim away. No wailing falsetto from White on the warpath, twisting his mustache in both hands until hairs fell out on the drawing board or spitting out the splinters from a pencil chewed on his back teeth. No booming *"cyma recta, cyma reversa,* fillet above, fillet below, dentils, modillions" from McKim as he designed aloud at his drawing board. No calls for Letarouilly's *Édifices de Rome Moderne,* the firm's office bible, for if a particular combination of moldings was not included in this 1849 reconstruction of Renaissance Rome, then McKim would not use it.[1]

McKim was mostly in Boston at the firm's temporary office there, working on plans for the Boston Public Library. After the firm was awarded the library commission based on his designs, it made sense for McKim to be situated in Boston full time. Perhaps adding some comfort, the library site was located just across Copley Square from the Trinity Church for which he had drawn the first set of plans more than a decade earlier, and where a stunning stained glass window of *The Presentation of the Virgin in the Temple* by John La Farge, commissioned in 1888 after his late wife's funeral, had recently been dedicated to her memory.

Despite his professional success, McKim's personal life had continued to be a troubled one. After his first marriage was dissolved among scandalous charges on both sides and his daughter kept from him, he suffered a continuing round of illnesses, both psychosomatic and otherwise. Then at a dinner party in the spring of 1883, McKim met the Boston-born Julia Amory Appleton. A few months later, Miss Appleton inquired about his designing a summer home for her in fashionable Lenox, Massachusetts.

After many architect and client consultations, an engagement was announced. They wed in June 1885, but after a year and a half of happy married life, Julia Appleton McKim died delivering a stillborn child.[2]

•

By October 1889 Stanford White had returned from Europe. He was in the office, and his staff was on alert. So much for the "delicious quietude," Joseph Wells mused, but he had to admit more work was accomplished when White was on board to manage the crew.[3] Due to the firm's growing prestige, McKim, Mead & White had its pick of applicants, and it was considered a great privilege to be admitted to the offices as a draftsman, tracer of plans, or clerk—although all draftsmen were required to pass a six-month trial before they were paid their first weekly wage of eight dollars.[4] In terms of internal organization, McKim, Mead & White was far more casual than other large New York firms in that there were no formal division heads, no squad bosses, and no chief superintendent other than Stanford White to manage the men on his projects.[5]

Manage the draftsmen? According to accounts by members of his staff, he was more likely to simply terrorize them. White preferred to design from the outside in, putting a great deal of primary effort on the overall beauty of a façade—on color, form, and texture—while leaving the more practical organization of parts to the last or to others to somehow be fitted together. Thinking with his pencil, he would hand off rough sketches of a project's dimensions, façade, and interiors to one of the younger draftsmen to translate into working drawings and then cover yards more tracing paper with other suggestions. Ever impatient when the work did not proceed as quickly as he desired, White would take a run from his private office, slide through the double doors along a groove he had worn smooth in the floor, and plunge into the "Holy-of-Holies" drafting room, also known as the monkey cage for its rather intense odors, all the while singing opera, cursing, and yelling at the men to push the work along.[6]

He might suddenly appear at one of the draftsmen's elbows and shoulder him off his stool shouting, "What do you got?" and exclaim after a quick look, "Beautiful! Fine as the Parthenon!" Then after a second, grab a piece of tracing paper while shouting, "Dammit, if it isn't we'll make it so." Or he might exclaim, "That was the goddamndest lookin' thing I ever saw," crumpling the drawing while reaching for a pencil and yards more tracing paper. In five minutes, he would have produced a dozen sketches of some detail, his long, blunt fingers flying across the paper. Then, slamming his hand down on one or two or three of the sketches, he would say, "Do that!"

Other times White might stare at a sketch he had first dismissed, then twisting his mustache admit, "Oh, I don't know—that's not so bad," then begin to whistle, and finally cry, "All right! All right! That's perfectly all right—go ahead! Go ahead!" If he called out for thumbtacks to post the drawing, one of the younger men would reach for a long T square, drag over a stool, and pry a couple of brass thumbtacks out of the wooden ceiling. It was something of a cultivated skill around the office, tossing them up there by the joint of the thumb.

They called him "the Indian" when he went on the warpath, and if he scratched his head and rumpled his hair while slapping his thighs together, his staff knew to flee the scene. Working for Stanford White could be a fearful experience, but still the draftsmen were terribly loyal to him. By all accounts, he was often brusque in his manner and rarely offered praise, but when praise did come it was generous and sincere, and the men knew they would break their necks for him. Eventually, however, a few of his staff, including Joseph Wells, came to resent White's seemingly growing arrogance and complained among themselves as he began to claim sole credit for what had been accomplished by his crew.[7]

In addition to working on the Madison Square Garden project, draftsman Wells had also taken over responsibility for planning the prestigious Century Association Clubhouse on West Forty-Third Street at Fifth Avenue.[8] Said always to be a meeting ground for people worth meeting, the Century counted both Stanford White and Charles McKim among its membership of noteworthy authors, artists, architects, and musicians. The Century Association had been originally limited to one hundred men when it was founded in 1847 down on East Fifteenth Street—hence the appellation—but the rolls had swelled to eight hundred worthies, and it

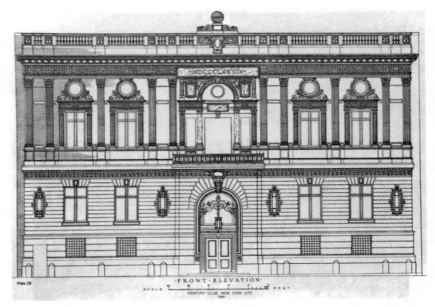

20. Century Association Clubhouse front elevation, 1889. *A Monograph of the Work of McKim, Mead & White 1879–1915* (1915, repr., New York: Dover Publications, 1990).

was in need of a new and elegant building in a more fashionable neighborhood. Its very handsome, well-ordered design in the firm's preferred Italian Renaissance style would soon come to be influential in the final design of Madison Square Garden.

•

In the late twentieth and early twenty-first century, scholars have noted a strong sense of connection among McKim, Mead & White's staff and the likelihood that some of the bonds between them were more than platonic. Evidence seems to indicate that McKim, Mead, White, and draftsmen Wells and Thomas Hastings, as well as Augustus Saint-Gaudens, enjoyed mutual sexual attraction if not actual intimate relationships.[9]

While working on a proposed biography of Stanford White in the 1960s, Aline Saarinen apparently came to the conclusion that White was homosexual and eventually abandoned the book.[10] In his 1989 seminal biography, Paul R. Baker writes that no doubt some in the group were

21. William Mead and office-boy and apprentice Royal Cortissoz in the offices of McKim, Mead & White, ca. 1885. Royal Cortissoz Papers, Yale Collections of American Literature, Beinecke Rare Book and Manuscript Library.

homosexual and others, like Saint-Gaudens and White, "probably had bisexual inclinations"; yet despite much circumstantial suggestion, Baker finds direct evidence lacking.[11] In her extensive 2010 examination of the firm, *Triumvirate: McKim, Mead & White, Art, Architecture, Scandal, and Class in America's Gilded Age*, Mosette Broderick states, "It seems clear that White was bisexual" and at times "part of an active gay circle," despite the efforts of his son Lawrence Grant White in the early 1930s to excise any suggestive correspondence from the collection the family donated to the Avery Architectural and Fine Arts Library at Columbia University.[12] Suzannah Lessard sums it up with a sense of exhaustion in *The Architect of Desire,* her

1996 examination of the White family and her great-grandfather Stanford White, by noting that "the question whether Stanford was bisexual seems irrelevant," that his activities seem more "a form of compulsive consumption," and that he was "merely all over the place, sexually."[13] And perhaps it was so for Saint-Gaudens, as well, that the pursuit of beauty and sensation was far more important than any specific labels.

Some observers may find the discussion of such sexual preference or identification irrelevant to the study of an artist's creative work. But no artist lives or works in a vacuum. And it is an unlikely assumption that an artist's personal life never interacts with or influences the creative one. As *New York Times* editorial writer Frank Bruni notes in the public examination of gay lives, "oppression is an act of omission rather than commission: not letting people give voice and vent to much of what moves them and to all of what defines them." Bruni also points out the observation by author Nathaniel Frank that to "erase whole chunks of people's existences" is as cruel "as it would be to leave out someone's life work or what country they lived in." While writing more specifically of obituary practice, Bruni concludes that erring on the side of saying nothing may be "a decision born of courtesy but steeped in prejudice. All of this adds up to an incomplete picture of our society and who shaped it. It adds up to a lie."[14]

•

Outside of the office, much of the McKim, Mead & White staff shared a social life centered around the Benedick, a residence nicknamed for Shakespeare's famed bachelor and the first apartment house in the city designed solely for single men. It was one of McKim, Mead & Bigelow's inaugural projects, opening formally in 1879 as the Tuckerman on the southeast corner of Washington Square. The building was officially named for Lucius Tuckerman, an iron merchant and developer who sought to provide comfortable and even luxurious homes for bachelors weary of the boardinghouse, furnished room, or hotel—a place where men might conveniently and comfortably chum together, with breakfast, boot blacking, and maid service provided. As vice president of the Metropolitan Museum, Tuckerman was particularly partial to the needs of artists, and with its four light-filled studios situated on the top floor, the building soon developed a reputation for catering to the artistically inclined.[15]

Residents included Joseph Wells, a confirmed bachelor said to evidence little interest in the female of the species and a raging bias against marriage, particularly for anyone engaged in the arts. Before his very private and childless marriage to Hungarian-born Olga Kilyeni in 1883, William Mead was also a resident in one of the thirty-three apartment suites,[16] and Charles McKim lived there between marriages. Winslow Homer, Albert Pinkham Ryder, John La Farge, and Louis St. Gaudens also had rooms at the Benedick. While still a bachelor, the wine-red brick building with its iron-clad Queen Anne bay windows served as the center of Stanford White's social life as well, and he spent most evenings there.[17]

The pleasures at the Benedick may have still been innocent ones in the early 1880s, when the young architects and their friends first gathered in Wells's rooms to pore over old volumes on Renaissance Rome and then continue the evening at Augustus Saint-Gaudens's quarters a block north on Washington Place or Thomas Dewing's on the north side of the square.[18] On Sunday afternoons, White, Saint-Gaudens, and Wells could be found at the weekly meeting of the Concert Club, also known as the Quartet Club, indulging their love of music. The tradition started in 1882 when the men found a better-than-average trio playing the violin, clarinet, and piano in a beer saloon on Broadway, three blocks east of the Benedick. Since the saloon was closed on Sundays, Saint-Gaudens offered the musicians the chance to come perform at his studio on Thirty-Sixth Street. He and Wells invited some forty of their pals—painters, sculptors, architects, and writers—to attend and chip in on the expense. The next year, Wells thought they could do better and negotiated with a string quartet from the Philharmonic Society to play for twenty-five dollars a concert.[19]

The performances were dubbed "smoking concerts," as everyone had a cigar or pipe filled with tobacco or perhaps something more potent. In a letter to White, Saint-Gaudens referred to the architect's dependence on "KIFE."[20] While a sexual connotation is possible, the word may have also been related to the Arabic *kif* or *kief,* a term for cannabis. At the time of his death, White was widely reported to have routinely "excited his blood by unnatural stimulants."[21] According to friends, these concert nights were one of the rare times that White the dynamo stopped buzzing. When he finally settled down to listen to the music he was absolutely motionless;

not even an eyelash fluttered as he happily puffed away on a long pipe, as seen in one of Augustus Saint-Gaudens's rather Bacchanalian caricatures.[22]

•

Despite Stanford White's marriage in 1884, the Benedick group had remained close. White, Wells, Saint-Gaudens, and the others were working together in some configuration nearly every day, with Tommy Dewing painting the murals for the Hotel Imperial and Frank Lathrop creating the glasswork for the Century Association Clubhouse, while Saint-Gaudens was hired as an official consultant to McKim, Mead & White on the Boston Public Library project and recommended his brother Louis to sculpt the great stone lions in the main hall. At night, however, they were united in pursuits of a different, if unusually tangled, nature.

Contemporaries noted Stanford White's "almost feminine" tenderness toward his friends, describing him as a warm, generous, lovable comrade with a delightful sense of humor.[23] Yet Joseph Wells had noted in White a certain lack of interest in his old friends and a change for the worse in his designs. "The work of all artists was destined to fail after marriage," he insisted. "But how long can the novelty of marriage last," Wells wondered, "when all new sensations have been exhausted?"[24]

Seemingly not all that long. The men started up something called the Jugged Club, apparently open to those who had been in "the jug," meaning they had been incarcerated or perhaps had just committed (or imagined they had committed) jail-worthy crimes. Then there was the Badger Babb Club—named for Benedick resident, old friend, and onetime McKim, Mead & White draftsman George Fletcher Babb—which met in his rooms or those of Louis St. Gaudens. As chief draftsman for architect Russell Sturgis, Babb had taken young Charles McKim under his wing in the 1860s during his first employment and then did the same for William Mead in his student days. Babb was one of the first draftsmen hired when McKim and Mead joined together, and he maintained a desk in the 57 Broadway building, working sometimes for McKim, Mead & White, sometimes on his own, and sometimes with his partners Daniel Cook and Walter Willard.[25]

The origin of Babb's nickname "Badger" is unclear—perhaps for his red hair or his cynical and sometimes unrelenting sense of humor. It is also possible that Babb may have once been the victim of the old "badger game" frequently played on men visiting the byways of the Tenderloin district—the old, "What the hell were you doing here with my wife?" (or husband), and everything smoothed over with a quick payoff.[26]

In 1887, Stanford White organized a select group of men—Gus Saint-Gaudens ("always a charming companion")[27] and his brother Louis, Joe Wells, and artists Tommy "Up-and-Dewing" and Frank Lathrop—into the Sewer Club. They took a separate apartment at the Benedick, and all were required to pay dues, although White and Saint-Gaudens shouldered most of the expense. Few details of these secret clubs exist, but there were rumors of illicit relationships and sexual exploits.[28]

"Physiological interests and investigations" was the way Dewing described their activities. "I'm your man," Saint-Gaudens wrote to White, "to dine, drink, fuck, bugger or such, metaphorically speaking." "S.M.C.," for "Suck My Cock," signed White in his letters to "Horgustus." Saint-Gaudens drew penises on his notes to White, as many as thirteen at one time, and signed "thine and thine only," or addressed "Beloved Beauty"[29] or turned a huge "A" for Augustus into a smiling phallus.[30]

To add to the complications, in correspondence Joseph Wells was Stanford White's "ever beloved." But then Saint-Gaudens wrote Wells love notes in French, "My adored love, My beautiful girl, I love no one but you, you alone in the world, your beautiful smile makes me die of love," accompanied by a sketch of himself carving to the tune of naked male musicians while Stanford White puffed on that pipe in a corner.[31]

Stanford White, known by his cablegram name as "Giddydoll,"[32] had other crushes, including Thomas Hastings, the son of a prominent Presbyterian minister who had performed the marriage between Charles McKim and his second wife and whose grandfather had written the venerable hymn "Rock of Ages." Hastings had known Joseph Wells while a young student and draftsman in New York and then later in Paris at the École des Beaux-Arts. On his return to the States, Hastings joined McKim, Mead & White through Wells's good graces. In the office, he reconnected with John Carrère, another draftsman and fellow graduate of the École. The two left the firm in 1885 to begin their own practice as Carrère & Hastings, but they remained part of the inner circle.

Described as "high strung and twittering about like an excited spar-row,"[33] Hastings also made quite clear his lack of interest in females. He sent notes to Stanford White signed, "Ever and ever thy beloved," and "Forever and ever thine."[34] And like Wells, he too received letters filled with love words from Augustus Saint-Gaudens. When he finally married at age forty, it was to wealthy sportswoman Helen Ripley Benedict, with her million-dollar dowry. Charles McKim served as best man, Stanford White as usher, and White's son Lawrence as the bride's only attendant. In later years the couple lived apart, she with a female companion to whom she left her fortune.[35]

•

It was likely acknowledged that Joseph Wells was what was commonly known at that time as a "fairie," a man who preferred other men as sexual partners and practiced what Saint-Gaudens so bluntly referred to as "bug-gery." In the second half of the nineteenth century, behavior that had pre-viously been ascribed to wickedness began to be examined from a medical and sociological point of view. Its first public defense was explored in "The Riddle of Man-Manly Love," a series of twelve tracts in German by Karl Heinrich Ulrichs, published from 1863 to 1879. The term "homosex-ual" was coined in 1869 by Hungarian journalist Karl-Maria Kertbeny to replace "sodomite" or "pederast" in describing what he now observed to be inborn and unchangeable male behavior. Homosexuality was further explored and institutionalized by the German sex researcher Richard von Krafft-Ebing in his seminal *Psychopathia Sexualis*, published in 1886. To the majority at the time, however, it remained deviant or "inverted" behavior if it was discussed at all, and certainly not in polite society.

Yet it was widely recognized that men were lustful creatures with urgent passions and that their continuing good health might actually be impaired if they were not able to find physical relief, whether with a male or with a female. Some argued that a "fairie" was as good as a female prostitute when needed, and those "sisters" for hire were cheaper and often more easily available. It was said that even married men who were very highly sexed might find women insufficient and could only be sat-isfied by other men. Furthermore, it was acknowledged that there were some things that a wife would not do and even many prostitutes were hesitant to perform but were the specialties of man-loving men.[36]

Needs of this or virtually any sort were easily met in New York City in the late nineteenth century. Columbia Hall, the so-called epicenter of "fairiedom," was located just a few blocks east of the Benedick. Better known as "Paresis Hall" after the medical term for syphilitic insanity, it was the place where "fancy gentlemen" might dance and drink with the powdered and painted "sisters" who sat for company.[37] Armory Hall also figured prominently among a number of saloons, social clubs, and dance halls in the city's homosexual culture, where powdered and rouged waiters, some attired in female dress, would circulate through the crowd singing, dancing, and joining the best-paying customers upstairs in private curtained booths. Other establishments in the Bowery and the Tenderloin district offered a variety of similar entertainments with pansexual and heterosexual partners, and among the circle of artists in the city, group excursions to such places were fairly routine.[38]

•

As for Augustus Saint-Gaudens, aside from his early days as apprentice to the brutal Avet and then the kindly Le Brethon with his well-known reputation for pursuing young boys, there were a few episodes in his past that reveal a particular closeness with his male friends, especially during his student days in Paris. There was his fellow art student and lifelong friend Alfred Garnier, who first spotted Augustus Saint-Gaudens in the street during the winter of 1868–69, attracted, as he wrote, "by his eyes, so frank, so candid." Garnier followed him to his lodgings and later to the gymnasium where Saint-Gaudens went each evening. He recounted with barely contained emotion how finally one night they wrestled, their bodies "all naked except for a pair of trunks," and after rolling each other around, crushing each other's skin, "after the sweat of one had run down with the sweat of the other," after having thrown each other a dozen times into the black sawdust, they rushed into the showers where they stayed until the gaslights dimmed.[39]

Later that year, the two men traveled to Switzerland with another friend, Saint-Gaudens and Garnier sleeping in the nude in a shared bed.

Saint-Gaudens also recalled sleeping on a single cot with a friend in need of lodging, and "in order not to spill over on the sides we had to stick to one another as tight as two spoons. To save space Thierry lay with his head on my arm. In the middle of the night we turned over and I put my head on his arm."[40] This sort of arrangement was not so terribly unusual in the nineteenth century, particularly during travel where private quarters and separate beds were not readily available. The very fact that these episodes remained in Saint-Gaudens's *Reminiscences*, which were heavily edited by his son Homer Saint-Gaudens, may indicate that these experiences did not seem out of the ordinary among Victorian male friendships. But they may also reflect a claimed innocence or denial of even the possibility of a homosexual relationship.[41]

Art historian Alexis L. Boylan notes in her 2016 examination of Saint-Gaudens's relief portrait of a reclining Robert Louis Stevenson in his bed that Saint-Gaudens "had numerous intimate relationships with men," although not specifically sexual, including Stanford White and Charles McKim. She suggests that Saint-Gaudens chose to depict Stevenson in bed as a manifestation of his need for male intimacy and "as a socially acceptable arena for representing queer and masculine restorative desire."[42] And according to Mrs. Daniel Chester French, Saint-Gaudens was "very fond of having young men about him, and of going about town with them . . . 'whooping it up,'" and doing things that seemed to some observers beneath him.[43]

•

If Stanford White and Augustus Saint-Gaudens were with the same person in turn, perhaps it was almost like loving each other. Whether it was boys, girls, boys who looked like girls or vice versa, or even a virgin goddess of gilded copper—the same partner mutually enjoyed would cement the bonds between them.[44] A number of men in their close circle, like Francis Millet, Thomas Hastings, Edward Austin Abbey, and John Singer Sargent, alternated between partners of their own sex and romantic crushes on and sometimes even marriage to females. The formal, heterosexual wedded state was generally expected, improved one's standing on the social scene, and reassured potential clients of one's respectability. As artists, they could do whatever they "darn please,"[45] wrote Stanford

White. Augustus Saint-Gaudens similarly wrote of the pursuit of happiness as "an inalienable right, God-given . . . I'm damned if I don't think I've a right to be so provided I don't injure any one."[46] And in September 1889 Augustus Saint-Gaudens's Swedish mistress gave birth to his son. He was named Louis after the baby's uncle but called Novy.[47]

10

The Walls Go Up

AS THE ACTUAL CONSTRUCTION of Madison Square Garden approached, the working drawings, the specifications, and the mechanicals now rested largely in the hands of McKim, Mead & White's senior draftsmen, but the logistics of the project were tremendous. Partner William Mead stepped in once more, scheduling and supervising the staff and keeping a close eye on expenses while Stanford White continued to oversee the design, with all under a great deal of pressure.[1]

An article on the Garden project in *Harper's Weekly* put into words what surely must have been buzzing through Stanford White's head, that "the day will certainly come when at the same hour 15,000 people will congregate there. Think of this tonnage of humanity, and the risk . . . of any unforeseen calamity!" And aside from questions of safety, made so vivid by the disasters at the old Garden, there were still the exigencies of the modern world that, as a contemporary critic noted, "would have hurried a Brunelleschi to the madhouse."[2]

The 40-foot-high common brick walls began to go up in the fall of 1889 while most of the plans were still in flux. It became something of a contest, as White and his draftsmen raced constructor David King and his building crew. King was what Mead described as "a rusher,"[3] and he happily left dealing with him to White. "When we begin to hit, we hit heavy, and keep on hitting all the time,"[4] King stated with some confidence. While the actual construction was under the superintendency of Charles E. McDonnell, David King scheduled and supervised the building trades that supplied labor and materials, and for those he did not supply himself, King coordinated the bids, awarded contracts, and negotiated with the trade unions that might otherwise have shut down the worksite.[5]

When word came from the Garden board that, due to dramatically rising expenses, the tower had been cut from the plans, "all bloody hell broke loose." An outraged Stanford White told reporters that they could say anything they liked about the building, but "for any sake, say it needs a tower," for he fervently believed it was the tower that would make a landmark of the place.[6] He kicked furiously to each member of the building committee and then to everyone connected with the Garden, even down to the bricklayers, until King could no longer take it and complained to the committee that White was hounding him into his grave. King offered to put up $225,000—half the amount needed to complete the tower—if the committee would raise the rest. The great glass dome over the amphitheater was traded away, but the tower was secured, and it was noted that Stanford White immediately became reasonable again.[7]

King's complaint to the committee must have been tongue-in-cheek, as he and White had been friends and colleagues since 1883 when the firm designed a shingled summer home for him in New Rochelle on Long Island Sound.[8] Over the next seven years, Stanford White had worked with King-the-constructor as well as King-the-real-estate-developer on a number of projects, including a five-unit tenement on Eighty-Third Street in the newly developing Upper West Side. The firm was about to begin work on the King Model Houses, another development scheme even farther up in Harlem intended to create an upper-middle-class townhouse complex, with McKim, Mead & White responsible for a block to be executed in the Italian Renaissance style. And on a personal level, King would soon be partner in the exploration of matters sexual, sharing a Manhattan hideaway with White where these interests would be pursued.

•

It was not unusual for Augustus Saint-Gaudens to drop by Stanford White's office for a powwow, bringing along his son, with whom he was sometimes saddled for the day. As Homer Saint-Gaudens later recalled, he was once playing with the swinging gate in White's outer office when the architect glared at him under those bristling red eyebrows and told one of his men to "go buy Gussie's son a golf bag and sticks," just to keep him out of their hair.[9]

At some point Saint-Gaudens and White had decided that the crowning figure for the tower would indeed be the Roman goddess Diana, eternally young and beautiful daughter of Jupiter and Leto, sister to Apollo the sun, queen of the open sky, lady of the hunt, protectress of women, and patroness of fertility and childbirth. In her sacred grove, her priests engaged in mortal combat, not too unlike the pugilistic displays that would one day fill the new Garden. And perhaps there was a bit of irony involved, considering their sexological explorations, in their choice of the goddess ever virgin.

●

It was likely that among Saint-Gaudens's earlier considerations was the creation of a figure of Atalanta, the beautiful maiden of Greek mythology who raced like lightning and was a fierce warrior with bow and arrow. For years he had hoped for the chance to create his own version of the figure popular with the ancient sculptors as well as the artists at the court of Louis XIV.[10] Like Diana, Atalanta was a sporting figure—young, strong, beautiful, independent—and either one would have been perfectly appropriate for the top of the Madison Square Garden tower.

But Diana was the better-known image in myth and more clearly associated with the use of bow and arrow, which would help the figure function as a weather vane. Diana, the virgin mistress of the wild creatures, the woodlands, and of the chase, would be depicted upright, moving through the air, her drapery catching the wind while the arrow in her bow neatly pointed directly into it, much as rusty old Indian chiefs had done over New England's barn roofs for centuries.[11]

●

Meanwhile, work continued at the Madison Square Garden site. Millions of bricks, shiploads of cement, lumberyards of floor plank, and miles of water, gas, and steam pipes were ordered and on their way. Ten foremen oversaw a thousand men, pounding away ten or twelve hours a day with steam drills and shovels, digging out the main body of the Garden, a rectangle 465 by 200 feet. Broken stone and cement were tumbled down and rammed 30 feet deep. Then one hundred men with trowels laid on mortar to support the brick foundation walls.[12] Steam-lift derricks of heavy steel raised huge stone blocks as easily as bales of hay and set them on top of the concrete footings to bear the wrought-iron columns that would carry the trusses that would hold up the amphitheater roof.[13]

When it came to bearing walls, Stanford White had chosen not to use the iron or steel skeleton frame, which resembled a steel bridge stood on end, or the even more stable cage frame, which supported floor beams as well as walls and was quickly becoming more common for taller buildings of the day.[14] Instead, these walls at the Garden were being built solely of traditional Hudson River brick, rising 28 inches thick.[15] However, steel was indeed being used for the main trusses and wrought iron in the amphitheater for the floor girders, I beams, and joists that would all aid in making the structure more fire-resistant.[16]

All the steel and ironwork at the Garden was to be erected by Post & McCord, a prominent New York civil engineering firm and one of the first to employ steam-powered derricks for the task. Ironwork was generally acknowledged as the most troublesome part of any building's design and construction, causing McKim, Mead & White to seek out such a large and well-established firm. Post & McCord was able to manufacture the required daily 100 tons of structural iron and steel at their huge plant in Brooklyn for the arena's finished interior space, 324 feet long by 194 feet wide.[17] The invention of the elevator had allowed architects to build tall, but as stone or brick walls rose upward, they needed to increase in thickness to support their height, consuming interior space as they climbed. Rolled wrought-iron structural beams were first produced by inventor Peter Cooper at his rolling mill in Trenton, New Jersey, in 1854. Cast-iron columns, in use in the 1850s, and hollow cast-iron fronts, common from 1860 to 1880, helped to relieve the load and open up interior spaces.[18]

Rolled and wrought columns, used to create an inner core of support, proved much superior to earlier cast-iron structural work, for although cast iron had a high compressive strength, it also had its weaknesses. In the process of manufacture, defects and variations like blowholes and cinders could appear, or unequal cooling could contribute to unequal thickness, as could the use of inferior pig-iron on the part of some unscrupulous founders.[19] However, the amphitheater's interior columns were to be of a type known as built-up Phoenix, manufactured by the Phoenix Iron Company of Phoenixville, Pennsylvania, and formed from hollow, rolled mild steel built up of four, six, or eight flanged segments riveted together.[20]

The rolled Phoenix column, apparently first conceived around 1860 by railroad engineer Wendel Bollman and then patented in 1862 by the Phoenix Company,[21] had greater rigidity than the typical cast-iron column due to its riveted flanges and circular section. These allowed the column to carry a more even load distribution, particularly in the center of a building where floor loads were the greatest. In addition to its uniform thickness and its rigidity, the rolled Phoenix column was also lower in cost because of its simpler construction. "A maximum of strength with a minimum of weight," as the company advertised.[22]

Rolled iron Phoenix columns had been well tested in the second half of the nineteenth century and put to good use supporting New York's Second Avenue Elevated Railway Line, as well as various bridges and viaducts around the country. In the 1880s they were used in many of the city's new office buildings, including the twenty-story World Building on Park Row in 1889.[23]

When the now-steel columns rose on their cast-iron pedestals and girders were put in place at the Garden site, the beams made a scaffold for the additional stories so that the structure nearly built itself up.[24] It is likely that the steel columns used in the construction of the Madison Square Garden were among the first manufactured by the Phoenix Company, as they had just effectively converted their manufacture from iron to steel in 1889.[25]

As the 300-foot-long brick walls began to rise inside the amphitheater, two rows of twenty-eight 60-foot-high Phoenix columns supported the six main Pratt steel trusses and the sixteen radial half-trusses that spanned the arena and would carry the 167-by-277-foot oval roof.[26] This truss system was said to be the largest and lightest ever constructed and was responsible for its remarkable ability to carry such an immense roof without any central support. It thus allowed the creation of this monumental interior space and eliminated the need for additional supporting columns that would have otherwise obstructed the view from a fair number of seats.[27]

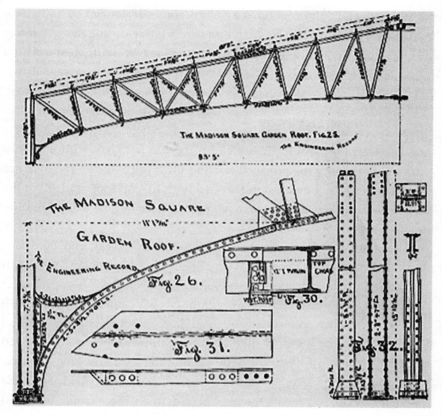

22. *Building Construction Details*, Madison Square Garden, *Engineering Record* (Jan. 24, 1891).

Like the Phoenix column, the Pratt truss was invented by railway engineers, in this case Caleb and Thomas Pratt, a father and son from Boston who had developed the principle in 1844. Thus the railroads, so crucial to America's continuing economic growth, contributed as well to the development of new and remarkable technical applications in other nineteenth-century fields of endeavor.

•

The riveting of beams involved quite a remarkable effort in itself that was vividly documented in a 1901 *New York Times* article titled "Would You Like to Catch Red-Hot Rivets All Day?" According to the *Times*, a portable rivet forge was set up at a construction site, tended by a furnace-man, most typically Irish by birth and careful to wear goggles to protect his eyes from the white-hot heat. An ironworker would then stand on a ladder so that his head was a little above the level of the truss that was being riveted. When ready, he would shout out to alert the furnaceman, who opened the door and with a long pair of pincer tongs pulled out a glowing piece of iron that he dropped on a wooden tray. His assistant, the rivet boy, would then pick up the red-hot rivet with a shorter pair of tongs, swing the pincers back and forth until he had the distance gauged right, take a quick step forward with his left foot, and shoot the rivet out with a slow, deliberate movement, almost as if he were throwing horseshoes.[28]

The rivet would sail across in a graceful red streak and land ker-plunk into the nail keg held by a begrimed riveter's assistant, who then dropped it into the rivet hole on the beam. The rivets flew through the air all day long, one a minute or so, to ten or twelve young men toting nail kegs. Once in place, the ironworker held a heavy set against the head of the rivet, while the hammer man took his ball-peen hammer to the tail end, causing it to mushroom tightly against the joint and hold in place. When cool, the rivets contracted to tighten even further. Aside from the main trusses, other connections were bolted. In all, there would be a total of 3 million pounds of wrought iron and steel and 500,000 pounds of cast iron in place in the amphitheater before they were through.[29]

•

The span of the finished trusses was not as wide as those at the Palais des Machines that Stanford White had seen the year before at the Exposition Universelle in Paris, but as with the Palais, there was no attempt to conceal or gussy up these structural elements with decoration. The trusses inside the Garden were left fully exposed, although White would have them painted a light buff tint like the rest of the girders and beams.[30] In a very modern sense, they served simply as the plain metal setting against which the color and movement of both the staged spectacle and the audience would be allowed to sparkle.

As the work continued, a tank for water spectacles was excavated four feet deep under the removable arena floor. Thousands of tons of earth

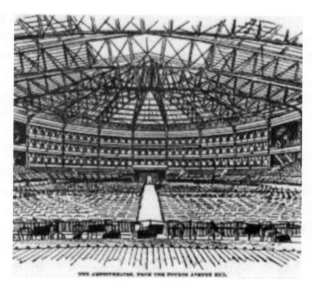

23. Interior, Madison Square Garden Amphitheatre, *New York Sun* (Sept. 27, 1890). Chronicling America, Library of Congress.

were then trucked in to raise the circus ring and track three feet. Finally, the upper floors were laid and partition walls built, both lined with hollow terra-cotta blocks that were covered with a thick coat of solid concrete to hold and lock the building together. The same material was used as wall furring and as floor arches between the structural steel beams, with the exception of the sloping area of the amphitheater around the arena created by oval corrugated metal arches and concrete fill.[31]

•

During the construction phase there was some concern expressed in the press regarding the sheer number of new places of amusement that were being built. In addition to the Madison Square Garden, there were three new theaters and two music halls simultaneously under construction that taken in total would offer 35,000 new seats.[32] In October 1889 an article by well-known actor and playwright Dion Boucicault warned against the extravagant plan for the Garden. "Doesn't the Board realize that a venue must be self-supporting," he demanded, "must generate some sort of profit to survive?"[33] It was certainly true that a huge hall like the Garden required more musicians in the orchestra, more gas for heating and lighting, more ushers, more canvas and wood for sets, and generally more and more of everything in every department. A smaller venue would have been easier to fill—seats as well as stage—and far more cost efficient to run. But apparently the board of the Madison Square Garden Company was little concerned with the notion of sustainability, and small and simple were clearly not part of White's design vocabulary.

Stanford White, Herman Oelrichs, and several other board members paid a visit to New York Mayor Hugh J. Grant in November 1889, asking his permission to build the proposed exterior arcade. The state legislature had voted its approval in June that year, but the mayor still refused, fearing that it would become a loitering ground for unsavory elements. For White, not only would the arcade provide shelter for arriving and departing audiences and a clear link to the architecture of the Italian Renaissance, but its deep voids alternating with the openings of the colonnade planned above would set up a graceful visual rhythm, and so he refused to abandon the scheme.[34]

By Christmas of 1889 great progress had been made on the site, thanks largely to a mild autumn that had allowed double shifts to work night and day. At nearly 40 feet, massive walls had risen to nearly two-thirds of their expected 65-foot height and were being faced with the pale yellow Roman brick supplied by Welch, Gloninger & Maxwell of Welch, Pennsylvania.[35] Interior structural supports were in place, girders and gallery divisions were rising along with them, and the roof was expected to be set within two months. King's contract had called for completion of the amphitheater in March of the following year, when Barnum's circus would inaugurate the house. A timely completion was expected, but as King blamed sudden cold weather for a slowdown, completion would come with a cost override of nearly $100,000.[36]

•

In late January 1890, as he was detailing the façade for the Garden, Joseph Wells fell ill with the grippe complicated by pleurisy. Never strong in constitution, he had long been plagued by toothache, dyspepsia, and gout.[37] February 1 was a cold rainy morning, but Wells managed to come into the office, looking frail yet full of enthusiasm. He dropped by the Century Club and then was off to inspect the work the firm had undertaken on the dining room remodel of the Plaza Hotel at Fifty-Ninth Street and Fifth Avenue. To add to the chill and damp of the day, the dining room was still reeking with wet plaster. The next morning—to the great shock of his many good friends—Wellzey was dead of pneumonia.[38] And Stanford White would recall that while he lived, his hand could be seen all through their work.[39]

11

Diana Defrocked

ALTHOUGH AN ARTIST might insist a work of art springs unique from their hand, much like Athena from the forehead of Zeus, a critic in the late nineteenth century might proffer instead that every work of art has a lineage, a line that can be traced back in time to antecedents, foreshadows, and influences. Not that every preceding work must be directly known to the artist—for one object might influence the next like a run of cards, accumulating attributes through time and space. Nor need every example seen by an artist during a lifetime of study and observation be specifically or consciously recalled as they commence their work.

It might have been a fleeting glance—in a crowded gallery, at a souvenir photograph, a well-thumbed volume, or a quickly made sketch hardly remembered by the conscious mind. Yet after the artist had put hand to canvas, clay, or whatever material, a discerning eye might yet uncover this familial tree of image, style, pose, and subject. And so it was with the goddess Diana and with the figure that would emerge under the hand of Augustus Saint-Gaudens.

•

While "working like a beaver"[1] on the *Adams Memorial* for Rock Creek Park in Washington, DC, also in collaboration with Stanford White, Augustus Saint-Gaudens continued to consider the Madison Square Garden Diana. One early version, incised in clay, reveals a quick sketch of the proposed figure holding a bow and arrow, clothed in a short-sleeved top and full skirt pleated rather like a ballet tutu.[2]

Although this was not the usual depiction of a Greek or Roman goddess, Saint-Gaudens no doubt had consulted his well-thumbed and marked *Dictionary of Greek and Roman Antiquities,* his five-volume *Dictionnaire des antiquités,* and Edmund von Mach's *Greek Sculpture*[3] to learn that in classical times Diana was typically shown clothed for hunting in either a short or a long chiton hiked up under a fawnskin girt tied beneath her breasts, with high-topped buskin hunting boots on her feet and a short himation cape draped over one shoulder.[4] That he was well familiar with rendering Greek dress and drapery, from a simple Doric chiton to the pleated Ionic style, is documented by drawings found throughout his student copybook from the École des Beaux-Arts.[5]

As many afternoons as he could spare in those student days in Paris, Saint-Gaudens would be across the Pont des Arts, the small iron footbridge over the Seine that linked the École to the galleries of the Musée de Louvre. Among the museum's treasures was the so-called *Diana of Versailles,* a Roman copy in marble of a lost fourth-century-BC Hellenistic Greek bronze that depicted Artemis as huntress in short chiton with leaping deer at her side. The piece was given to the French King Henry II by Pope Paul IV in 1556, apparently as an unspoken nod to Henry's mistress, Diane de Poitiers, who loved to pose like her namesake with bow and arrow.[6]

During the sixteenth and seventeenth centuries it became quite the fashion for ladies of the European nobility to take up archery, a diversion with appropriate classical associations that was said to have been invented by Diana's brother Apollo and well-adapted to accentuating the gracefulness of the female form. Ladies of high standing, from Anne Boleyn to Isabella of Brabant, the reigning duchess of Belgium, happily let fly their arrows as the goddess's devoted disciples.[7] And following the fashion and its well-treasuried enthusiasts came a new flood of such sculpted Dianas, depicted mid-stride and toting her bow and arrows.[8]

•

At some point it was decided that the figure for the Madison Square Garden tower would be a nude one, and Saint-Gaudens no doubt could not have been more pleased. He had long said that if he ever had a moment free, he would want to create an idealized female nude.[9] While a nude *Diana* set on top of a great tower might set New York City on its ear, it was not without historical precedent. Aside from the contemporary versions of Diana by Falguière and MacMonnies that he had seen at the 1889 Exposition Universelle, literary sources dating back to Ovid's book 2 of the *Metamorphoses* recalled the oft-told story of Artemis-Diana caught in her bath,[10] and nude depictions of the goddess did occur in the classical world.[11] This sort of image was particularly found in antique engraved gems and medals, which Saint-Gaudens, the master of low relief, may well have known. But for him, inspiration only began with the ancient world. The more relevant sources were the great fifteenth- and sixteenth-century marble, bronze, and terra-cotta sculptures of the Italian Renaissance, wherein long-abandoned treasures of Greece and Rome were rediscovered, reimagined, and reinvented by artists who looked with fresh eyes at the human figure and its place within the grander scheme of things.

As noted, during his early days in Paris and then in Rome, Saint-Gaudens found common ground with the other young, contemporary sculptors known as Neo-Florentines who were inspired by the figures produced by High-Renaissance fifteenth-century and Mannerist sixteenth-century Italian sculptors—their fully rounded figures worked in warm bronze, moving, twisting, feeling, and breathing. Among the Mannerist examples were two strikingly nude Dianas with which Saint-Gaudens was surely familiar. The first was Benvenuto Cellini's 1543 muscular, high-relief bronze *Nymph of Fontainebleau*, originally made for the palace of King Henry II in 1543 but placed instead above the entrance to Diane de Poitiers's Chateau d'Anet. The second, even more monumental sixteenth-century example, the *Fountain of Diana*, was likely inspired by the first and carved by an Italian or Italian-trained artist in smooth white marble to decorate the courtyard of that same chateau. Here the 7-foot-high Diana semireclines, a dog between her legs, her arm around a majestic stag— perhaps Actaeon after his transformation or more metaphorically her royal lover as king of the herd.[12] Long removed to display in a secluded upstairs gallery of the Louvre, the fountain was said to be a favorite meeting place for late nineteenth-century lovers.[13]

No doubt many Dianas were thus inspired by Diane de Poitiers, as created by the Italian-tutored painters and sculptors of the school of Fontainebleau as an ideal figure of beauty in an intriguing blend of neoclassical restraint and realist sensuality. Nude depictions of Diana had also been particularly popular with French artists who made a specialty of stripping down the chaste goddess to her most basic attributes and

24. *Diana the Huntress,* Jean-Antoine Houdon, 1790, bronze.
Musée du Louvre, © RMN-Grand Palais / Art Resource, NY.

accouterments—her bow, arrow, and crescent moon—and then gifting her
with the voluptuous body of Venus, goddess of love. By the late eighteenth
century, she had become a rather seductive figure, daring a gaze upon her
naked body yet remaining the ever unattainable, well-armed virgin.[14]

The most scandalous example of a nude Diana was created by the late
eighteenth-century sculptor Jean-Antoine Houdon, otherwise famed for
his realistic portraits of fully clothed Enlightenment-era luminaries like
Voltaire, Rousseau, Molière, and even George Washington. There is little

doubt that Saint-Gaudens had seen Houdon's 1790 stunning bronze *Diana the Huntress*—whether featured at the 1867 Paris exposition, on view in the Louvre, or replicated for the 1889 exposition. Originally intended as a garden ornament for the German Duke of Saxe-Gotha, Houdon's *Diana* was 6 feet tall, totally nude, and in motion—gracefully balanced on the ball of her left foot, her right leg flexed behind as she departs for the chase, bow and arrow in hand and crescent-moon crowned.

Houdon based his pose on the observations of German antiquarian Johann Winckelmann, who wrote that Diana was always represented among the ancients as walking or running, thin of waist as becomes a virgin, her gaze straight forward, with her hair gathered up on top of her head.[15] Houdon completed a whole series of Dianas beginning in 1776 executed not only in bronze but in plaster, terra cotta, lead, and marble.[16] When Houdon's *Diana* was first displayed, some praised its elegant pose and purity of powerful form, yet many viewers were stunned by her anatomical particularities. Diana's graphically depicted female parts were so horrifically offensive to museum visitors that when the piece was acquired by the Louvre in 1829, her cleft was filled with six bronze plugs, hammered down and filed smoothed before she could be put on display.[17] And if the French had had their issues with a nude Diana, how would she fare in America?

●

Given the country's puritanical roots, it was understandable that nineteenth-century American sculptors might have been more hesitant to depict full figure nudes. However, Saint-Gaudens's predecessors—the expatriates working in Italy during the first half of the nineteenth century—did not hesitate to produce female nudes in the coolly refined neoclassical style. Their impassive faces and the smooth and idealized contours of their bodies carved in pure white marble were far removed from any hint of life. Whether it was an enslaved virgin, a Psyche of Greek mythology made to represent the immortal soul, or an American Indian girl staring with wonder at a newly found cross, their nudity was depicted with an almost unseemly relish, while coyly draped about them a thin, protective gauze of Christian morality and illuminating titles proclaimed their higher purpose.

In the 1840s, Hiram Powers produced a completely unclothed *Eve Tempted*, but it was his second piece, *The Greek Slave* of 1847, that made his reputation. Shown in his studio in Florence, at the Crystal Palace International Exposition in London, and then in galleries and on tour in America as well as purchased in replica,[18] it was the best-known and most popular sculpture of its day, setting a standard for the full-figured carved female image.

The sculpture's popularity was due in part to sympathy with Greece struggling for its independence from Turkey, as well as its relevance for the American antislavery campaign. The small cross that dangled from one hand proclaimed an underlying Christian theme to the piece, thus allowing her nude figure to be unapologetically viewed by all for its moral and geopolitical lessons.

Twelve years later Erastus D. Palmer—a self-taught former carpenter who began his artistic career like Saint-Gaudens by cutting cameos—produced the rival *White Captive*. This more naturalistic yet still neoclassically depicted American girl was shown cruelly bound to a post by her Indian captors. The piece proved so popular that it was put on display in a gallery in New York City where viewers paid twenty-five cents to view her from all angles on a mechanically rotating pedestal.

As for the goddess Diana, she had not been a particularly popular subject with the midcentury neoclassical American sculptors working in Italy. While nymphs and other hapless virgins of mythology made regular appearance in the altogether to much acclaim, Diana had been represented by American sculptors as a seemly and sedate symbol of feminine chastity. Hiram Powers carved a heavily draped bust of Diana around 1863 that did not sell, although his bust of Proserpine, virgin daughter of Ceres and devotee of Diana—with her breasts fully displayed—became the best-selling bust of the century, replicated more than one hundred times.[19]

As nude sculpture became more popular in the later nineteenth century, it no longer required an attached moral lesson. American viewers became more used to seeing the naked form not only in sculpture but on the canvases of Paris-trained painters, whether viewed in the great museums on the European grand tour, on the gilded walls of Fifth Avenue mansions, or in a fancy hotel bar on Madison Square.

•

Meanwhile, Augustus Saint-Gaudens continued to make pencil sketches for the proposed Diana, a habit ingrained at the École des Beaux-Arts. As a student first enrolled in the antique class, he worked endlessly from the "flat," copying the nude in charcoal pencil over and over from the school's collection of engravings and drawings, and then modeling from plaster casts of the Greek sculptors. It was this knowledge and mastery of the unclothed human figure—considered the highest achievement in Western art—that was the goal of every artist's education at the École.

These lessons had stood him well, and an undated sketch undoubtedly reflected more of what he and Stanford White had in mind for the top of the great tower of the Madison Square Garden. A slim, almost boyish, unclothed goddess, one foot forward, one extended behind, left arm outstretched to hold her bow, right arm flexed, her hand grasping the arrow's tail. Saint-Gaudens tried out the view on paper, from the side, as most would see her, and from head-on. *Diana Smiling* he titled the drawing.[20]

25. *Diana Smiling*, Augustus Saint-Gaudens, undated drawing, photograph by DeWitt Clinton Ward. Courtesy of the US Department of the Interior, National Park Service, Saint-Gaudens National Historical Park, Cornish, NH.

•

Now that he had a pose in mind, it was time for Saint-Gaudens to begin thinking about hiring a model.

His mistress, the one known as Davida, might well have been the obvious choice as it appears that was how they first met. Born Albertina Hultgren, she emigrated from Sweden in 1879 at the age of seventeen.[21] There is no direct evidence as to their very first meeting, but it was likely in 1880 when Saint-Gaudens was in Manhattan modeling angels for the planned Morgan family tomb, one of Stanford White's architectural projects that had been in the works for several years.

The former New York governor Edwin D. Morgan knew Saint-Gaudens's work, having commissioned his marble *Hiawatha* while in Rome in 1873, and when he embarked on the project premortem, Morgan agreed with White's suggestion that Saint-Gaudens execute the sculptural work.[22] There were to be 9-foot-tall marble angels standing all around the granite mausoleum planned for the Cedar Hill Cemetery in Hartford,

26. Davida Johnson Clark. Courtesy of the US Department of the Interior, National Park Service, Saint-Gaudens National Historical Park, Cornish, NH.

Connecticut. The project had been overshadowed by Saint-Gaudens's work on the *Farragut Monument* among others, as well as numerous portrait reliefs of friends and clients, until the summer of 1883 when Morgan, now dead more than a year, was lying beneath the still undecorated monument. Finished plaster models were required for the marble carvers Saint-Gaudens had contracted in Hartford, so nearly half-sized, 39-inch plaster models were what he produced, modeling Albertina in the nude as was his method and then draping and pinning the clay figure with moistened muslin in preparation for the plaster cast.[23] Three angels were completed with classical features, strong but not indicative of either sex, as befitting genderless angels. And Albertina's face, handsome but not terribly feminine, was the perfect model.[24]

Saint-Gaudens had another commission he had also been nursing along, the assorted decoration and sculptural details for the Cornelius Vanderbilt II mansion on Fifth Avenue, designed by society architect George B. Post with the interior decoration under the direction of John La Farge. When it came time to design the monumental fireplace in the front entrance hall, he went to the Morgan angels and to their model for inspiration. In the very same sort of drapery, his *Amor* and *Pax* support the massive mantelpiece with arms upraised and heads bowed under the weight, their bodies as sturdy and straight as classical Doric columns.

Yet when Saint-Gaudens's old friend the painter Kenyon Cox studied these figures, he recognized beyond the obvious classical reference a much more modern sensibility. Filled with tender feeling, "they were not goddesses," he said, "but women; if they were not women who have lived, they were women who might have lived and have loved and, assuredly, have been loved."[25]

•

It is possible that Gus and Albertina became lovers late in the summer of 1884, when—like most summers—wife Gussie was away, holed up with young Homer at a clinic in Nova Scotia being treated for a floating kidney, dosed with 12 drops of arsenic a day, and forbidden conjugal visits. The housekeeper left behind to take care of Augustus Saint-Gaudens was inattentive to her duties, and an invasion of bedbugs drove him to sleep most nights at the big white studio on Thirty-Sixth Street,[26] or so he claimed.

Those finished plaster casts for the Morgan angels were a bright spot that summer, and Saint-Gaudens thought them his finest work to date next to the *Farragut*. They were shipped off for the carvers in Hartford to use as models as they worked on the huge blocks of costly Carrara marble Saint-Gaudens had selected in Italy. He traveled frequently to Hartford to check on the work, sometimes joining in with chisel to finish the details.[27]

Then in August 1884, just as the angels were nearing completion, the temporary shed constructed to protect the carvers from bad weather—and the angels from public view—caught fire. The heat was sufficient to destroy the plaster casts as well as the nearly finished marble figures. The origin of the fire remained a mystery, although enemies of Governor Morgan or Saint-Gaudens, a fired workman, tramps, and ghouls were all suspected. Saint-Gaudens visited the site with his then-assistant Frederick MacMonnies and returned nearly prostrate from the loss.[28] Although Saint-Gaudens had plaster duplicates for two of the angels, Morgan's widow decided they would no longer be needed, and the angels were finally abandoned.[29]

The balance owed him on the job was slow in coming, and so Saint-Gaudens could not make his payroll. It was at this tremulous point that MacMonnies departed for the École des Beaux-Arts with back pay owing, and the studio assistants quietly hocked some of Saint-Gaudens's medallions hanging on the wall. With family gone and Stanford White away in Europe on his six-month honeymoon, Saint-Gaudens had been deserted by all those he loved. And so perhaps it was that summer of 1884 that he reached out to embrace a surviving Morgan angel made flesh.

As to the transformation of Albertina into the more elegant, Italianate, yet somewhat masculine "Davida," it was said that Saint-Gaudens bestowed the nickname because of her resemblance to Michelangelo's *David*.[30] However, she seems to bear a much closer resemblance to Saint-Gaudens's old friend Antonin Mercié's 1878 *David*, which he greatly admired,[31] and whose tilt of the head and lowered eyes might also be detected in the Vanderbilt caryatids.[32]

By Christmas of 1885 "Albertina Hultgren" was no more, at least among their New York circle of friends. As a gift, artist Will Low gave her a copy of *Lamina*, a newly published edition of the epic poem by Keats that he had illustrated, and it was inscribed to Davida Johnson.[33] As for the "Johnson" surname, it was more Americanized, although it might have been derived from the Swedish Jonson, which was possibly her mother's maiden or remarried name.[34] Or "Johnson," a very old slang term for the male member,[35] might have been just another jibe at Davida's rather masculine persona, with her broad shoulders and strong arms said to be like a man's.[36] Saint-Gaudens arranged with Stanford White to forward letters from Davida in a plain white envelope, and so he continued to keep Davida a secret,[37] or at least he so believed.

12

Baked Earth

MADISON SQUARE GARDEN's brick walls had barely been erected as the new year 1890 began, and already there was conflict, controversy, and a threat to the Garden's financial future. Barnum's Circus, since 1881 joined in partnership with James Bailey in what by then had become Barnum & Bailey's "Greatest Show on Earth,"[1] had always been a mainstay of the old Madison Square Garden, and it was assumed that they would ever continue to signal the arrival of spring with the "March of the Elephants" from Grand Central Station down Broadway to the Garden and their annual sellout engagement. But in 1890 it appeared not to be the case, and a circus war threatened.

Phineas Barnum complained that the design of the new Garden would make it wholly impractical for his use; the new amphitheater would be too small to hold their crowds while its central arena floor space was insufficient for their new spectacle, "Nero," with its huge 450-foot stage set and cast of 1,400.[2] Regardless, it was clear that construction of the Garden would not be completed in time for the spring engagement, so Barnum & Bailey threatened to abandon the city and move to Brooklyn instead. After meeting to discuss the crisis, the directors of the Madison Square Garden Company vowed to import the Paris Hippodrome troupe as a rival attraction and then voted in a rather lordly way to pay no further attention to Messrs. Barnum and Bailey, who would eventually present their show that spring under tents at the old polo grounds at the north end of Central Park.[3]

But still, a shadow was cast. Those investors who bought stock—the visionaries, the gamblers, the men drunk on dreams of equine flesh—could scarcely imagine that those dreams alone would not be sufficient to carry the Garden. A $1.25 million mortgage was taken on the property, and advertisements for gold bonds on the mortgage, at 5 percent per annum for thirty anni and described as "an exceptionally safe investment," turned up in the classified pages of *Harper's Weekly*[4] among those for ladies' corsets, double breech-loading guns, and Cuticura skin cure.

T. Henry French, of the theatrical management firm of Samuel French & Son, bought $100,000 in stock and was elected general manager of the Garden by vigorous vote.[5] Despite his famously cool disposition, "as demonstrative as alpine edelweiss," French had managed to get himself punched in the nose the previous year by theater owner Oscar Hammerstein over the payment of a twelve-dollars-due bill,[6] so a careful rein on expenses was surely to be expected.

•

After Joseph Wells's sudden passing in early February 1890, detailing of the plans for Madison Square Garden's decoration was taken over by seasoned draftsman William Mitchell Kendall, a graduate of Harvard and MIT who had been with McKim, Mead & White for eight years. At work at his board, Kendall continued to refer to Wells's earlier drawings for the Century Association's sixteenth-century Renaissance palazzo for inspiration, borrowing its golden Roman brick and graceful terra-cotta ornament, and designing the detail as he imagined Wells would have desired.[7]

In the 1880s there had been growing interest in building in lighter, brighter colors, with sober, old-fashioned brownstone and red brick abandoned in favor of buff or yellow brick and similarly light-hued terra-cotta ornament. McKim, Mead & White embraced if not led the charge with the American Safe Deposit Building from 1882–84, the 1888 Judson Memorial Church, and the contemporary Hotel Imperial in even lighter white-glazed brick, marble, and white terra cotta.

The use of ornamental terra cotta, literally "baked earth," dates back to Roman times and was subsequently revived to spectacular effect during the Italian Renaissance. In the United States, hard-fired, hand-molded unglazed clay was first used to a limited degree at the end of the eighteenth century, imported from England where the embellishment—as in much of Europe—was painted red to imitate brick. Terra cotta had been used for ornament in New York City with varying degrees of success since at least the 1850s but primarily as a means of reducing cost, with rather inferior quality product serving as a substitute not only for brick but for carved stone, iron, and wood.[8] Despite being more economical in both labor and materials by at least half, terra cotta had a poor reputation in the city, and many believed it could not hold up for long in the brutal East Coast winters.[9]

"Architectural" terra cotta, distinguished by the fact that it was left plain and valued in itself for its decorative embellishment, found some favor in the 1850s but then blossomed in the city of Chicago during the wave of rebuilding after its great fire in 1871.[10] The late nineteenth-century New York interest in architectural terra cotta has been attributed to the prominent architect George B. Post and his decoration of the 1877 Henry M. Braem house on West Thirty-Sixth Street, which he followed with major terra-cotta-embellished public buildings, such as the 1880–81 Post Building and the 1883 Produce Exchange.[11] However, McKim, Mead & White was the first firm to work consistently with this material molded solely for ornament.[12]

Madison Square Garden's four exterior street facades were to be elaborately ornamented with white terra cotta manufactured by the Perth Amboy Terra Cotta Company of Perth Amboy, New Jersey, the premier innovator and leading manufacturer of terra cotta on the East Coast and regular supplier to McKim, Mead & White. The company had previously developed a line of thin "old gold" bricks copied from an antique Roman brick Stanford White had carried home from his honeymoon trip, as well as lines of gray brick, speckled Pompeian terra cotta for the 1885 Tiffany house, and now unglazed white terra cotta. Along with Wells's and Kendall's detailed scale drawings and plans for the molded decoration, White also provided photographs from Italy for inspiration. In return, the company sent shop drawings back to McKim, Mead & White for approval before they would proceed to the modeling.[13]

Stanford White made frequent visits to Perth Amboy to personally supervise the process. He would regularly storm into the modeling room like a whirlwind, quickly inspect the semidry clay models, and invariably proclaim, "Terrible!" He would then hail the workmen, calling out to "Guido, Giuseppe, Luigi"—which might have been the names of the

Italian craftsmen but never actually were. Sometimes he would grab a carving tool and change a line or sharpen a detail himself.

After the ornament was modeled, carved full-scale for final approval, and judged acceptable to White's high standards, it would still take another good eight to ten weeks to cast the plaster molds, pack in the clay, dry each piece, unmold them, harden them, smooth the edges, slip and glaze them, fire them in one of the twenty-two kilns in three stages over ten to twelve days, finish them, check them for fit, number them according to the setting beam, and pack them in hay for delivery to the site.[14] And William Mead had issued the strict order that no matter what, the total cost for the terra cotta must come in at under $40,000.[15]

•

Amid the travails and tedium of ongoing construction, there were still a few bright spots during the winter of 1889–90. In December 1889 old friend John Singer Sargent arrived in New York, where Stanford White had lined up a number of commissions for him.[16] None were as appealing a subject as the Spanish dancer Carmencita, "The Midnight Passion Flower of Seville," who had performed at the 1889 Paris exposition and was currently appearing at Koster & Bial's Music Hall a block west of Madison Square.

Sargent was entranced and began to paint her portrait at his borrowed Twenty-Third Street studio just across the square, bribing her with jewelry and keeping her amused by eating cigars.[17] Bare-armed and full-bosomed, Carmencita sang gypsy songs and swayed and swirled, whirled and twirled, fluttered and quivered in short, bespangled skirts that revealed perfectly formed ankles sheathed in high-heeled boots. The crowds cheered as she became the hottest ticket in New York, at least among the artistic crowd with enough sophistication to appreciate her rough and what some had called even barbarous charms. Soon she and her guitarist were regularly performing in private homes and at late night studio parties that Saint-Gaudens and White were pleased to attend, although Carmencita's sensual shivers and torsal upheavals still proved too much for some in polite society.[18]

Meanwhile, Stanford White was at his desk, working days and most nights on the final plans for the Garden and its splendid grand opening.

At least that was what he told his wife, and it was undoubtedly mostly true, for, like Saint-Gaudens, White rarely ceased working and reworking a project. At the end of those short winter days, when office lamps were lit and all but a few draftsmen had gone home, White would still be there, softly whistling to himself as he added a detail to his work. Late evening diversions also continued,[19] however, and aside from the studio parties and Carmencita's performances, there was a jolly bear-steak dinner party at Edward Austin Abbey's studio at which White commandeered all the fruit on the table to erect a model of the Garden—which he explained would no doubt pay for itself with admission fees to its roof garden and tower.[20]

As a likely result of all this candle-burning, White suffered a succession of colds, and in March 1890 he and Bessie traveled to a health resort in Asheville, North Carolina, for some southern sunshine and quite possibly a look at George W. Vanderbilt's fabulous Biltmore House, designed by Richard Morris Hunt and just under construction.[21] Back in the office by the end of the month, White once more entered the fray in a rush, his focus solely on the Garden until it was in better shape.[22] "I'm not worth much myself at night on account of it, which is enough work for one man without having anything else to do,"[23] White's "anything else" being the monumental Washington Arch on Washington Square, set to break ground one month later.

•

By mid-April, the city finally had warmed up from its deep-freeze, and the Madison Square Garden Amphitheatre was rapidly approaching completion, with more than 1,200 carpenters, plumbers, bricklayers, masons, plasterers, and countless others at work from early morning until late at night. The flat roof was within one week of being finished, with dressed hemlock tongue-and-grooved planks covering the steel members and sealed with roofing paper covered by felt and tar pitch, with tin flashing inserted between the roof and parapet walls.[24]

Then the rush began to complete the architectural ornament, carefully building it into the walls and filling the voids tightly with brick and high-quality hard mortar.[25] The Garden's 65-foot-high façade was divided into three stories and three distinct architectural zones. The first level was left quite plain, awaiting the construction of the attached arcade, except for

27. Madison Square Garden, Madison Avenue main entrance, 1925, Wurts Bros. The New York Public Library / Art Resource, NY.

the planned entrance on Madison Avenue. As the Garden's main entrance, it was the most elaborately designed, with pairs of Ionic columns supporting a high enframed arch.

Above a surrounding open balcony rose the second and third stories, which were cleverly united in a single band of design with groups of three or four two-story round-arch, archivolted windows separated by shallow pilasters and a row of circular bull's-eye windows above, very much like the Century Association Clubhouse façade. Again the focal point of the second floor was the Madison Avenue entrance, where a slim window arch framed in polished lavender marble was surrounded by blank niches and a profusion of floriated and foliated terra-cotta ornament. This design would closely remind some observers of the Parisian Académie Nationale de Musique-Théâtre de l'Opéra,[26] whose dome was perhaps coincidentally topped by a monumental nude statue of Apollo, god of the sun and brother to Diana of the moon.

The roofline third stage of the elevation was composed of open Ionic colonnades on Madison Avenue and 100 feet along two sides. These would eventually screen the roof garden and beyond it transform to a shorter, colonnaded parapet. At the third-floor level above the Madison Avenue entrance a panel was inserted with the date of erection, and at the very top a towering flagpole was to be installed from which Old Glory would fly. As a rather chauvinistic symbol of the republic's position in the world at that point, Saint-Gaudens designed a colossal eagle, 15 feet across, that perched on a globe intended to be set before the flagstaff, but it was never actually installed.[27]

The corners of the building were anchored by great broad piers that were each crowned above the roofline by a belvedere. Columned and turreted, these eight small domed structures—said to be among the Garden's prettiest details—were not physically accessible and served no practical purpose except to break the flatness of the Garden's roof, add interest to the skyline, help to create a playful, festive air, and eventually re-echo the verticality of the great tower when it was finally erected.

Each rather fantastical belvedere—or cupola or tourelle or turret as they were variously termed in the press[28]—had a gallery course of twelve Corinthian and Ionic columns with projecting pilasters at the corners that were strengthened by interior wrought-iron pipe encased in mortar. The caps of some were covered with red terra-cotta tile, while others were left with copper open-work. They were clearly finished in a rush, framed by wooden ribs covered with sheathing boards at the very top, the terra-cotta tiles nailed to the sheathing with iron wire nails.[29] Most observers at the time would quite appreciate the belvederes, while a few, harsher critics would find them to be "trivial" and "illiterate."[30] As for their design inspiration, a Latin American influence was suggested, or Byzantine, or perhaps Moorish, or even New England meetinghouse.[31] It was not unexpected that Stanford White would mix his epochs with a certain daring charm.[32]

28. Madison Square Garden roofline belvederes, northeast corner, 1890. The Museum of the City of New York / Art Resource, NY.

The Fourth Avenue façade that would serve as a secondary entrance to the amphitheater was very much plainer, although it boasted a small portico to shelter visitors and taller, more substantial double-storied towers at its corners. To some observers these towers suggested a miniature version of St. Paul's Cathedral in London, which, like the serpent biting its own tail, were late seventeenth-century English Baroque cribbed from Bernini's ill-fated early seventeenth-century towers for St. Peter's late Renaissance basilica in the Vatican, which could in turn be traced back to Roman examples like the Temple of Vesta.[33]

But it was not just the details of the Garden's decoration or its stylistic pedigree that was of importance to Stanford White. It was said that he

29. Madison Square Garden, Fourth Avenue rear entrance, ca. 1890, from *King's Handbook of New York City* (1893).

would explain to anyone who would listen that he was not only concerned with the design of the building, "but how would it look, how it would feel, when the cigarette smoke curled up into the yellow spotlights—how would the color sound when the band struck up, how would the arena smell when the scents of powder and perfume and the acrid odors of excitement were all mixed."[34]

•

Even though the building was far from finished, the critics did not hesitate to continue to offer preliminary judgment. Aside from debating the vast range of historical sources, some also argued that the Garden walls lacked a sufficient massiveness. As for the terra-cotta decoration spread like a skin over the building—shallow yet intricately carved in rather the manner of

Spanish sixteenth-century Plateresque silverwork design[35]—reviews were once again mixed. Some found it too feeble and hardly appropriate for the Garden's vast dimensions, especially where it was spread rather thinly across the back, Fourth Avenue side, while others complained the ornament was a little too heavy and overblown, perhaps even smothering.[36]

Writer and architectural critic Mariana Griswold Van Rensselaer pointed out another source of critical discomfort that the Garden's very large and solid rectangular exterior violated a fundamental precept of architecture in that it did not at all reflect its interior parts or functions. The great straight-angled rectangle, 465 feet long by 200 feet wide, gave no hint of the elliptical arena or the various other divisions within—the theater, concert hall, restaurants, and so forth—that would cleverly fit around the arena on three floors.[37] But still, like McKim, Mead & White's other commissions, Madison Square Garden stood out for its solid construction and overall quality, the choice of fine materials, the play of texture and light over its surfaces, and the overall uniqueness of character that somehow each of the firm's structures conveyed.[38]

And when considering the Madison Square Garden in toto, as Van Rensselaer stated, despite any perceived fault, there was absolutely no question that "we are in the presence of a great amusement palace."[39] However, as a relative by marriage of contractor David King and dear friend of Augustus Saint-Gaudens, she may not have been entirely the most impartial of judges.[40]

13

An Irksome Spring

IN THE FREEZING COLD nearly spring of 1890, Stanford White scurried to attend to Madison Square Garden's last architectural details, both inside and out. By mid-April the Garden's walls were complete, most of the roof was on, and the huge pillars at the front entrance had been installed. Inside the amphitheater, the elegant boxes were being fitted up while the upper tiers were ready for the thousands of seats to be installed. The planned May 15 opening seemed assured.[1] Of course, there was to be a lavish celebratory opening for the Garden, and who better to plan a spectacular show than White himself.

After checking in on the ongoing work at the Garden site, he would often pop into John Singer Sargent's nearby studio to warm up, arriving "as though shot from a cannon." White would express various opinions ("mostly absurd in nature," according to Sargent), and then depart as suddenly as he had arrived. "It was best to stand back," Sargent found, "and let the tornado blow itself out."[2] On one of his blow-throughs, White informed the painter that he had asked the inimitable Carmencita to dance for the Garden's opening, generously offering $250 a week, but that she had quite rudely refused.[3]

Luckily, two ballets were already in the works, to be imported, along with the ballet girls, from England. "Peace and War" and "Choosing the National Flower" had been devised by the very British Captain Alfred Thompson, formerly of the Enniskillen Dragoons but schooled in art in Paris and currently a well-established playwright and costume designer in London. The dancers were under the direct supervision of ballet master Leon Espinosa, late of the Imperial Theatre, St. Petersburg, and the score would be by French composer Paul Cressonois.[4] To perform the music as starring attraction, Eduard Strauss, son of Johann the elder and brother of waltz king Johann II, would make his New York debut with his Vienna orchestra on opening night.[5]

But in April 1890, news of Strauss's engagement resulted in a huge protest by both the city's Federated Trades and the Musical Mutual Protective Union, which claimed it was clearly unpatriotic—and quite possibly illegal—to sign a foreign orchestra to open an American edifice of such importance, "especially when there are a dozen orchestras right here in the city that are equal or superior."[6] They insisted that Eduard was merely the Johanns' nephew who traded unfairly upon his famous family name and that the orchestra was composed of cheap musicians who scraped by playing in one of Vienna's beer gardens. Soon, however, it was revealed that the complaint against Strauss had been launched by the leader of a rival band who had lost the bid to the Austrians, and the protest was soon forgotten.[7]

•

Toward the end of April, there was distressing news that Bessie White's mother had died of pneumonia. However, she left a substantial fortune of some $8 million to be divided among her five surviving children, with Bessie inheriting likely more than $500,000 in cash as well as part ownership in some 130 properties, including several hotels and the popular Niblo's Garden on Broadway a few blocks south of Washington Square. Husband Stan was, as expected, named trustee in charge of her funds and purchased 1,100 shares of the Madison Square Garden Company for himself, as well as another 350 for McKim, Mead & White. This investment brought with it a spot on the Garden board, and he would soon be elected vice president.[8]

•

Augustus Saint-Gaudens had his own distractions that spring of 1890. The house he and his family had been renting on Washington Square was put up for sale, and a new residence needed to be quickly found. It was the worst possible moment, for Saint-Gaudens was still searching for a suitable life model for the *Diana*. If Davida would not do, with her recent pregnancy and his wife's suspicions, perhaps one of the models on hire at the Art Students League might fit the bill.

At least twice a week Saint-Gaudens traveled from his Thirty-Sixth Street studio down to the old Sohmer Building on Twenty-Third Street, a few blocks east of Madison Square. Once a piano factory, since 1887 it had been home to the Art Students League of New York, the largest and best of the city's art schools, with both male and female students enrolled from all over the United States. Here Saint-Gaudens had been teaching for the past year and a half, in full charge of the sculptural modeling classes.

The league was first established in 1875 as a cooperative association when the free classes offered by the cash-strapped National Academy of Design were temporarily suspended. A fair number of the founding two hundred students chose to remain at the league even after the academy reopened, preferring the league's more democratic approach. They also chose to reject the academy's hidebound focus on landscape painting in favor of a more progressive, Continental-style education based on the study of the human figure. Since its founding, such illustrious alumni as Charles Dana Gibson, Frederic Remington, George Inness, and Frederick Church had all paid the two-dollar monthly tuition to study at the league in this more modern method. By 1890 there were some eight hundred students enrolled in nineteen different classes in figure sketching, painting, and sculpture as taught by the European-trained faculty led by William Merritt Chase. With no grades or degrees offered and no time limit on the course of study, some students continued to attend year after year throughout their professional careers.[9]

While the very first life classes employing nude models were available to male students at the National Academy in the 1830s, a separate course was not open to females until 1871. Gender-separate classes in life drawing and sculpture had been available at the Art Students League since its founding, and more hours of study from live models were available there than at any other art school in the country.[10]

•

Although in negotiations to build a permanent home uptown, in the spring of 1890 the league was still renting the narrow old brick-box building on Twenty-Third Street, redolent of the lingering odor of the many nearby stables.[11] While Kenyon Cox taught the separate men's and women's life drawing classes, Saint-Gaudens taught life sculpture to both male and female students—which was apparently something of a secret and unknown to the administration, or so they would later claim.

Upon entering the building, Saint-Gaudens would have climbed up a short flight of stairs past the office, the library, and then the reception room decorated with framed photographs of old master portraits as well as the exemplary work of its instructors, including his own Morgan tomb *Angels*. Past a morgue of stark white plaster casts of classical figures, then up another flight of stairs to one of the life classrooms, large, open, and skylit yet secluded from public view. Here too the walls were hung with photographs and studies, while dictums like "Draw firm and be jolly" were painted on the rafters.[12]

As he entered the life modeling classroom each Monday, Saint-Gaudens's students quickly came to attention. One would run with a special hook for his hat, another with a clean towel for his hands, while others prepared the day's fresh clay. As was the case in most art schools since the Civil War, the majority of the class were women who were making the most of newly opened opportunities, not just in studio work but as decorators, designers, illustrators, portraitists, draftswomen, and teachers.[13]

When all was settled, the students would quickly take their places at the clay model stands scattered around a low platform in the center of the room, ready for the week's pose. While female models stepped onto the platform or "throne" fully nude, male models kept a piece of cloth draped over their loins or wore a pair of bathing tights when studied by female students. As was typical of instructors, Saint-Gaudens would no doubt approach the model with absolute detachment, as if she or he were "a wax doll," to quickly arrange their limbs into an appropriate pose to be copied in clay.[14]

At the end of each week, Saint-Gaudens would return to the classroom once again to offer his advice and criticism of the student efforts. Despite the demands of his own work, he was quite devoted to his students at the league. According to his son Homer, he took an almost paternal interest in the development of their talent, hiring a gifted student in need as an assistant at the big white studio and paying not necessarily what they were worth but what they needed to get along. Although only two visits

30. Augustus Saint-Gaudens with his life sculpture class at the Art Students League. Courtesy of the US Department of the Interior, National Park Service, Saint-Gaudens National Historical Park, Cornish, NH.

a week were required, he might have dropped by the league any day and even on Sundays. As soon as a new idea occurred or problem was solved in his own work, he would rush downtown to share it with his students. The students were quite devoted to him as well—dubbing him "Gaudy St. August"—and appreciative of his rather shyly made comments on their work. Unlike his behavior in the studio, Saint-Gaudens strove to restrain his temper, although he had been known on occasion to pick up a tool and slash an irritatingly inferior work to pieces.

Among the students, Saint-Gaudens had no patience for mere cleverness or superficial surface modeling or tool marks left behind, or figures that appeared heavier than the model, or fat rumps, or short legs, or thin wrists, or turned out toes, or excuses of any kind. Urging his students to study the work of the ancient Greeks, the Italian Renaissance, and the French—from Praxiteles to Michelangelo to Houdon—he admonished,

"You cannot reproduce things absolutely. So since you must err, err only on the side of beauty."[15]

•

With the turn away from landscape painting and toward the figure among younger American artists, and the growing enrollment in life classes, there was an ever-increasing need for models. In the late nineteenth century, there were several hundred female and fewer male professionals at work in the city. Modeling for a group of students was quite different than posing for a single artist, and the better, more professional models often refused to pose for classes. Thus, the league had a reputation for hiring the relatively inexperienced, for which they were able to pay the lowest rates, likely fifty cents an hour for a female, forty cents for a male.[16]

Most of the female models at the league worked part time as dress models or ballet girls and were quite used to showing off their figures, while others may have been office or shopworkers tired of the daily routine and in search of a bit of adventure. Still others may have come to modeling after finding themselves in desperate straits, out of work, widowed with children, stranded, perhaps even near starvation. Male models were more difficult to hire, as few men possessed the stamina for it, or those that did considered the work too girlish, or too confining, or they were too suspicious of the whole process. In general, it was said that men who were fit and well-muscled preferred to box for a living or play baseball.[17]

Whatever the gender or motivation, modeling at the league was primarily a business proposition, with the pay still better than what was to be found working in a shop or factory, in domestic service, or at the needle. In general, models were treated with respect, and newcomers were shown particular kindness and consideration.[18]

In his search for an appropriate model for the *Diana*, Saint-Gaudens may have run through the listings on the league's model engagement books; perhaps there were one or two that might do, although their identities were carefully guarded, even from the faculty, to prevent embarrassment and the possibility of relationships outside the studio walls. Many models used assumed names or wore masks or veils to ensure their modesty. A distance of 18 feet from the students was carefully maintained in the studio, and for a time the students were not even permitted to see the models dressed so that their station in life could not be guessed.[19]

•

Over the previous few years, attendance in Saint-Gaudens's life modeling course had increased as well as the quality of work produced under his guidance,[20] but in the spring of 1890 there was trouble. There had been some general hullabaloo in the press regarding art classes that employed nude models, the more sordid details of the models' lives, and the fear that proximity of young students of either sex to those persons might "stimulate looseness of morals and awaken licentiousness."[21] However, the character of New York's Art Students League had always been unimpeachable, and nothing unseemly had ever been discovered about the league's policies, particularly since male and female students had always been kept apart in separate classes.[22]

This changed in the spring of 1890, when it was publicly revealed that Saint-Gaudens had been offering mixed classes, apparently for the first time in the school's history. When one of the female students quit the school in protest over the use of a fully undraped female model, Saint-Gaudens was called before the league's board of control. He explained that it was simply a matter of economy and that separating the male and female students would have necessitated the hiring of a second model. Under pressure from the membership, the board ordered him to divide up the class at the end of April, teaching the women in the morning, the men in the afternoon. But this, Saint-Gaudens responded, would have taken up far more time than he intended to spare.[23]

His students protested the decision, confessing that mixed classes had actually been going on without incident even before Saint-Gaudens's tenure.[24] In his defense, the students also pointed out that a fair number of the females in class were over thirty years old and "hardly impressionable maidens."[25] Furthermore, they feared that their separation into male and female classes would surely affect the quality of instruction and their famed spirit of competition in vying for the achievement prize Saint-Gaudens offered at every term's end.[26]

Saint-Gaudens resumed the class in secret, but word soon spread, leading most of the faculty to oppose him. Some argued against mixed classes of any kind, fearing that the courtesy and deference "naturally" paid by men to women was not conducive to the best work of either sex. Some appealed to patriotism, claiming that mixed classes were repugnant to American ideals.[27] Only Kenyon Cox supported Saint-Gaudens, noting that the presence of male students and their "stronger" work would surely inspire the female students in their own studies, while reminding the board of control that artists simply look upon a nude model as one would an undraped horse, adding that, after all, "it is the tendency of the times to uphold the similar treatment of men and women."[28]

There was some real danger that Anthony Comstock, the former postal inspector and now secretary and special agent of the New York Society for the Suppression of Vice, would descend upon the league and drag the students off to jail. Endowed with police powers to enforce public morality, he was armed with the eponymous 1873 Comstock Law that allowed him to confiscate materials he deemed obscene, indecent, lewd, or lascivious—at gunpoint if need be. Two years before, Comstock had nosed around the women's life class, frightening the students with the possibility that they were to be arrested for violating obscenity laws.[29] The fear was not completely unwarranted, but it would not be until 1906 that Comstock launched a full-scale attack on the league, seizing its art magazine for the inclusion of ten nudes from the students' annual art exhibition, destroying all copies, and eventually incurring widespread ridicule for arresting the league's female bookkeeper for distributing it.[30]

Complaints by the membership regarding Saint-Gaudens's class continued until once more the board of control took up the question in early May 1890, and with a tie vote among the twelve members, they were forced to cancel his class.[31] The story soon erupted in the national newspapers with headlines like, "Art Students Agitated," "Study Not the Nude Together," and "Nude Models Must Go." Saint-Gaudens resigned in protest, but when his class threatened to disband without him, he agreed to teach the two classes separately for the remaining two weeks of the term without pay, simply as a member of the league and a friend. It was assumed that he would not be returning in the fall, so his October class, divided in two, was soon reassigned to fellow sculptor Daniel Chester French.[32]

•

While Augustus Saint-Gaudens was struggling in the spring of 1890 with this scandal of national proportions, Stanford White was facing continuing concerns. In early April a strike was in progress at the Madison Square Garden construction site by the asphalt layers who demanded an eight-hour day and a wage of fifty cents an hour. Reasonable working hours and fair wages were issues that had sparked violence for some fifty years and formed a plank in the growing labor movement.[33] Just four years earlier, the Haymarket Square riot had erupted in Chicago over the same issues when a bomb was tossed, shots were fired, and the Knights of Labor, trade unions, socialists, and anarchists battled the police to leave eight dead and scores injured. By 1890 the country was in the midst of strike fever: in New York, it had affected everyone from messenger boys to cigar makers, in Chicago it was the hotel waiters and the stockyard workers, in Boston the building trades, and out west the miners.

No doubt fearful that the strike at the Garden might spread, constructor King agreed to all demands, and the asphalt workers returned to the job alongside the painters, paper hangers, and marble cutters.[34] Another positive note was struck in early May when 1,500 interior incandescent lights were given a test run, successfully illuminating the amphitheater "as bright as noon."[35]

Although the Madison Square Garden opening had been originally scheduled for May 15, a new string of crises made that an unlikely proposition.[36] In early May, 240 costumes that had been created in London arrived in New York in the possession of the forty European-born ballet girls. But in a matter of days the costumes were seized by special agents of the Treasury Department on charges that the outfits, which were valued at $10,000 in total, had been smuggled in. Apparently while on board ship en route to New York each girl had been given a locked wicker basket with a costume packed inside and told to swear in customs that it contained nothing but her own fancy dresses. Acting on a tip, special agents kept the baskets under surveillance, then seized them in a raid on the theatrical boardinghouse where a dressmaker had been altering the costumes to fit—thus revealing that they had indeed been new to each dancer.[37]

The girls claimed innocence, as did all members of the Madison Square Garden board. It was clearly a shady scheme, "no doubt the work of some unknown agent in London," Police Captain Thompson helpfully suggested. The criminal charges were dropped when it was discovered that the agents had acted on a tip furnished by Dazien & Co., a prominent New York costumer who had unsuccessfully bid on the job. As with all other aspects of the Garden's opening spectacle, "European-made" still had its cachet with Stanford White, who had preferred to import the gowns. The case was finally settled by the payment of over $7,000 in duties and fines,[38] which might have made the American-made outfits a better bargain but would scarcely have generated the publicity.

•

In the midst of the brouhaha over costumes, Eduard Strauss and his Vienna Orchestra arrived in New York on May 14 only to face a complaint lodged with the district attorney. The problem was that labor inspectors could not clearly determine whether the fifty musicians should have been classed for entry as laborers or as artists. If laborers, then White and the Madison Square Garden Company had violated the protectionist Alien Contract Labor Law by booking in Europe for concerts to be performed in America. At a hearing by the US Congress Immigration Investigating Committee, Strauss's musicians were accused of being neither soloists nor composers, which might have exempted them, but as hacks who played the most common sort of dance tunes.[39]

While still in quarantine, Maestro Strauss complained to the press that art should be international and all artists welcomed with open arms.[40] After an examination by the labor inspector, the musicians were allowed to come ashore provisionally for a year's time. Once again it was discovered that the complaint had been lodged by the leader of a local band who had hoped to open the Garden himself. Strauss's orchestra soon departed for a monthlong tour on the East Coast but would return for the Garden's opening night and a following three-month engagement.[41]

•

The next crisis arose within a few days when lawyers for a group of prominent theatrical managers, including Oscar Hammerstein, still annoyed after his dustup with Mr. French, sent letters to the mayor, the president of the Board of Fire Commissioners, and the superintendent of the New York Bureau of Buildings to protest the issuance of a theatrical license to the Garden. Their claim was that the absence of a proscenium arch in the amphitheater made the new structure a fire hazard and a menace to public safety.[42]

After a number of disastrous theater fires in the city, new laws had required that any building used for theatrical purposes must have a proscenium arch supporting a fireproof steel or asbestos curtain and a brick firewall with fireproof shafts that extended 4 feet above the roof—all of which were absent from the amphitheater. Since all other New York City theaters were required to comply with the law, the lawyers demanded, should not the Garden conform as well?[43]

It had not helped the case that men working all night on the Garden's interior that very cold spring of 1890 had lit huge bonfires in the center of the amphitheater, frightening the public with the illusion that the place truly was on fire.[44] However, upon further examination, details of the Garden's plumbing system executed by Byrne & Tucker of New York and published in the *Engineering Record* clearly showed that it possessed a more than adequate fire suppression system, including a fire tank located on the theater roof and sprinkler heads installed 10 feet apart over the amphitheater's stage that would automatically open when the temperature in any part of the building exceeded 160 degrees. In addition, the house pump, steam boiler pump, and elevator pumps were all connected to the fire main and its fire pumps, which completely surrounded the amphitheater on its foundation walls.[45]

Once again it turned out that fire safety was just a pretext, and the real issue that had raised hackles among the city's amusement moguls was the Garden's intention to sell liquor throughout the premises, including a mammoth public bar that would service the amphitheater. This could be in violation of a New York State law that not only forbade the sale of liquor in a house given to dramatic entertainments but also attached a penalty to so much as having a doorway cut between a theater and a saloon. So if the Garden could be compelled to install a proscenium arch, then it could clearly be judged a theater, and then could be found in violation of the liquor laws. Thus, the opening was postponed to mid-June until the situation could be unraveled and any necessary modifications made.[46]

On May 29, just two weeks before the scheduled opening, the mayor finally granted the Madison Square Garden Company a city license to permit amusements and entertainments in the amphitheater, except those in which stage scenery and appliances were employed, thus banning scenery for the opening spectacular.[47] With just a large, 3-foot-high platform allowed, well-known scenic designer Matthew Sommerville Morgan began to create a simple painted background. The English-born artist, cartoonist, correspondent, founder of Matt Morgan Art Pottery, actor, linguist, and father of sixteen children, unfortunately caught a fatal summer cold while doing so, perhaps from working long hours amid damp plaster, and was buried days later.[48]

•

The amphitheater's acoustics were tested on May 29 when the orchestra and singers from the Metropolitan Opera arrived to perform various selections for the board of directors. The board proclaimed themselves delighted with the results and reassured that the effects would be even better with a full house.[49] On the night of June 7 a second test run and preview were held for a select audience, including the mayor, various politicians, the Madison Square Garden board, neighboring clubmen, and, most important, the press. The forty-eight imported ballet girls—reported to be mostly young and pretty—were trotted out to a piano accompaniment just to give a flavor of the upcoming extravaganza.[50] The newspapers happily reported that there was no trace of the circus, the walking match, pugilism, or the dog show about this Garden. It was all new, clean, and very inviting.[51] The next day tickets for the June 16 opening went on sale, and within four days every arena and orchestra seat and every box in the giant amphitheater was sold out.[52]

14

Opening Night

MONDAY NIGHT, June 16, 1890. Finally, after a terrible week of heat and thunderstorms, all of New York turned out for the grand opening of the Madison Square Garden Amphitheatre. After the seemingly endless delays, there had been some concern that by June everyone who mattered would be out of town—on their way to Newport, Saratoga Springs, Narragansett Pier, or the Continent. The June opening was said to be the reason so many of society's leaders had either put off their summer departures or run back to town just for that night, and why members of the Madison Square Garden Company and the National Horse Show Association had "ordered back" their wives and daughters to help fill the seats.[1]

In spite of the planned opening festivities, the new Garden remained only two-thirds complete, still lacking the street arcades, theater, restaurant and bar, concert hall, and the landmark tower. With its creamy terra-cotta ornament, the plain rectangle of a building was said to rather resemble a "titanic cake covered with dusty frosting."[2] As to its particular architectural style, discussion had continued in the press with the source of its ornament variously attributed to the middle Spanish Renaissance, Northern Italian Renaissance, French or English Baroque, and French Second Empire. Regardless, from the exterior at least Stanford White appeared to have accomplished his mission, to create a place grand enough to befit a great city yet graceful enough to convey its purpose—pure enjoyment regardless of historical precedent.[3]

The mob disgorging from carriages, cabs, and the Madison Avenue omnibus began to gather in front of what they assumed to be the Garden's main entrance.[4] But there was a good bit of confusion among the sellout crowd as to where or how to enter the structure, until the triple doors on Madison Avenue were finally thrown open at seven o'clock in the evening in anticipation of the eight o'clock performance. Most everyone had already purchased their tickets, except for a few seats left in the fifty-cent unreserved balcony and the one-dollar seats in the parquet section of the rear floor. J. P. Morgan had allowed no free passes, and scalpers were reselling at premium prices, with thirteen-dollar tickets going for as much as fifty dollars apiece. The lines were long at both the ticket sellers and the takers, who obviously lacked sufficient experience to move things along quickly.[5]

General manager T. Henry French stood at the entrance shouting to the crush of box and ticket holders to go around to the side doors on Twenty-Sixth and Twenty-Seventh Streets.[6] Many did, but the crowd was so dense that most attendees were still trapped in place amid a sea of flowered bonnets and silk top hats. After a half hour the police arrived, and officers were able to relieve some of the jam, keeping at bay with the threat of billy club the gawkers who had come solely to view society folk in evening dress while still keeping a close eye out for pickpockets. An observer for the *Philadelphia Times* described the fashionable crowd as "the most brilliant and showy collection of beautiful women" since the opening of the Metropolitan Opera House seven years before. (The men, however, were said to be quite ordinary and lacking in Continental style and polish.)[7]

When finally ushered in by doormen in sky-blue jackets with red facings, first-nighters passed under an elaborate arch of terra-cotta ornament—of swags and festoons, cartouches and garlands, cornucopia and shields, lion's heads and wreaths—set between pillars of polished granite. They continued into the large marble entrance hall or foyer lobby 100 feet long, its walls lined with polished yellow Siena marble, its floors decorated with mosaics. The still-unfinished Garden Theatre to the left of the hall was expected to open sometime in the fall. On the right, overlooking Madison Square, would stand the café bar and restaurant, still being fitted up in elegant style. At 10,000 square feet, it would be double the size of any such fashionable establishment in the city. Nearby rose the wide stone and marble staircase that would carry visitors to the still-unfinished hall upstairs where classical music concerts would be presented by the end of the year.

Progressing straight ahead up a long, broad ramp, the huge amphitheater space presented an immense elliptical arena floor enclosed within the rectangular walls. At some 265 feet long, 125 feet wide,[8] and 60 feet high to the rafters, it was capable of holding more people than any other hall on earth, a greater crowd than history had seen since the open-air arenas of the ancient Romans.

Attendees were surprised by the virtual absence of ornament or decoration within the amphitheater, except for the immense yet graceful steel and cast-iron columns and arches that supported the roof, now spectacularly strung with thousands of tiny balls of electric light. Beneath every arch and girder hung bare incandescent electric lamps about a foot apart, with additional clusters suspended from the ceiling, the central chandelier alone containing six hundred lights. For fire safety, the entire building was illuminated solely by these four thousand lamps, which were powered by their own rather remarkable generating station in the basement. The flood of white light thrown down upon the boxes, the gallery, and the floor was described in itself as an astounding sight, although some complained in the press about the blinding glare reflected off the painted white ceiling.[9]

It was not only electric light that warmed and decorated the amphitheater, but Stanford White's rather remarkable use of color. Walls were variously painted ochre, chrome orange, and pale red, with bright amaranth-red drapes swagging the amphitheater's many windows and boxes.[10] The ushers contributed to the scheme with their chrome-yellow-orange swallowtail coats, dark trousers with a stripe of scarlet down the side, flame-colored waistcoats with sixteen huge buttons, white satin scarves, and white gloves—designed by White as well (and perhaps inspired by those worn at the Paris Hippodrome).[11]

However, the ushers "kicked like steers" over their outfits, some quit, and a strike was briefly threatened after first-nighters were heard to exclaim, "over here, red and yaller" or "hurry up, rainbow," much to the ushers' embarrassment. Business manager James Morrissey explained that the ushers were meant to be conspicuous so that they could easily be found when needed,[12] but it was well known that Stanford White had always loved color. As reported by William Dean Howells, William

Mead's brother-in-law, he and White were once standing together on the deck of a Staten Island ferry when a stoker fell from a nearby tug and was mangled by its screw. "The poor devil!" exclaimed White as he was torn to pieces, "My God! What color!"[13]

•

As for the interior arrangement of the amphitheater, a three-tiered honey-comb of more than one hundred plush-trimmed boxes ringed the western end of the floor, each with five to nine seats. Above the boxes and just under the roof ran a 36-foot-wide promenade balcony for strolling about the house. Along the sides stood a row of simpler, open boxes and galleries of fixed general seats, all connected by iron stairways with slate treads and landings. Fixed seating totaled near 5,000, but the multiple rows of removable, all-iron firesafe seats that filled the amphitheater floor in both orchestra and parquet sections allowed for 10,000 comfortably, 12,000 with a bit of crowding. On opening night the galleries were full and the floor was nearly so with several thousand in standing room. Final attendance figures varied greatly, with the total number estimated in the newspapers between ten and seventeen thousand.

On that night in June the private boxes that towered above the amphitheater floor were filled with New York society, including Vanderbilts, Roosevelts, Cuttings, Belmonts, and Van Rensselaers, as well as delegations that had traveled in from Philadelphia, Washington, Baltimore, and Boston. Well-known actors, politicians, merchants, and various members of the professions filled more of the good seats, the men in evening clothes, the women in evening gowns and jewels that were said to rival the ceiling's electric fire. Scores of police detectives were scattered about, keeping a sharp eye out for thieves, loose women, and bomb-tossing anarchists, particularly among the standing room crowd.[14]

Amid the tiers sat the presidential box of state, placed directly over the main entrance, 14 feet wide and capable of holding up to fifty dignitaries. On opening night it was occupied by New York's bushy-whiskered "boy mayor," Hugh J. Grant, the son of an Irish saloon-keeper and, at thirty-three, the city's youngest mayor ever. Sharing the box was New York governor David B. Hill, who would run against Grover Cleveland for the Democratic presidential nomination two years later; Chauncey M.

Depew, president of the Vanderbilts' New York Central and Hudson River Railroad and recent candidate for the Republican presidential nomination; and General William Tecumseh Sherman, a longtime resident on Madison Square. Levi P. Morton, vice president to Benjamin Harrison and a former New York congressman, was expected to inaugurate the box of state but at the last moment was unable to attend. Stanford White occupied his own permanently reserved box when not rushing about the house, settling all the final details.[15]

As the house lights dimmed, electric lights up in the ceiling were said to shine "like stars in a fairy land." After a collective gasp of surprise and a sigh of delight, all eyes shifted to the huge, slightly raised stage at the far Fourth Avenue end of the amphitheater, said to be the largest in the world. At a quarter after eight there was a buzz and then a frenzy of applause as Herr Director Eduard Strauss and his forty-three-piece Vienna Imperial Court Orchestra appeared. Strauss stepped jauntily to a slightly raised platform at the front of the stage and held his violin bow aloft, ready to begin, his slender figure trim in a jacket hung with ribboned medals. *Der Schoene* Eddie, the papers called him, a veritable prince charming, with a strong, handsome face, a broad and lofty forehead, keen and twinkling eyes, and a carefully groomed moustache and small patch beneath his lower lip.

The concert began with the delicate, shimmering notes of the overture to *Si j'etai roi*, an opéra comique by Adolphe Charles Adam and enduringly popular since its first presentation in Paris in 1852. Over the years, however, Adam would achieve more lasting fame for the ballet *Giselle* and the Christmas carol known as "O Holy Night." Adam's overture was followed by selections from Gounod's *Faust* and Von Weber's *Der Freischutz* conducted in the usual manner, and then Strauss's own and his brother Johann's Vienna waltzes and polkas, conducted while facing the audience, occasionally playing his violin while swaying his body and pattering in little waltz steps around the stage.[16]

Applause for the orchestra was generous at first, and there were numerous encores, including his brother's enthusiastically received "Blue Danube" waltz accompanied by much toe tapping and head nodding among the crowd. However, the press later reported that Strauss's workmanlike performance was something of a disappointment—his end-less pattering, the dipping of his shoulders, and the nodding of his head soon a great bore. A more serious complaint concerned the acoustics: the orchestra could not be clearly heard beyond the front rows, the sound was blurred and dull and far too small for such a vast space, the reverberation from the instruments was actually quite painful for those in the orchestra seats, and for disappointed thousands the orchestra's performance was more a pantomime than a performance.

•

Following the intermission came the opening night's first ballet, "Choos-ing the National Flower," which was also something of a disappointment, beginning with the painted set that seemed cold and barren.[17] Reaction warmed once the dancers entered in those notorious costumes, which were described in the press as both beautiful and brilliant in design as well as color. Their striking appearance also served to hush some of the audience, who had insisted on chatting through most of the concert, which they could not hear. Strauss and his men had been relieved on the band-stand by the Garden's house orchestra led by Jesse Williams, formerly musical conductor at the city's Casino Theatre, playing the accompanying music by the late French composer Jules Cressonnois.

The dancers themselves were also rather disappointing to the audi-ence. All of the girls except for two were foreign born—French, Belgian, German, and Spanish—including the star, Mlle. Rodman of the State The-atre in Hamburg. Their faces were not what New Yorkers deemed pretty, their black tresses differed from the typical American bleached blonds, and their figures seemed a little too heavy, their movements ungainly. By contrast, the two American girls in the cast—sisters Ray and Louise Allen—were judged quite graceful, light, and expressive in their move-ments, providing ammunition for those who had argued for purely American talent to open the Garden.

Oddly enough, the European designed and performed ballet dealt with an American subject, and it soon became the audience's favorite. As the first ballet unfolded, the figure of Columbia searched for an appro-priate floral emblem to represent the United States. The goddess Flora arranged her garden of long-legged lilies, pansies, violets, and daisies who swayed to and fro in the summer winds while winged dragonflies, butterflies, and bees hovered about. Stunning the audience, one Mlle. Azella took a little leap and was off like a bird, lifted and swung around the arena by means of India rubber springs and a hidden wire operated by the dancer's husband.[18] The ballet continued until Columbia selected the goldenrod as America's symbol and placed it in the center of a revolving fountain, all lit up by electric lights.

Another intermission followed, then more Strauss waltzes and polkas, and finally the second ballet, "Peace and War." This began with a country wedding scene soon interrupted when the groom was suddenly called to soldierly duty. Then came the grand military spectacle with a cast of hundreds of gold-spangled platoons: Bellona, the Roman goddess of war, rode in a dragon chariot dragged by the fierce dogs of war while barbarians of the Iron Age, ancient Egyptians, Roman legions, Templars of the Crusades, Hungarian hussars, Etrurians in animal skins and light-flashing helmets, and a fire-juggling machine all paraded past.

When the performance finally concluded near midnight in a grand electric apotheosis, there was concern that the huge crowd's egress from the Garden might be as chaotic as its entry and likely quite dangerous in case of fire or a panic. However, the egress was far better planned, and the entire amphitheater was vacated safely within four and a half minutes via inclined ramps that led to ten street exits.[19]

•

By the following day the New York newspapers were filled with stories that described the great opening. The critics complained primarily about the size and sound of Maestro Strauss's orchestra, the ungraceful ballets, and the nearly indecently garbed ballet girls. As for the Garden itself, the reaction was quite positive. There was much praise for the architect's design and the builder's execution, particularly in the structure's proportion, its interior light, the warm color scheme, and the sense of "combined strength and gracefulness in its constructive details,"[20] which were made more impressive by their simplicity. The *New York Sun* lauded Stanford White's taste and genius in the harmony of design and decoration that balanced simplicity with richness and named it one of the best of the new American school inspired by the great buildings of Italy and Spain.[21]

The *New York Times* reported a perfect consensus on the building's safety, convenience, completeness, and "perhaps, most of all, upon the comfortableness of the place."[22] Much of this praise was due to its pleasant temperature during the warm summer months, achieved by two 26-by-55-foot fixed glass skylights and ten 26-by-26-foot rolling skylights covering more than half the amphitheater's roof.[23] These could be silently rolled open to admit fresh evening air along with ten large fans and more than one hundred opened windows. Even the toilet rooms were described as charming, with their ceramic-tiled mosaic floors and white glazed-tile-covered walls.[24]

The *Times* assumed that the Madison Square Garden would soon become one of the must-be-seen sights of the city, along with Central Park and the Brooklyn Bridge, while the *Daily Tribune* declared it to be the inauguration of a new era in popular summer entertainment.[25] Newspapers around the country also reported on the opening of the Garden and its architecture. Most opinions were similarly quite favorable, with the *Chicago Tribune* proclaiming it Stanford White's masterpiece and the finest combination of utility and beauty anywhere.[26] And General Sherman was heard to loudly exclaim that as for the building, he could conceive of nothing more perfect.

Raves were not unanimous, however. The *New York Herald* conversely found the building "too stiff, too conventional," and criticized the "crude terra cotta walls, its cold iron pillars and girders, the bare deal boards, its wooden chairs, and the hideous proscenium with its tawdry red curtains."[27] *Harper's New Monthly* complained about the amphitheater's lack of interior ornament and the visibility of its constructive parts, deeming it "more like a big barn than a garden, neither handsome nor prettily finished but rather thin and cheap."[28] But these were minor compared to New York's ability to now claim equal footing with London, Paris, and Vienna as the proud possessor, newspaper ads touted, of "the largest, most magnificent amusement place in the world."

•

For the rest of the summer, the musical program was reordered, shortened, and dubbed the "Strauss sandwich," with the orchestra playing concert selections in between the two ballets.[29] Critics continued to find the Vienna orchestra unimpressive, although moving it off the main stage to a smaller, raised circular stage constructed in the center of the house greatly improved its sound. Ticket sales began to fall off in July, so prices were reduced to three dollars and six dollars for boxes, with five thousand seats now selling for just fifty cents. Concertgoers complained that the great house was still and rather depressingly only half-full, but in fact there were as many people at the Garden every night as could fill *all* of the first-class theaters in town.[30]

To distract attention, a press notice from the Garden's management praised the charm and grace of the ballet girls, claiming most were from Paris or had danced there, and tipped off clubmen that Tuesday was salary day when scores of the young beauties might be spotted lounging about Madison Square as they waited to be paid.[31]

In late July a full liquor license was finally granted by the New York Excise Board for the cafe bar, grand enough to serve champagne, wine, and lager beer to seven hundred patrons at once.[32] "So the big, bare, cheerless Madison Square Garden is to become a beer hall, after all,"[33] sniffed the society gossip rag *Town Topics*, but ticket sales immediately increased.[34]

•

Eduard Strauss presented his last concert September 13, 1890, departing the city with some rancor. "That Madison Square Garden was a circus hall, not a concert garden," he complained to the *Times*. "The echoes off the vast space interfered with the musicians and marred the delicacy of my music—it would have been easier to play in the open street," he declared.[35] The *New York Sun* responded with the reminder that Strauss's orchestra was just a temporary summer amusement, and surely any intelligent New Yorker would realize that the Madison Square Garden Amphitheatre was not designed for concerts but for grand spectacles like the circus, the horse show, political conventions, and great athletic competitions.[36]

The Garden closed for a week in September in preparation for a monthlong season of promenade concerts in the style of London's Covent Garden, during which the audience was free to stroll about the house. Strauss's central bandstand was removed and one three times its size was placed further back toward the stage at the eastern Fourth Avenue end to accommodate Anton Seidl's substantially larger Metropolitan

Orchestra while allowing more space for tables and for promenaders on the floor.[37]

In another attempt to stimulate attendance, alcoholic drinks of all kinds were sold in every part of the building and served by scuffling waiters to parties seated at the small round tables and chairs now installed on the floor. Admission was again reduced to more popular prices of twenty-five and fifty cents.[38] Seidl and his seventy-five musicians found much greater favor with the audience and the critics, as the crowd cheered and waved handkerchiefs following their performance of classical concert favorites.[39]

Good music, good beer, and a place to enjoy a cigar. "What more could the spirit of mortal desire?" demanded the *Times*.[40] "Working as many hours a day as Americans of all classes do . . . why not enjoy the pleasurable relief of light music, merry comedy, gay costumes, graceful actors and songstresses, and freedom through it all to get up . . . and walk around. . . . Give us air and liberty in the theaters. We are learning to be merry and wise."[41]

15

More of the Pieces

WITH SO MANY PARTS of the complex waiting to fall into place, New York's eye was still very much on Madison Square Garden in 1890, and as the year progressed and each of the remaining elements was added, it was carefully examined, debated, and discussed in parlors and clubrooms as well as in the press. The first to be completed was the Garden Theatre, spelled British-style like the Garden Amphitheatre, and dedicated to popular drama, high-class farce comedy, and light opera. A leased operation, it possessed its own separate entrance on Madison Avenue at the northwest corner of the Garden's ground floor. The theater opened Saturday night, September 27, 1890, with the American premiere of *Doctor Bill*, a British version of the French farce *Le docteur Jo-Jo*.

While the production received middling reviews—with the text judged more suggestive and salacious than witty—there were nothing but raves for the theater itself: for the suitability of the stage, the tasteful decorations, the comfortable arrangement of the seats, the excellence of the lighting, the number and width of the aisles, the safety of its fourteen exits, and the perfection of its ventilation system. Stanford White the theater buff and well-known first-nighter had incorporated into its plan virtually every modern theatrical improvement, including multitiered dressing rooms and a mechanical shifting double stage, for which the bedrock had been blasted down 25 feet.[1] Nearly fully lit by electric light, except for part of the huge ceiling chandelier, it was also guaranteed fireproof.

The theater stood three stories high, with a row of eight boxes—swagged, fringed, and tasseled—as well as a balcony, a gallery, and a side colonnade that functioned as a promenade in place of the traditional dress circle, an idea freely borrowed from White's design for the 1880 Casino

Theatre in Newport.[2] Although the theater was grand enough to seat 1,200 with room for another 400 in standing room, it was said to still feel warm and inviting. At 80 by 120 feet, the stage was the largest in the city and richly framed by four immense Corinthian columns and a proscenium arch that was brought forward to the level of the side boxes, creating the impression that even the rear seats were near to the stage. There were no pillars or posts to obstruct the view, and the floor was pitched to eliminate the craning of necks and allow every seat an open view of the stage.

The theater's acoustical design was inspired by the famed 1876 Festspielhaus in Bayreuth, Germany, built to the specifications of composer

PROSCENIUM ARCH OF THE NEW GARDEN THEATRE.

31. *Proscenium Arch of the New Garden Theatre, New York Herald* (Sept. 21, 1890). Newsbank / Readex and the American Antiquarian Society.

Richard Wagner. As Wagner decreed, the orchestra was invisible, sunk below the line of vision to eliminate unnecessary distraction from the stage and improve the balance in sound between the singers and the orchestra. In addition, a solid masonry wall was erected from cellar to roof that, along with its cushion of airspace, would provide insulation from the din of the adjacent amphitheater.[3]

•

The theater's style of decoration was neither Italian nor Spanish but the exceedingly fashionable Louis XVI. As the last king of France, Louis and his period were favorites with New York's very rich, who may have imagined themselves living as eighteenth-century royalty, envied and admired by the still-grateful peasantry. Cornelius Vanderbilt's music room and Mrs. Ogden Goelet's drawing room were judged among the finest examples of Louis XVI decor, furnished by American decorators like Stanford White who had ransacked Paris on behalf of their clients.[4]

The walls of the Garden Theatre were hung with striped coverings in soft cream and pale yellow; the seat covers and imported English carpet installed in crimson plush; and ceiling, walls, and pillars painted creamy white with the delicately modeled papier-mâché decoration picked out in gilt[5]—a favorite color scheme that led to the firm's well-known soubriquet, "McKim, White-and-gold."[6]

The side proscenium boxes were festooned with papier-mâché roses, and the coffered ceiling above was decorated with large rosettes and basket weave designs also borrowed from Newport's Casino Theatre. Atop the golden proscenium arch perched the soaring female *Angel of Fame* and her attendant naked putti, modeled in papier-mâché by Philip Martiny. A young émigré born in Alsace to reputedly French but more likely Italian parents, Martiny was another former pupil of and assistant to Augustus Saint-Gaudens. His remarkable talent was discovered by the master while wood-carving on the Vanderbilt mansion decoration in the early 1880s, and he would continue to be employed on a number of important projects.[7]

The grand drape curtain by prominent New York scenic designer Henry Hoyt continued the French allusion by reproducing one of Italian society painter Giovanni Boldini's views of the gardens of Versailles.[8] Although he did much work in Paris, Boldini painted more in the representational style of the old masters rather than the Impressionists, a style Stanford White did not appreciate or much care to collect. White was a friend and patron of Boldini, and the portrait the artist painted of Bessie White in low-cut evening gown, feather boa, and wistful smile would be a great favorite.[9]

Full judgment of the theater by New York society would have to wait for a few weeks, however, as most were still enjoying the beautiful autumn weather out of town and would not be back in force until November. It was only the relatives and friends of the stockholders and those with homes in the nearer suburbs who bid on the auction sale of the theater's opening night seats and boxes.[10] But opening night plans were nearly derailed at the last moment when the unions threatened but did not enforce a strike of all their musicians, stage carpenters, property men, and sceneshifters unless general manager French agreed to hire only union men for those jobs.[11]

The Garden Theatre, with its stately colonnades, delicately modeled decoration, and joyful air combined with a sense of refinement, was soon judged the prettiest theater in the city, if not the world.[12] Stanford White was particularly fond of the place and was often spotted in his box wearing a fashionably bobtailed tuxedo jacket in the style of the Prince of Wales, having abandoned the more formal and fusty old swallowtail.[13]

•

For many New Yorkers, the real test of Madison Square Garden came mid-November with the first horse show in its new home. This was, of course, the very raison d'être for the Garden, to serve as a suitable showplace for New York's greatest annual exhibition, the first full appearance of society after summers away, and the most prominent event of the winter social season. At no other time or place during the entire year would society be seen in fuller force or more splendidly arrayed.

By mid-October 1890, the amphitheater was in the midst of transformation—hardly recognizable to anyone who had swayed with Strauss or hummed along with Seidl during the opening summer season. The stage had been removed as well as the floor seats, and the whole place transformed from concert hall to arena. A sawdust-covered track was laid around a center ring covered by tanbark, and in the very middle a judges' stand was constructed.

32. *At the Horse Show, The Century* (Mar. 1894).

A clear promenade was left open around the arena floor, set off by an open 7-foot fence to protect the spectators who desired a closer inspection of the horseflesh. No need to dirty one's shoes for a view of some of the gentler horses and ponies, for the promenade was fringed by a row of three hundred elegantly finished box stalls for the more notable thoroughbreds, each stall decorated with a bundle of golden straw tied with red and blue ribbons. An additional six hundred horses were more casually stabled in the lower caverns below the arena floor. Nose to nose with the upper stalls, so to speak, and within petting distance, were the first-level arena boxes, quickly snapped up at auction by the Astors, Whitneys, Vanderbilts, de Peysters, Webbs, and Roosevelts, while single seats and less desirable boxes went on sale the first of November for as much as $350 apiece.[14]

Aside from the horses and the fashions, the chief focus of speculation was obviously the new Garden and how effectively the show would be carried off in its now quite palatial space. After years of planning, months of preparation, and weeks of anxiety, the sixth annual exhibition of the National Horse Show Association of America opened to well-deserved fanfare on November 10 and to positive reviews for the commodious arena, the ample room for exhibitions and exercise, and the row of sparkling new stalls encircling the field—all well lit, drained, ventilated, and heated. The grooms were in colorful livery, the horses brightly decked out, and the crowd said to be as good-natured as it was well-bred.

According to the newspapers, there was truly no event in New York that brought out such a crowd of handsome women, well-dressed men, and pretty children. "Are you exhibiting at the Horse Show this year? Yes, I'm sending my daughter,"[15] the joke ran. Dowagers cozied up in boxes they had furnished with comfortable wicker chairs and Turkish rugs, employing binoculars to survey the social scene as well as the horses.[16] Night after night thousands of "the very best people" in the country were spotted in smart new evening dress. Ladies wore long gowns with full, ballooning shoulders and enormous hats covered with velvet blooms, while for gentlemen horsey fashion included a white topcoat, brilliant necktie, high top hat, multicolored boutonnière, and silver-headed cane in hand. John Lander's society band, so popular at the Saratoga track and all the best parties, furnished the background for the throng of laughing, chatting spectators filling the promenade, parading for the benefit of those less famous or fortunate.[17]

As the fancy traps clogged the avenue in front of the Garden, one quite sympathetic policeman was heard to wish aloud that he were rich enough to pay admission to the show for every man who sat on a driver's box shivering in the street. "Those fellows pass their lives among horses and love them far better than the rich men who speculate in horseflesh," he said. "The rich men of the town would never do more good or give more pleasure than if they would all stay home one night to let their coachies go to the show."[18]

Despite the obvious circumstances, the air in the Garden was surprisingly sweet, thanks to the efficient in-house ventilation system first tested out in Stanford White's Methodist Church in Baltimore. The system was helped along by slanted floors for drainage and liberal doses of Sanitas-brand disinfectant in the stables below the arena, the most popular and best-known product of its kind, acknowledged to be so effective that even the Prince of Wales had endorsed it.[19]

The horse show was judged a great success, with more than a thousand entries, scores of prizes offered, record-breaking attendance, and receipts with a profit estimated at $50,000. By the last few days, seats were being scalped for three times their price, and on the next to last night the crush inside was so terrific that the fire department had to halt the sale of seats. The *New York Times* acknowledged there was no place in America that compared with the Garden in offering such accommodations for both people and horses.[20] However, it was clear to many participants that despite the best planning the Garden was almost at its limit. In just two years there would be stalls enough for only half the participating horses, with the other half forced to board elsewhere and be brought in solely for judging.[21]

•

Three days before Christmas 1890, the handsomest banquet room in New York—Madison Square Garden's new Concert & Assembly Hall—opened with the eighty-fifth-anniversary dinner of the New-England Society of New-York. Five hundred men were packed in the 110-by-75-foot rectangular hall at tables laden with baskets of roses. A massive crystal electrolier hung from the center of the ceiling, with additional lights built into the elaborately coffered ceiling and spread over the walls. J. P. Morgan, president of the society, presided from the speaker's table installed on the stage and with a nod acknowledged Stanford White and his latest architectural triumph.[22]

Public banquets were something of an institution in New York, where men tied by occupation, alma mater, home state, religion, political preference, or ethnic background gathered to dine together and then later in the evening, over drinks and cigars, hear a round of speeches. While the open floor of the new hall held the required banquet tables, the upstairs balcony and side gallery's private boxes now, for the first time, allowed several hundred women to arrive later, after the catered terrapin and green turtle soup had been served, and to enjoy the evening's program[23]—a clear acknowledgment that women might also appreciate an educational presentation.

The hall, along with its attached ladies' and gentlemen's withdrawing rooms, toilets, reception room, and kitchen, was located at the southwest corner of the Garden on the second floor. While there were interior connections to the Garden Amphitheatre and Garden Theatre, allowing patrons to easily move from one event to another, the official entrée to the concert hall was still under construction at the time of its opening. When the work was completed visitors would enter through the doors on Twenty-Sixth Street and climb up a broad marble staircase to the hall's reception room, which, like the main hall, could also double as a smaller ballroom, supper room, or, when fitted with opera chairs, concert hall for an audience of up to three hundred.[24] The Concert & Assembly Hall was thus cleverly designed to host a variety of events, as its name implied. When set fully with its sea-green velvet chairs, an audience of 1,600 could be accommodated at musical recitals, lectures, or meetings, and when the floor was completely cleared, the room was neatly transformed into a ballroom. In addition, when a large ball took place in the amphitheater, the music hall could then become its supper room.[25]

The hall complex sat directly above the space that was intended to be leased out as the Madison Square Garden's restaurant, although it still remained vacant. For a brief time a local caterer tried to serve meals there at popular prices, but it did not last.[26] The space had been offered to Delmonico's rent free, but even they were not up to the challenge of satisfying such a wide range of events and palates on a nightly basis.[27] Instead, it was leased for the night by various restaurants and caterers to serve guests attending special events, such as the midnight supper for six hundred prepared by Sherry's Fifth Avenue restaurant on January 8, 1891, on the occasion of the Assembly Ball, the first of many such society balls to be held in the complex.[28]

While the Stanford Whites were invited to various balls, they were not included among the social elite and the mythical "four hundred." Bessie White's inheritance from the A. T. Stewart empire did not greatly grease the wheels, as Mrs. Astor once replied regarding the admittance of "shopkeepers" to the city's social scene, "I buy my carpets from them, but then is that any reason why I should invite them to walk on them?"[29]

Like the Garden Theatre, the Concert & Assembly Hall was decorated in lush gold-and-white Louis XVI style with sage green accents, and it was likely the most lavishly decorated room within the Garden complex. Portière curtains of sea-green and gold cloth draped the doorways, and the sumptuous high-relief plaster and papier-mâché decorations on the walls, columns, and arches—all festoons, wreaths, and swags—had also been modeled by sculptor Philip Martiny.[30] Particularly notable was the frieze of life-sized female figures united by garlands of flowers that hovered above the stage and stretched along the walls of the balcony's deeply arched bays, five on each side. The *New York Times* noted the "beautiful and shapely women"[31] that created an effect the *New York Herald* described as "singularly soft, charming, and sensuous."[32]

The forty-four balcony boxes afforded a fine view of events on the floor below and, with their steep sides, provided a cozy and rather private respite for weary ballgoers. Their pale green upholstery and hangings of figured silk repeated the white, green, and gold color scheme of Stanford White's just-opened Hotel Imperial on Broadway across from the Metropolitan Opera House, while also recalling once more his design for Newport's Casino Theatre, similarly furnished with deep balcony niches and movable floor seating that could be whisked away. The Madison Square Garden Company proudly advertised the facility as the most beautiful music hall in the world, "more like an emperor's throne room,"[33] and it was likely the most elaborately decorated party hall or music room in the country.

•

Perhaps it was in celebration of the Garden's success or simply boredom during a long winter, but in January 1891, Stanford White took a lease on Studio 8 in the Holbein Studio Building off Broadway on West Fifty-Fifth. Furnishings from the old Sewer Club's haven at the Benedick were carried up the long, narrow staircase built over a row of old stables. Painter Thomas Dewing shared the rent for what became known as the

"Dewing-White" studio, and a servant named John was hired to take care of the place that White and his friends called "the Morgue."[34]

The origin of the name is uncertain. Perhaps it derived from the French term *le petit mort*, or "little death," that began to be used as a synonym for the orgasm in the 1880s.[35] Or it might have derived from the warning reformers gave to girls considered too free and easy that they were surely "on the way to the morgue."[36] In any case, coded "mask notes" kept their wives in the dark as to their secret assignations and their "scenes of mirth and physiological interest,"[37] as Dewing had once termed them. More girls, perhaps boys. Two years later Stanford White would move the activities to Studio 1 and share the rent with Madison Square Garden constructor David H. King Jr.[38]

•

On the evening of January 30, 1891, Carmencita finally danced for thousands on a temporary stage set up in the Madison Square Garden Amphitheatre. During the daytime, her steps re-echoed in the construction of the Garden arcade, which had finally begun. Despite the fact that the governor of New York had signed the special legislation approving its construction in 1888, the actual arcade permit was not issued by the city until the spring of 1890, when the mayor's objections were assuaged with promises of sufficient lighting and regular police patrols.[39] In addition to the threat of thieves and loose women, the city's real estate moguls had been concerned that the arcade, a concept so new to the city, might grow in popularity, and that by blocking light to storefronts the trend would eventually lower the value of street-level rental space.[40]

The Garden's arcade was composed of polished granite Ionic columns and thick brick piers that supported a line of arches attached to the building. Focused on the main entrance, the arcade ran along the Madison Avenue sidewalk and then for 150 feet down Twenty-Sixth and Twenty-Seventh Streets. Aside from visually adding balance to the Garden's upper stories, the arcade would also offer shelter in bad weather to those entering, departing, or waiting in queue, while in warm weather it would serve simply as a cool and pleasant spot to stroll. In addition, the top of the arcade, edged with a balustrade for safety, formed a second promenade with a fine view over Madison Square.[41]

33. Madison Square Garden arcade. The Museum of the City of New York / Art Resource, NY.

That the arcade was modeled in the Italian Renaissance style was clear, as it was of a type found in many fifteenth-century Italian examples from Bologna to Milan, but the exact inspiration was up for debate. Perhaps Brunelleschi's Ospedale degli Innocenti in Florence or the Cortile at the Ospedale Maggiore in Milan, or any number of other similar examples.[42]

The Madison Square Garden arcades were most likely constructed by a new crew of men that had begun to build the arches and their curved vaulted ceilings in a very new way known as the Guastavino Tile Arch System. Patented in 1885 by Spanish-born architect and builder Rafael Guastavino, the system derived from a type of tile and mortar building dating back to Roman times and more fully developed in Spain during the fourteenth century as the *boveda catalana*, or Catalan vault. Guastavino then revived and refined the system while working as an architect in Barcelona.[43] When addressing the Society of Arts at MIT in the early 1890s, he referred to it as "cohesive construction,"[44] but it was also known more

34. Scene under the Madison Square Garden arcade, W. T. Smedley, *Harper's Weekly* (July 18, 1891).

popularly as timbrel vaulting for its likeness to the stretched papyrus skin of a timbrel, the ancient Middle Eastern instrument brought to Europe by the Crusaders and now commonly known as the tambourine.

Architectural commissions had been few after Guastavino emigrated to New York in 1881, but he found work as a building contractor and installed vaulted ceilings for other, more established architects.[45] Real success came in 1889 when Charles McKim took a chance and signed the Guastavino Fireproof Construction Company to construct the vaulting for the Boston Public Library. McKim had been "more than pleased" with the quality of workmanship and assured other architects of his complete confidence in the Guastavino vaulting system.[46]

After preliminary drawings were made for the Garden, workmen moved quickly to set a herringbone first layer of thin, interlocking terra-cotta tiles in plaster of Paris; then the second and third layers were set in a mixture of Portland cement and glacial sand from Cow Bay on Long Island Sound.[47] A British invention but manufactured in the United States since the mid-1870s, strong and durable Portland cement was created by a compound of ground limestone mixed with riverbed clay and water, dried to paste, burned in a kiln to expel the carbonic acid, and then ground to a powder that set when mixed with water.[48]

The arcade's arched spans were broad and graceful, the vaults virtually self-supporting and able to sustain a great deal of weight—rather like the natural strength of an eggshell—yet they required less buttressing and support than stone. There was no need for a keystone, and little or no wood-framed centering support or scaffolding needed to be erected during construction. While the style was visually striking, it was also eminently practical—not only were the structures strong, but they were cheap and quick to erect and were fireproof as well.[49]

Oddly enough, however, evidence that the Guastavino firm itself was truly responsible for the construction of the vaulting is largely circumstantial. The McKim, Mead & White account books for that period show no payments to Guastavino, and Guastavino's advertisement in the May 2, 1891, issue of *American Architect and Building News* failed to list it among its other projects.[50] Yet an article on the triumph of Spanish architecture published in *Las Novedades*, a New York Spanish-language newspaper dated May 14, 1891, did include the Garden project, and a September 1891 Guastavino ad listed it as "among the contracts now on hand."[51] While it is possible that the contract fell through, architectural historian John A. Ochsendorf, author of *Guastavino Vaulting: The Art of Structural Tile*, does credit the vaulting to the Guastavino firm based on photographic evidence, drawings, and other documents, as well as the absence of tile vaulting competitors.[52] And even if the arcade had not actually been constructed by the Guastavino firm per se, it was still clearly executed in its style.

•

The Madison Square Garden management was surely thrilled the morning of February 13, 1891, when the largest gathering of people ever seen at the first day of ticket sales queued up at the Garden Theatre box office to purchase seats for the appearance of Sarah Bernhardt, the world's greatest living actress, in the play *Cleopatra*. The line—estimated at seven thousand long—wound from the box office on Twenty-Seventh Street down Madison Avenue and across and around Madison Square. The remainder of Bernhardt's monthlong engagement was also tremendously successful, with additional shows added and her run extended.[53] A few weeks later the Madison Square Garden directors proudly issued a summary of the Garden's first season that reflected a handsome profit.[54]

The horse, dog, poultry, and flower shows, the athletic games, and the return of the Barnum & Bailey Circus—heralded by one thousand torchbearers and a parade down Fifth Avenue[55]—did much to establish the Garden's popularity as New York's palace of pleasure in its first six months. The assembly and ballrooms were filled during the social season by the most elite gatherings in the city, along with concerts, dinners, and lectures. A full schedule of offerings was planned for the spring, summer, and fall, including an engagement by Lillian Russell, the foremost singer in America, and the Garden's first boxing tournament. But there were a few sour notes as well. The first dog show clearly indicated that accommodations were too limited, not only for horses but for smaller animals as well, with 450 canine competitors relegated to the basement with the chicken incubators.[56] And soon New Yorkers were complaining about the Garden's unfortunate location tucked off to the side of Madison Square rather than a more open and fashionable site further uptown.[57]

PART THREE

The Virgin and the Tower

March 1891

*She is New York's proper deity, for she exults in life, she is always
a-tiptoe with restlessness; she is gilded and graceful; and she twirls
with every breeze . . . Diana, huntress of pleasure, long may you
pirouette above the pleasure-hunting town!*[1]

35. *Diana*, Augustus Saint-Gaudens, on the tower of
Madison Square Garden, ca. 1915. The Museum of the
City of New York / Art Resource, NY.

16

On the Model Stand

IF NUMEROUS FIRST and secondhand accounts are to be believed, the model likely arrived promptly at Augustus Saint-Gaudens's big white studio on West Thirty-Sixth Street and walked directly to the disrobing screen, stepping behind to remove her feathered and flowered hat, detach the high collar and cuffs from her ruffled shirtwaist and unfasten the hooks down its back, step out of her long bell skirt and then her petticoats, unhook the binding corset and the small pad bustle designed to round her derriere, and finally untie the strings and drop her drawers. A cotton wrapper had undoubtedly been provided, and she would have quickly slipped it on until the moment Saint-Gaudens would call her to the model stand.

It is also likely that the rest of the studio was in its usual state of chaos that day. The clay model for the huge, low-relief *Shaw Memorial* filled one entire end of the room, having been in process for the past seven years or so. For Saint-Gaudens, absolute perfection was the ever-elusive goal, and he confessed, "I make every sculpture seventeen times."[1] A loud whinny and a neigh might well have added to the confusion, as the live horse prancing in the corner took its turn posing as Colonel Shaw's brave steed. Saint-Gaudens had been telling his wife that he simply must spend his nights sleeping at the studio to look after the horse, while actually it was being stabled nearby between modeling sessions and exercised in Central Park by his old friend the painter J. Carroll Beckwith.[2]

No doubt used to the typical sound and fury of a busy artist's studio, the model shed her wrapper on command and strode up to the stand without the slightest bit of hesitation, stretched her limbs a bit and prepared to take her place. She was most certainly professional, experienced and trained beyond the amateurs who may have dabbled at the modeling

195

game. Furthermore, she was not simply running through the typical repertoire of poses for an art school classroom of students but was working
for one of the finest artists in the country, and much would be expected
of her.

The pose Saint-Gaudens had chosen for his *Diana*—requiring her to
balance solely on the toes of her left foot while holding out her arms as
an archer—was exceedingly difficult, and it simply could not be held for
more than a minute or two. So, after experimenting with a variety of supports, he settled on a framework of two braced ladders that allowed the
model to prop herself up by draping her arms over two rungs, the left arm
out straight as if gripping the hold on Diana's bow, her right arm flexed as
if grasping the bowstring and the arrow's feathered fletching, her right leg
bent at the knee and slightly extended behind her, and the other leg lightly
touching the floor. Dubbed "the torture pose," Diana's stance was widely
acknowledged as not only the most difficult but the best for discouraging
an amateur.[3] It would have certainly taken skill and some nerve to get the
twist and the tension of it and then stand absolutely still all day, staring
straight ahead while impersonating a goddess. But for the model, it was
acknowledged as just the day's work.[4]

•

According to their published accounts, asking the impossible of a model
was hardly out of the ordinary on the late nineteenth-century art scene.
Every artist wanted a strong female model, and a girl applying for a job
was always asked, "Can you stand long?" But that was just the beginning.
Despite a perfect command over her muscles, the model could not be too
stiff and lifeless, nor let her muscles relax so that the pose lost all tension.
In addition, after a break allowed every half hour or so, she needed the
muscle memory to return to the stand and instantly reproduce the pose.[5]

Symmetry of form and a strong, supple figure were among the most
basic requirements for a nude model, with the ideal female figure said to
be 5 feet 4¾ inches tall, 32 inches at the bust, 24 inches at the waist, and
only 9 inches from armpit to waist, but with proportionately long arms
and neck.[6] Among the several hundred professional models in the city,
maintaining this perfect form required endless effort, living as carefully
as athletes to stay in good health and spirits, or so it was reported. No late

nights, no falling ill, no excess of any kind. Yet, they had also to live like princesses. A broken fingernail or a sunburnt nose might throw a model out of a job as surely as a broken leg. Neuralgia or rheumatism would prevent good posing, and poor digestion might spell the end of a career. Baths and cosmetics, toilet soaps and perfumes came high, yet they were all part of the tools in trade.[7]

But beyond the purely physical, there was still a great deal more. Painter Thomas Dewing insisted that all his models must have brains, for a good model could also be a coworker and helper.[8] Popular illustrator Harrison Fisher concurred that if a model lacked intelligence, she was useless, no matter how pretty or well-formed she might be.[9] For it was also her job to realize the artist's intent and then use her mind and spirit to convey it, serving as both groundwork and guide. Proud of the part they had played, some models would linger in the gallery on opening day of an exhibition near "their" work of art, listening for favorable comments and sharing in the praise.[10]

Only artists who had already achieved a high level of success could afford to pay a professional model for the amount of time required to create a work of significance. Among the professionals, there was also a hierarchy, and of those top models with the luxury of a preference, it was for "nice men" like Saint-Gaudens who behaved toward them "as would a reputable physician to his female patients."[11] According to William Merritt Chase, a true artist was as respectful to his model as to any other woman who entered his studio.[12] It was a small world among the artists and models in New York, and stories of meanness or improper behavior circulated as quickly as did small acts of kindness.[13]

As for an artist finding an appropriate model, there was no central listing of professionals, no real gathering place or model market as in Paris, Rome, or Munich.[14] Many artists did keep a detailed listing of some of the several hundred available models, with notes describing the merits of each—a beautiful arm, a perfect shade of hair, a handsome carriage, and so forth. But models would also more assertively go around to the studio buildings, knocking on doors and offering their services.[15]

Five years was about the maximum a young woman was able to make a living making the rounds, with few continuing to work past the age of thirty. In addition, modeling was still considered a rather suspect profession in the outside world, even in New York. It was said that when a young woman was seen headed regularly for the National Academy or the Art Students League without palette or paints, she might well be evicted from her boardinghouse or apartment, purely on suspicion. Furthermore, the market for live models was shrinking by the 1890s, for with the development of impressionist styles and new technologies, there was less and less interest in or need for the actual figure. A reasonable substitute, such as a photograph, lantern slide, manikin, or joined wooden lay-figure—if not the artist's own imagination—might have served just as well.[16]

•

As for posing in the altogether—the "toot-and-scramble," as the models referred to the French *tout ensemble*—that too was considered just part of the job. Again, according to published firsthand accounts, the first time she disrobed a model might have steeled herself with a stiff drink. But for an experienced model who likely would have stood as Diana, with her leg drawn back and thighs parted, her female parts fully exposed on the stand, those parts would have seemed hardly different from any other. It may well have had something to do with the model stand itself, an island of sorts between nakedness and nudity.[17] As was often said, "a model is undressed only when she is half dressed,"[18] and should an artist be foolish enough to peer over the disrobing screen while the model was in mid-dishabille, they would likely be greeted by a scream.[19] But once the model was on the stand there was neither shame nor modesty, and as far as most artists were concerned the model might as well have been a bowl of fruit.[20]

Except, of course, when she was not. Beyond the New York art scene, artists' models were a continuing source of fascination for the American public in the late nineteenth century, fed by a tremendous curiosity as to what sort of creature would willingly place herself in such a position for fifty cents an hour. In particular, a great deal was written for popular consumption about the romantic side of studio life and the relationship of male artists to their female models, from Titian to Monet. In Saint-Gaudens's case it had been true, he having fallen in love with the handsome Davida Johnson. But then there were the sad stories as well, of love affairs gone awry and the ruin of both parties—the model left to work the street, the artist lost to drink.[21] There were a few cases in New York where an artist actually did marry a model—William Merritt Chase, for one—but it did not often occur, and quite rarely among female artists and their male models, of whom there were far fewer. The commonly held belief was that an artist should never marry a model, any more than a gourmet should marry a cook.[22]

•

Back in Saint-Gaudens's studio, the day's work came to an end, and "Diana" was released to dress behind the screen. As for her identity, the talk at the time, at least at the Art Students League, was that she was a popular model, one he had used before, and surprisingly one who still posed for the life drawing classes there. An illustration of what was claimed to be a sketch of her figure on a student's easel at the school was published several years later in the *New York Sun*.[23] But whomever she may have been, she most likely emerged from behind the disrobing screen as a plain, independent businesswoman[24] and stepped out the door into the

36. *With the Art Students,*
New York Sun (May 26,
1895). Chronicling America,
Library of Congress.

GIRL STUDENT AT WORK IN THE LIFE CLASS.

passing crowd, no longer the virgin goddess but once more very much of the everyday world.

•

The *Diana* would be Saint-Gaudens's only public and monumental female nude, but it was not truly his first or only female nude. In Paris, while waiting for admittance to the École des Beaux-Arts, he modeled both male and female figure studies in clay at the École Gratuite de Dessin, including a youth kneeling to kiss a mermaid in a fanciful design for a fountain, a nude Mozart playing the violin, and a little Greek girl kissing an infant.[25] While working in Rome in the 1870s, as his nude *Hiawatha* sat waiting for a buyer, Saint-Gaudens supported himself by making bare-chested portrait busts of visiting Americans and copies after the antique busts of illustrious classicals in the collection of the Vatican Museum and other locations in Rome. Saint-Gaudens had a few buyers for copies in marble of the *Psyche of Naples* (a Roman copy of a Greek rendition of the maiden loved by the god Eros), as well as Greek philosophers, Roman emperors, and the *Apollo Belvedere*.[26] According to an account book, Saint-Gaudens also reproduced in marble the greatly admired and endlessly copied *Venus de' Medici* for a client. Like much of his work completed in marble during this period, the rough cutting was done by his Italian assistant after Saint-Gaudens's model in clay, with Saint-Gaudens finishing the details himself.[27]

These unsigned, never-exhibited pieces would be among Saint-Gaudens's first and last attempts at sculpting the nude figure for many years, although his 1873 *Silence*, destined for the New York Grand Lodge of the Masonic Order, was modeled first in the nude, as would become his practice for other clothed figures, with the drapery added later.[28] There were also the rather skimpily clad figures that flanked Admiral Farragut on his stone base in Madison Square Park. Although they may have been actually finished by brother Louis St. Gaudens, they were certainly created under Augustus Saint-Gaudens's guidance.

•

With *Diana's* figure well underway, it was time to address the goddess's visage. This time he did look to his mistress Davida, perhaps not only for her classical features but as a gesture of consolation. He had modeled her face many times over the past few years, beginning the head in clay as he always did from the back and outlining the profile carefully as he shifted to the front, laying a good foundation for the details to come. Fired to terra cotta, this portrait was a little less than life size, 10½ inches high.[29] Perhaps following the pronouncements of renowned German classicist Johann Winckelmann that Diana's hair be smoothed upwards on all sides around her head and then gathered in a knot behind after the manner of virgins, Saint-Gaudens pulled back her hair and placed rough curls on her forehead,[30] accentuating Davida's long nose, prominent cheekbones, deep-set eyes, and the stuck-out chin she hated.[31]

37. *Davida Johnson Clark, Study for the Head of Diana,* Augustus Saint-Gaudens, ca. 1886, plaster, shellac. Metropolitan Museum of Art, Gift of Alice and Evelyn Blight and Mrs. William Payne Thompson, by exchange, 2003.

Saint-Gaudens had a shellacked plaster copy made of the bust as a gift to Davida,[32] and then a marble version was likely carved by the Piccirilli brothers, Tuscan stone carvers in New York who had worked with him on a number of other projects. In exchange, he apparently gave them the terra-cotta head, perhaps to get it out of the house.[33] The dating of the heads is uncertain, as is whether it began simply as a portrait of Davida. Saint-Gaudens scholar John Dryfhout dates the marble bust to 1886, which was a year before the commission for the Madison Square Garden was ever awarded to McKim, Mead & White, while Homer Saint-Gaudens dates a study for the head of Diana to 1891, although he does not specify for which version and in what material. In any case, Augustus Saint-Gaudens would keep the marble version on his desk, and when the project was underway, he likely told his wife, true or not, that it was a just a study for the *Diana*.[34]

•

When Saint-Gaudens was more or less satisfied with his small, quickly modeled clay sketch of *Diana's* figure, he then carefully modeled it again in clay, this time a foot high. Her legs were fashioned longer than they would be in nature, an old trick dating back to the Greeks, who understood that an extra bit of length, particularly between the knee and the sole of the foot, added a great deal of grace to the human figure.[35]

Saint-Gaudens no doubt continued to study his *Diana*, set on her left foot atop a half sphere. He would pose the figure, then make a change, and then another, moving the bits until it suited his idea of just how the figure should stand.[36] As Margaret Adler observes, the goddess Diana challengingly must appear as a balance of opposing tensions—of restraint juxtaposed with potential force, tautness of muscles with seemingly endless patience as she is eternally about to let her arrow fly.[37]

When Saint-Gaudens first added the drapery that would catch the wind, it flew straight out from the shoulder. But when some visitors to the studio spoke out that they did not much care for it, Saint-Gaudens—so sensitive to criticism that many friends refrained from making comments after seeing weeks of work destroyed before their horrified eyes—changed the line so that the drapery bellied out in a circular fashion, quite in the style of the sixteenth-century Italian Mannerist painter Parmigianino.[38]

38. Model of *Diana*, Augustus Saint-Gaudens, ca. 1891, plaster,
10 in. The Museum of the City of New York / Art Resource NY.

This *Diana* was quite well suited for a weather vane: lithe, lean, long-waisted, and long-limbed. However, except for the high, firm breasts, the figure may have seemed a little boyish. In the day of the corset-induced full hourglass figure, this was clearly not the female form that fashion decreed. No plump monobosom, tiny waist, and wide flaring hips here.[39] But was it truly just a matter of function? The scholar Winckelmann had also declared that Diana's figure must be as light and slender as befits a virgin, thinner than that of Juno or Athena—a form that no doubt won the approval of Stanford White.

39. *Circe Drinking*, detail from woodcut by Ugo da Capri, mid-sixteenth century, after Parmigianino. Library of Congress, Prints and Photographs Division, LC-DIG-ppmsca-18708.

The most beautiful figure is that "of a twelve-year-old boy,"[40] declared White, who often warned his wife that "fat is indeed fatal."[41] As for the female form, it was young girls that he favored, preferably in their teens, and it was the very slim figure of a young girl that predominated aesthetically among their circle, with one reviewer complaining that Thomas Dewing's painted figures were positively bony.[42]

Saint-Gaudens had his clay figure of *Diana* cast in plaster and then cast one in bronze without her drape and the bow, wearing only a crescent moon on her forehead. It was a sweet little nude—two feet tall—that he presented to Stanford White as a gift.[43]

17

The Tower Rises

IN THE MEANTIME and by the spring of 1891, the tower was slowly rising on the Twenty-Sixth Street side of the Madison Square Garden. In the previous year, the huge stone foundations had been sunk 15 feet below ground and covered with a mat of sand, gravel, and strong and durable Portland cement. Just as the oaks were turning color in Madison Square, hundreds of workmen had begun laying nearly two million building bricks and then covering them with pale, buff-yellow facing bricks set in a subtle diaper pattern of interlacing diamonds. As the tower rose course by course, each joint was carefully filled with higher-priced Rosendale Natural Cement carted in from the Hudson River Valley in paper-lined wooden barrels and used to make the very same mortar that had so successfully secured the Brooklyn Bridge stone piers, their superstructure, and the base of the Statue of Liberty.[1]

Art critics like Mariana Van Rensselaer appreciated the subtle patterning caused by the slight divergence in the color of the facing bricks.[2] Dismissing any aesthetic intention as "rot," however, William Mead attributed the variation in shade solely to the bankruptcy of the original brickmaker and the required use of a second source.[3] An interesting patterning on the surface of the tower also occurred in the insertion of the narrow windows in an arrangement that differed on each side. On the north side, a single window alternated floor by floor with three that were widely spaced; on the south, just two adjoining windows were placed at the center of the tower wall on every floor; on the east, two adjoining windows alternated with two widely spaced; and on the west, one window alternated with two widely spaced.

Although it might have appeared at this preliminary stage that Stanford White had chosen not to follow the new trend in construction for using skeleton steel framing to bear the weight of walls and floors, it was not entirely the case. While the walls were being laid thick enough to support the great height on their own, running from 12 feet thick at the 38-foot-square base to 3½ feet at the top,[4] his plan also required that the tower's upper loggias and lanterns be framed in heavy steel with structural iron beams enclosed within protective terra-cotta sheathing and securely tied into the brick shaft.[5]

The use of steel skeleton framing for such a tall, narrow structure was a highly controversial and much-debated decision among engineers, architects, and the public, who feared that a composite brick and iron structure might simply blow over.[6] That damaging winds might pose grave danger to tall structures was a very real concern, particularly after a tornado struck Louisville, Kentucky, in March 1890, leveling nearly eight hundred buildings in a square mile of the downtown, and skeleton construction would not be universally accepted until the end of the 1890s.[7]

The US Weather Service had devised a formula for determining the pounds of pressure per square foot of exposed surface exerted by wind velocities, and in 1888 the Royal Meteorological Society in England determined and confirmed the constant in the formula. This method of computing and overcoming wind load pressure was successfully tested by Gustave Eiffel in the erection of the iron and steel framework for the Statue of Liberty. But there were some who still argued for caution,[8] and White might have considered complete dependence on skeleton framing still a little too risky to attempt. With the decision to simply strengthen the top of the Garden tower, it was hoped that no hurricane or other terrible force of nature would ever be able to affect it.

White's choice to firmly set the tower on massive brickwork was also an aesthetic one, as the taper of the shaft's walls would serve to increase the visual impression of straight and soaring height.[9] It also turned out to be a wise one from a practical point of view, for the wrought iron and structural steelwork in the upper portions of the tower would severely corrode and nearly crumble away over its thirty-five-year lifespan.[10]

•

Stanford White's firm commitment to the concept of a tower for Madi-son Square Garden was likely attributable to several factors. Towers, in general, are tall, rigid, muscular, attention-grabbing symbols of power—whether religious, military, or economic—that serve to dominate the landscape.[11] Aside from its design opportunities, a tower would serve as a practical means of advertising the Garden as well as a source of rental income. "The tower that's the real thing,"[12] White had stated without hesi-tation, but it would not be the only impressive tower in Manhattan.

There were several well-known structures that recalled the grand towers of the Italian city-states, such as Richard Morris Hunt's copy of Florence's late thirteenth-century Palazzo Vecchio campanile for his 1873 Tribune Building on Park Row. It had been the tallest occupied structure in the city until the erection of George Post's neighboring and journalistic rival World Building, with its Saint Peter's–like dome, in 1890. Another promi-nent example was the Tower Building, eleven stories high but just 21½ feet wide and said to be New York's first skyscraper. Designed by Bradford Gilbert in the Neo-Romanesque style and completed in 1889, it was the first to employ a steel skeleton structure and was erected on lower Broadway, directly across the street from the offices of McKim, Mead & White.

•

By the time the Madison Square Garden tower was under construction, Stanford White had already designed some fine towers of his own, but they had been ecclesiastical rather than commercial in nature. His 1883 granite bell tower for the Lovely Lane First Methodist Church of Balti-more was a reworking of the eleventh-century Romanesque campanile of the abbey church at Pomposa in northern Italy.[13] In New York, the nearly completed campanile of the Judson Memorial Baptist Church on Wash-ington Square was clearly and closely inspired by the towers of several twelfth- and thirteenth-century churches built in the heart of Rome, including San Giorgio in Velabro, San Lorenzo in Lucino, and Santa Maria in Cosmedin.[14]

These two earlier structures by Stanford White had also been quite useful as proving grounds for features that would appear in the Madison

Square Garden tower; it was at the Baltimore church that White first tested his ventilation system, and at the Judson church that he executed his plan for filling a tower with apartments, one stacked upon the next.[15] As aesthetically pleasing as these earlier examples might have been, towers in the purely Italian manner had thus been done—by White and by others, for churches and for commerce—so perhaps New Yorkers would welcome something rather different and more fanciful in style for the city's new palace of pleasure.

As *Harper's Weekly* pointed out, it would be the tower "that will be all-important, the feature that will raise Madison Square Garden from a handsome structure with a good deal of cleverness and taste to an ornament to a city very much in need of beautiful buildings."[16] While the original plan had called for the tower to be located at the front corner of

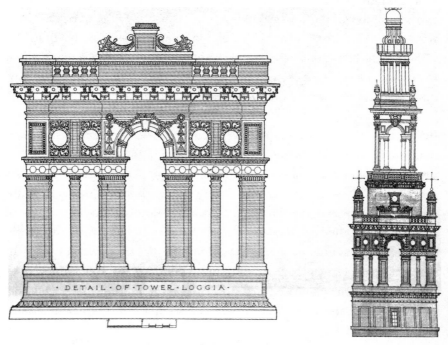

40. Drawing of the upper section of the Madison Square Garden tower and details of its loggia, 1891. *A Monograph of the Work of McKim, Mead & White 1879–1915* (1915; repr., New York: Dover Publications, 1990).

Madison Avenue and Twenty-Sixth Street, it was now set back 100 feet down the street, between the still-unleased restaurant and the amphitheater, thereby presenting a much more striking perspective when viewed across the Garden's vast mass. Here there was breathing space for the tower, an interesting rhythm and pattern set up with the smaller towers and belvederes that lined the roof, and from the intersection of Broadway and Fifth Avenue, an impressive view that filled a vacant spot in the city's landscape.[17]

There was some complaint that, lacking bells or a clock, the tower would serve no real purpose other than to draw the eye and visitor to Madison Square Garden, although that was surely considered by the governing board to be a most worthy cause in itself. In terms of directly generating income, the tower was planned to house eight floors of living and working space filled with artist studios and apartments, as well as a pay-to-ride elevator for sightseers.

•

But there was a dispiriting moment on May 1, 1891, when the Madison Square Garden Company presented its financial report for the fiscal year just ended. Despite a good opening season, the Garden posted a loss of $18,000 for its very first year and, in fact, would not show even a small profit for another five years.[18] The problem seemed to be the high operating costs, of some $20,000 per month. So the new board, which now included Stanford White and constructor David King Jr., responded rather fancifully by spending more money to transform the amphitheater into a fairyland for the summer season's promenade concerts and then hosting a private reception for the press and well-connected guests. The arena floor was converted into a garden with avenues of firs and cedars, parterres of hydrangeas, garlands of evergreens draped from the skylight, and one thousand colored electric lights twined around the rafters. In addition, business manager James Morrissey let it slip to the press—he could not imagine how—that the management planned to dispense free beer at the coming summer band concerts.[19]

•

As the tower was rising, the firm of McKim, Mead & White was in the process of moving its offices up from lower Broadway to a sublet very near Madison Square. Over the previous twelve years virtually all their clients had moved or were in the process of moving uptown, and the new address just blocks from the square would be both more convenient, less than a block from White's home, and far more prestigious. Their offices would remain there, on the top floor of an old brownstone at 1 West Twentieth Street, at the corner of Fifth Avenue, for another three years.[20]

These new offices of McKim, Mead & White were much larger and more appealing to their clients, who could now await the ever-tardy White on a settee in one of two handsomely furnished reception rooms. Along with more spacious offices for the partners and their stenographers, there were additional rooms down a private corridor to house bookkeeping, drawing storage, a photographic darkroom, and an extensive architectural reference library. The number of draftsmen had doubled since work on the Garden began, with some sixty employed at thirty drawing tables.[21] Always "in a hell of a hell of a hell of a hurry,"[22] White might appear pounding on the door before seven o'clock in the morning, arms full of rolled drawings, or bound in late at night in full evening dress, throw off his cloak, and set to work.[23]

•

By June 1891, the tower presented an imposing sight as it loomed up above the trees in Madison Square Park. As each new story was added it surely seemed that it must be the last to New Yorkers, continually surprised by its rising height.[24] Eight stories finally reached the level of the blind arcade that would serve as the base of the great loggia and the vertical limit of the diaper-patterned brickwork and alternating narrow windows. Powerful electric searchlights were already in place and shining brightly. From here up a series of columned lanterns would be constructed in iron framework sheathed in copper for another 80 feet, finally reaching 341 feet into the sky.[25]

The *New York Times* reported an amusing incident that occurred early that month when a fire broke out around eleven o'clock on a Saturday night on Madison Avenue, just a little north of the Garden. Suddenly a flood of light from the tower loggia's searchlight was directed toward the fire, and instantly the street became as bright as day. Just as instantly the occupants of the neighboring houses, each of whom was leaning out of their windows in various stages of undress, were suddenly revealed to those standing in the street below. The crowd roared out with laughter, causing a score of startled exclamations and the violent pulling down of curtains by those who had been so unexpectedly exposed. A fine time was had by those in the street, while another round of victims would be chalked up to modern times, the intrusion of vertical architecture, and the hidden dangers of electrical lighting.[26]

18

Diana, Doing and Making

UNLIKE THE PAINTER who may well work in peaceful solitude and whose considerations are primarily two-dimensional and aesthetic rather than physical, the sculptor's art, particularly the monumental, is ultimately produced by the rigorous labor of others. The sculptor does not create merely an illusion of form but is ultimately responsible for the actual three-dimensional reality in a studio that is designed more like a factory than an artist's retreat. Attendant to this reality in the late nineteenth century were a myriad of practical problems as to the size of the piece and weight of the materials. Along with the bins of clay and the bags of plaster came a reinforced floor, dollies, track, planks, derricks with block and tackle, ladders, and scaffolds set against the background sawing of wood and the bending of iron for armatures. All this "while trying to soar into the blue,"[1] as Augustus Saint-Gaudens pointed out.

A sculptor like Saint-Gaudens was quite dependent not only on studio assistants for the actual production of a piece, but molders, casters, and foundrymen who might work geographically quite distant from the studio and from his control. In addition, there were steps in the process when the destruction of the artist's working model was required and the complete destruction of a piece by accident a very real possibility.[2]

In the case of the *Diana*, Saint-Gaudens created the rough clay sketch, or maquette, perhaps as early as 1889, which was followed by the more detailed foot-high study in clay. Based on the accounts of his studio assistants and other late nineteenth-century sculptors, it can be assumed that once the second study was finally finished to his satisfaction, his assistants took careful measurement, not only of width and length but of the exact position of *Diana*'s chin, nipples, navel, thighbones, kneecaps, and so forth. Then, with enlarging calipers and a simple mathematical formula, they pointed up[3] a half-sized version, building the figure over an iron and lead pipe armature nailed to a wooden plinth set on a modeling turntable. Copper wire may have been enough to support the small clay sketch, but such a large figure required a substantial inner framework. The main supporting iron rod, or "standard," would have likely entered at *Diana*'s dorsal vertebra and passed up through the core to the nape of her neck. Wrought-iron crosspieces supported the weight of *Diana*'s hips and shoulders, while additional lead pipe braced her head, neck, arms, and legs as needed. Smaller wooden crosses and copper wire also served to support the clay as it was added to the figure.[4]

Assistants no doubt kept a sharp eye out for drying and cracking as the work continued, wetting the clay with hand pumps to keep it soft and malleable and draping it at night with damp cloths. It was also likely they who accomplished all of the rough modeling until it was ready for Saint-Gaudens to carefully refine. Working in a smock customarily thrown over his shirtsleeves and cravat, Saint-Gaudens would complete the pose and details to his satisfaction, while brother Louis might step in for the final surface finish.[5]

Still, there was doubtless a great deal of labor ahead and a good share of worry as the *Diana* progressed. There were the long, intense days and nights in the studio as Saint-Gaudens typically struggled with the work, studying it from every angle, worrying with it, puzzling over it, tinkering endlessly to achieve perfection.

When work was going well, Saint-Gaudens sang out, but when he was struggling, when his nerves took over and he was in one of his moods, assistants knew better than to disturb the master. Friends and assistants recollected that should a workman drop a tool, Saint-Gaudens would explode, yelling and swearing. If an unexpected visitor rang the doorbell at the wrong moment, Saint-Gaudens would shout out, "I would be left in peace!," hurl oaths and curses, and grab a stick to beat whoever dared disturb his near silence.[6] Or if Saint-Gaudens—always chilly—sensed the temperature had varied by two degrees, he went after the assistant who tended the stoves, shouting and swearing and throwing across the studio his tools, lumps of clay, packing boxes, and anything that came to hand, while all would duck for cover. He called himself the "boss lunatic." "Sometimes I'd cry, then I'd laugh, then I'd do both together, then I'd rush out into the street and howl," he recalled.[7] When the strain completely overwhelmed him, Saint-Gaudens would fire his assistants, smash everything, and disappear for days at a time until he finally returned, morose and discontent but ready to move ahead. Finally, after the storm had run its course, Saint-Gaudens would once more offer the jokes and songs, and again the studio would be filled with laughter.[8]

●

Because clay was so unstable and likely to crack or crumble, a copy of the *Diana* would next be made in the more durable plaster of Paris.[9] The studio boys would mix up a huge batch, gently sifting the dry white plaster powder into warm water, smoothly stirring the mixture in just one direction until it reached the consistency of thick cream. Saint-Gaudens trusted the next step to the supervision of only one man: Gaétan Ardisson, his much-vaunted mold-maker. A big man with a temper to match, Ardisson was later recalled as one who seemed to enjoy stirring up jealousies, rivalries, and rows among the assistants. Yet he was so tenderhearted toward animals and insects that he once refused to make a casting for fear of disturbing a spider who had spun its web around it. While the French-speaking Ardisson claimed to have studied sculpture in Paris, Saint-Gaudens had found him a few years before modeling ornament at a New York clock factory.[10] Saint-Gaudens believed him to be the best modeler in the world,[11] and it was to Ardisson's supervision that he would later entrust the first reduced version of *Diana* made for commercial sale. Ardisson's life would sadly and rather dramatically come to an end in August 1926 when he leapt like one of his flying creatures from the top of a 100-foot water tower on the Long Island estate of Mrs. Harry Payne Whitney.[12]

If it can be assumed that the usual practice was followed in Saint-Gaudens's studio, Ardisson and the studio boys would have removed the damp cloths draped about *Diana's* clay form and slathered the plaster in sections beginning at the top of her head, then over her breasts, her flat belly, and long thighs, blowing the liquid plaster into her eyes, ears, and other intricate places until it was 2 inches thick. After a half hour or so of drying time, they would have cracked each piece-mold apart to dig out the clay, rinsing every last bit. Thus, the object of Saint-Gaudens's labor would have been reduced to bits and tossed into a waste barrel, his great work now existing solely as the hole inside a plaster of Paris mold.

The washed molds were likely set aside by the stove until they were completely dry, painted with a coat or two of linseed oil, and then filled to about three-quarters of an inch with freshly made plaster. After an hour or so, the studio crew would turn the molds over and begin to chip away, carefully cracking off the outer shell with chisel and mallet until at last the *Diana* was cast in plaster.

Assistants no doubt would have scurried to clean up the mess, for now the studio would have resembled a sort of battlefield littered with pieces of plaster, planks, dirty tools, oil-soaked brushes, and plaster dust.[13] Back at work, the assistants now needed to point up from the half-sized plaster model a full-sized version, 18 feet tall, to send to the foundry.

After the figure was laboriously enlarged in clay on a wood and iron framework twice the previous size, Saint-Gaudens would have likely refined it once more. Then a great batch of plaster would have again been whipped up, and assistants would have likely blocked out with rolls of clay sections of about 3 feet in length that could be easily maneuvered without damaging the model's surface. This time they would work from the bottom up, brushing oil on each section to be cast, applying the plaster, removing the clay "fence," removing the mold, cleaning the edges, refitting to be certain it was a perfect fit, and then setting a new "fence" for the next section.[14]

•

After the last of Saint-Gaudens's tinkering, Ardisson and his crew packed up the full-sized plaster cast and shipped it off to the W. H. Mullins Company in Salem, Ohio, for fabrication. Since the figure was destined to be constructed in hammered sheet copper rather than the more traditional bronze, Mullins was an appropriate selection. Far-off Salem was an old Quaker town in the northeast corner of the state, not far from Youngstown, and was once the center of the abolitionist movement and the Ohio Underground Railroad. It was there in 1872 that Kittredge, Clark & Co. set up machinery and labor from France and Germany to stamp out sheet metal cornices, capitals, moldings, and various other ornaments for Victorian homes and public buildings. In 1875 the company produced the country's first life-sized, stamped sheet-zinc architectural statue, a figure of Justice for a Michigan county courthouse. They soon expanded to stamped sheet copper statuary under the direction of William H. Mullins, who joined as a partner in 1882 and renamed the firm after buying it outright in 1890.[15] Mullins was rather well connected, with a cousin the editor of the *New York World*, so good coverage of the *Diana* once back in the city would likely be assured.

Unlike cast bronze or carved stone, stamped statuary in zinc, copper, or brass is far lighter in weight and can be made faster and cheaper. Catering to a growing market for memorials, monuments, and new civic architecture, the W. H. Mullins Company was on its way to becoming the most prominent producer of stamped statuary in the country, turning out a flood of semiclad personifications of civic virtues and social ideals, piety-instilling saints, and a head-spinning inventory of domestic and commercial decoration, from stately lawn elk to Indian warriors to the *Flying Dutchman*.[16]

When the 18-foot plaster model of *Diana* arrived in Ohio, it was carefully unpacked under the direction of the German-born brothers Hubert and Alfons Pelzer, who oversaw the sculpture department and would supervise its preparation for the manufacturing process. Instead of simply hammering sheet metal into shape by hand, the company had developed an entirely new and quite original process that began with Mullins workmen taking additional plaster of Paris piece-molds, section by section, from *Diana*'s full-sized plaster figure. The molds were sent down to the foundry, where zinc and iron dies were then cast from them.[17]

The finished dies were installed in a powerful yet very accurate drop press, the iron male die bolted to a drop hammer, the zinc female die installed in the press bed. Cut sheets of copper that had been rolled flat to 22 ounces to the square foot were gently heated in a brick warming oven and then ferried over to the press by derby-hatted workmen in shirtsleeves and vests. Under the watchful eye of a dark-suited foreman, the sheets were slipped between the dies. With a great roar, each sheet was struck up by a succession of steam-powered blows, smashing the copper into the female die below that was continually replaced by one of greater

41. First *Diana* at the W. H. Mullins foundry, 1891. Courtesy of the US Department of the Interior, National Park Service, Saint-Gaudens National Historical Park, Cornish, NH.

depth. Amid the blows, the copper was annealed to keep it malleable by heating it red hot with a gas torch and then quickly quenching it with water. By this process, the workmen were able to far more accurately execute each detail, and Mullins declared their work "finer than anything made elsewhere in the world and full equal to cast bronze."[18]

As each section of *Diana*'s figure was formed, shallow rabbet grooves were worked on alternating edges. Mullins's men trimmed each finished section, lapping the rabbets and riveting them together in countersunk joints that were made watertight by high-heat brazing, a method that was stronger than ordinary soldering. Seams were then copper plated to make them invisible.[19] As an individual section was completed, it was built upon and supported by an intricate interior framework of 7-inch wrought-iron pipe that ran up through the center of the *Diana* to her head. With each addition, extra pipes, bars, and iron stays were attached to various parts of the figure and secured to the main armature. Unfortunately, it was at the very last of the assembly that the end of the wrought-iron mounting pipe was erroneously put through the heel of *Diana's* left foot, rather than the ball. Neither Saint-Gaudens nor apparently his representative was on-site at the time, and the W. H. Mullins Company must have assumed or perhaps just hoped that no one would notice the error. Assembly complete, the hammered sheet copper *Diana* was packed up and shipped back to New York City with a bill for $7,380.[20]

19

Oriental Fantasies

BY JULY 1891 the Madison Square Garden tower was approaching completion. Just above the first eight stories, work focused on the classically inspired five-bay open loggia that was formed by alternating piers and columns. This would be the most elaborately decorated section of the tower, with garlands of stucco draped over its central arch. As the four niches between its columns and piers stood empty, Stanford White proposed that they be filled with statues. Likely with a wink, *Harper's Weekly* nominated figures of Commodore Vanderbilt, P. T. Barnum, John L. Sullivan, and White himself, in acknowledgment of all they had done to draw crowds to the Garden.[1] But the niches would remain empty.

Above the loggia rose an elevated base flanked on four corners by belvederes of the type found on the amphitheater's roof. Upon this base, one atop another, stood three columned, open "lanterns," or small windowed towers or turrets, each of diminishing height, with the middle lantern circular in the style of a Roman temple.

As the tower neared completion, it became clear that its plan was not quite the one McKim, Mead & White had first submitted when the contract for the Garden was awarded. Stanford White's original design was for a massive, top-heavy structure, grandly elaborated with three rectangular loggias, a stacked, doubled-domed circular lantern, and a giant clockface 22 feet in diameter.[2] The rendering was reminiscent of the Italian and Spanish Renaissance but truly differed from any known tower in existence.

Instead, the tower that rose, with its obviously simplified design no doubt dictated by rising costs, had a much lighter, more festive air. While the planned tower may have been reminiscent of the famed Giralda tower of the cathedral of the city of Seville, Spain, it was clear to most critics that

42. Madison Square Garden Tower, George P. Hall & Son, ca. 1905. George Eastman House Collection, Wikimedia Commons.

the final version was "related to," "inspired by," "derived from," or even "copied off" the same structure.

The still-enduring Giralda tower is itself a rather odd composite, resulting from the work of three different architects over a period of nearly four hundred years. The tower's first version was erected in the late twelfth century by the Berber Almohad Empire of northwest Africa

43. *Street Scene in Seville under the Shadow of the Giralda,* from a watercolor by David Roberts, 1906, in the University Galleries, Oxford. Wikimedia Commons.

during the Islamic occupation of the captured capital of the rich and fertile land they called al-Andalus.

In the late nineteenth century, this historical allusion to Islamic Spain conjured up exotic visions: the scent of Seville's orange blossoms and tales of its Caliph Abu Ya'qub Yusuf, the great Almohad patron of learning and scholarship who, when not raptly discussing the finer points of philosophic thought or Spanish art, architecture, and literature, relentlessly led jihad in that subjugated land.[3]

In 1172 the caliph commissioned the architect Ahmad ibn Basu to design a great mosque laid out near his palace in the Spanish city the invaders called Ishbiliyah. Builders and craftsmen came from their home capital of Marrakech—located across the Strait of Gibraltar and just down the coast of Morocco—to aid them. Eight years later, after securing the conquered cities of Cordova, Malaga, and Granada, Yusuf ordered the construction of a minaret at the northeast corner of the mosque in Seville from which the call to prayer would be issued over the rooftops of that city. Ahmad ibn Basu drew up the plans for a square-shaped minaret attached to the side of the mosque and decorated with raised-brick sebka patterning. It was a long-popular design in North Africa dating back to the tenth century but more directly inspired by the tall, elaborately patterned minaret at the Kutubiyyah Mosque in Marrakech, completed under Yusef's reign a few decades earlier.[4]

•

Caliph Yusef died from wounds received at the 1184 Battle of Santarém, so the actual erection of the minaret in Seville was left to his sixteen-year-old son and heir, Abu Yusuf Ya'qub al-Mansur. Construction began, using old stones from the walls of a nearby palace, some dating back to Roman times. After the tower had risen 6 feet, work stopped, perhaps due to the death of the architect. When it commenced again in 1188, a new architect, Ali al-Ghumari, built succeeding courses in baked brick on top of the stone base.

After winning a great victory against the insurgent forces of the Spanish King Alfonso VIII in 1195, Ya'qub al-Mansur celebrated by ordering four enormous gilded bronze balls to be stacked in graduated size atop the minaret. More than 77 pounds of gold were used to gild the "apples," as they were called, and when the sun struck them, the reflection could be seen a full day's march from the city. When completed in 1198, the 213-foot minaret reigned as the tallest tower in the world.[5] Aside from issuing the call to prayer, the minaret in Seville was also said to be used by Arab astronomers to observe the heavens. On a more practical level, attached as it was to the rather low and horizontal mosque, it also served to clearly mark a sacred place in the crowded cityscape and came to symbolize the city itself.

After centuries of conflict, Seville was retaken in 1248 by the Spanish King Ferdinand III. The set of four gilded apples that topped the tower crashed to the ground during an earthquake in 1356 and was replaced with a small bell gable that officially converted the minaret into a bell tower, for the former mosque was then consecrated as the Cathedral Church of Santa Maria de la Sede. In 1401 the old edifice was demolished, and by midcentury a Gothic-style stone cathedral was begun on the site, although the tower was happily spared by the forces of man and nature.[6]

In 1568, when New World gold and silver had made Seville the richest city in Europe, it was decided that a symbol of the city's new prosperity needed to be constructed. Rather than demolish the Moorish tower, the architect Hernán Ruiz the Younger created an imposing 100-foot addition of five stories, including a loggia for the cathedral bells and one for a sundial. The loggia was then topped by two classically inspired circular lanterns—likely by the fourth century BC Choragic Monument of Lysicrates in Athens—that were built of ashlar, brick, and glazed tiles. Stylistically, however, they were all executed in the manner of the Italian Renaissance, for Seville had become culturally the most Italian of Spanish cities,[7] and Ruiz a leading practitioner of the style.

So that it might blend more harmoniously, the lower part of the tower was also modified with the addition of Italianate balustraded balconies to the lobed Islamic archways over the paired horseshoe windows.[8] With the addition at the top of a weather vane, or *giraldillo* (from the Spanish verb *girar*, to turn)—in this case the 13-foot-tall bronze female figure *Faith*—the tower had a new name, the Giralda, and the city a new symbol of the triumph of faith, the victory of the Christians over the Moors, and, by extension, the Catholic Church over the Reformation.

•

Stanford White had always been fascinated by the exotic and the "Oriental," at least since his first trip to Paris in 1878. There he hurried to see the riches of the Exposition Universelle and fell in love with the Palais du Trocadéro that had been specially built on a nearby hillside.[9] Until its eventual destruction in 1936, the huge Hispano-Moorish-style exhibition hall remained in place, topped by a magnificent dome 23 feet taller than Saint Peter's. Its twin towers, 45 feet taller than Notre Dame and accessible by a speedy, water-powered elevator, were inspired by the Giralda of Seville and doubled for good measure.

When White revisited Paris in 1889, the summer the old Madison Square Garden came down, he no doubt saw the Trocadéro again. Its

Moorish interior may have also recalled the evenings he spent on his first visit to Paris at painter Francis Millet's Montmartre studio, in those days stuffed full of hanging lamps, damascened scimitars, brass- and ivory-inlaid furniture, and other souvenirs of the artist's Middle East travels.[10] Then there was the unforgettable honeymoon trip to Constantinople, a city White termed the most wonderful place in the world. And a mosque full of antique tiles he had bought there but were lost in a shipwreck.[11]

A love of the exotic was something Stanford White shared with many other artist friends in the second half of the nineteenth century, including Louis Comfort Tiffany, who began his artistic career as a landscape painter traveling through North Africa and Spain, fascinated by Byzantine and Islamic pattern, light, and color. Upon his return to New York, Tiffany continued to paint scenes of mosques, camels, and snake charmers that he displayed with some success, while developing a passion for acquiring objects of Near, Middle, and Far Eastern manufacture. Tiffany also began experimenting with glass in an attempt to create decorative tiles inspired by the dazzling Byzantine mosaics he had seen on his travels.[12]

In late 1879 Tiffany had approached Stanford White to serve as consultant on the decoration of the new armory for New York's Seventh Regiment, the "silk stocking" home guard known for its socially prominent members. The fortress-like structure had just been completed at an uptown location at Park Avenue and East Sixty-Seventh, where its members believed protection might be needed from the waves of seemingly less-civilized, anarchist-leaning masses streaming in from southern and eastern Europe.

Tiffany had just entered a partnership with textile designer Candace Wheeler and painter Samuel Coleman to create the firm L. C. Tiffany & Associated Artists, with the purpose of encouraging good taste in America. The idea of a group of artists working together to create harmonious interiors of fine quality, much in the manner of the medieval guilds, had been the goal of the Arts and Crafts Movement, born in England in the 1860s and introduced to America in the 1870s through the art and writings of the Pre-Raphaelite Brotherhood, the art and architectural criticism of John Ruskin, and the reprinted lectures on the decorative arts by William Morris, the movement's most influential designer.[13]

Associated Artists also took direction from the British Aesthetics Movement, with its ideal of beauty for its own sake that helped to make the decoration of rooms an endeavor worthy of fine artists. It was believed that every bit of decoration placed in a room—floor, walls, and ceiling— should be handmade, of finest quality, and a thing of beauty. The perfection of such rooms not only reflected the owners' high level of cultivation but was also said to inspire moral improvement.[14]

Tiffany and his firm began work on the Seventh Regimental Armory in April 1880, decorating the Veterans' Room and its adjoining library. When it was complete, most agreed that the sumptuous and quite fanciful mélange of the Greek, Moresque, and Celtic, with a dash of the Egyptian, Persian, and Japanese, was quite remarkable.[15] More commissions would come to Associated Artists based on the success of the Armory, including the 1881 redecoration of the White House at the invitation of President Chester A. Arthur. The new, romantic, and primarily Middle Eastern "Orientalist" mode of good taste that incorporated the exotic, the sensuous, the sumptuous, and the unexpected, was now in play.

44. Sarah Bernhardt as "Cleopatra," Napoleon Sarony, 1891. Theatrical Cabinet Photographs of Women (TCS 2), Harvard Theatre Collection, Harvard University, PD-1923, Wikimedia Commons.

The Oriental and the exotic quickly spread from the world stage of politics, trade, and colonial expansion to the make-believe world of arts and amusement. The influence was evident in the 1882 New York Casino Theatre inspired by Moorish Spain, Sarah Bernhardt's widely performed role as Cleopatra so triumphantly offered at the Garden Theatre, and the painted harem scenes of John Singer Sargent, as well as the "Turkish corner" with a pile of fringed pillows found in every well-decorated American home.

•

But it was not just the generically Oriental and the exotic that influenced Stanford White. His more particular love of Spain was something he shared with Augustus Saint-Gaudens and John Singer Sargent among his many artist friends.[16] Spanish art and architecture—whether seasoned with a Moorish influence or not—had always intrigued White, who had also begun collecting Spanish painting and would come to own *Head of an Infant* by Velasquez, along with more formal portraits by sixteenth- and seventeenth-century artists.[17]

The Madison Square Garden was not his first reworking of a Spanish tower. His first real triumph while still in the office of H. H. Richardson, the tower of Trinity Church in Boston, provided an impressive precedent. Inspired by a photograph of the *torre* of the twelfth-century Old Cathedral in Salamanca, Spain, young White drew the final design, shortening the original tower and lightening it up while reinforcing its upward thrust, broadening its support base, improving its proportions, and reemphasizing its pyramidal lantern.[18]

Although White had reportedly traveled widely in Spain,[19] it was unclear whether he worked from primary or secondary sources in his final rendering of the Madison Square Garden tower. The Giralda had been illustrated in an enthusiastic 1882 article in *Harper's Magazine* by George Lathrop, a friend of both White and Saint-Gaudens, and then published in great detail along with a floor plan in an 1885 issue of *American Architect and Building News*.[20] Doubtless, it also appeared in some of the volumes in McKim, Mead & White's fine library of architectural reference works, or the notebook of drawings White always carried on his travels, or the one hundred scrapbooks of photographs and sketches the three architects amassed on their visits to Europe.[21]

•

The last stages of the Madison Square Garden tower were finished in a rush, and perhaps not quite up to the firm's usual standards, with short-cuts taken and sheet iron and copper used where brick might have been better employed.[22] Finally, at the end of the summer of 1891 after two years of construction, the tower was declared finished.[23]

"How do you like the tower?" was the question everyone asked, and no one in Manhattan needed to be told which tower was meant. Most joined the New York Sun in praising White for "the greatest artistic achievement of the nineteenth century." "If this community can put any token of honor and esteem on Stanford White, now is the time to do it!"[24] the newspaper proclaimed. But others declared White a mere copyist if not an out-and-out plagiarist.

Whether the tower was a quite literal copy of the Giralda or an inno-vative hommage was a matter for continuing debate.[25] The opposing camps acknowledged that both towers were square in shape and that there was a similarity in the general scheme, outline, proportioning, upper loggia, and rather lacy set of lanterns. The Garden tower was also nearly the same height as the Giralda. But it was 6 feet narrower at the base and had a simplified shaft with subtler diaper-pattern brickwork than the Giralda's high-relief sebka panels of arches and interlaced rhomboids.

Among their other differences, the Garden tower was faced with light buff-yellow brick rather than soft rose, and its plain windows were scat-tered in a rhythmic pattern over the tower, in contrast to the Moorish horseshoe windows, arched frames, and Renaissance-style balustrades down the center of the Giralda. Where the Giralda's five-bay loggia holds the cathedral's bells, the Garden loggia was quite vacant, and although the top five stories of both towers were basically similar, White had elongated and lightened the upper stages by replacing heavy piers with delicately columned arcades that were more graceful and perhaps even playful. The Garden tower was, therefore, a much more unified whole than the mismated half-Moorish, half-Renaissance Giralda. While it might indeed have been reminiscent, not a single individual feature of the Giralda had been directly copied onto the Garden tower.[26]

Furthermore, while the Giralda served a spiritual need, as minaret and then cathedral bell tower, the Garden tower primarily filled an aesthetic one, as a lovely ornament to a palace of pleasure, and commercially as a signpost for Madison Square Garden. Small distinctions, perhaps, but important to those who defended the tower as "the most New Yorkish thing in town."[27] It was widely held that there was no reason to begrudge White's debt to Spain for the tower, for as that critic of modern architecture Mariana Van Rensselaer pointed out, White had borrowed what was best in the Giralda and then very cleverly recast it in a new mold.[28]

Some critics found that White's tower was truly more beautiful than the Giralda, reminding their readers that it was far better to borrow a good design than originate a bad one.[29] In any case, the Garden tower was certainly unique in the city, if not the entire nation, and a rather different riff on the Beaux-Arts classicism that had been so much associated with the firm of McKim, Mead & White.

•

At last, the tower awaited only its crowning glory, the female figure that still remained something of a mystery to the public. In July 1891, Charles De Kay, art critic and friend of both White and Augustus Saint-Gaudens, wrote in *Harper's Weekly* that the tower would soon be topped by a statue holding a lance with a pennon flag, perhaps created by Saint-Gaudens, and that there was presently a statuette in his studio, about three feet high, which if enlarged would just match the figure on the tower's plans.[30] Whether he was writing on the fly or intentionally adding to the surrounding mystery is not clear.

Some expected that the figure would be a copy of that striking image known variously as the *Triumph of Faith*, *Christian Faith*, or simply *Faith* that tops the Giralda and serves as its weather vane, or *giradillo*. Clad in Roman helmet, strap sandals, and a clinging, transparent tunic, that broad-hipped female figure clearly appears more pagan warrior than Christian paragon, with a palm frond in one hand symbolic of conquest, and in the other the Roman standard and pennon flag of Constantine, the first Christian emperor. This monumental figure boasts a lengthy pedigree dating once again to classical roots. The figure was cast by Spanish Renaissance sculptor Bartholomé Morel between 1566 and 1568, after a model by Juan Bautista Vázquez the Elder, after a design attributed to Luis de Vargas, from an Italian engraving of the helmeted Greek goddess *Athena of War and Wisdom* by Marcantonio Raimondi, from an original likeness by either Italian artist Giulio Romano or Perino del Vaga.[31] To many minds, the tower was and continues into the twenty-first century to be secondary to she who gave her nickname to the structure.

•

Madison Square Garden's own crowning statue was to be delivered on September 29, 1891,[32] carefully wrapped and concealed from view until the figure's unveiling on November 1 and the tower's formal dedication the following day. With the subject and its specific representation still uncertain, all of New York remained in suspense.

20

The Virgin Installed

ON SEPTEMBER 28, 1891, a beautiful fall Monday, the statue of *Diana* arrived by train and then truck at the Madison Square Garden ready for installation. But by the end of the day, the discretely wrapped *Diana* had been raised only as far as the top of the arcade on the Garden's Twenty-Seventh Street side. There she remained for nearly a week until preparations were complete for the great haul upward when the figure would be hoisted some 350 feet in the air to the very top of the Garden tower.[1]

Oddly enough, Augustus Saint-Gaudens was not in the city and would not be present to inspect the figure upon its delivery from the foundry in Ohio. The plan, as detailed in a letter from Stanford White, was that *Diana* would arrive in New York gilded and "balanced to a hair," yet carefully wrapped and crated. Knowing Saint-Gaudens's penchant for perfection and fearing another round of his fiddling, White had hoped that this would make it "virtually impossible to unpack her in the street for an examination." Although the sculptor had pressed White for the opportunity to inspect the figure one last time before it was installed, White begged off. He did warn Saint-Gaudens that the Mullins people "probably have not done anything more than make a passable copy," realizing that a close look would likely make Saint-Gaudens "mad as the devil, but when it is way up in the air it will probably look all right." White added, "If you wish it unpacked, Amen; I will try and arrange it, only, if it can be avoided, I should like it more than I can tell you."[2]

The whole situation was really quite strained, with White dreading a delay of any sort. Over the previous three weeks, work on the tower had come to a standstill due to Saint-Gaudens's tinkering with the drapery that had delayed *Diana*'s delivery to the metalworks in Ohio and therefore to New York. White took all responsibility for rushing the figure back to the city on time and offered to cover the extra cost incurred by its monumental size. Saint-Gaudens agreed to White's request and remained sequestered at his country home in New Hampshire for the installation.

The engineering firm of Post & McCord had been hired to accomplish *Diana*'s installation, but first the necessary apparatus needed to be set in place, including an outrigger that projected from the top of the tower, a mast lashed to the ironwork, a boom hung from the mast, and attached to the boom 1,000 feet of steel rope. Because of the anticipated difficulty and danger of the work, the men from Post & McCord insisted upon completely free access and clear space around the figure, chasing the Mullins foundry workers and deliverymen back to Ohio before they could interfere. To further ease the installation, mechanics were called in to extend the 7-inch-diameter wrought-iron pipe that ran through the figure, stem to stern, for another 9 feet.

•

On Saturday, October 3, 1891, temperatures and tempers rose as crowds of workmen gathered to attempt the remarkable feat—the heaviest hoist of the city's largest sculpture and the world's largest weather vane onto the top of New York's tallest tower. The *Diana* was secured around the waist with ropes, and with much creaking was awkwardly swung up in the air by a steam-driven boom derrick.

Stanford White superintended the entire process with his usual energy, taking care that men were placed at the tower's windows and on its ledges, ready to prevent the goddess from bumps and bruises on her journey. Members of the Madison Square Garden board, who had been meeting inside the building, streamed out into the street as soon as they received word that the *Diana* was about to rise.

•

By that time it was midafternoon and the distinguished actor Richard Mansfield—known for his arrogance and bad temper—was performing a matinee of *Prince Karl* in the Garden Theatre. During the intermission, manager Jimmy Morrissey was handed a message summoning him to the actor's dressing room, or so he recalled. "Mr. Morrissey, what's that horrible noise?" the actor demanded. With some effort, Morrissey heard a faint tapping sound, like the ticking of a watch under one's pillow. "I cannot stand it!" exclaimed Mansfield. "Unless it is stopped the audience must be sent home."

Morrissey hurried down to the street to discover that it was the sound of the derrick's engine that had driven Mansfield mad. So Morrissey approached Stanford White and with some embarrassment told him of Mansfield's demand. White listened with an expression of astonishment on his face. He was apologetic, but he explained that once the job was underway, it was crucial that *Diana* reach the top of the tower while there was still light.

Morrissey expected this response and was mentally preparing himself for the task of canceling the performance when White surprised him by changing his mind. "We must make allowances for the high nervous tension of the genius, I guess," said he so accustomed to the vagaries of the creative mind. White gave the order to suspend operations until the conclusion of the matinee, and the goddess dangled ingloriously in the air, halfway to her pedestal, until the play concluded.[3]

•

When the *Diana* finally touched down, the long pipe that extended through her left heel was slipped onto a slender tube that emerged from a larger 10-inch-diameter wrought-iron tube that would be attached to the very top of the tower's arched lantern's skeleton frame. The pipe was then set through a hollow metal ball 22 inches in diameter and again through a second ball more than 3 feet in diameter. To reduce friction and easily allow *Diana* to turn in the wind, two horizontal ball bearings were engineered at either end of the long pipe, each consisting of two grooved flanges between which ½-inch polished steel balls worked. The *Times* claimed there were forty ball bearings involved, all the size of billiard balls,[4] but this was something of an exaggeration.

Mechanics then installed a great crescent moon, measuring about 12 feet from tip to tip and nearly 2 feet wide, upon an angle iron frame set between the two balls beneath her feet. Immediately above the crescent moon, ten gas pipes were set to fuel reflecting lamps that would cast their rays upward onto the figure. *Diana* was then connected by a mechanism to the large dial on the south side of the tower, intended to more clearly

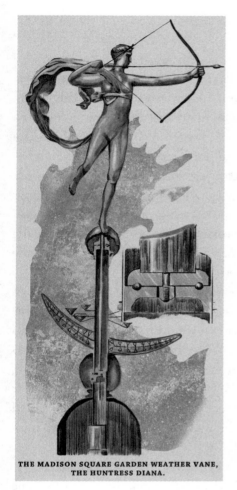

THE MADISON SQUARE GARDEN WEATHER VANE,
THE HUNTRESS DIANA.

45. *The Madison Square Garden's Weather Vane, the Huntress Diana, Scientific American* (Dec. 26, 1891).

indicate the wind's direction. A lightning rod was attached under the upper ball, from which six copper rod arms extended upward. The entire apparatus—*Diana*, her armature, and counterpoise—weighed a good 1,800 pounds, yet it was figured that it would take less than a quarter of a pound of wind pressure per square foot to move her about.[5]

Diana's great swirling drapery had been separately cast and soon followed the goddess up the tower, along with her bow and arrow, and all were riveted into place.[6] At the close of the day, Stanford White—known for his kindness to working crews—very gratefully rewarded the supervising foreman with a chain and engraved gold charm for his pocket watch.[7]

•

On October 5, fearless workmen on ladders once more climbed the tower to redrape the figure in huge cotton flannel sheets. She had been briefly undressed behind protective scaffolding so that her gilding could be retouched and then rewrapped to help keep the gold leaf in place. The drapes would also serve to conceal her form until the great and ceremonial unwrapping on November 1. One leg, then the other, and then her waist were swathed, but it was a terribly windy day, and before her upper torso could be scaled, a gust blew the wrappings far over the housetops. Struggling against the wind, the workmen tried to drape her from the shoulders down, but again the flannel sheets blew into the howling gale until the effort was finally abandoned.[8]

The following day more brave workmen hauled up a crescent crown of two hundred electric lights for *Diana*'s head and a double crescent mirror to be set on her forehead. The crown would reflect light onto the tip of her arrow that pointed into the wind so that her practical purpose, as a wind vane, could serve all night long. Due to the difficulty in reaching them, these lights in her crown were engineered to burn for a full year without replacement. Cut-glass prisms to catch the sun's rays were added to the crescent moon at her feet, along with fittings for another two hundred incandescent lamps.[9]

•

Finally the heavy scaffolding surrounding the goddess began to come down, partially revealing her figure. The *Times* had rather obliquely reported that *Diana* was "clad in the hunting costume mythology dictates,"[10] but nothing more specific. On October 14, drawings appeared in the *New York Sun* and the *Recorder* that claimed to actually represent her, nude except for a drape wound beneath her breasts.[11] Apparently, under pressure from the press, Stanford White had gone to Saint-Gaudens's New York studio, picked up a small model of the figure, and had it photographed for *Harper's Weekly*. The newspapers then made "hellish" drawings of it, or so White explained to Saint-Gaudens, still up in New Hampshire. More photographs were taken at the Kurtz Studio on Madison Square, but Saint-Gaudens remained "in a lather" that the pictures displayed the figure "in a bad light and wrongly set." So a second set of photographs was taken and sent out.[12] However, the issue of the *Diana's* likely nudity seemed to generate little public comment or protest.

On October 28, three workmen climbed up once more to install additional electric wires around the sculpture. While turning on the current to test it, a spark suddenly flew from the wire to the flannel covering that still concealed the figure, and it burst into flames. The workmen were able to extinguish the blaze before any real damage was done, but *Diana's* wrappings had been badly singed. Cognizant of the need to keep the figure draped, the workmen scrambled down from the tower to scavenge whatever cloth they could until the official unveiling just four nights away. After the wrappings were replaced, one of the workmen swore that upon seeing the damage to her covering, he felt *Diana* aim an arrow at his breast![13] The anthropomorphization of the figure that would soon become the city's own patron deity had begun.

•

On the late afternoon of November 1, 1891—nearly a year and a half after the dedication of the Madison Square Garden Amphitheatre—great crowds once more gathered on Madison Square. In just a few hours, the tower would be presented to New Yorkers as a pyramid of light and the figure of *Diana* unveiled. Meanwhile, lights were still being added, with half a dozen workmen, electricians, and their assistants scurrying to string additional wires up onto her head, around her still-draped limbs, and out to the point of her arrow.[14]

Officers of the Madison Square Garden Company, including Stanford White and a select number of the press, had been ushered up through the Twenty-Sixth Street entrance into the tower itself, riding the elevator to the top of the loggia and then up the winding iron staircase at the 225-foot mark that led to the outlook at the uppermost lantern. Master Van Rensselaer King, the eleven-year-old son of constructor David King, led the way, having had the honor of being the first to officially climb the tower stairs.[15]

•

A brisk breeze was blowing at nearly five o'clock when one of the workmen began climbing upward from the tower's topmost lantern, up the

Diana and over the drapery that still concealed her figure. As word spread that the spectacle was about to begin, crowds piled out of the Hoffman House and the Fifth Avenue Hotel, and sidewalks were jammed along Broadway as far as West Thirty-Third Street. The workman—just a tiny figure to the crowd—slowly climbed up the back of the goddess like a sailor up a mast, to her arms, and then, to the cheers of the thousands now in the streets, sat astride her shoulders. He loosened the fluttering drapes that covered her shoulders, then her arms, and then her bare breasts. As he worked his way downward, he continued to pull away her wrappings piece by piece, until finally, standing on her bent back leg he dragged away the last bit of clothing and the virgin goddess, as the newspapers reported, was "stripped bare."[16]

As breathlessly described in these accounts, the beauty of *Diana*'s golden figure against the sky was absolutely stunning as she swung in the wind, pointing one way and then the other, while people in the streets and on the square stopped to stare and point. Most of the crowd thought the show to be over, but at exactly a quarter after five, as the shadows deepened, the two hundred incandescent lamps in the cut-glass crescent at her feet were lit,[17] while the great searchlight in the topmost lantern rode on rails around the tower to illuminate her figure against the night sky. On came the lamps on *Diana*'s forehead, and then the fifty incandescent bulbs strung around her head and outlining her bow and arrow. As the first public sculpture to be illuminated by electric lights, the effect appeared simply breathtaking.[18] The tower itself had been fitted out with a total of eight thousand incandescent lights and one hundred arc lights in addition to the searchlights, and when all the switches were pulled and the building became bathed in a flood of light, the square was brought to an absolute standstill.[19]

21

Diana Reigns

THAT NEXT NIGHT'S official dedication of the tower and the great show of red fire, bombs, and rockets choreographed by Stanford White quickly became headline news around the country. Typical of the enthusiasm for the tower, the *New York Sun* described the whole construction as "a marvel of beautifully calculated proportions, beautifully contrasted effects, beautifully disposed details."[1] Within the city, the tower and its goddess had become the focus of all eyes and an object of some adoration.[2]

Walking in Madison Square or on one of its surrounding streets became almost hazardous, as pedestrians collided while gazing upward.[3] There were tales like that of the driver of a Fourth Avenue horse car who decided to stay on the job even though he had been denied a wage increase, saying that he would not miss passing that tower for fifty cents a day.[4]

As an editorial writer at *The Century* pointed out, *Diana* was happily symbolic of nothing. She carried no patriotic or social sentiment and commemorated nothing, but was simply her own beautiful excuse for being.[5] "A real American girl," said the *New York Times*, all day long rushing this way and that, active and independent with a definite personality of her own.[6] Poems were written, satires penned, and cartoons published, all depicting the city's new patroness partaking of its vibrant life—startling ballgoers with a personal appearance, taking in the horse show, endorsing a local haberdasher, and chatting with the Goddess of Liberty across the bay.[7] "Is that you, Miss Diana? Excuse my not turning my head. I'm not as flighty and whirly-whirly as some," said Miss Liberty in O. Henry's short story "The Lady Higher Up."[8]

Newspapers all over the country—thousands of miles and light-years away from the city—were carrying the story of Madison Square Garden's goddess with gushing praise and with hardly a word about her state of undress. The *New York Daily Tribune* appreciated the power of the tower's beauty to affect the social order, promising that it would "remain a constant and permanent force to elevate, refine and refresh all who gaze upon it."[9] Papers as distant and as circumspect as the *Salt Lake Herald* in Utah called the tower a magnificent monument and proclaimed the sculpture a great work of art.[10] According to *The Century*, the typical comment on the streets of New York was simply "splendid."[11]

Some complaint did come from a few self-proclaimed connoisseurs of feminine pulchritude who criticized the flatness of the figure, both fore and aft, finding it "almost sexless."[12] Other critics noted the inauthenticity of the pose in that should the *Diana* ever actually shoot an arrow, the bowstring would cut right across her left breast. While Saint-Gaudens may have taken the point under consideration and then ignored it for the sake of aesthetics, Henri Marceau, curator at the Philadelphia Museum of Art, suggested that Saint-Gaudens was simply not sufficiently familiar with the fine points of archery to realize the seriousness of his error.[13]

•

Within a few weeks, as observers had a bit more time to consider all the angles, comments of a more critical nature began to appear in the press. With *Diana*'s breasts and strongly muscled buttocks standing in relief against the sky, every detail of her anatomy appeared startlingly visible. The *New York Mercury* bemoaned the change in quiet Madison Square, formerly a daily gathering place and quiet playground for the young. But now, the rare child who ventured there was said to be rushed through at breakneck speed by a nursemaid dodging the flood "of young Casino Johnnies, pop-eyed dudes, Grandpa Hayseeds from Westchester, and bald-headed clubmen armed with field glasses." A local policeman on the Madison Square beat warned that parents should no longer let their children be "immoralized" by a figure far too brazen to have been installed in a public place.[14]

More voices joined in the chorus. The Woman's Christian Temperance Union lodged a formal complaint to Anthony Comstock of the New York Society for the Suppression of Vice. He had made his views on the nude in art quite clear when he published *Traps for the Young* in 1883 and *Morals versus Art* four years later. According to Comstock, the nude figure of a beautiful woman might in itself be chaste and sweet and not necessarily obscene, lewd, or indecent when legitimately exhibited to cultured minds in an art gallery.[15] But when it was paraded in public before the eyes of young men and boys—the uncultured and inexperienced, as it were—it created an appetite for the immoral and provided food for impure imaginations. And if appropriated for lewd purposes, it would fan the flame of secret vices and desires, thus creating a demand for that which was far worse. Furthermore, to expose a female nude in public to such a vulgar gaze, he asserted, was to rob her of her modesty and to degrade her entire sex, for the proper place for a woman's body to be denuded was in the privacy of her own apartments, with the blinds down.[16]

Inspector Comstock had long conducted his attack on publishers, booksellers, art academies, galleries, and even art supply stores that violated his principles. Saint-Gaudens had already assigned himself to Comstock's list of enemies in 1887, along with other so-called liberals and free thinkers, when he signed a petition decrying Comstock's raid on the Knoedler Gallery located a block south of Madison Square, in which more than one hundred photographs of French paintings that happened to include nudes were seized for fear they might be acquired by young men.[17]

It was true that the public display of *Diana*'s nude figure outside of the rarified confines of a museum or gallery was something quite new. When such a figure was displayed in an enclosed venue, it was argued, the viewer made the conscious decision to enter and to look upon it. But those who passed by in the street had no choice, and women and children could hardly be prevented from gazing upward. Deeper thinkers conceded that nude art was not necessarily offensive in itself, but wondered if it became so when put to an offensive purpose. Could *Diana*, ever-virgin champion of chastity, remain pure when she was being forced upon the public as a commercial advertisement for the week's show at the Madison Square Garden?[18]

The Rev. Dr. Benjamin Franklin De Costa, rector of St. John the Evangelist Church and president of the White Cross Society—dedicated to elevating public morality, discouraging immoral amusements, encouraging

46. *Created by St. Gaudens. Purified by St. Anthony Comstock*,
E. M. Kemble, *Collier's Magazine* (Aug. 25, 1906).

respect for women, and promoting male chastity—expressed the angst
felt in some circles in decrying "the brazen heathen goddess's" nudity.[19]
However, neither Comstock's nor De Costa's comments regarding *Diana*
were given much credence, nor were their opinions widely shared by New
Yorkers.[20] In a story titled "The Comstock Nuisance," the *New York Times*
reminded its readers that "the true problem is the impertinence of reformers who are themselves coarse and fancy that all others must see things

through their own vulgar spectacles."[21] But more than that, Manhattan claimed *Diana* with a touch of bravado—a symbol of its coming of age, of the sophistication that set it apart from clearly more provincial cities like Boston, Chicago, or Philadelphia that would not have dared to display her.[22] While it might be reassuring to imagine from the implied superior perspective of the twenty-first century that the public display of a nude figure in the late nineteenth century would produce widespread shock and scandal among Manhattanites, in the main it simply was not the case.

•

The positive public response to the *Diana* was no doubt gratifying to both Stanford White and Augustus Saint-Gaudens, but there were some real and concerning issues with the sculpture. Within days of the figure's installation, Saint-Gaudens realized that aside from the error of the mounting pole through her heel, her drapery needed to be modified into a more graceful contour. The quite stiff line of the scarf wound between her breasts billowed out too far behind her shoulder, like the handle of a teapot "or the loop of a pretzel," the *Times* chided, and "the sooner mended the better."[23] Saint-Gaudens simply placed the blame for the unattractive drapery on another error made at the foundry.[24]

But a far more serious flaw soon took center stage. Even though the ancients recorded that the goddess was taller than any of her attendant nymphs, it became apparent that this *Diana* was far too large in scale for the delicate concoction of Italian Renaissance columns, loggias, cupolas, and lanterns that topped the Madison Square Garden tower. Stanford White confessed to Saint-Gaudens that the very day *Diana* had been installed, as pleased as he was with the sculpture, his heart "contracted at the thought that she was going to be too big."[25] He recalled that it had been Saint-Gaudens who had argued for a height of 18 feet, and he had only acquiesced.[26]

The *New York Sun* agreed that *Diana* was a good deal bigger than was perhaps expected, but offered that she should be more than a finishing touch. Why not assert her own importance and the importance of the sculptor's art? "It would have been a blunder to make the tower a mere pedestal for her, but neither would it have worked if she were just a finial for the tower. Now they have equal rights and equal significance."[27]

Others joined in the conversation, and even the press in Salem, Ohio—the city of her manufacture—warned that *Diana* might be rather too large.[28] The *New York Herald* went so far as to call the figure a mastodon, "a remarkably handsome mastodon to be sure," but a mastodon nevertheless.[29] *The Collector*, a journal of art and antiquarianism, blasted Saint-Gaudens and White for their apparent ignorance of the laws of relation and appropriateness, insisting that the figure "should have been just a light detail, not the most ponderous feature of the entire building. Even if it is not indecent in the physical sense, it is certainly artistically so." Alfred Trumble, the journal's editor, added that in the interest of good taste he "should not be sorry to hear that the next blizzard has blown Diana down . . . As egregious a humbug as was ever fostered on a confiding lot of stockholders by an architect in league with a sculptor," thundered Trumble, who must surely have been Saint-Gaudens's most vocal and vicious critic. "Grossly disproportionate, clumsy, ungainly, and ungraceful," he added. "If only John Quincy Adams Ward had been called upon to create the sculpture, instead of someone like Saint-Gaudens, so overly concerned with feeling rather than pure form."[30]

Saint-Gaudens's regret at her size was reported in the newspapers along with additional excuses: that he had been forced to model the figure without a proper allowance for the tower's height, or that it was a clerk's blunder in making calculations.[31] Stanford White frankly conceded that until he saw her hoisted up and unveiled, he had not anticipated that *Diana* would become such a noticeable and perhaps too prominent feature of the tower.[32] Soon everyone was calling it *"Diana's Tower,"* and friends were making jokes about "that statue with a tower on the side."[33]

One Saturday afternoon after the staff had left the office for the half-day, White locked the office door, and he and Francis Hoppin, one of his favorite office assistants, made a scale silhouette of the tower and cut-outs of differently sized *Dianas*, from 18 feet down to 9 feet. One after another was tried until White was satisfied that the 13-foot model looked right. Charles McKim, working there that day and only too aware of the disproportionate size of the figure, emerged from his private office as White was striding back and forth. "White," he said with a smile on his face, "that was a very beautiful pedestal you made for Saint-Gaudens' statue, but I thought that he was going to make a finial for your Tower." McKim quickly retreated to his office, shaking with laughter at the explosion that followed.[34] In fact, Thomas Dewing had warned White and Saint-Gaudens that the *Diana* was going to be too tall, but they refused to listen, pointing out that he was "only a painter and what could he know" about sculpture placed on great towers.[35]

•

Within six weeks of her installation, the *New York Herald* reported the shocking news that *Diana* might be coming down off the tower and go instead to the World's Columbian Exposition being planned in Chicago for 1892 to commemorate the four-hundredth anniversary of the European discovery of America. Stanford White quickly insisted to the press that the claim was a completely unfounded rumor. "It may be possible," he admitted, "that a duplicate may be made for one of the fair's buildings," but *Diana* was staying put. "If Chicago wants a copy, Chicago ought to have one," but, as the *Sun* asked, "What would Diana do in that grimy and murky place?"[36]

But rumors persisted that Saint-Gaudens was dissatisfied with the virgin's less-than-graceful pose and planned to replace her. Back in Chicago, Daniel Burnham, chief of construction for what would quickly become known as the Chicago World's Fair, informed the press that Saint-Gaudens was planning to design a smaller statue for the Garden tower and, significantly, one with additional drapery. Burnham indicated that this would be done to satisfy the demands of Anthony Comstock, who had been threatening the Garden's board of directors, Saint-Gaudens, and White with prosecution under the laws relating to immodest exposure. Stanford White smiled broadly and said that Burnham's statement was all "false rumor. If we had to put up another *Diana*," he laughed, "she would have even less covering!"[37]

Reporters visited Saint-Gaudens's studio to grill him on the situation. "Not much to say about her," he replied, adding that there were no plans to make a replica for Chicago. When asked whether the rumor was true that he had simply copied the actually quite different nude figure of *Fortuna*, the late seventeenth-century bronze weather vane perched on the golden dome of the Dogana da Mar customs house in Venice, he made it very clear that the *Diana* was neither copied nor suggested by any other statue anywhere in existence. The idea and result, modeled in clay by his own hand, were most emphatically his own.[38]

•

In early January 1892 the *New York Times* reported that McKim, Mead & White had offered to sell *Diana* to the Committee on Grounds and Buildings for the Chicago fair at the bargain price of $2,000, with transportation to Chicago, installation, and a regilding included, but the committee had rejected the offer as an unwanted expense.[39] So it seemed that *Diana* most definitely would not be going west. Meanwhile, true to form, *The Collector* expressed hope that *Diana* "is headed to the melting pot" and noted that "residents around Madison Square are praying that the ungainly Diana will soon be taken down in any case, fearful that a high wind may blow her off her perch and thereby demolish some of the houses across the way."[40] There was indeed some concern about such an occurrence, until a test proved she would withstand wind pressure of approximately 5,000 pounds per square inch.[41]

At the end of January 1892, the goddess herself consented to an interview with the *New York Times* to discuss her role as the city's patron divinity. Olympus, she informed the reader, had grown dull and distasteful, Jove fairly bald, Juno shrewish, and everyone cross. Vesta had been put out of business thanks to gas and electricity, while Mercury had become the district telegraph boy. *Diana* adored seeing and being seen here in New York, although she did not care much for silk hats or bicycle riders who turned their backs on her, or the sooty air she had to breathe, or those abominable cigarettes. And why, she asked, were the houses huddled so closely together, all alike and all so hideous? Why was that darn goddess of Liberty ever constructed to ruin the harbor's view? New Yorkers were a strange race, she noted, so full of kindness for those in distant parts of the globe, yet so oblivious to the suffering in their own city.[42]

While *Diana* mused in the press, White was afflicted with a high fever and a severe urinary tract and bladder infection, a recurrence of his troubles that had begun in the spring of 1890. He remained ill for five or six weeks, suffering through two minor surgeries and barely managing to crawl down to the office for meetings. "The water works are still not working right," he noted.[43] These problems continued to recur, and some-time later Saint-Gaudens would write, "I am glad to know that your BALLS are all right. Sometimes mine wobble and sometimes they clink, clink."[44]

•

By March 1892, three months after the rumors of *Diana*'s departure began, a decision had been made and made public. The newspapers announced that chaste *Diana* had been chased from the Madison Square Garden tower at last, but only to be replaced by a smaller edition, somewhere around 13 feet high.[45] Stanford White told reporters that "height was the only prob-lem," making his tower look too slender, but "artistically she was per-fect."[46] When questioned, Augustus Saint-Gaudens confirmed that all he and White had done was to decide that the change would be made, how soon he could not say. It would certainly take some careful work to haul the present goddess down, for installing her at that dizzying height was one of the great engineering achievements of the day.[47]

It would also take a great deal of money. *Diana* would have to be swung down, a new version modeled, sent to Ohio and forged again in copper, gilded, sent back to New York, and then once more hauled up America's tallest tower and installed. It would only be a difference of 5 feet in height for the new figure—and seen at a distance of some 300 feet at that. But for both architect and sculptor money was merely a tool to achieve the beau-tiful, and they were willing "to empty their pocketbooks" once more.[48] According to his staff, White never stopped studying his work until actual construction began, while the only way to stop Saint-Gaudens from tin-kering on a piece was to cart it away to the foundry.[49] Scale "was the hard-est thing in the world to judge," White confessed, and calling on heaven, he and Saint-Gaudens vowed never again to work without first making a scale model that had been carefully scrutinized in place.[50]

22

Up under the Stars

AS THE EARLY SPRING of 1892 progressed, Stanford White was over-seeing the completion of the last bit of the Madison Square Garden complex—the new roof garden. He had laid out a rectangle measuring 200 by 80 feet that ran north to south the full length of the roof from Twenty-Sixth to Twenty-Seventh Street and west to east from Madison Avenue to the amphitheater's glass skylights. It was certainly a unique location, with a stunning view over Madison Square and beyond, over the roofs of the city in all directions.

From the beginning White's intention had been to make the roof garden the sort of pleasant place for light entertainment that could easily be found abroad—an enjoyable spot to spend a summer evening after the theater, eat a light supper, have a drink, and smoke a cigar, all while listening to good music. Something like a beer garden, perhaps, but for a rather different class of people and a refuge of sorts for those unfortunate New Yorkers forced by their labors to remain in the city during the long, hot summer months.[1]

This, however, would not be the first theatrical rooftop summer garden in Manhattan. That distinction belonged to the Casino Theatre, that Moorish fantasy with the quite distinctive if not downright phallic red-tiled tower thirteen blocks up Broadway at West Thirty-Ninth, catty-corner to the Metropolitan Opera House. Owner and conductor Rudolph Aronson had been inspired by the street-side concert gardens he had enjoyed in Paris along the Champs-Élysées and had hoped to open a similar establishment in town. But when he considered Manhattan's summer heat and the high cost of its square footage, a garden on top of the roof of a building he already planned to erect seemed like the perfect solution.[2]

While the Casino Theatre proper continued to entertain a rather high-brow audience by presenting European operetta on its main stage, since 1883 its summertime roof garden had served as a pleasant spot to lounge to the tunes of a Hungarian band before and after the theater's main event, or even watch the theatrical performance through an opening in the roof. Although the weather obviously affected attendance—with the roof garden packed to overflowing on a warm evening and relatively deserted on a cool or rainy one—it was not unusual for more than eight thousand patrons to crowd onto the Casino's roof each week.

Spurred by the planned opening of the new Madison Square Garden roof, the old and rather rustic Casino Roof Garden was in the process of being enlarged, improved, and totally made over into an elegant Parisian café chantant. A 30-foot stage was being erected, the old garden plantings torn up for added seating, European variety acts booked, and a very French cuisine being planned in the kitchen.[3] Once again Stanford White was engaged in a contest, a race to complete and open his own roof garden for the season before the Casino on May 30, following the annual Decoration Day military parade down Fifth Avenue.

•

To begin, the floor of the Madison Square Garden's roof garden was laid with paving brick from W. A. Underwood of Croton Point, New York, just up the Hudson River.[4] Stanford White surrounded the garden with a row of buff-colored brick Ionic and Corinthian columns, stiffened for safety's sake with iron pipe through their centers, just as the columns of the belvederes had been, and then decorated with Pompeian white terra-cotta trim. While a glass roof was originally planned to protect customers from the vagaries of weather, White had had to settle for red-and-white striped canvas side curtains as barrier against cool breezes and for similar awnings that could be quickly spread out over the crowd in case of rain.[5]

The small jewel box of a stage was installed on the east side of the roof garden, enframed by an elaborate entablature and Corinthian pilasters, the grand curtain decorated with another painted scene of Versailles. The unsightly ventilator shaft over the Garden Theatre and the skylight over the alleyway between the theater and the amphitheater were disguised by creeping vines, ferns, and flowers.[6] Soon to be added were rows of settees and theater seats accommodating 250, as well as scattered small tables for those desiring a light supper, with beer or wine to be served from the big kitchen and long bar set behind the stage.

•

As was to be expected, the roof garden was just one of a multitude of projects occupying Stanford White's time and mind. White had a typewriter hauled up to the roof, where for several weeks he would work from ten in the morning until midnight dictating notes and letters as he dashed about, finalizing various details.[7] Aside from the imminent completion of the Washington Memorial Arch on Washington Square, White was also considering a scheme with several other Garden investors to build a permanent, year-round home for the circus away from the Garden. They scoured sites farther uptown, around Fifth Avenue and Forty-Second Street, and White sketched out some plans. But with the cost estimated at $600,000 and the news that the Garden had again lost money that fiscal year—some $14,000—with no dividends yet paid, the project was dropped.[8]

With the architectural and decorative aspects of the Madison Square Garden largely complete, White had also discovered a new outlet for his more theatrical side. With the Garden serving as backdrop, he enjoyed the role of impresario extraordinaire, creating, directing, and producing extravaganzas like the Actors Fund Fair that opened in the amphitheater on May 2, 1892. White recreated an entire fantasy world with entry through a triumphal arch and Roman colonnade into a charming village featuring reconstructions of Shakespeare's home, the Globe Theatre, Dickens's Olde Curiosity Shop, a Japanese tea garden, and a Moorish mosque in a setting studded with gardens, fountains, and a towering maypole, all illuminated by brilliant multicolored electric lights.[9]

On the more personal side, White was still suffering from various physical ailments when he learned that the rented brownstone on West Twentieth Street—where he and his family had long been in residence—was to be torn down by the owners and that the Whites needed to vacate by May 1. In April he found another suitable brownstone a block up on Twenty-First Street, but since it was not yet fit for habitation, at least not to his standards, his wife and son moved to their house on Long Island for the summer, leaving White to find rooms in town. Coincidentally, a vacancy opened in the Garden tower, allowing him to lease a sixth-floor apartment. Of course, it too was uninhabitable until he painted the walls in shades of umber, sienna, and vermilion, with accents in chrome yellow and green. White had, in actuality, been camping out in the tower for a while, using sculptor Daniel Chester French's studio as an office while he continued to supervise the construction of the roof garden. Ever mindful of his privacy and annoyed by stories leaked in the press of his taking rooms there, he solved the issue by having his name removed from the tower's directory board.[10]

•

In mid-May 1892, the grand opening of the Madison Square Garden's summer season was being advertised in all the newspapers, with the new roof garden touted as the most magnificent open-air resort in the world.[11] Fresh air could be had for the price of a band concert,[12] with a fifty-cent admission granting access to both the roof and the reinstated "Gilmore and His Famous Band of 100 Musicians" concert in the amphitheater, with an elevator ride to the top of the tower added as well. Garden Theatre attendees might also enter the roof garden free of charge between dramatic acts and at the end of the performance, but they were required to pay extra for the tower elevator and were not allowed to enter the amphitheater. A complicated system of coupon tickets was used to distinguish the varied rights conferred on each purchaser.[13]

Stanford White met his deadline, and the formal opening of the roof garden took place as planned on Monday night, May 30. Some 150 tables, each set with four to six Windsor chairs, dotted the floor. Tall palms, potted plants, and rare flowers were arranged over the roof, the fountains were filled, the last of the brightly colored Chinese lanterns hung, and red, white, and blue bunting swagged from the parapets. In addition, hundreds of red, white, and yellow incandescent lamps were strung over framed latticework arches, ready to blaze away.[14]

The day before tickets went on sale, advertisements informed the public that music and dance performances were to be offered on the new roof garden, but this barely described the entertainments that were planned. Like the Casino Theatre roof, the summer-only entertainment here would be more of the vaudeville type, lighter in tone than the concerts Gilmore would be presenting downstairs.[15]

Despite the damp and rather chilly weather, opening night was jammed to the fainting point, and a number of angry ticket holders were turned away. Management had counted on seating 800 comfortably and 1,200 in a pinch, but there was a crowd of at least 3,500, with an interesting mix of the usual society folk and those less so. The crush was so great that when Gilmore's bandsmen attempted to dedicate the roof garden at eleven o'clock with a ceremonial blast of their horns, they were unable to fight their way to the stage. Reason prevailed when it seemed clear that the addition of Gilmore's band and its one hundred members might have fatal results and that the roof garden might better remain undedicated than risk merrymakers being crushed to death.[16]

●

In the days that followed, the June crowds continued to pack the roof garden. At first the waiters were stymied trying to force their way through the crowd to serve drinks, but they soon learned how to juggle their cocktail trays through the crush, and table service was judged quite good. As for the entertainment, the crowd enjoyed the sweet tinkles of the Tipaldi Brothers' twelve-piece Mandolin Orchestra, while famed banjoists Brooks and Denton plink-plinked a new twist on Chopin.[17]

But the star of the evening was no doubt the rapturously applauded Minnie Renwood, clad in violet tights and flowing white skirts, who gyrated away in her mysterious serpentine and other fancy dances to the jingle of a bright-ribboned tambourine. Her performance was rather a coup for the new roof garden, as White had managed to win her away from the Casino, where she had previously appeared. Her dance on the small stage was difficult to see over the heads of the crowd, forcing many women to stand on their chairs. But a better look revealed that her movements were strikingly similar to the famed serpentine dance pioneered by the renowned Loie Fuller. The new combination of swirling movement and lights had been developed by the dancer under Rudolph Aronson's direction and first performed by Fuller at the Casino Theatre in February 1892. After a disagreement over billing and pay, Fuller then took her

THE MADISON SQUARE ROOF GARDEN.

47. *The Madison Square Roof Garden, New York Herald* (May 29, 1892). Newsbank / Readex and the American Antiquarian Society.

dance to the Madison Square Theatre. Following the Renwood appearance on the roof garden, Fuller tried unsuccessfully to legally enjoin her imitator from performing the serpentine dance, which made it all the more appealing to the crowds.[18]

The rooftop crush was largely manageable most evenings until the concert program in the amphitheater ended and thousands began to file out toward the stairs and the elevator to reach the roof, just as crowds from the roof began their way downward. Every night, mobs were turned away disappointed, and rumors were hotly denied by management that the fire department had ordered the closing of the roof garden until additional exits could be constructed.[19]

Management did respond by opening the large stone staircase that led from the roof into the Garden Theatre and then onto Madison Avenue, but it was not enough. Ten days after the roof garden's opening, the city's building department ordered the erection of two more fire escapes, one each on the Twenty-Sixth and Twenty-Seventh Street sides of the building. Still, as the *New York Herald* observed of the roof garden, "it has been neither pleasant nor safe to take a delicately bred woman there—and it has been quite unpleasant enough for a stalwart man to get up and down."[20]

Finally, the only remedy was to increase the price of admission, at least for a few nights of the week, thereby limiting access to a more restricted crowd. It was not until a full week had passed that bandmaster Gilmore and his men were able to make their way up to the roof garden and to the stirring strains of the "Grand Army of the Republic March" finally and officially dedicate the spot.[21]

Once the crowds were limited, the Garden's garden soon became one of Manhattan's most appealing spots for summer entertainment,[22] with the *New York Herald* comparing it to Babylon's hanging gardens. With music, flowers, fountains, dancing, and wine and other refreshments enjoyed from sunset to midnight, the roof garden soon outstripped the amphitheater in attendance. Café society, "hard-working husbands deserted by their wives" for the summer, and "visiting country cousins" on holiday filled the roof while the "management happily raked in the shekels," or so the *Herald* wrote.[23] And when the weather was cool and rainy, it was reported that management would pay a young man in a straw boater to sit in the front row to make those shivering in warm coats feel a little more festive.[24]

Prior to the second summer, improvements were made for "the greater safety and peace of mind" of the audience, including a passageway through the brick wall to the roof of the amphitheater, the addition of fireproof iron staircases leading to the amphitheater's upper promenade, and two elevators to the exits on Twenty-Sixth Street.[25]

When the Casino Theatre opened its enlarged and much-improved roof garden just five days after the Garden had opened, with a ballet, various musical specialties, and a bird warbler, it too received positive reviews. But with limited seating and its tone more Frenchified and a bit more elevated, it would not pose much of a threat to Madison Square Garden's success, nor would any of the nine other roof gardens that soon followed—among them the Majestic, the Ansonia, the Café de Paris, Hammerstein's Paradise Roof Garden, the Terrace Garden, and the Cherry

Blossom Grove.[26] Rudolph Aronson may have come to regret his failure to patent his quite novel idea for the rooftops of New York,[27] especially as the idea spread to clubs, hotels, department stores, and hospitals to reclaim the "choicest part" of their buildings, and New Yorkers charted the summer breezes to determine at exactly which spot they might best spend their evening.[28]

23

A Home in the White City

IT WAS JUST AT THE END of that first summer season on the roof garden, on September 12, 1892, that *Diana* vanished from the top of the tower at the Madison Square Garden. All that evening the crowds on Broadway, on Madison Avenue, and crossing through the park sadly exclaimed, "Where is *Diana*?" or so reported the *New York Tribune*. The glittering goddess, a much-loved sight familiar to all New Yorkers, was gone. Twelve hundred pounds of divine had come down after just three days of preparation, and reportedly with less fuss than might have been imagined.[1]

•

Frank R. McCord, the contractor who had hoisted her up the Madison Square Garden tower almost exactly a year earlier, agreed to cover the $300 cost of her descent. Preparations began when he ordered a ship's mast, 57 feet tall, hauled up the tower and lashed firmly above the uppermost lantern. A boom, 35 feet long, was then rigged up with tackle and extended at right angles from the top of the mast. After the figure was bound with protective red flannel to prevent bruising, thick ropes were wound around her waist and heroic thighs. J. B. Knight, the foreman who had received the gold chain and charm from Stanford White for so smoothly landing the *Diana* on top of the tower, hitched up the five-strand ropes with a big hook and pulley. In place of the steam-driven engine, seven workmen hauled away, and the statue was lifted up and off the great iron spike that ran up through her left heel and leg. Gently they lowered the figure on her side to the floor of a small platform at the top of the tower, removed the crown of electric lights from her brow, released the hand that held her giant bow, and unfastened the drapery that flared out beyond her shoulders.[2]

Foreman Knight caught the rope and clambered up the topmost lantern to its topmost platform, while the crowd in the square and on the streets held their collective breath as the workmen followed. Then Knight suddenly lurched in pain with a sprained hand and had to be helped back to the lantern's parapet.

With the men on the pulleys, the boom once more lifted the *Diana* up, gently swinging it clear of the tower, swaying over the heads of the anxious crowd. Then, very slowly—as nearly two hours passed—she descended down the south side of the tower to briefly rest on the roof of the Twenty-Sixth Street arcade. Once again, workmen manned the ropes until the figure finally came to rest on the biggest wagon they could find, padded with an immense straw mattress 5 feet thick. But the wagon was only 15 feet long, leaving her feet to hang ingloriously out the back.

For once, Stanford White was not on-site to oversee the work. It appeared he was traveling, although the location remained rather vague; he told some he was sailing for Europe, others that he was heading south, and the newspapers that he was in Chicago working on plans for the fair.[3] By a quarter past four in the afternoon a team of heavy draft horses had hauled their precious cargo to the Pennsylvania Railroad Station where the figure was boxed for shipment back to Salem, Ohio. There at the foundry William Mullins would oversee repositioning the pipe through the ball of her foot and then her regilding before shipping the *Diana* off to Chicago.[4]

Bereft New Yorkers, bemoaning her absence, turned to poetry, reading through their tears "To *Diana* off the Tower" by W. J. Henderson, published in the September 18, 1892, *New York Times*, which included the verse:

For poised aloft in thy transparent air
She'll typify to all Chicago's fair.
Great is Diana in the boundless west!
(I hope they'll buy her a new flannel vest,
For there rude Boreas is at his best.)
Farewell Diana! by the limpid lake
A fitter home for virtue thou shalt make.

•

It was to the Windy City that *Diana* was headed and the Chicago World's Fair, or, more formally, the World's Columbian Exposition. As the celebration of the four-hundredth anniversary of the European discovery of America, it was to be the country's first great fair since the 1876 Centennial in Philadelphia and the first time the United States had invited the rest of the world to join in, with more than five thousand displays planned from forty-six states, fifty-one nations, and thirty-nine colonies. The fairgrounds were scheduled to be dedicated on October 21, 1892, although they actually would not be opened to the public until the first of the following May. The US Congress had committed the federal government to support a major celebration two years before, but an assortment of federal and municipal committees dillydallied long enough that the fair would miss the actual anniversary year of Columbus's arrival.[5]

New York had hoped to host the fair—as had Washington, DC, and St. Louis—and the city fought hard for it. But in the spring of 1890, when Congress made the final decision as to location, the vote on the eighth ballot went to Chicago with its $10 million offer to underwrite. Chicago's appeal was magnified by its location near the center of the country's population at the hub of both water and rail transportation. It also possessed the open space the fair would demand. To those representatives from the West and the Midwest who cast the deciding votes, Chicago may have also seemed more "American" than New York and more typical of the county's remarkable growth, particularly after its recovery from the great fire of 1871 that had destroyed thousands of buildings.[6] So *Diana* was actually New York's second painful loss to the Windy City, so dubbed for both its lakeshore breezes and its blowhard boosters.

•

Once Chicago had secured the fair, a group of prominent local businessmen formed the World's Columbian Corporation and hired Frederick Law Olmstead, America's foremost landscape architect and designer of New York's Central Park, to survey possible locations. On his recommendation, they selected the dreary, desolate, and wind-beaten morass along the shore of Lake Michigan seven miles south of city hall known as Jackson Park. Under Olmstead's direction, armies of workers drained the swampy hollows by dredging new lagoons, ponds, and basins linked by canals.[7] Daniel Hudson Burnham, partner in the prominent Chicago architectural firm of Burnham and Root, was made chief of construction and invested with virtually all control. With two hundred buildings to design for the 633-acre site, he reached beyond Chicago and called upon the country's best-known architects in New York and Boston.

McKim, Mead & White was invited to participate, as were prominent New York architects Richard Morris Hunt and George B. Post. But following the keen disappointment of losing the fair to Chicago, all were hesitant to commit. On January 10, 1891, the architects met in Chicago for the first on-site gathering, examining the inauspicious location on that cold and overcast winter's day.[8] After a good dinner, Burnham passionately proclaimed that the Columbian Exposition would certainly be the third greatest event in American history, following the Revolution and the Civil War, and that the same sort of self-sacrifice and teamwork would be required to make a success of it. He also promised that each architect would exercise full artistic control over their designs, and then sweetened the offer with a $10,000 recompense for working drawings and just a required visit or two to Chicago.[9]

Now won over, the architects confirmed the general plan suggested by Olmstead and Burnham, which envisioned grouping the fair's largest and most significant buildings to form the Court of Honor around the Great Basin, a rectangular body of water 350 feet wide by 1,100 feet long that would serve as the fair's centerpiece. As plans unfolded, buildings of slightly lesser importance would dot the shores of a meandering lagoon. The structures contributed by each of the states and foreign countries would cluster even further north around the Palace of Fine Arts set on the North Pond.

Finally, the more common amusements and attractions would be concentrated on a strip of parkland to the west named the Midway Plaisance. These would include a variety of exotic villages representing a number of foreign countries and peoples, most popularly Little Egypt with her "hoochie-coochie" belly dance. The standout feat of engineering, planned to rival the 1889 Paris Expo's Eiffel Tower, would be George Ferris's Great Wheel on the Midway, a 250-foot-high steel structure with cars the size of trolleys carrying more than two thousand passengers at a time and studded with three thousand blinking lights.

With the goal of order, harmony, and unity in plan and design, the architects agreed with Charles McKim's suggestion that all buildings in the Court of Honor and all major adjacent buildings be executed in the Greco-Roman classical style, as interpreted by the masters of the Italian Renaissance, with its grand proportions, festal style, and rich decoration. It was no accident that this was the style with which these mostly École des Beaux-Arts–trained architects were all familiar, and so would save time and money at the drawing board.[10]

Interestingly enough, the five architects assigned to the Court of Honor constituted a bit of a family through long-established ties and aesthetic sympathies. By dint of seniority, Chairman Hunt was given the focal Administration Building at the head of the court and basin; George B. Post, his onetime student, took the huge Manufactures and Liberal Arts Building, destined to be the largest building in the world under one continuous roof; the Boston firm of Peabody and Stearns—students of Post's students—requested Machinery Hall, which would house the huge electric dynamos that powered the fair; the Electricity Building was assigned to the Boston firm Van Brunt & Howe, now relocated to Kansas City; and to McKim, Mead & White went *Diana's* future home, the massive Hall of Agriculture, no doubt so assigned based on its size and location rather than any implied familiarity with its subject.

•

In February 1891 Charles McKim traveled to Chicago by private Pullman car, the first of his twenty-three fair-related visits, accompanied by architects Hunt and Post as they met to review preliminary sketches. Augustus Saint-Gaudens had also come along to Chicago. Initially offered $15,000 by Daniel Burnham to take charge of sculpture,[11] but far behind on a long list of commissions, Saint-Gaudens agreed instead to a consulting fee of $6,000 and recommended as primary sculptors old friends Daniel Chester French and Frederick MacMonnies.[12] During the second day of the meetings, Saint-Gaudens sat in a corner, silent as he often was, hardly moving. At last, he got up and walked over to Burnham and, taking hold of both of his hands, famously said, "Look here old fellow, do you realize this is the greatest meeting of artists since the fifteenth century?"[13]

Charles McKim eventually became Burnham's chief advisor on aesthetic matters, putting aside all other work and giving himself completely to the fair.[14] On McKim and Post's recommendation, an old friend, the painter Francis Millet, was hired as chief of decorations. He would earn his $15,000 fee by overseeing all the painted and sculpted decoration as well as much of the actual construction, serving as eyes on the scene for the New York architects now making only periodic visits to Chicago.[15]

The building facades were truly more like stage sets than architecture, for the pitch-pine lath and iron structures were quickly covered with a layer of stucco-like substance called staff, an inexpensive mixture of plaster of Paris, gypsum plaster, water, and jute fiber that was almost as stiff and tough as wood and could be cast or molded, colored, bored, sawed, and nailed. An eighteenth-century French invention that had long been used in Europe for such temporary structures, staff created the illusion of granite or marble when oiled, polished, or painted, but it would soon begin to crumble away unless kept up.[16] It was the 30,000 tons of staff, Millet explained, "that has allowed the architects to indulge in a veritable spree . . . to create a vision no monarch could have ever carried out, to erect temples, colonnades, towers, and domes of surpassing beauty and of noble proportions."[17]

•

For much of 1892 it had been rumored that *Diana* was likely headed to the World's Columbian Exhibition then under construction. However, despite being offered to fair officials at a cut-rate price, the figure of *Diana* had been refused and her fate left up in the air while Augustus Saint-Gaudens prepared a newer, more refined version for the Madison Square Garden tower.[18] In August 1892, just one month before her descent, the fair's executive committee board of directors announced a change of mind, finally agreeing to purchase the figure for the somewhat inflated price of $2,500. Soon she would take up her place on top of the great dome of the Hall of Agriculture.[19] Ever critical of Saint-Gaudens's sculpture, Alfred Trumble of *The Collector* noted that *Diana* would probably be less of a disappointment there in Chicago "where she would not be so absurdly disproportionate, although nothing," he added with his usual rancor, "would ever make her a great work of art."[20]

•

While the figure of *Diana* was deposed from her perch for being just a little too big for the Madison Square Garden tower, McKim, Mead & White's Hall of Agriculture was a broad enough base to amply support her. A $699,000 project, the hall was the third largest building at the fair and flanked the entire southern side of the Court of Honor, directly facing the gigantic Manufactures and Liberal Arts Building across the Great Basin. On the west side the building was linked by a colonnade to Machinery Hall and its dynamos, while on the east side lay Lake Michigan.[21]

Two stories tall and 500 by 800 feet, the hall covered 9 acres, with a total of 15 square acres of floor space. Designed by Charles McKim as a temple dedicated to Ceres, goddess of agriculture, it was also said to be the most Roman of all the buildings at the fair.[22] Constructed of wood and staff over a steel shell, the hall's central section was crowned by a great Pantheon-like dome 100 feet in diameter and 130 feet high, which some critics would dub a soup tureen,[23] but it would quite adequately serve as a home for the *Diana*.

Stanford White was also involved to some degree in the design,[24] and, superficially at least, there were certain resemblances to the Madison Square Garden in the facade, particularly the piers, the large arched windows, the continuous colonnade around the top of the building, and the use of corner pavilions. But unlike the Madison Square Garden, the Hall of Agriculture was literally covered with masses of statuary, most designed by Philip Martiny, Saint-Gaudens's onetime protégé who had also created the sculptural decoration for the Madison Square Garden Theatre and Concert & Assembly Hall.[25]

The hall's temple-like front, measuring 65 feet across, carried a festive pediment scene representing *The Triumph of Ceres*. Executed in staff by William Mead's Florence-based sculptor brother Larkin, it was filled with cavorting deities, including "a drunken looking Silenus, a sprightly young Bacchus, a lively Satyr playing cymbals, a gay young Bachante on the flute, a rather stunning Flora, a pretty good Jason, and a reclining Gaea, although Mercury may look a little sick at the stomach," as the *Boston Herald* described them.[26] Visitors entered the huge building under the pediment, passed between mammoth Corinthian columns 50 feet high and 5 feet in diameter into a vestibule filled with more of Philip Martiny's agriculturally themed statuary, and proceeded into a rotunda 100 feet in diameter under its great glass dome and then on to view its multitude of displays (including a mammoth cheese weighing more than 20,000 pounds).

•

Augustus Saint-Gaudens had sought for the western end of the Great Basin a "tremendous fountain, all movement, gaiety, and exuberance," and he had hoped that Frederic MacMonnies would assist him in the design. When MacMonnies refused, Saint-Gaudens realized that he was too busy to undertake the project on his own. MacMonnies then chose to submit his own design for the Columbian Fountain, intended to represent the triumph of the American Republic. The fountain, executed in gleaming marble-like staff at MacMonnies's studio in Paris and shipped across the ocean in pieces, was rather remarkably composed of a young, bare-breasted *Columbia* enthroned on the barge-of-state, with *Fame* trumpeting her arrival from the prow as *Father Time* steered at the stern, all accompanied by another thirty-five barely clad male and female allegorical figures, each 12 feet high, illuminated at night by electric fountain jets shooting crystal and gold, sapphire, ruby, and emerald-colored sprays.[27]

Stanford White called the fountain "howlingly swell,"[28] while Saint-Gaudens praised it as the most "beautiful conception of a fountain in modern times."[29] Saint-Gaudens wrote to MacMonnies, swearing it "the swellest fountain" that had ever been made. "You have done the fountain forever, G.D. you."[30] But when the fountain began to rival the *Diana* as the artistic talk of the fair, the old resentments erupted, and Saint-Gaudens privately recalled his suspicions that MacMonnies had stolen the idea for his goddess back in the day. He reminded his artist friend Paul Bion to "hide your devices or others more light-fingered will carry off the fruits of Victory. . . . I do not mean that my treasures have been stolen from me, only unconsciously others have deprived me of their lustre."[31]

•

Soon after the *Diana* had swung down off the Madison Square Garden tower, reports came from Chicago that the fair did not want her after all, at least not if the Woman's Christian Temperance Union had anything to say about it. They denounced the scheme to place a nude figure on the agricultural building's very prominent dome as a disgrace to both civilized womanhood and the American people. Plans were made to flood Anthony Comstock's Society for the Suppression of Vice with petitions to prevent it.[32] A boycott of the fair was also threatened if nude *Diana* was raised, and the pastor at the Wabash Avenue Methodist Episcopal Church preached a sermon on "Christ or Diana?"[33]

Aside from any moral grounds, there was concern that Chicago was "to be made a dumping-ground," the *Chicago Herald* thundered, "an asylum for all the cast-off statues, the errors in judgment of New York."[34] The art critic of the *Chicago Daily Tribune* concurred, calling the figure "unsightly, out of proportion, and unstatuesque."[35] Some papers poked fun at the moralists, noting with tongue firmly in cheek that those viewing the *Diana* at a height of 120 feet would need to rent field glasses in order to be shocked. "When decency is compelled to go to an expense of three or four dollars in order to be outraged, it is indeed time to hold indignation meetings and adopt resolutions." Similarly facetious suggestions were made in the press that *Diana* be painted sky-blue so that she blended into the landscape or be furnished with a skirt.[36]

Calling upon Comstock did not help the Woman's Christian Temperance Union's cause, and exposition president Harlow N. Higinbotham quickly assured the press that *Diana* would be placed in position just as she was, with no drapery added.[37] "Diana sans chemise may still be chaste—so curiously are modesty and clothing confused in the partially civilized mind,"[38] sniffed the *New York Sun*. The prominent Mrs. Potter Palmer, president of the fair's Board of Lady Managers, put the matter to rest by supporting *Diana*'s installation, adding that if there had been a suitable dome or tower on the Woman's Building the statue would have found a welcome resting place there.[39]

During all the hubbub, *Diana* remained at the Mullins foundry in Ohio. In addition to repairs and regilding, Stanford White had requested some modifications before the figure was shipped. "I don't wish *Diana* same as New York," he wrote to Mullins, "shorten her drapery to balance the figure. Make a ball 24 inches in diameter for her to balance upon."

48. *World's Columbian Exposition: Court of Honor,* Chicago, 1893, lantern slide. Brooklyn Museum Archives S03i2163l01_SL1. jpg, Goodyear Collection, Wikimedia Commons.

Fearing that she might be delivered late to the fair, he instructed Mullins to hurry the work and deliver as quickly as possible. "Push the *Diana* through on time at all hazards," he insisted.[40]

But once the *Diana* was delivered and installed on the top of the Hall of Agriculture, there was little discussion in the newspapers of her suitability. The fair was so "littered" with nude sculptures, both male and female, that the *Diana* faded from the national discussion. The *New York Sun* noted that the nudes might have been somewhat startling to those unsophisticated viewers of the Midwest, but it was particularly the male nudes "of heroic size and very boldly executed" that caused concern. "Worship of the beautiful may pardon the nude female figure, but the nude male figure never. . . . To place nude male figures indiscriminately about the great Fair buildings . . . is the very apotheosis of brutality."[41] Still, the article concluded with the hope that the shock of exposure to both male and female nudes "will work wonders in cultivating and refining them, and they will learn to love the beautiful in art."[42] Beyond that, there was little official or public reaction.

•

Stanford White was once again fully occupied doing double duty. In addition to his role in the Chicago fair, he was on the Honorary Advisory Committee for New York's own October 1892 Columbian celebration, serving on the art committee with Augustus Saint-Gaudens, Richard Hunt, Francis Millet, John La Farge, William Merritt Chase, and Louis Comfort Tiffany, among others. They were furiously working on the decorations for Fifth Avenue, which would serve as the line of march for the greatest military parade since the Civil War. White had designed an elaborate trellis arch to be constructed over the Fifth Avenue parade route at Twenty-Second Street, supported by twelve columns and decorated with flags, banners, bunting, and lighted lanterns. Over the next twelve blocks north on the avenue, he installed one hundred 60-foot poles topped by eagles, flags, shields, and streamers. For White it was the usual burst of frenzied energy the week before the celebration, staying up forty-eight hours without sleep and working in the rain on the final details, as well as supervising a fireworks display from the Madison Square Garden's roof garden and the illumination of both the Garden tower and city hall.[43]

Aside from his other projects, such as the new Columbia University campus, the New York Herald Building, and the Players Club, White had also designed two buildings for the Chicago fair—a temple-like pavilion for J. P. Morgan's White Star Lines Steamship Company and one for the humor magazine *Puck*.[44] "If it were not for the Roof Garden & the ballet girls I should have been dead long ago," he explained. But it all caught up with him a few days before the celebration, when he was confined to bed in howling pain, packed in ice and under morphine, unable to eat or drink—the victim, perhaps, of a bleeding ulcer. A lengthy recuperation followed, with minor surgery, daily visits to the doctor, and a strict milk diet, all intended to quiet the "little buzz-saw" still going on inside him.[45]

Saint-Gaudens was similarly occupied with Columbian celebrations in both Chicago and New York, but it is also likely that he was dealing with the messy complications of his wife discovering the existence of his mistress.[46] In an undated letter he rather high-handedly assured Augusta that "the quiet dignity of Mrs. MacMonnies and Mrs. White toward the gross actions of their husbands is far finer and commands a deeper respect than any other attitude they could possibly have taken and way down deep in their hearts their husbands respect them all the more. Although my action is a mere peccadillo in comparison to them, it has caused me a misery of mind you do not dream of. . . . [F]or a mutual peace of mind on this earth I beg of you not to come down from the high place you hold in my heart."[47] Then he moved Davida out of the city to a three-story clapboard home in the Noroton Heights section of Darien, Connecticut, which he visited often as "Mr. Clark, a traveling agent."[48]

•

The original plan had been to hand paint the architectural ornament on all the buildings at the Chicago World's Fair in different colors, but time ran out. There was already discoloration and weather damage to the staff before the fair even opened. Someone, it remains unclear who, suggested they paint all the buildings cream white, which, as it happened, evoked the marble of ancient Greece and Italy. Francis Millet met with Joseph Binks, a former maintenance worker at Marshall Field & Company wholesale store in Chicago who had invented a quick way to whitewash its enormous basement. Millet assembled a paint gang and hooked up Binks's hand-pump-operated, hose-and-nozzled-wand paint-spraying machine to a 5-horse-power electric engine–driven compressor that allowed two men to do the work of twenty-five. With white lead- and oil-based paints, they quickly painted all the buildings—and the glorious White City was born.[49]

•

In April 1893, just before the opening to the public, Stanford White, Charles McKim, and Frederick MacMonnies visited the fair, rowing out in a little boat along the Great Basin and among the lagoons, viewing the magnificent buildings, the rich sculptural decoration, the great vistas. White was so taken with the fair that he soon returned with his wife and son and described the Court of Honor, with its thousands of electric lights and lanterns, as "almost the finest thing I have ever seen in my life." He returned again in October for one last look and became so enchanted by the Commissioner's House in the Java Village that he bought it on the spot and had it reassembled on his estate on Long Island.[50] Augustus Saint-Gaudens was equally taken with the fair and later recalled the days that he passed there "linger in memory like a glorious dream."[51] And as Charles McKim wrote, it was "a beautiful time . . . and it would be pleasant for the rest of our natural lives to be able to look back to it and talk it over and over and over again."[52]

24

A Second *Diana*

BEFORE THE FIRST SCULPTURE of *Diana* was ever set upon the Madison Square Garden tower in late 1891, there were whispers that Augustus Saint-Gaudens had a new figure already in mind, that it would correct the earlier defects—the oppressive height, the stiff and awkward drapery, the misplacement of the mounting post through her heel—and that perhaps he was already at work modeling a new version.[1] Those rumors proved to be true, as once again, in the spring of 1892, a model took the stand in Saint-Gaudens's studio.

As for her identity this round, there were several prime candidates among the fifty or sixty or so top professional female models in New York.[2] One was eighteen-year-old Lillie Daly, popular for her petite yet well-proportioned figure and said to be one of Saint-Gaudens's favorites.[3] After briefly trying a career on the stage, Daly began posing at the National Academy of Design and at the Art Students League. However, she found to her distress that although the male students behaved well while she was on the "throne," after class was dismissed and rules not in force they were quite the pests, impertinently offering to walk her home or take her to supper.[4]

Then she tried modeling for the ladies' classes, but there were rude remarks made about the "common figure-model,"[5] or so she felt. The moment she came up onto the stand, their eyes seemed to say, "How can you? Don't you feel dreadfully ashamed?"[6] Oddly enough, it was said that the women's classes tended to choose the most painful poses, keeping a model long in place and ignoring her signs of fatigue—reflecting perhaps a certain unease on the part of the students with working-class women.[7] "Nobody knows what we have to put up with," Daly complained to a reporter. "Do they suppose we stand on one foot in a badly heated studio all day just to amuse ourselves?"[8]

Then there were the duffers and dilettantes—society men with money to spend and fancy fixed-up studios who did not know how to paint but offered ten dollars a day plus supper with champagne, or the dabblers who hired Daly and then preached "it's wicked to pose."[9] Finally she vowed only to pose for well-known, established artists like Saint-Gaudens, and Daly swore it was she who provided *Diana*'s strong back.[10]

According to the many newspaper accounts aimed at the public eager for details of studio life, it was common knowledge that the best models were girls of Irish heritage like Lillie Daly, prized for the delicate texture of their Celtic complexions, their fine coloring, and their slim figures.[11] Aside from Daly there had been rumors that the model for the second *Diana* was another Irish girl named Nellie Fitzpatrick, picked out of the chorus line to model by Stanford White himself, yet said in later years to be employed as a charwoman at the Hotel Plaza.[12] A certain Netta Wildey, also known as Annette or Antoinette, spread the story that she was the poser, citing dates, times, and places to whomever would listen.[13] In fact, nearly every model in New York would eventually claim to have stood for the second *Diana*.[14]

The most likely candidate, however, was actually the slim, well-muscled, nineteen-year-old Julia Baird, known to most as "Dudie" for the childish way she pronounced her own name when very young. She was a favorite of Thomas Dewing's, but she also worked for Charles Dana Gibson, Kenyon Cox, and Edward Austin Abbey, among others of their circle. Baird would claim herself as the only model to ever pose for *Diana*, and Saint-Gaudens would never publicly deny it.[15] "The thrones that I haven't sat on are so few that you could count them on your fingers,"[16] she stated quite proudly. And it was rumored that Baird might have modeled for the first *Diana* as well.[17]

Like many other young women making their own way in the 1890s, the auburn-haired Dudie came from a hardworking, Scotch-Irish Catholic family fallen on difficult times. A native New Yorker and the second-youngest of seven children, she began to pose in her teens when a neighbor, an artist, spotted her through an open door, made a sketch,

49. *Reclining Nude Figure of a Girl*, Thomas Wilmer Dewing, modeled by Julia Baird, undated pastel on paper mounted on paperboard. Smithsonian American Art Museum, Washington, DC, Gift of John Gellatly / Art Resource, NY.

and suggested that if she were ever in need of money she might find a job modeling. When times grew harder, Baird headed for the uptown studio buildings, knocking on doors until one of the artists took her on. Her parents discovered that she had been posing in the nude and disowned her, but more engagements followed, and she was soon earning fifty cents an hour.[18]

According to Thomas Dewing, Dudie Baird was a lively free spirit with a down-to-earth manner who seemed to get the hang of a pose right off, knew how to keep perfectly still, and kept silent. Even more important, she seemed to know just the sort of feeling and effect an artist sought to capture.[19] She would soon pose in the nude for a series of thirty pastels by Dewing, the most openly sensual of the group purchased and framed to his own design by Stanford White. White was rapidly building a collection of "young, sweet, and alluring nudes with firm little bubs that stand up,"[20] intended to shock all the straightlaced people in town. Recalling the fuss Comstock and others made about the first *Diana*, White stated that he "got so mad that I'm going to make a little collection of nudes and when I die give it to the Metropolitan Museum of Art!"[21]

•

Back in the studio, if Baird's quite detailed but somewhat dubious account in the *New York Herald* is to be believed, she took up her position as *Diana* supported between two ladders in the full pose as if she were about to send the arrow flying from its bow. But this time, instead of modeling a small figure that would be mechanically enlarged, Saint-Gaudens decided to begin with a life-sized model. Thus, six assistants applied plaster directly to Baird's various body parts, section by section. She described the four or five minutes when the lime began to warm up and the plaster began to set as quite peculiar. She dared not move, for the slightest motion would have spoiled the mold. Then, finally, when it was solid hard they cut each mold with a thread and removed it in two sections. By her recollection it took three-quarters of a day to finish casting her figure, section by section. When all the parts were assembled, according to Baird's rather fanciful retelling, the 5-foot 6-inch exact cast of her body was sent back to the W. H. Mullins Company in Ohio to be enlarged.[22]

•

It was generally accepted, at least in the New York art world, that Dudie Baird probably did pose for some or perhaps much of the *Diana* figure but that she was not the only model.[23] Artists were well aware that few models were fully proportioned according to their aesthetic needs or preferences. Due to the crushing high corsets in the late nineteenth century, firm breasts were said to be the hardest thing to find, and *Diana*'s had to be firm indeed. Equally difficult was finding a model who had not injured the muscles of her back and waist with the pressure of those corset stays that would break down the smooth, firm sweep of line. Another great problem was knock-knees, and few were the girls who, whether from high heels or "careless walking," did not have the slight outward tendency of the calves. Equally difficult was finding the perfect foot that, despite the current footwear, was flexible, round, firm, and muscular.[24]

Thus, it was a very common practice for artists to choose one model for her limbs, another for her torso, and so forth, with many models known for one specific aspect of their anatomy, as William Merritt Chase's notebook revealed. Artists frequently required as many as five or six different models to sit for a single nude figure, in addition to another for the face.[25] In confirmation of Saint-Gaudens's practice, model Kate Clark claimed to have posed for him on many occasions, but said he regularly used just her waist, hips, hands, and neck.[26]

As for the large number of candidates who claimed to have been Saint-Gaudens's *Diana*, it is also possible that he played a bit of the deceiver, allowing a whole string of models to sincerely believe that hers alone was to be *Diana*'s perfect figure. Stanford White seemed to confirm this theory; when questioned as to the model's identity in early 1893, he insisted there was no one figure on which she was based and that "she's just a fancy sketch."[27] After Julia Baird's claim was published, the *Boston Herald* reported that some seventeen women from various parts of the country each swore that it was she who had been the model.[28] To further confound matters, in 1956 Homer Saint-Gaudens declared that he had never heard of Baird and that he was quite certain that she had not posed for the figure.[29]

The second *Diana*'s face seemed little changed from the first version, long believed to represent Saint-Gaudens's mistress Davida. But an "unnamed society woman" was also suggested for this go-round, and if so, a likely candidate may have been the writer and art critic Mariana Griswold Van Rensselaer, for whom Saint-Gaudens created an 1888 low-relief portrait and with whom he was said to have had a close, affectionate, and possibly flirtatious relationship.[30] However, as Jennifer Hardin points out, Diana's facial features were still somewhat abstracted and idealized, and perhaps Saint-Gaudens "deliberately avoided fidelity to the model in order to distance himself from the actuality of the body . . . enhancing the platonic qualities that an ideal female nude ought to possess."[31]

In addition, a most shocking claim emerged in newspapers nationwide in 1894. Dailies from San Francisco to Saginaw reported that the actual model for the *Diana* had been a young British gentleman! Was it possible that this paragon of ideal and innocent young American womanhood had been portrayed by a man, and a foreigner at that, the press demanded?[32] Regardless of whether this was the actual case for the *Diana*, there was artistic precedence for this sort of gender play. For instance, in Donatello's famed *David*, of which Saint-Gaudens was quite fond, this Italian Renaissance sculptor did incorporate elements of female anatomy, broadening his figure's thighs and pelvis, widening and rounding the buttocks, and adding fatty tissue to the chest to create small breasts.[33]

If Saint-Gaudens did indeed use a male model or incorporate masculine bits of anatomy, those features are likely to be found in the torso and the legs. As Saint-Gaudens himself observed, "long-leggedness is not common with women, although it is an essential requirement for beauty."[34] A male model may also have accounted for the *Diana*'s wide waist, very firm and rather flat buttocks, and exceedingly long arms. Interestingly, in 1910, when a female Australian swimming champ compared her athletic physical measurements to *Diana*'s, she declared the figure to be quite masculine, measuring a good bit larger proportionately than her own at the waist, thighs, calf, ankle, upper arm, forearm, and wrist.[35] *Diana*'s body is also longer proportionately to the head than is typically found in the female figure.[36] The possible use, at least in part, of a male model might also explain why the original clay model and the resulting plaster cast, now in the collection of the Saint-Gaudens National Historical Park, is significantly taller than Baird's 5 feet 6 inches.[37]

As for the identity of the unknown young British gentleman, the name of W. Graham Robertson might be considered. A set designer and playwright, he was a constant companion of Oscar Wilde and a dear friend of John Singer Sargent. Robertson did indeed pose for the British painter Walter Crane in 1881 for a painting of Diana and other immortals of uncertain shape and sex because, according to Robertson, the artist's wife objected to his use of female nude models.[38] Since there is no direct evidence that Robertson ever visited New York or actually posed for the *Diana*, the story of his modeling for a Diana in England might have simply become entangled among the gossip surrounding Saint-Gaudens's figure and confused in the press.

•

Augustus Saint-Gaudens continued to work on the slightly less than half-sized, 6-foot clay model of *Diana* into the summer of 1892, although

50. Model of the second *Diana* in Augustus Saint-Gaudens's New York studio, 1891. The Museum of the City of New York / Art Resource, NY.

passing on some of the detailing to brother Louis.[39] The clay figure was at last delivered to John Walthausen, the plaster molder on West Forty-First Street, where additional casts were made and the work completed by the end of September 1892.[40]

For months White and Saint-Gaudens had held long and secret consultations in well-guarded studios where no one spoke above a whisper and their assistants were sworn to secrecy, all more mysterious about their plans and intentions than if they were plotting to blow up the Garden with dynamite, or so the newspapers reported.[41] It was the size and proportion of the *Diana* that had them concerned. Just to be certain that all was correct, in December 1892 Saint-Gaudens suggested that they make an enlarged dummy and haul it up somewhere high for a look. Stanford White investigated a few tall buildings nearby, and then it struck them— why not the Madison Square Garden tower itself?[42]

At a freezing cold dawn in January 1893, a half-dozen workmen hauled up three big boxes delivered from Walthausen and pulled three huge and shapeless bits of yellow-painted plaster of Paris from their beds of hay. Stuck together they formed a rude yet identifiably female figure that men from Post & McCord hoisted up the tower for just a few moments, so as not to give it all away. Was it true, as rumored, that White and Saint-Gaudens were hiding behind trees in Madison Square to squint at the figure's proportion by the light of the rising sun?[43]

"No, it doesn't look anything like the new *Diana*," White assured the curious press, "it's just a trial." Would the new *Diana* differ much from the old one? they asked. "She will be entirely different," White assured them. "We haven't yet decided on her drapery, which is only a device for catching the wind, as she is a weather-vane you know."[44] Saint-Gaudens confirmed the difficulty in estimating the figure's optimum height. "We're not certain if the new *Diana* should be 11 and a half feet or 13, but this test should decide it." The trial figure came down, and 13 feet was confirmed.[45]

Meanwhile Lillian Russell, the grand stage star, was so taken by the prospect of the new *Diana* that she asked if she might place a gold bracelet on the statue's arm when it was finally installed. "Just a bracelet and a sweet smile will probably complete the goddesses' attire," the *Evening World* observed. "Please excuse us while we blush,"[46] added the *Boston Daily Globe*.

•

Back in the chaos of the studio, Saint-Gaudens and his ten assistants continued to tinker with *Diana* and her accoutrements through the spring of 1893 until Walthausen's final plaster casts were complete and ready to be sent off to the W. H. Mullins Company for fabrication.[47] William Mullins

sent a quote for casting the figure—this time in either bronze or aluminum—which he assured Stanford White would be made exactly in accordance with the plaster model, would be properly gilt with their best gold
leaf, would be made to his and Saint-Gaudens's satisfaction, and would be
shipped to New York for the sum of $1,650.[48] His bid was accepted, but the
two men did not trust the shipping of the molds to just anyone, including
Mullins. With detailed instructions as to value and care, only Walthausen
was allowed to pack the precious cargo for the trip to Ohio.[49]

At the Mullins foundry the half-sized plaster model of *Diana* was
enlarged to full size and plaster casts made. After seriously considering
the use of lighter weight aluminum, the sculptor and architect resorted
once again to 32-sheet copper. Fifty pairs of male and female dies were
cast, and the sheet metal was stamped by drop presses with hammers
varying in weight from 50 to 1,000 pounds.[50] The stamped sheet copper
pieces were then cut, riveted, and soldered around a central iron armature
with two spoked wheels[51] in the torso. Then the figure was primed and
sized with a mixture of linseed oil, shellac, and conifer oil.

51. Second *Diana* at the
W. H. Mullins foundry,
1893. Courtesy of the
US Department of the
Interior, National Park
Service, Saint-Gaudens
National Historical Park,
Cornish, NH.

During the process, White kept in close contact with Mullins, and when it was time to cover the figure with a layer of gold foil, he sent instructions to gild the drapery in a lighter, whiter gold, and "I do not mean a green gold," he wrote. "Be sure to notify me or Mr. Saint-Gaudens before the Diana is boxed up so that someone may go and approve. Again," he insisted, "be very careful, make extra good job of gilding and properly protect."[52]

•

Diana reborn was safely delivered back to the city by November 1, 1893, and the half-sized model ready to be photographed for *Harper's Weekly*.[53] All New York was eager to know exactly how this second figure would differ from the first, aside from the obvious reduction of some 5 feet in height and 500 pounds in weight. Saint-Gaudens described her as "light and breezy and far more becoming than the tall and heavy original."[54] In general the figure was slenderer, more natural, and more buoyantly poised. Her face was thinner and more elegant, with her hair more smoothly rendered and swept up into a fashionable Psyche knot at the back of her head. The crescent forehead piece had been removed, while her stylish pompadour bangs seemed to form a crescent of their own.[55]

"So artistically has she been molded," the *New York Advertiser* sighed, "that each little dimple about the knees and arms, the curve of the limbs, the rounded shoulder and the shapely bust (the sort greybeards dream about) are revealed with minute faithfulness to nature."[56] Her breasts did seem smaller and more firm, as befits a virgin goddess, and the torso rather more elongated. The waist was more defined, although the hips were straight and slender, and her buttocks perhaps flatter. The modeling of her legs—which some found to be coarse in the first version—was thinner and far more refined, and they were gracefully extended, especially the right one with its less acute bend.[57]

In answer to the public's most pressing question, *Diana*'s drapery was as scant as ever, with the objections of Anthony Comstock and other protestors completely ignored.[58] There were, however, a few small differences. The scarf was attached by a bit of ribbon below the breasts and draped over her left shoulder, rather than between her breasts and over her right shoulder, and it rose higher above her more elongated torso, flowing out behind her in the breeze.[59] Although the line of the drape was still rounded to function as a rudder, it was less exaggeratedly so and was shaped more like a water cracker this time than a pretzel.[60]

This second *Diana* also carried a different type of bow in her straightened left arm, a recurve with flattened riser or center section of the type employed by Roman imperial archers. However, it was equipped with a Mongolian-style release, with the thumb draw and arrow located on the right side of the bow.[61] The arrow held at the ready was positioned lower across her neck so that it did not obscure her face but angled higher up. The figure's mounting rod was correctly placed through the ball of the left foot, and the bearings upon which she rotated were also improved and augmented.[62] This smaller and lighter figure would revolve more easily and more accurately, with a better connection made to the wind dial on the south face of the tower.

As art critic Royal Cortissoz observed, "The little goddess now has movement and elasticity as well as dignity; there is more strength in her limbs than there was, and there is more grace." According to Cortissoz, an old friend and former McKim, Mead & White office boy, the final bill—somewhere between $5,000 and $6,000—was indeed paid by Stanford White and Augustus Saint-Gaudens from their own pockets.[63]

•

On Saturday morning, November 10, 1893, the new *Diana* was ferried back to Madison Square Garden and set down to rest on Twenty-Sixth Street, heavily wrapped in what appeared to be bed coverlets and burlap. Her bow, arrow, and the copper globe on which she was to stand were wrapped separately. Members of the Garden's staff rigged up a derrick with block and fall tackle, and *Diana* was hoisted to the top of the roof garden's colonnade and then to the tower loggia, where she was stowed on her stomach atop burlap stuffed with hay. The figure would be assembled here and raised complete, rather than attaching the bow and arrow after she had been installed. It was also at this point that a coat of sizing and additional sheets of gold leaf, hammered thin, would be layered on and gently brushed into place.[64]

The plan was to haul her to the top of the tower a week later, on November 17, but the installation had to be postponed one day until all arrangements were complete and the wind calm. And perhaps the fracas across the square at Delmonico's the previous night had left nerves a bit raw, after an unemployed, "socialist-leaning" stonecutter shot up the restaurant with cries of "Down with the rich" while formally dressed diners dove under tables and out through open Twenty-Sixth Street windows. No one was injured in the incident, but the concern that some "radicalist crank" might cause damage to the *Diana* could not be completely ignored.[65]

On the eve of her installation, Stanford White issued a rather overblown statement to the press on the figure's history, with or without Saint-Gaudens's acquiescence, to explain that neither he nor the sculptor had any idea that the original *Diana*

> would become the noticeable and prominent figure that it afterward became. We both felt a new figure must be made, in proper proportion to the tower and one that Saint-Gaudens would be willing to have his name connected with. He certainly was not willing to do so with the old statue as this was very quickly made from a small model not over 18 inches high, which was hastily enlarged without superintendency on the sculptor's part, and the pose of which was seriously altered by a metal worker with the post through the heel, etcetera, etcetera. Rest assured that the new *Diana* has been very carefully modeled life-size and carefully thrown up under his supervision to its present height. While the figure is practically the same in idea as the old one, it is entirely different in poise and proportion.[66]

Just after dawn on the morning of November 18, 1893, the second *Diana* finally began her rise to the top of the tower, unceremoniously hauled up by her ankles to a horizontal position, the bulk of her weight resting upon her left ear. Additional ropes were then placed under her chin to sling her upright and into midair. By this time the streets around the Garden were once again crowded with onlookers. As the windlass on the derrick creaked, the figure rose slowly until noon, when finally she was swung upright over the iron rod on the top of the highest lantern. There was a slight hitch in trying to set her down squarely, as a section

52. *Diana* on the Madison Square Garden tower, ca. 1912, photograph by DeWitt Clinton Ward. Courtesy of the US Department of the Interior, National Park Service, Saint-Gaudens National Historical Park, Cornish, NH.

of the mounting rod had been wrought too thick, but with some twisting and pressure the workmen succeeded in setting her toe down plumb.[67]

When the figure was in position her covering was removed, and as the sun broke through the clouds a few minutes later she once again "shone forth in all her splendor."[68] A wind from the northwest began to blow, and she gracefully spun about, pointing her arrow into the wind for the rest of the day. As the sky darkened, a circle of incandescent light appeared at her feet. As a surprise for the crowd, this *Diana* had gone up fully wired and illuminated from top to bottom. The tower also was fully lit to honor her return. "Hail to the new *Diana*," cheered the *Evening World*, "and if any man attempts to haul her down and pack her off to Chicago—make him go too!"[69]

•

However, for Augustus Saint-Gaudens, the perfectionist who lagged years behind on the completion of a slew of projects, this was hardly the end of modifications to the figure. Just one week after she was installed on the tower, Saint-Gaudens decided that her scarf did not seem large enough or properly draped to function effectively. So down came the drapery. At the same time, her right leg was temporarily removed, as it had been battered during the installation process and needed to be smoothed.[70]

Still Saint-Gaudens was dissatisfied. Now the drapery was too voluminous and it floated too freely, so the scarf was lightened by the loss of a fold or two and its rounded outline made more of an oval by cutting away at its interior. In addition, the tail of the scarf was lightened to a more flowing, dynamic S curve. When the alterations were complete, the scarf was then hauled back up and reattached.[71]

Although some may have considered the second *Diana* a bit of a usurper,[72] soon most New Yorkers were once again in love with their virgin goddess, as evidenced by the *New York Sun*:

> Some persons can tell you the exact height and weight of Diana. The length of her bow, the girth of her waist, but New York is really not concerned with these statistics. It is her airy poise, her grace, her glory, her unapproachable aloofness, her goddesshood of the air that attracts and tantalizes and delights. She has cultivated the imagination of the whole city. From her airy height, poised seemingly on tiptoe, and lifted high above the sordid struggle of ant-like men below, she teaches in eloquent silence her daily aesthetic lesson.[73]

25

Within the Tower

THE NIGHT the Madison Square Garden's roof garden opened, on May 30, 1892, Stanford White topped off the evening by inviting a group of best pals to view his new tower apartment. "I don't know of anything like it in the world or so chic," he confided to a friend. "It is quite like Fairyland," he added, and his guests were tickled to death.[1] White bristled in the following weeks, however, when word got out to the newspapers about the delights of his new place. He gave orders that no one should be admitted in his absence under any circumstances, and he tried to squelch any further publicity, hoping that his residence would remain anonymous.[2] When summoning the private elevator and discovering another passenger already in the car, he would bellow at the night operator, "When I ring, the elevator is to stop at no other floor!"[3]

Virtually always on the spur of the moment, White would issue invitations by telegram or messenger boy asking invitees to attend the following evening at eight for a "shindig" or supper "with frills."[4] White did host evenings just for gents, when "the pigs are in the poke," as he put it, and "ready for sausage making,"[5] but there were other sorts of evenings as well, particularly post-theater dinners where wife Bessie, well aware of his rooms in the tower, often played hostess.

Arriving perhaps in one of those new green and red motorized taxicabs, guests would be delivered to the Garden's Twenty-Sixth Street tower entrance. Once inside, they would be confronted by two great staircases, each 9 feet wide, one winding above the other. One staircase led solely to the Concert & Assembly Hall, while the second staircase of 602 steps led to the roof garden. Unlike the general public, invited guests were able to use the tower's private elevator to reach White's apartment on the sixth floor, situated as were all apartments between the roof garden and the first lookout gallery.[6]

The tower's thick, brick walls left an inner space on each floor of just some 30 by 30 feet. Described in newspaper advertisements as bachelor apartments, each of the seven units took up the entirety of its floor, wrapping around the elevator shaft to include three full rooms, along with a kitchenette, pantry, and bathroom that could be arranged to suit. Most tenants, however, chose to use the space for offices or studios rather than living quarters, and the tower was nearly deserted at night.[7] The rent was steep, precluding all but the very few who could afford such a unique address and its stunning views: the shining silver East River and the low line of the Long Island shore on one side; Madison Square, Broadway, and Fifth Avenue on the other side, and beyond that the Hudson and the higher, greener line of the New Jersey hills.

Stanford White's apartment was indeed quite remarkable, finished in hardwoods and luxuriously appointed. The space was arranged into an elegantly furnished parlor, two bedrooms, and a bathroom. Sheets and towels of the best quality were ordered from Lord & Taylor while W. & J. Sloane provided the carpet and heavy drapes.[8] The rest of the apartment's furnishings were as artistic as would be expected. Here, away from the more formal home he and Bessie kept on Gramercy Park, White was able to indulge his leopard skin-draped fantasies. The rooms were warm and cozy, heated by steam and lit by a few well-placed electric lamps tucked among the flower vases and bay and palm trees draped with twinkling electric lights.[9]

•

On a typical evening, waiters would pass glasses of dry champagne and sparkling Apollinaris water, while White, restless as a whirlwind, flashed around the room.[10] The dinner ingredients would have been packed up and trucked over from Sherry's restaurant at Thirty-Seventh and Fifth Avenue and prepared by a cook working madly in the small kitchenette. The typical first course of oysters would be spread upon a great crescent-shaped table covered with golden damask and bunches of orchids. Thereupon might follow in head-spinning profusion a cream of lettuce soup, lobster à la Newberg, a timbale of grouse in puff pastry, sorbet, roasted beef, salad, cheese, and elaborate desserts, while two waiters continuously filled the glasses with burgundy.[11] The meal would be followed by continued good conversation, cigars for the gentlemen, and dancing to the accompaniment of a Neapolitan mandolin band.[12]

The crowd was typically a mix of society, theater, and art, with John La Farge, Frederick MacMonnies, photographer James Breese, and partners McKim and Mead regular guests. Even Augustus Saint-Gaudens often attended, dressed in the previous year's rough cloth suit, tucked into a corner and looking shy. For him, it would have to have been a casual evening, not a "sassiety" affair where the social rigmarole caused him more pain than pleasure. A chummy dinner with White and a friend or two at the Players Club was much more to Saint-Gaudens's comfort and liking.[13]

Some of the tower's other tenants might also drop by, like Daniel Chester French, who rented a studio, or inventor Peter Cooper Hewitt, who had turned his rooms into an experimental laboratory. Newly arrived from Paris to claim another of the studios was the ever-opera-cloaked architect Whitney Warren, who signed his notes to White as "Bibi la Poupette" and to whom White was exceedingly devoted. Warren's sister, the witty Mrs. Harriet Louise Warren Goelet, wife of client and friend Robert Goelet and herself a painter, had acquired the top-floor studio that White would eventually take over and turn into an even more exotic playland when she vacated the space in 1899.[14]

•

During the winter months of 1893–94, if the topic of the Chicago World's Fair came up, there would likely be a sudden, strained silence among the dinner guests and a heartache in that silence. It had been universally acknowledged that the White City was built to be temporary, a fleeting dream, nothing more substantial than a few moments of beauty that could never last and "should all be swept away in the same magical manner in which it appeared,"[15] wrote Charles McKim. When the fair ended in October 1893, Daniel Burnham had considered blowing up the buildings with dynamite or burning them down to save the expense of professional deconstructors and the hauling away of debris.[16]

But the gods of fire saved him much of the effort. It began on July 10, 1893, while the fair was still in progress, in the Cold Storage Building and warehouse, designed by Franklin P. Burnham and erected by the Hercules Iron Works of Aurora, Illinois. The structure served to demonstrate their famed ice-making and freezing machinery and to provide refrigeration for food and drink served at the fair. One of the larger buildings at the site, it was located just outside the fair proper, to the west of the Great Basin and Court of Honor, behind the Central Railroad Station.

Rather remarkably, the Cold Storage Palace, as it was known, was a quite literal copy of the Madison Square Garden, with belvederes at each of the four corners of the five-story structure and a replica of the Giralda-inspired tower, 225 feet high, which for aesthetics' sake concealed the coal-fired boiler's iron chimney within. Like Stanford White's tower, it was topped with a decorative loggia and lantern, but this tower was built entirely of wood covered with staff that reached just 30 inches above the chimney's upper rim. The tower and its lantern top were to have been constructed of wrought iron and lined with asbestos as protection from sparks and heat, but whether for the economy of time or funds, this part of the plan was ignored.[17]

On the day the fire began a newly created skating rink on the top floor was being iced up, which may have caused the boilers to overheat. After the fire broke out at the top of the tower flue stack, some twenty firemen quickly climbed ropes to the loggia roof. Just before they reached the summit, suddenly and to the horror of the tens of thousands of gathered spectators, there was a fierce outburst of flame 50 feet below. Realizing they only had seconds to escape before the tower collapsed, a few were able to slide down ropes or hoses before they snapped or burned through. Fourteen firemen were left trapped on top of the tower with no means of escape. They clasped hands in their last farewell, and one by one jumped 100 feet from the loggia to the main roof as the spectators below wailed in anguish. A few were left on the tower when it tottered and fell, crashing through the roof. In all, sixteen men died and twenty-two were injured. There is no evidence as to how White may have felt about this architectural homage intended for such a mundane purpose. But when photographs and drawn images of the tower in flames circulated around the table, surely they must have been quite nightmarish.[18]

53. *Chicago Fire-Burning of Cold Storage Warehouse—Worlds Fair*, Charles Graham, *Harper's Weekly* (July 22, 1893). Keystone-Mast Collection, California Museum of Photography, University of California, Riverside.

Then in January 1894 fire struck the fair once again. The Court of Honor had been deserted since the fair had ended three months before, although a guard occasionally toured the grounds. On the afternoon of January 8, he chased out several vagrants who had been camping at the northern end. They headed off to the opposite end of the peristyle, just east of McKim, Mead & White's agricultural building, and it was widely assumed that it was they who had accidentally or maliciously set the fire that began there. When the guard discovered the flames, he could not find a working fire-alarm box to send in the call, and by the time the first engines arrived the fire was already beyond control.[19]

As a crowd of fifty thousand watched from along the lakeshore, the peristyle's great plaster cornices and columns gave way and crashed like thunder through the streets of the White City, taking with them much of the Great Basin's heroic sculpture. The flames soon spread to the roof of George B. Post's hugely imposing Manufactures and Liberal

Arts Building, destroying with the structure its mural paintings by well-known New York artists Kenyon Cox, J. Carroll Beckwith, Walter Shirlaw, Francis Millet, J. Alden Weir, and others. The entire peristyle end of the Court of Honor—said to be one of the most beautiful architectural creations of the day—was completely destroyed. "Athens has crumbled," bemoaned the *New York Times*.[20]

One month later, a small fire was found set in a remote corner of the Hall of Agriculture when flammable material was stuffed down a wiring hole. It was quickly extinguished, as was a second, much larger fire set later that afternoon. The second blaze did do some damage to the dome and begrimed the building's white facade. Inexplicably, firebugs struck again on February 14, setting fire to the colonnade that ran between the Hall of Agriculture and Machinery Hall.[21]

Finally, ten days after that, in February 1894 the arsonists fully succeeded, setting a fire at the Hall of Agriculture's grand entrance. The flames ran up the columns to the roof and quickly spread toward *Diana's* central dome. Burning through the roof's interior, embers soon began dropping to the floor, and the supports gave way with a crash, bringing down the dome in ruins and leaving nothing but scorched walls and blackened columns.[22]

The identity of the perpetrators and their possible motive for the fires remained a mystery. No practical reason was clear for the destruction of the fair's Court of Honor and even more determinedly the Hall of Agriculture, as there was no salvage value to the buildings, no insurance, no work for the unemployed in rebuilding them, no great interest on the part of the public in preserving them. The newspapers debated whether the fires might have been set by revolutionaries or anarchists. Or perhaps as part of a criminal conspiracy to attract crowds of spectators through which pickpockets might run free. Or simply as an act of ordinary mischief.[23]

As for Augustus Saint-Gaudens's first and original *Diana*, which had reigned from the top of that now-destroyed dome, Lawrence White believed it lost to the flames. However, the *Chicago Tribune*, the *Chicago Daily Inter Ocean*, and the *New York Times* reported that the figure had been wisely removed from the building about six weeks earlier—at the time of the first arson—to the safety of the Columbian Museum,[24] established in September 1893 in the former Palace of Fine Arts. Or so it was believed.

•

After such events had likely been discussed far into the night at one of Stanford White's shindigs, the dancing would commence once more in his tower apartment, and in the early hours of the morning a few brave souls would head for the top of the dining table to demonstrate their fancy footwork.[25] On some occasions a last guest or two would be ordered out into the private elevator for a run-up to the second loggia outlook at 225 feet above the ground, wide and comfortable with a surrounding stone balcony. From there an iron staircase led to the highest outlook, nearly 300 feet above the street. This would have been the terminus for the ordinary paying visitor, among the telescopes, wind gauges, and weather signals presided over during working hours by a guard who would point out sights and operate the most powerful searchlight in the country. But White's guests might climb higher still, up a long, narrow spiral staircase, round and round the center pole with no backing to the stair treads until reaching the highest outlook atop the circular gallery of Corinthian columns.[26]

Then up an iron ladder, hand over hand, and out through a small opening in the circular platform just below the *Diana*'s left foot, at a height of 304 feet. Below, the lights of New York, Brooklyn, Jersey City, and boats on the East River twinkled in the dark. The *Diana* towered above, and a guest, as onetime mistress Evelyn Nesbit later recalled, could reach up and hold tight to her heel and feel it trembling with the wind.[27]

PART FOUR
Epilogue
The Last of the Story

And so passes one of the fine things of which New York was proud;
One of the things which proved that New York is not altogether sordid.[1]

54. *Diana Moves,*
Trenton Evening
Times (May 12, 1925).
Newsbank / Readex
and the American
Antiquarian Society.

26

Diana Redux

TWO VERY UNPLEASANT SCANDALS erupted in early 1894 revolving around several nude figures by Augustus Saint-Gaudens, but this time they were male. First came a representation of the Spirit of America "in the full vigor of life,"[1] as he described it, displayed on a commemorative medal for the Columbian Exposition. Amid that brouhaha came the quite public discovery of a pair of high-relief nude young boys installed over the main portal of the new Boston Public Library that were attributed to Saint-Gaudens and then loudly and distressingly criticized in the press.[2] He would never create another fully nude figure of any gender[3]—except for a whole line of reduced bronze reproductions of the Madison Square Garden's second *Diana*.

•

The earliest reductions, which dated back to small studies for the first version of the figure in its experimental state, were produced in both plaster and bronze in 1889 and gifted by Saint-Gaudens to Stanford White.[4] The pieces remained in White's collection until his death, when they were sold at auction with the rest of his art collection, the bronze for $300, the plaster for $130. The bronze *Diana* was eventually donated to the Smithsonian Institution and is now in the collection of its American Art Museum.[5]

In the spring of 1894 Saint-Gaudens had a half-sized, 6-foot version of the second *Diana* cast in Portland cement by Herman Walthausen, his New York plaster modeler, for White's new country home on Long Island. Still fussing with her drapery, Saint-Gaudens wryly thanked White for his suggested modifications. "You must know that the drapery I had designed could not make me any more sick than the design you sent me for the drapery; however, I shall go ahead and do it and be g.g.d. to you."[6]

55. *Diana*, Augustus Saint-Gaudens, 1889, bronze reduction, 25 in., given to Stanford White as a gift. Smithsonian American Art Museum, Washington, DC, Gift of John Gellatly / Art Resource, NY.

The home, named Box Hill after the boxwoods that grew on the property, was an old farmhouse in St. James that White had purchased for $25,000 two years before. There, wife Bessie, mother Nina, and son Larry, would spend their summers and early fall months, while White would travel out from the city most weekends. White had added gable roofs, dormers, cornices, Palladian windows, twisted Bernini columns, and a continuous porch to the structure, as well as laying out the gardens. His cement *Diana*, mounted on a 4-foot-high pedestal at the top of a knoll on Carman Hill, was set among other similar pieces just below and directly in front of a low, classical sort of concrete exedra bench facing the sea.[7]

•

Realizing how well known and very popular his iconic statue of *Diana* had become not only among New Yorkers but nationwide, Saint-Gaudens decided to produce in volume a series of small bronze reductions of the figure suitable for decorating the fashionable Gilded Age parlor, library, or boudoir.

The reduction of artworks produced in multiple editions had become something of an industry in France during the mid-nineteenth century due to popular demand by those who had viewed favorite pieces at the various grand expositions. The 1893 Chicago fair had introduced Americans to decorative painting and sculpture on a grand scale and to amazing technical advances that provided fine take-home souvenirs. The Collas machine, for example, invented by French engineer Achille Collas in the 1830s, thus employed a pantograph or pointing system for the exact reduction of three-dimensional sculpture, eventually reducing, for example, Falguière's 1882 life-sized bust of *Diana* to the size of a paperweight.[8]

Now fueled by the desire for bits of art to add just the right luster to well-decorated domiciles, new art foundries in Europe and in the United States, operated primarily by French and Italian émigrés, were manufacturing the popular *bronze d'art* for sale to the bourgeoisie.[9] "Good objects of art give to a room its crowning touch of distinction,"[10] counseled Edith Wharton in the 1897 *Decoration of Houses* she cowrote with architect Ogden Codman Jr.

There was actually a long tradition of reduced sculptural reproductions of the goddess Diana as precedent. In the late eighteenth century, French sculptor Jean-Antoine Houdon had created reduced versions of his *Diana* in plaster, metal, and marble that continued to be reproduced and sold posthumously into the late nineteenth century. By this point, French sculptors Paul Dubois, Albert-Ernest Carrier-Belleuse, and Antonin Mercié were all marketing reduced reproductions of the Virgin Goddess of the Hunt, as was Frederick MacMonnies with his own *Diana* cast by 1890.[11]

Finances were tight with Saint-Gaudens, as always, and he confided to White that "every blooming cent is all poured out." He did not see how he would be able to fix it except by selling reproductions of his work, and Saint-Gaudens had high expectations for their appeal.[12] "What are you singing to me about your *Diana* and your *Puritan*," wrote his old friend Paul Bion from Paris in the fall of 1893, that "they're going to line your pockets with a Niagara of gold?"[13]

•

Figuring out the sums, Saint-Gaudens realized that it would be more economical to have reproductions cast in Paris and then shipped to the United States for sale. In May 1894 he sent a plaster model of the second *Diana* to Paul Bion to be reduced and cast. Lodged in the depths of a poorly packed box, "as if in her casket," the model arrived in Paris with a broken arm and one leg crushed. Bion arranged to have it repaired and a mold made. Standing 21 inches high and now devoid of drapery, since it obviously would not be functioning as a wind vane, the figure held an arrow at the ready in her small and simple recurve bow.[14] While waiting on a carved wooden bow from Saint-Gaudens, Bion had devised a temporary design that in later editions would be replaced by a larger bow with a flattened, articulated riser at the handhold.[15]

Like the very first bronze *Diana* made for Stanford White, the figure stood on a sphere, but now one that was set on a tiered bronze plinth. The base was engraved "Augustus St. Gaudens 1894" and carried the foundry stamp of E. Gruet, for Edmond-Paul Gruet, younger brother of Adolphe Gruet, who had cast the *Farragut* sculpture for Madison Square in 1880. He now ran his own foundry at 44 Rue de Chatillon in Paris, where he had also cast reductions of MacMonnies's *Diana*.[16] After shipping the figure back to Saint-Gaudens for approval in September 1894, Bion warned a few weeks later that profits "would not be as prompt or as simple as opening the beak to swallow," resentful that MacMonnies's brother Frank, an importer-exporter living in Paris, would be taking a third of the profits for his work on their behalf.[17] Saint-Gaudens received the first *Diana* reduction in late November and rather thoughtlessly gifted the piece to wife Augusta for Christmas "to do whatever you please with it."[18]

56. *Diana*, Augustus Saint-Gaudens, ca. 1894, gilded bronze reduction, 28¼ in. Gift of Lincoln Kirstein, image copyright © The Metropolitan Museum of Art / Art Resource, NY.

•

With counterfeit plaster versions of *Diana* in faked bronze finish being hawked in front of the Madison Square Garden for seventy-five cents,[19] Augustus Saint-Gaudens registered US copyright number 6782AA on the reduced figure of *Diana* in January 1895. A variety of versions would follow, but he made certain that each bore a copyright mark, incised by hand until 1901 when it was replaced by a small stamp or plug, either cast separately and inserted or cast directly with the model.[20]

For the next iteration, a large *Diana* measuring 31 inches in height was cast by the French-born brothers Ernest and Charles Aubry at the Lorme-Aubry bronze foundry in downtown New York in 1895. Holding a heavy recurve bow with a large, flat, articulated riser, this *Diana* now stood on a half sphere set on a square plinth incised with the copyright symbol. Some were stamped with the words "Augustus Saint-Gaudens 1895,"[21] while on others the same date was expressed in Roman numerals.[22] This edition was sold at both H. Wunderlich & Co. and the Frederick Keppel Gallery in New York, as well as in Boston at Doll & Richards Fine Arts and the silver and fancy goods store Bigelow, Kennard & Co.[23] There was also an extra-large version, 41 inches high, of which Charles McKim may have been the first owner.[24] His unstamped piece appears to have been followed in production by those stamped 1895, 1899, and 1905 and bearing the title *Diana of the Tower* on the base.[25]

•

In 1897 Saint-Gaudens moved to Paris to breathe again "the art atmosphere of Europe" and to "view the new influences in sculpture" that had "sprung up," as Stanford White explained to the press.[26] But, in truth, Saint-Gaudens had become disaffected with America and yearned to be free of "the infernal noise, dirt, and confusion of New York City."[27] Over-work had also taken its toll, as had the affair of the Chicago World's Fair medal, his clients' efforts to rush him along in his work, factional quarrels among American sculptors, and the inevitable political wire-pulling behind the awarding of large sculptural commissions.[28] Saint-Gaudens's well-known years of delay on projects had tarnished his reputation a bit, and it was time to make a fresh start while restoring his standing in the art world.[29] He had also learned that in France his work was practically unknown, and he felt that by showing at the annual Salon he might learn where he truly stood among his contemporaries.[30]

In Paris and wildly impatient to begin work, he rented a studio in the Rue de Bagneux, an out-of-the-way corner in Montparnasse not far from the Luxembourg Gardens and his old studio. Here he continued to toil away on a mounted *Sherman Monument* destined for the Grand Army Plaza in New York City, on figure groups for the Boston Public Library, and on several winged memorial figures among others—all while supervising the casting of the *Diana* reproductions.[31] An exhausted Saint-Gaudens wrote to brother Louis that he was "jumping from branch to branch" like the red-headed monkey that he was, hanging on by his tail and "throwing coconuts at the other apes."[32]

But somehow Paris was not the city Saint-Gaudens remembered, and he was depressed and blue and missing New York. He consulted a physician, who diagnosed neurasthenia. He seriously considered creating several other nudes, including a Venus carrying a winged figure of Love on her shoulders and a little Cupid shooting his bow, but nothing came of them.[33] "All this struggle for beauty seems in vain and hopeless,"[34] he wrote to his wife back home.

Augusta Saint-Gaudens came and went, visiting spas then traveling back and forth to the States to ensure son Homer's acceptance into Harvard after his failure to pass the entrance exam.[35] In the summer of 1899, the sale of a half-sized version of *Diana* for $1,200 was cheering, and Augusta returned to France to oversee further castings and shipping of reproductions back to the States. Augustus was happy to let her iron out the marketing details, as when the Second Boer War interfered and three different steamers set for Boston were confiscated by the English to carry their troops to Africa rather than the *Diana*s to their retailers. "So we won't have any money for Christmas presents," Augusta added, "which is a great 'Boer.'"[36]

•

In August 1899, Saint-Gaudens informed Augusta that he had designed a new edition of the small *Diana* with a very different pedestal and carefully remodeled hairdo and bow. This time the roughly 21-inch figure was poised on a sphere set atop a tall tripod that added another 15 or so inches to the piece, an effective means of giving the figure a greater sense of height and re-creating the Madison Square Garden tower effect in miniature. The tripod base was embellished with a line of rosettes, scrolls, and the raised letters spelling out "Diana of the Tower." There were various stampings of the sculptor's name, the copyright date of 1899 spelled out in Roman numerals, and Edmond-Paul Gruet's foundry mark, "E. Gruet Jeune."[37] Some, or perhaps just one special version, included a floral knob on the back of the tripod to control a hidden gear-driven device that allowed the figure to turn gracefully on its toes.[38]

57. *Diana of the Tower*, Augustus Saint-Gaudens, bronze reduction, cast 1899. Courtesy of the National Gallery of Art, Washington, Pepita Milmore Memorial Fund.

In this new edition, each corner of the tripod base was embellished with a winged, lion-headed beast, wingtips joining at the center of each side. While the design may have been something of a little joke, for Saint-Gaudens often thought of himself as a lion, such composite and ferocious motifs dated back to ancient Egypt, Greece, and Etruscan Italy. The winged lion of St. Mark, the symbol of the city of Venice that Saint-Gaudens no doubt saw on a trip to Italy in 1897, was another possibility. He may also have been taking a cue from Frederick MacMonnies, who had appropriated an Etruscan-inspired triangular base with bear-headed, ram-headed, and goat-footed sphinxes for his small bronze *Running Cupid with His Bow* of 1894 and his *Standing Cupid* of 1895, also produced by E. Gruet.[39]

There were other significant changes in this 1899 figure of *Diana* as well: her hair was more in the style of the contemporary Gibson girl, with a higher, more prominent back knot, fuller sides, and less of a front pompadour. Her bow was also remodeled with a much smaller riser at the handhold and a bit less recurve where it was connected to the string.[40]

Before they were ready for market, the bronze *Diana*s were usually electroplated with a matte-gold finish, achieved with the addition of copper and zinc that might vary in color into shades of brown, green, silver and blue-gray.[41] Saint-Gaudens discovered and then suggested to Stanford White that the gold effect could be improved by mixing together a little burnt sienna paint with turpentine, rubbing it over the figure, and then partially wiping it off.[42] In any case, a fresh patina was easily damaged, and despite warning his dealers, Saint-Gaudens found that damage to the surface, as well as to *Diana*'s delicate, twisted wire bowstring, was a fairly regular occurrence for which he was forced to accept the charges for repair.[43]

In October 1899, Saint-Gaudens contracted with Tiffany & Co. to allow their showroom on Union Square exclusive sale of his reproductions in New York. The firm requested enough pieces to impress visitors in their great bronze room, and in return for a 20 percent commission they agreed to launch a maximum $200 advertising campaign. True to their word, in January 1900 Tiffany's offered an exhibition of some of Saint-Gaudens's recent bronze reductions, including the *Diana*. The large figure was priced at $200–$225, depending on the type of base, and the small tripod-mounted figure priced at $175. If requested, the figure could also be mounted on a block of marble.[44] Saint-Gaudens informed Doll & Richards in Boston, his only other current dealer, about the new edition and urged that they too raise the price of the revamped small *Diana* from $150 because of the added expense of production.[45]

Saint-Gaudens himself hand-modeled and refined each new version of *Diana*, a selling point that his dealers did not hesitate to make.[46] In the summer of 1899, Saint-Gaudens happily reported to brother Louis that he had quite a little income now from these pieces. Not shy as far as the marketing, Saint-Gaudens also urged his friends and patrons to purchase these "charming little works of art" as gifts.[47] He even pressed Stanford

White, sending him the new 1899 *Diana* along with a bronze reduction of his bedridden portrait of *Robert Louis Stevenson* so that he would have them on hand as Christmas presents, "and for Heaven's sake," Saint-Gaudens wrote, "don't feel bound to take these things because after having filled yourself with cock-tails you felt like ordering copies of everything that I and all your friends ever have done or ever will do."[48]

Saint-Gaudens discovered that although the bronze reductions had sold very slowly at first, the sales increased once people began seeing them in friends' homes, as on the drawing room mantel of Stanford White's Gramercy Park townhouse.[49] White did enjoy giving the *Diana*s as special gifts and placing them in the homes he designed,[50] while Saint-Gaudens was happy to supply him as needed at cost.[51]

•

Saint-Gaudens left France for the United States in 1900, a self-described patriot fully appreciating "what a bully country this is and what bully friends one has at home,"[52] but in physical pain so intense that he felt on the verge of insanity. When Parisian doctors told him he had cancerous tumors of the lower intestine and rectum and must return home immediately for surgery, he fell even deeper into depression and nearly committed suicide by jumping from a bridge over the Seine until he was dissuaded by the beauty of the scene.[53] After Saint-Gaudens departed for Boston "to be cut up,"[54] longtime assistant Gaétan Ardisson remained behind to supervise the bronze reductions. But by the following year, frustrated by carelessness at the foundry and damage in shipping, Saint-Gaudens decided to have the bronze casting done in New York and had Ardisson return the models of both the large and small *Diana*s. Saint-Gaudens shopped among the foundries he had previously used in New York and nearby New Jersey, and he finally selected Charles and Ernest Aubry Brothers Foundry as the most competitive bid and on whose quality of cast he could rely.[55]

•

In midsummer of 1907 Augustus Saint-Gaudens lay on the porch watching a sunset behind Mount Ascutney at his home in Cornish, New Hampshire, and spoke out of a long silence, "It is very beautiful, but I want to go farther away."[56] He died several days later, on August 3, following years of additional surgery, nervous exhaustion, and terrible pain. Despite his failing health, he had desperately tried to complete projects still unfinished, working from a litter carried into the studio by assistants and surviving on morphine.[57]

Saint-Gaudens bequeathed to his widow all rights to reproduce his works, and she soon had a number of new bronzes cast for sale and presentation as gifts.[58] Along with the *Victory* from the *Sherman* group and the heads of *Lincoln, Farragut,* and *Shaw,* emerged a new bust of *Diana* that she copyrighted two months after Saint-Gaudens's death. Much in the style of the commercially successful Dianic busts by Houdon and Falguière, this new piece, at only 7½ inches high, reproduced the remodeled hairdo, shoulders, and upper chest from the 1899 edition, but it was set on a pedestal-type base with the inscription *Diana of the Tower* within a scrolled cartouche and the stamped monogram of "A ST G." On the back of the bust was stamped "copyright by A[ugusta]. H[omer]. Saint-Gaudens MCMVIII."[59]

In January 1908 Augusta Saint-Gaudens followed up by copyrighting and issuing a roughly finished bronze head of the second *Diana,* 9½ inches high and cast by the Aubry Brothers from Saint-Gaudens's plaster half-sized model with a bit of remodeling, perhaps by brother Louis.[60] She was once again retailing through Wunderlich and other firms besides Tiffany's, as well as selling directly from the studio in Cornish, with the large *Diana* now priced at $300, the smaller at $200 to $225. *Diana* on the tripod also continued to be manufactured and sold long after Saint-Gaudens's death, carefully supervised by Augusta, who kept a close eye on costs and profit margins while allowing no casts to be made without her written order.[61]

When the Aubry Brothers ceased production in 1909, plaster patterns for the new head and bust of *Diana* along with bronze master models for the small *Diana* and tripod base were transferred to Tiffany Studios, which cast from their foundry in Corona, Queens. In the early 1920s Augusta Saint-Gaudens was dealing with the Roman Bronze Works, a subcontractor to Tiffany that would be installed in their Corona foundry in 1927 and would take it over in 1932.[62] Augusta Saint-Gaudens enjoyed the fruits of her marketing skills and, until her death at Aspet in 1926, was often

58. *Diana of the Tower*, ca. 1907, plaster bust, 7½ in. Courtesy of the US Department of the Interior, National Park Service, Saint-Gaudens National Historical Park, Cornish, NH.

spotted being chauffeured around the Cornish environs in a big black automobile.[63]

•

While smaller versions of *Diana* were being added to the repertoire, copies of the 6-foot, half-sized model were also generated well into the twentieth century. In 1927, alarmed by their cement figure's deterioration, the Stanford White family commissioned Osterkamp-Mead to cast a bronze from White's 1894 garden ornament at the firm's Priessmann, Bauer Foundry in Munich, Germany. Still mindful of *Diana*'s loss to the city, Daniel Chester

59. Half-size *Diana* in Saint-
Gaudens's Cornish studio,
plaster cast. Courtesy of the
US Department of the Interior,
National Park Service, Saint-
Gaudens National Historical
Park, Cornish, NH.

French—who served as a trustee of the Metropolitan Museum of Art—
urged that a half-sized replica also be cast for the museum so that she
might always be present for New Yorkers to enjoy. As a result, the following year Bessie White allowed the Met to make its own gilt bronze cast at
a cost of $1,300.[64]

Despite Osterkamp-Mead's aviso to the museum that the figure would
need to rest for six weeks in order for its gold leaf gilding to set properly, the *Diana* was immediately taken to the attic for antiquing when it
arrived in May 1928. When the figure was brought down to the sculpture
gallery just three weeks later, an inspection revealed that its surface had
been scratched by buttons on the workmen's overalls. Back to Osterkamp-
Mead, and an extra charge to regild and antique the damage.[65]

Still revered for the beauty of her lines and her history, *Diana* continued to be reproduced at half size in the 1970s and 1980s. These models,
based on the White family's cement cast, were intended for the Madison

Square Garden Corporation, various museums, and sale to individual collectors via private galleries, from which casts continue to be made. A half-sized bronze was cast in Italy in the 1970s for the Saint-Gaudens National Historical Park.[66] It was taken from the site's half-sized plaster model made from plaster piece-molds that had survived a devastating 1904 studio fire and had been cast under the aegis of Homer Saint-Gaudens. The plaster figure was itself one of the few pieces to survive a second studio fire in 1944 at what had become by that time the Saint-Gaudens Memorial.[67]

Over the years the smaller bronze reproductions were also acquired by numerous museums and galleries through purchase and donation, including the National Gallery of Art, the Brooklyn Museum, the Indianapolis Museum of Art, the Amon Carter Museum of American Art, the Cleveland Museum of Art, and the Fogg Art Museum at Harvard.[68]

27

A Murder at the Garden

STANFORD WHITE'S Madison Square Garden would, of course, be remembered in many ways and for many things aside from its great tower and the *Diana* that twirled on top. Among the historic first exhibitions held in that grand arena were those that celebrated the finest canines, felines, poultry, orchids, and automobiles to be found in the city, if not in the entire country. Such events generated substantial national interest, appreciation, and subsequent commerce. Any turn-of-the-century New Yorker's fond memories most certainly would have included the sights and smells of Barnum's Circus, Annie Oakley shooting glass balls out of the air in Wild Bill's Wild West Shows, the heartbreaking six-day walking marathons that gave way to heart-stopping cycle races, the steel and brick bully pulpit that served many a prophet and politico, the expositions and conventions showcasing hardly believable developments in science and invention, the brutal slugfests, and the fairylands created for fetes and festivals beyond number.

But more than anything else, Madison Square Garden would always be remembered as the place where—in an almost unimaginable twist of fate—Stanford White was shot to death in 1906 on his roof garden, beneath *Diana*'s very shadow. Many details of the so-called "crime of the century" remain vivid in American popular culture more than a century later, reported, re-examined, and revisited in literature and films: the celebrity architect-about-town, the beautiful young model he had seduced and presumably ravished years before, the angry and certainly insane millionaire husband with the itchy trigger finger, the thousand eyewitnesses to White taking three bullets point-blank while the murderer shouted, "You

305

60. *Scene of the Stanford White Murder Drama and the Chief Actors, Belleville (IL) News Democrat* (July 2, 1906). Newsbank / Readex and the American Antiquarian Society.

ruined my wife" and the opening night chorus girls of *Mamzelle Champagne* danced around a giant bottle of bubbly.[1]

Seven months later came the "trial of the century": the revelatory tales of White's tower rooms and his secret nights, the defense's plea that Harry Kendall Thaw had merely defended the sanctity of his home and the purity of his wife, the stunningly beautiful Evelyn Nesbit, and the trial's culmination in a hung jury. Then came the second trial and Thaw's acquittal by reason of insanity, his committal to a luxury suite in an asylum for the criminally insane, the baby Thaw claimed he could not have fathered, and Thaw's escape to Canada, followed by his extradition, acquittal, and victorious return to Pittsburgh in 1917. Then came the divorce, Nesbit's unsuccessful suicide attempt and his, and Nesbit's comeback on the stage and subsequent remarriage.

Much of the murderer's defense, however, appears to have been based on falsehood. Another surprising view of the motive and the murder puts the story in a quite different perspective.

To briefly review the details, the famed young beauty in the case, Florence Mary "Evelyn" Nesbit, was born in 1884 in Tarentum, Pennsylvania, the daughter of a Pittsburgh lawyer who died young and an ambitious mother who did not hesitate to do what was needed to advance their situation. After being left nearly penniless, Mrs. Nesbit brought fourteen-year-old Evelyn and her younger brother to Philadelphia, where she hoped to find work. But it was the daughter who achieved success as an artist's model, with her beautiful face and slim, boyish body.[2] In search of greater opportunities, Mrs. Nesbit moved her family to Manhattan in late 1900. Letters of introduction brought work for the fifteen-year old, first from J. Carroll Beckwith and then from a growing number of painters, sculptors, and commercial photographers as Stanford White's circle of friends sought to use her face and figure.[3]

Stanford White first met sixteen-year-old Evelyn Nesbit in 1901 after she had netted a role as a Spanish dancer in the hugely successful musical play *Florodora*. Apparently, White had previously snipped photographs of her from the newspapers for an album he kept of contemporary beauties. In August of that year Nesbit was brought by a fellow cast member to luncheon at White's hideaway on Twenty-Fourth Street, the one that backed onto and above the FAO Schwarz toy store. After having her try out the legendary velvet swing—still fully clothed at this point—Stanny (as she called him) took her under his all-encompassing wing.[4]

As he had for other young girls, the now forty-seven-year-old White served as devoted father-protector, kindly benefactor, and thoughtful teacher.[5] Invitations soon followed to lavish and quite proper parties in his rooms in the Madison Square Garden tower, where Nesbit met among others Augustus Saint-Gaudens, Frederick MacMonnies, and Charles Dana Gibson, for whom she famously modeled. It was also at this time that

White had her photographed by Rudolf Eickemeyer, who created some of the most iconic images of this model, now known as "the angel child." Mrs. Nesbit saw White, a frequent visitor to their home, "as a heaven-sent friend of the family, a veritable second father"[6] who supported them generously, while others like Saint-Gaudens viewed White's interest as more opportunistic, and her mother as little better than a procuress.

According to Evelyn's recollections, one night at the Twenty-Fourth Street apartment, after her mother had turned her over to White's protection, one too many glasses of champagne caused her to pass out on his bed, and she awoke to find them both naked and blood on the sheets. He had taken her virginity without her knowledge or permission. Nesbit intimated during the trial that she had been drugged but later denied this, and in her 1934 memoir stated that it had probably been due to her unfamiliarity with champagne.[7] White explained that she was "so nice and young and slim" that he could not help himself, and "only young girls were very nice, and the thinner they were the prettier they were."[8] Much, it seems, like the figure of *Diana*.

With assurances that "everybody did these things," he warned her that the important thing was not to be found out and swore her to secrecy about that evening. She forgave his assault, and they remained lovers, Nesbit often perched upon that red velvet swing, now quite naked. When they found themselves at the Madison Square Garden tower apartment in the early hours of the morning, they would climb to the very top and, at *Diana*'s feet, gaze out on the city, holding hands and talking softly.[9]

About the same time, Nesbit began receiving letters, money, and flowers from a rather mysterious admirer. When she finally met the sender at an arranged dinner in early 1902, it turned out to be the Pittsburgh-born, nouveau and very riche Harry Thaw—an explosively tempered profligate and generally loony playboy.[10] Thaw was an extravagant spender with an $80,000 per year allowance that came primarily from his father's $40 million estate, which included coalmine leases and significant investment in the Pennsylvania Railroad. "A crazy dope fiend" was the way White characterized Thaw, known about town as "Mad Harry."[11] His use of both morphine and cocaine fueled often-violent escapades in the

States and abroad that had for years been well reported in newspapers across the nation.[12]

While courting Nesbit later that year, Thaw proposed. According to Nesbit, she declined, revealing to him in dramatic detail the story of her defloration. This, she insisted, perhaps with some relief, precluded their nuptials, but Thaw persisted. Evelyn Nesbit and Harry Thaw finally married in the spring of 1905, moving into the Pittsburgh family mansion. The following year, in late June, the couple came to New York for a few weeks' stay on their way to London and a visit with Thaw's sister, who had been more or less sold in marriage to the rouged and perfumed Earl of Yarmouth for a reputed $1 million. There were rumors that the earl and Harry had been very close friends, and that Thaw had introduced him to his sister, although the earl was known not to prefer women.[13]

On the evening of June 25, 1906, Mr. and Mrs. Thaw dined at the very fashionable Café Martin on Madison Square, in the building that had some years before housed the famed Delmonico's. They were joined by two friends, one of whom, Thaw confided (falsely, as it turned out), had killed his wife's lover in California but had been acquitted on the unwritten law that excused murder in defending a man's sexual honor and was then generally hailed a hero.[14]

During dinner, Stanford White, who had been dining up on the balcony, passed behind Thaw's chair unnoticed. Nesbit slipped Thaw a note of warning, "The B" (as in "blackguard" or "beast") had just slipped out.[15] White had come for a pretheater dinner as well, joined by his son, Larry, and a classmate who had both just completed their freshman year at Harvard.

Thaw finished his dinner in a funk, staring straight ahead and biting the nails on his trembling hands before all four walked over to Madison Square Garden for the premiere of a new musical, *Mamzelle Champagne*. It was an odd choice since, prior to that evening, Thaw had refused to set foot in any building connected with White, and even odder because despite the June warmth, he wore a long, dark overcoat that he would not remove even after they were seated at their table on the roof garden. After a few moments gazing up at the looming tower "whose size seemed to grow in the darkness"[16] before his eyes, he spotted White's brother-in-law, James Clinch Smith, and strolled over for a rather awkward chat.[17] He then passed several times by the table down front where White, as usual, was seated. Thaw returned to Nesbit's side, but she complained of boredom and asked to leave. He agreed, and the pair, along with their two friends, headed for the elevator.[18]

But as the twenty chorus girls in tights brandished swords and paraded to the front of the stage to sing out the repeated line, "I challenge you, I challenge you to a duel, to a duel, a du-u-el," Thaw suddenly turned around, leaving Nesbit behind. He cut over to lurk in some greenery near White's table, then approached as the second-act chorus of "I Could Love a Million Girls" rang out. At about 15 feet away he pulled out from beneath the black overcoat a revolver, said to be a Colt .22, and held it at arm's length. As White turned toward him, half rising, Thaw fired a shot through the left eye. "Wanting to take no chances," Thaw walked closer and fired twice more, one through the upper lip and one through the shoulder. Never making a sound, White slid sideways from his chair, knocked over the table with his right arm, and collapsed on the floor.[19]

There was a moment of utter silence, an uncertain laugh or two, then screams, and then the crowd began to run for the exits. In the panic that followed, Thaw held the smoking revolver high above his head, broke the gun, and emptied its chambers. Amid the chaos, a doctor in the audience examined White and pronounced him dead. A waiter pulled a tablecloth over his powder-blackened face, but gushing blood seeped through. A dozen women fainted while men cursed and cried, "Catch the man!"[20]

Thaw moved toward the elevator, where a shocked and dazed Nesbit stood waiting for him. A fireman in the audience grabbed the gun, and then a police officer clapped him on the shoulder and declared him under arrest. As he was being taken away, Nesbit was heard to say, "Oh Harry, why did you do this?" to which he replied, "I have probably saved your life." Thaw then added, "He had it coming. He ruined my wife!"[21]

•

The autopsy revealed that the now portly, fifty-two-year-old Stanford White had been suffering from incipient tuberculosis, Bright's disease of the kidneys, and the fatty degeneration of the liver—all of which probably would have resulted in his death within a year or two.[22] His body was returned to his home on Gramercy Park for several days until it was taken by ferry across the East River (an hour before the announced time, to foil curiosity seekers), and then by private train to the north shore of Long Island.[23] A simple service was held at the St. James Episcopal Church in St. James, illuminated by three stained glass windows that White himself had designed.[24] Charles McKim and William Mead arranged the details, and a fair number of old friends attended. Augustus Saint-Gaudens had been in town the night of the shooting to receive X-ray treatment for his cancer, but he was too ill to make the funeral trip and two months later had a complete collapse.[25] It was reported in the papers that of all the mourners, only Bessie White remained tearless throughout the service and burial.[26]

Within weeks of the murder, relic hunters whittled up a dozen or more tables on the Madison Square Garden roof, thinking they had secured remains from the place where Stanford White last sat. Cleverly, the staff there had placed a new table on the spot as soon as its predecessor was so chopped up that it could no longer stand, and the roof garden chairs went almost as quickly.[27]

•

The story put forward by the defense at the trial, which began in January 1907, was that after Thaw learned of Nesbit's defloration, he simmered with anger for years, waiting for the chance to defend her honor. Stanford White was castigated as the despoiler of a poor little child to gratify a moment of passion and lust.[28] In rebuttal the prosecution claimed to have evidence proving Stanford White could not have committed the attack on the date Nesbit specified, and that three years earlier she had sworn in a deposition that the charge of rape was fabricated by Thaw, but the judge ruled it all immaterial to the case.[29]

During the trial many of White's friends and colleagues remained silent, but a fair number came to his defense, listing his architectural achievements and his devotion to beauty, as well as his kindness and generosity to all. Augustus Saint-Gaudens sent a letter to *Collier's Weekly* praising White's "almost feminine tenderness to his friends in suffering and his generosity to those in trouble or want."[30] Privately, to his old friend Alfred Garnier, Saint-Gaudens decried the death "of a man of great genius . . . right at the foot of one of his best works . . . for a woman with the face of an angel and the heart of a snake."[31]

But the scandalmongers held the day, printing countless accounts of White's predilection for young girls with those figures like "twelve-year-old boys,"[32] as well as the goings-on in his lavishly decorated tower apartment.[33] Nesbit claimed that White performed "unspeakably unnatural acts" upon young girls, and other witnesses reported him actively seeking out victims between thirteen and fifteen years of age.[34] White's privilege and power were claimed to have prevented Garden employees from interfering with the orgies that might have taken place in the tower,[35] and its shadow was said to have "darkened many a fresh young life."[36]

61. *Diana*, in the form of Stanford White shooting virgins, Robert Carter, *New York American* (June 29, 1906).

White was vilified nationwide as a profligate, libertine, and debaucher of young girls.[37] Headlines like "Stanford White, Voluptuary and Pervert, Dies the Death of a Dog"[38] in *Vanity Fair* turned White into a one-man symbol of the morally bankrupt elite, egged on by drugs and overspiced foods, who cared little for Main Street American values, the sanctity of the home, or the virtue of the American girl.[39]

●

While Stanford White was likely guilty of countless acts that today would be considered morally, legally, and socially reprehensible in regard to young women, it is possible that the murder had not actually been about his relationship with Evelyn Nesbit. What if it were really about an intimate relationship between White and Thaw? The truth of it was that the explosive, unstable Harry Thaw had been obsessed with Stanford White long before he ever met Nesbit. Even more remarkably, it seems that he made a great effort to cultivate her acquaintance solely because of her connection to White.[40]

In fact, the two men had known each other for years, and there had obviously been a raging resentment on the part of Thaw. It may have begun when the ever-erratic Thaw misbehaved at a Garden tower party and was scratched from White's guest list.[41] Nesbit acknowledged and attributed the feud to another party arranged years earlier for some of the girls who appeared in *Florodora*.[42] After the chorus girls stood Thaw up in favor of a party at the Garden tower, *Town Topics*, the city's gossip rag, printed the entire story under the headline, "Florodora Beauties Sing for Their Supper in White's Studio, while Thaw's Orchestra Fiddles to an Empty Room at Sherry's." Thaw blamed White for the whole fiasco. Nesbit believed it was then, long before she met him, "that the seed of that bitter hatred for Stanford White was born in the weird, unfathomable labyrinth of Thaw's brain."[43]

Whenever he spied Stanford White in New York, Thaw would break out in sobs. He also believed that White had blacklisted him for membership in the Knickerbocker Club, the Metropolitan Club, the Century Association, and the Players' Club, all of which had rejected him. Thaw hired detectives to follow White, and White hired detectives to discover who was following him, and when he learned it was Thaw, hired more for protection.[44] And so it went, back and forth. Even Nesbit admitted that Thaw's campaign against White and his determination to injure him was a mystery to her in many ways, and that at their very first meeting—long *before* she had shared any intimate details—Thaw had referred to White as "a beast." It seems that her relationship with White served only to justify Thaw's already simmering hatred.[45] But as anyone who had ever loved knows, hate was but a small step across.

The *New York Times* reported that as he was being taken away from the murder scene Thaw told the fireman, "He ruined my wife." Or was it "He ruined my *life*?" The fireman testified that he "really couldn't tell which." Another witness was in fact quite certain that Thaw had said, "He ruined my life."[46] Ruined his life in that White was such a long-standing object of fascination and obsession? It would probably come as no surprise to those who knew of Thaw's own predilections that he might have had a passion, unrequited or otherwise, for Stanford White, who himself was more than familiar with man-manly love.

It seems that Thaw long had been attracted to the male sex, and on that first trip to Europe with Nesbit he was nearly arrested for flogging a boy for pleasure in his hotel room. Apparently his affinity for boys had been discussed among certain circles since his late teens. However, vicious beatings with a dog whip he had reserved not only for boys but girls as well, including Nesbit herself, and she observed that his relations with women were "tinged with perversion."[47] And how could Thaw have possibly saved Nesbit's life by killing White? Perhaps because he did not trust himself not to murder her during one of his fits of jealous rage, as he had threatened in the past. And his rage over White's other young girls? Again, likely jealousy rather than any sort of moral indignation.

It also seems that Thaw and White's relationship might have actually been a continuing affair. According to one witness, during the 1904 trip to Paris, Thaw spent a good deal of time with Stanford White, who happened to be in town as well. Their local guide, who had been hired to show them the nightlife, said the two were close until they quarreled over something and afterward became quite bitter.[48] There was also an unsubstantiated report that Thaw and White met a few nights before the shooting at Burns Restaurant & Hotel on Sixth Avenue and huddled alone together until nearly 4 o'clock in the morning.[49] For whatever reason, it was only by whipping out a gun and shooting point blank that Thaw felt he could exorcize Stanford White from his life.

In 1917, after Thaw was finally freed from institutionalization, he was arrested on charges of kidnapping and flogging a young man into unconsciousness after luring him to a hotel in New York with the promise of paid tuition and a position. Evidence was also discovered that Thaw had similarly promised money or jobs to other boys if they would only join him for an evening.[50] Oddly enough, it turned out that White himself had quite an interest in flagellation, his extensive private library of erotica containing at least a dozen volumes on the subject.[51]

White had supported Nesbit's younger brother, Howard, paying for his boarding school education and then giving him a post at the office. Howard was so devoted to White that he admitted during the trial that if testimony should prove his faith in White was misplaced, "it would nearly break my heart." After various financial and legal problems, Howard Nesbit, whom Paula Uruburu believes to have been a homosexual, hung himself from a steam pipe in his Bronx kitchen in 1928.[52] And to further complicate things, it was possibly Evelyn Nesbit's slight and boyish figure and her striking resemblance to Howard, enhanced by the very short hair she wore under a wig for a time, that had entranced both White and Thaw.[53]

28

The Tower Falls

DESPITE ALL THAT WENT ON THERE, and despite its spot lodged deep in New York's cultural, social, and athletic heart, Madison Square Garden never really turned a profit. From that day during construction when Stanford White approved the first cost override, it had mostly run at a loss. It never paid those promised stock dividends, and the company's board of directors often had to dip into their own pockets to cover the ever-increasing taxes, salaries, insurance, advertising, and running of a plant that by the 1920s had an average operating cost of $1,500 a day. The Garden needed to make a profit of at least $10,000 a week to break even, and over the years this had occurred less and less often.[1] Not unexpectedly, Madison Square had been left behind as the city's new hotels and theaters and restaurants continued to be built northward, and New Yorkers had come to expect the all-too-frequent newspaper headline warning of the Garden's crushing failure, pending sale, and likely imminent demise.[2]

There was a close call in 1897 when the Garden found itself once again strapped for funds and in debt to the city of New York for $100,000 in taxes. When an attempt to place the Garden directly under city management failed, a reorganization plan and the assessment of stockholders deferred disaster for a few years.[3] In 1900 weary investors recognized once again that it was time to unload their financial burden.[4] The US Postal Service expressed interest in purchasing the Garden and turning it into the grandest postal station in the world but then passed on the opportunity, realizing the location was just too far downtown.[5] The Garden's neighbors on the square—particularly the merchants, restaurants, and hotels that profited from its events—urged the city to relieve the tax bill or obtain title to the spot, but the city passed again.

•

The Garden lumbered on for another eight years until its hundred or so stockholders decided that, after carrying the property for twenty years pro bono publico with virtually no return on their investment, it was time for drastic action.[6] In truth, the Garden complex had little to recommend it: its theater was now quite superfluous with the newer houses on Broadway's Great White Way; its restaurant had been abandoned; its concert hall faced too much competition; the bucolic charms of its roof garden seemed passé in the new century; and its tower, while beautiful, was truly of little use. There was no likelihood of the Garden *ever* being a profitable venture, and the prevailing thought was if staunching the losses meant disposing of the site to a party that would raze the complex and replace it with offices or shops, then so be it. The entire property was listed for $3 million, but the outstanding $2 million in stocks, $2 million in bonds, and two mortgages made it less than appealing. Prospective buyers needed also to consider the estimated cost of more than $200,000 to dismantle the Garden's iron, steel, brick, and terra cotta—and there were simply no takers.[7]

•

Three years later, founding board member J. P. Morgan made it known that the Garden was once again on the market, this time for $3.5 million, more or less, although it was rumored that the Garden could be had for just $1.5 million cash, provided the buyer was willing to preserve and improve the property as a whole and not divide it up into lots.[8]

In April 1911, Madison Square Garden was said to be sold or at least optioned to one real estate operator and then to another. Then it was rumored that a syndicate was planning to build at least two and perhaps four commercial skyscrapers on the site. This was not a great surprise, for the old brownstone residences on Madison Square and Fifth Avenue were rapidly giving way to tall business lofts, and the Garden's square block—a full thirty-two city lots—had become more valuable than its buildings.[9] Beginning in 1902 with the Fuller Building on the southwest side of Madison Square, designed by Daniel Burnham of Chicago World's Fair fame and more commonly known as the Flatiron Building, *Diana* would be overtopped on all sides by towering commercial structures as the square transformed from a residential and amusement center to a purely commercial one.

•

The 1911 buyer for the Garden, F. & D. Company, was indeed a syndicate—said to represent German business interests—while the mortgage would be carried by the New York Life Insurance Company. The syndicate's plan was to erect a twenty-five-story skyscraper around a central courtyard, creating the largest commercial structure in the world, with more than 50 acres of floor space.[10]

The plans for the huge commercial structure were eventually abandoned, although F. & D. Company retained ownership. Ringling Brothers leased the Garden for the circus, then the Garden Athletic Club took over the arena for boxing bouts. The horse show, dog show, motorboat show, and automobile show managed to bring in even greater crowds, but the major transformation was the remodeling of the roof garden, which was reopened for dining, dancing, cabaret theater, and motion pictures shown on an extra-large bed sheet.[11]

•

But none of this was quite enough, and in the summer of 1916 the Garden was once more in peril. The primary mortgage holder, New York Life Insurance Company, began an action for foreclosure against the F. & D. Company, which then filed for bankruptcy. At the foreclosure auction in December, Madison Square Garden fell back to New York Life, much to its chagrin, for there were no bidders despite the company's offer to loan $1.75 million to any purchaser willing to take the property off its hands. New York Life quickly placed the building back on the market. Less than a month later it was sold to another syndicate and then leased to Grant Hugh Browne, a horseman with a fancy for boxing who planned to hold matches there.[12]

But boxing in New York was still not fully legal. Under the stringent code mandated by the Frawley Law, the Garden lost its state license in 1917. With the country's entrance into World War I, however, boxing exhibitions were offered as benefit shows under the oversight of the Army, Navy, and Civilian Boxing Board of Control, which managed to circumvent the rules. Boxing proved helpful in preparing soldiers and sailors for combat, and all around the country the sport was attracting great crowds newly hardened to violence and ready for a distraction from the years of war.[13]

In the spring of 1920, the Walker Bill was jammed through the New York legislature to fully legalize prizefights under careful licensing and supervision. In signing the bill, Governor Al Smith noted that the stress of the times demanded healthy and wholesome amusement for the men of New York State,[14] and Madison Square Garden stepped up as the place to provide it. George Lewis "Tex" Rickard, a well-known sports promoter from out west whose bouts had brought in nearly $10 million, signed a ten-year lease with New York Life at $200,000 a year. Rickard took over the Garden on August 1, 1920, and within a month the sport of boxing had taken over the Garden as well.[15]

Rickard claimed the distinction of having promoted the most successful match in ring history, the 1910 "Fight of the Century" bout between John Arthur "Jack" Johnson, the first African-American boxer to claim the

62. George Lewis "Tex" Rickard. George Grantham Bain Collection, Library of Congress, LC-DIG-ggbain-32373.

heavyweight title, and James J. Jeffries, the "Great White Hope."[16] Rickard pledged that every old tradition would be preserved but that he planned to make the Garden the sport and athletic training center of America.[17] It was a new, postwar world; life was fast, hard, tough, and serious now. No more last-century fringe and fluff; no more lazing about on rooftops drinking beer and ogling chorus girls. Men *and* women needed to be strong and quick, and Rickard understood.

He began the process by transforming the Garden's roof into the world's largest gymnasium. The very spot where Stanford White breathed his last was paved over and turned into a tennis court encircled by athletic training equipment and the city's best running track. The place was not just for aspiring boxers but for businessmen hoping to become fit, and women too, stylishly clad in middy blouses and bloomers.[18]

While stripping the tower of much of its interior trappings, workmen found that it was honeycombed with a network of hidden stairways and secret passages, quite likely designed by Stanford White himself.[19] Newspapers across the country heralded the discovery with White's ghostlike image hovering above the Garden, perhaps irate in the afterlife that the arena's elegant floor boxes had been pulled out to allow for the installation of 5,000 more cheap seats.[20]

Amazingly, Rickard managed to make the Garden pay. Receipts from the first six months under his direction resulted in the most successful season the Garden had ever enjoyed. Fueled mostly by boxing receipts, the Garden hosted a series of unparalleled matches, including six championships, to an audience of nearly 300,000 who came to worship at the new "Temple of Fistiana."[21]

Rickard also found a way to make the Garden pay during the steamy summer months, when its sporting schedule was near dead. In July 1921, a new, white-tiled tank the full length of a city block opened as the world's largest and grandest indoor swimming pool. A variety of exhibitions, races (including swimming and diving contests among Broadway's showgirls), and water polo matches were regularly offered.[22]

Yet despite *Diana*'s protection, a cloud lingered over the tower. It was later revealed that Rickard's office had a back door through which he could step onto a balcony high up among the rafters and peer down on the new swimming pool, looking for young female prey. When Rickard spied a likely victim, he would take her upstairs for a glass of wine, make his assault, and then offer money for her silence. In 1922, eleven New York schoolgirls, ranging in age from eleven to fifteen, formally accused Rickard of abduction and rape. He was found not guilty, however, after a string of prominent men testified to his good character, and additional charges involving three other victims were suddenly dropped.[23]

And so the Garden hung on. While Rickard was proud to be the only man who ever made a profit off it, the black ink came at a cost. Needed upkeep and repairs were largely ignored. The *Diana* received a new coat of gold paint, but there was little effort to wash away the smoke, soot, and dust that now obscured the Garden's buff brick and terra cotta.[24]

•

It might have seemed inevitable that in the spring of 1924 Madison Square Garden's mortgage holder, New York Life, would announce plans for the erection of a new forty-story corporate headquarters on the site.[25] "What would you say if they tore down the Rheims Cathedral over in France to make room for an office building?" demanded one art critic. "We build up only to tear down, we have no regard for things merely because they are beautiful; they must return us six percent on our investment, or out they go."[26] And so it was with the Garden.

That the chosen architect for the project was the MIT-trained Cass Gilbert, who had apprenticed at McKim, Mead & White from 1880 to 1882, added a bit of irony to the plans. He had served as Stanford White's chief and personal assistant, supervising a variety of projects until he left to start his own practice, "a little sick of White's arrogance and claiming all the credit for everything done in his office."[27] He did remain, though, a great fan of Saint-Gaudens, who had treated "a young unknown and inadequate draftsman" so kindly.[28]

With his lease on the Garden suddenly terminated, Tex Rickard recruited investors and announced his plan to build a new Garden uptown at the site of the old trolley car barns on the west side of Eighth Avenue between West Forty-Ninth and Fiftieth, not far from Times Square. Buying up adjacent properties, his intention was to erect the largest building in the world dedicated exclusively to amusement, with twice the seating of the old Garden and in a far better location.[29]

•

The first preliminary sketch for the New York Life Building preserved the memory of Stanford White's Garden tower with a rendering of what would once again be the tallest tower in town. Cass Gilbert pushed for the tower, hoping to find a new home for *Diana* at its top, since the figure would obviously be homeless when the Garden came down. The twenty-story tower scheme was abandoned, however, over the feasibility of its rental space.[30]

As for the *Diana*, New York Life president Darwin P. Kingsley offered to donate the figure, valued in 1925 at $22,000, to any group of citizens interested in its preservation. More than one hundred offers and ideas flooded New York Life, with the most reasonable suggesting that the *Diana* be installed elsewhere in the city—from the top of the New York Times Building to the dome atop a hotel at Coney Island. Perhaps one of the most intriguing came from Lawrence White, who suggested to Kingsley, with a carbon copy to Homer Saint-Gaudens, that since *Diana* had always been associated with Madison Square she should be placed in the center of the square itself upon a pedestal built of fragmented columns and cornices salvaged from his father's Garden.[31]

Meanwhile, Gilbert considered placing her in the planned entrance foyer to the New York Life Building, but like Kingsley he soon realized the *Diana* needed to be placed where the figure might be seen at long range, poised high in the air.[32] Kingsley then offered the sculpture to the Saint-Gaudens Memorial in Cornish, New Hampshire, the private, charitable corporation formed by Augustus Saint-Gaudens's friends, family, and supporters in 1919 to preserve, protect, and maintain his rural home, studios, and the surrounding land as a living memorial. The site had been operating as a museum under the direction of Saint-Gaudens's son, Homer, who even more dramatically urged that the *Diana* be destroyed rather than set on a low pedestal or building. "She would be completely out of proportion at the Memorial," he wrote to Stanford White's son, "and her dirty little secret might be revealed"—that when seen up close, her seemingly smooth and sleek appearance was marred by seams and rivets thicker than those on the side of an ocean liner.[33]

Perhaps the fact that the *Diana* also bore the face of his father's mistress made it just too uncomfortable for Homer Saint-Gaudens to put her on display. There was also the sculpture's association with the lurid murder of his father's dear friend and collaborator, although privately he wrote to Lawrence White that the Saint-Gaudens Memorial might be willing to store the piece, adding he believed the memorial's other trustees would not allow it to be destroyed. Homer Saint-Gaudens also suggested that since models of the original still existed at the memorial's museum, the trustees might focus on producing smaller editions for sale, and then he quickly contacted his lawyer to check on copyrights, moral rights, and common rights, as well as a commission should a new replica be cast.[34]

•

In February 1925, New Yorkers learned that the *Diana* might well be donated to New York University on the condition that the institution acquire and rebuild the tower as her pedestal. The administration considered reconstructing it at one of several locations at the University Heights campus in the West Bronx, where Stanford White had designed a number of buildings—including the Hall of Fame for Great Americans, the Gould Memorial Library, the flanking Halls of Languages and of Philosophy, as well as one of the dormitories—"in which he took the greatest interest and pride," added Cass Gilbert in support of the plan.[35]

Kingsley immediately agreed to the proposal, promising the *Diana* to the university as soon as the tower had been reconstructed and offering in the meantime to store the sculpture free of charge.[36] Sighing with relief and citing *Diana* and the Madison Square Garden as one of the most successful collaborations of two of America's greatest artists, the National Sculpture Society resolved to support the move to NYU, as did the prestigious National Academy of Design.[37]

However, once NYU officials studied the proposal more carefully, they discovered that the cost of dismantling the old Garden tower and its flanking arcades and then transporting the bricks and terra cotta to storage would run as much as $20,000. After estimates rose to $25,000 and then $65,000, a committee composed of one hundred prominent men began to raise funds, and Cass Gilbert searched desperately for a patron while the work of reconstructing the tower, numbered brick by numbered brick, was placed under the purview of Professor Fiske Kimball, the university's supervising architect.[38] Moving ahead, New York Life signed a contract with the Joslin Construction Company of Bayonne, New Jersey, to take down the Garden, carefully dismantling the tower and storing the pieces until NYU was ready to receive them.[39]

•

In January 1925 four hundred housewreckers began razing the old car barns on Eighth Avenue to make way for the new Madison Square Garden, the third structure that would bear the estimable old moniker despite its location far from the square. The name was kept partly out of sentiment and partly because the new venue would continue to host the multitude of events that had become such a part of the old Garden's history. It would be owned and managed by the New Madison Square Garden Corporation, of which Tex Rickard served as president. The architect was Thomas W. Lamb, known for his designs for a number of new and lavish movie palaces in the area, although his design for the Garden was as stark and square as a boxing ring and equally free of all ornamentation.

Erected of steel, stone, concrete, and brick at a cost of $5 million, "The House That Tex Built" would open November 28, 1925. While the new Garden would dwarf the old in size and scope, it would consist simply of a main arena with an exposition hall located directly beneath it. All the newest mechanical systems were to be installed, including a spectacular ice rink designed to make the Garden a mecca for ice hockey and a fitting home for Rickard's new professional teams, the New York "Americans" and, for the 1926–27 season, a second team dubbed "Tex's Rangers."[40]

•

On the night of May 2, 1925, the last performance of the Ringling Brothers, Barnum & Bailey's Greatest Show on Earth at the old Madison Square Garden concluded with the circus band playing "Auld Lang Syne" as thousands in the arena joined thousands more on the street to watch the last parade down Twenty-Third.[41] Two nights later the old Garden heard the very last roar of the crowd with a boxing match—a fight between former lightweight champion and New York favorite "Italian" Johnny Dundee and an up-and-coming East-Sider named Sid Terris. Thirteen thousand seats were filled, but not solely by fight fans. "Old timers, the place is full of them," said Rickard, chewing on a cold cigar. "I swear I don't know who is here, some look like they may have been important in days gone by, and some are very old men. I am sorry to say goodbye to the old place myself."[42]

There was little ceremony to mark the end. Before the final main event the golden-voiced Joe Humphries, the official announcer for the Garden, stumbled amid sobs as he tried to read an ode that began "Good-bye forever, Temple of Fistiana, Farewell to thee, sweet Miss Diana."[43]

When the fight was over and the decision given to young Terris over the old veteran, Humphries signaled John F. Mullins, an army bugler of the fighting Sixty-Ninth Regiment resplendent in uniform and medals, to stand in the center of the ring and play "Taps." But the sergeant was nearly drowned out by a chorus of jeers and boos protesting the referee's call, and as the audience stomped out incensed, the end of the Garden was hardly noticed.[44]

Nor was the fact that the chunk of crowbar and pickax, the ring of hammer, and the buzz of saw had already begun in the adjacent tower, as the wrecking crew launched their assault. The ornate steel cage that was once the elevator shaft was taken apart and hauled off. Pine scaffolding was built on the tower exterior as temporary bracing and working space. The copper sheeting and decorative columns, bases, and moldings were torn off the lanterns' iron framework at the tower's upper reaches.[45]

Within the tower, Stanford White's apartment was the first to be tackled. These rooms dated to 1899, when he had moved from the sixth to the top floor and created an exotic snuggery, where costly tapestries covered the walls and a bronze reduction of *Diana* reigned over velvet divans and carved antique chairs from Spain and Italy, which—like the floors—were covered with bear, tiger, and leopard skins. Artificial orange trees held nestled electric bulbs that cast a rosy glow over the room, along with Tiffany azure and emerald-green sconces and a lit cardinal's red hat—since Shakespeare's time, a symbol of the tip of the erect male member. Workmen broke the rusted door locks and found little inside but dust and a few massive pillars, the lavish furnishings having long since been carried away and most sold at auction to pay White's debts.[46]

•

On the afternoon of May 6, 1925, the figure of *Diana* finally came down off her tower. In preparation, two derricks—one a 35-foot wooden gin pole with attached block and tackle and the second fitted with a sling ingeniously designed by boss wrecker Martin Ingeman—had been fixed to the top of the tower. After posing with his crew for the many gathered reporters, photographers, and motion picture cameras, wrecker Mose Cameron cut through the base of the statue with an acetylene torch. Steel ropes were then run from a steel bar under *Diana*'s foot to the base of her neck and fastened to the block and tackle. At 2:56 in the afternoon, as she was freed from her pedestal, a great shout rang out from the crowds filling the nearby buildings and craning from the windows. Gently lowered into the sling, her weight resting on her feet to prevent crushing of the thin copper plates, *Diana* turned gracefully in the wind and was swung slowly and carefully earthward.[47]

It took forty-five minutes for the sculpture to make the journey to earth. "I had no idea how lovely she was," said Cass Gilbert as she swung into view. "What a beautiful face! There is something about her eyes. I almost regret letting her go,"[48] added Darwin Kingsley. Among the crowd there to welcome her earthward were a fair number of the Garden's watchmen, cleaners, and porters, as well as NYU chancellor Elmer Ellsworth Brown, university architect Fiske Kimball, Tex Rickard, and Stanford White's now-grown son, the architect Lawrence Grant White.

Diana's condition was better than might be expected, with no rust or corrosion on her base or in the ball bearings that supported her. There were, however, many odd dents on her surface that were assumed to be damage from fast-flying birds that had struck the thin copper. After a brief examination, the *Diana* was swaddled in burlap for transport and trucked to the Franklin Fireproof Warehouse in Brooklyn, where she was to rest in storage.[49]

There was a bit of an anticlimactic moment later that afternoon when *Diana* was briefly replaced on the top of the tower by a visitor from Philadelphia, one Charles Drysdale, a baseball player who scaled the tower's fire escapes and scaffolding, removed most of his clothing and attempted to fill her spot. When ordered by the police to come down, he replied, "Statues do what they please!" After finally being pulled to earth, he was wrapped in newspapers and hustled off to the psychopathic ward at Bellevue Hospital.[50]

•

Following *Diana*'s descent, the razing of the Garden tower began in earnest, with the remainder of its framework removed by the gin pole and a portable, hand-powered Jinniwink derrick of the type commonly used in the 1920s to lift lighter weights.[51] In the course of the deconstruction, workers discovered severe corrosion some 30 feet below *Diana*'s base between the framework and the copper sheeting, with the vertical struts nearly eaten away by exposure to moisture, electrolysis, or both. Some beam connections were so rusted out that the wreckers had to brace and wire remaining pieces of the framework together before they could safely be removed. In several places some of the flanges of the corner girders were spongy, swollen, and peeling off like scabs, a loose, dirty mass that easily broke and crumbled in the fingers.[52]

While only a small section of the tower's structural framework was found be in such poor condition, there were a few other problems discovered in the remainder of the Garden. Some of the terra-cotta roof tiles, fastened with cheap wire nails to thin sheathing board, had fallen away from the small belvederes, affording comfortable homes for Madison Square's large flock of pigeons.[53] Elsewhere seeping water had disintegrated the tin flashing between the arena roof and parapet walls and created cracks in the surface of the decorative terra cotta. Virtually no maintenance had occurred over the years—except for the *Diana*, who had been regularly polished and the ball bearings cleaned of rust by an exceedingly brave steeple-climber.[54]

By the first of June 1925, the arena was roofless, but the remainder of the old Garden was "fighting to the last ditch."[55] Over the next three months, the walls had to be torn apart literally brick by brick by brick with sledgehammer, crowbar, and pneumatic hammer. Despite the lack of upkeep, the few structural problems, and its grimy, gray appearance, as the demolition continued Madison Square Garden was found to be in

63. *Demolition of Old Madison Square Garden*, William Charles McNulty, 1925. The Museum of the City of New York / Art Resource, NY.

generally excellent condition, solidly and carefully built. According to the expert engineers who examined it postmortem, had the Garden been permitted to remain and reasonable maintenance been performed, there was no reason why it should not have stood for hundreds of years.[56]

•

On June 18, 1927, President Kingsley of New York Life wielded a trowel to lay the cornerstone for the company's new, thirty-six-story "Temple of Humanity" on the old site, its gaunt steel frame already towering above its neighbors. While movie cameras rolled, still cameras clicked, and several hundred onlookers cheered, Kingsley promised that the figure of *Diana*, which had become dear to the heart of every New Yorker, would soon reign again on a worthy throne.[57]

29

The Last of the Story

INTO THE TWENTY-FIRST CENTURY, several mysteries continue to shroud Augustus Saint-Gaudens's *Diana of the Tower*. The foremost concerns the final disposition of the first and original version, installed on the Madison Square Garden tower in 1891, removed the following year, and then shipped out to Chicago to be set on the dome of McKim, Mead & White's Hall of Agriculture at the World's Columbian Exposition of 1893. Following a series of smaller conflagrations in early 1894, the White City was virtually wiped out of existence that July when fires visible from forty miles away broke out almost simultaneously in all the remaining structures in the Court of Honor and swept away Frederick MacMonnies's glorious Columbian Fountain. When the flames were finally extinguished, only the shell of the Hall of Agriculture was left standing along the Great Basin, amid a wasteland of ruin and ash. No suspects were ever arrested or a grand conspiracy proven, but since a railroad strike was currently underway in Chicago, it was widely agreed that the fires could likely be blamed on labor unrest.[1]

One of the few buildings that survived that last fire had formerly been the Palace of Fine Arts, rechristened the Field Columbian Museum, to which the *Diana* was reportedly moved in early 1894. However, the museum's records for 1894 and 1895 indicate no such acquisition, nor do those of the Chicago Art Institute,[2] while in May 1895 the *New York Sun* distressingly mentioned that New York's "first and most beloved" *Diana* had been dismembered in Chicago and offered for sale as scrap metal.[3]

Writing in 1982, preservationist Margot Gayle suggests an alternate possibility—that the *Diana* only took temporary shelter at the museum while negotiations were underway for its sale and had likely been stored with the other remnants of the exposition in the museum's basement.[4] A new tower was about to be constructed in Chicago as headquarters for Montgomery Ward & Company, a dry goods mail-order business that sold more than ten thousand items a day from its hefty catalog. Evidence found in the Ward files indicated the *Diana* had been admired by company officials as they passed to and from their exhibit in the Hall of Agriculture and was purchased by Charles H. Thorne, the son of Aaron Montgomery Ward's partner, George R. Thorne. The figure was to be held at the museum until the tower was completed.[5]

In the late 1890s architects Richard E. Schmidt and Hugh M. G. Garden had envisioned a weather vane in female form topping the ten-story tower set above the skyscraper on Michigan Avenue that would house Ward's offices and distribution warehouse and would become Chicago's tallest building at 390 feet. Sketches by Garden reveal a figure very much like Saint-Gaudens's virgin goddess. And like *Diana*, the figure installed as a weather vane atop Montgomery Ward's "busy bee-hive" Tower Building in October 1900 was a nude female poised on one foot, about 18 feet tall, made of gilded sheet copper constructed over a metal armature, and produced by the very same W. H. Mullins Co. of Salem, Ohio. Moreover, the heads of both figures were similarly positioned with similar features, and both bore a crescent moon on their foreheads.[6] Despite the fact that the Ward figure, officially christened *Progress Lighting the Way for Commerce*, carried a torch with a sweeping flame in one hand and a caduceus in the other, the resemblance was so striking that many began to call the figure "Diana" as soon as it was placed on the tower.[7]

Ward architect Richard E. Schmidt had hired sculptor John Massey Rhind to complete the design for the figure. Rhind was a Scotsman who emigrated to the United States in 1889 and was well known in New York for his monumental figural pieces that served as architectural decoration. However, he is not known to have created any other female nudes. Furthermore, Rhind never claimed credit for the piece and never listed *Progress* among his works, nor was it included in his lengthy obituary published in a London newspaper in 1936. Gayle speculates that Rhind may have designed alterations to transform the figure but did not originate the piece.[8]

64. *Progress Lighting the Way for Commerce*, 1900, Montgomery Ward Tower, Chicago, *Western Electrician* (Feb. 9, 1901).

Could *Progress* on the Ward tower actually have been *Diana* in disguise? The catalog for the Saint-Gaudens Memorial Exhibition at New York's Metropolitan Museum of Art in 1908 did indeed note that the first *Diana* now served as the weather vane for Montgomery Ward's tower.[9] But if that were true, why did Saint-Gaudens write to Stanford White in 1906, "As to the big Diana, all right, we will let the disposition of that go for the present,"[10] indicating that it was extant and within their control.

To further confound matters, how did the head and torso of the first *Diana* then briefly appear in 1909 in front of the Chicago Art Institute for the Saint-Gaudens Memorial Exhibition there?[11] A possible explanation is that after the *Diana* was purchased by Montgomery Ward the figure was sent back to Mullins to be bisected at their giant scrapyard while Rhind, who had done other work for Mullins,[12] designed a new upper torso with outreaching arms carrying the flaming torch and the caduceus.

For the head, perhaps a copy of *Diana*'s was simply struck off. It was well known that along with a stock of heads and limbs, Mullins often

65. Upper half of the first *Diana*, on display at the Chicago Art Institute, Augustus Saint-Gaudens Memorial Exhibition, 1909. DN-0054907, *Chicago Daily News* negatives collection, Chicago History Museum. Copyright © Chicago Historical Society, published on or before 2013, all rights reserved.

reused dies for other pieces as a means of minimizing costs. A Mullins advertising brochure, likely from the 1930s, clearly states that "there were so many statues left over from the Chicago fair that the city asked Mullins to buy them back for scrap," while alluding to the thrifty Mr. Mullins's tendency to reuse sculptural remnants "with a few changes." If this were the case with the *Diana*, then the various pieces of the figure would have been reassembled at Mullin's and simply riveted together.[13] Unfortunately, as Gayle observes, there is no conclusive evidence to support this theory, and it is possible that the Ward's executives simply asked their architects to commission a similar figure for their new building.[14]

The Montgomery Ward Tower Building was sold in 1908, when the company moved to new headquarters, but *Progress* reigned atop the tower until 1947, when the structure was judged essentially unsafe and demolished.[15] As reported by the *Chicago Tribune*, the figure was cut into thirty

66. Head of *Progress Lighting the Way for Commerce*, 1900, gilded copper. Eric J. Nordstrom Photography.

pieces to be claimed by Chicagoans and made into metal ashtrays or simply kept as souvenirs.[16]

As for the original *Diana*'s head, upper torso, arms, arrow, and partial bow, a 1925 article in *American Architect* reported on claims that the upper portion of the figure was still in existence, but it provided no details.[17] Perhaps after resting in storage at Mullins's or elsewhere it was hauled out for that memorial exhibition in Chicago and then taken away or left behind, melted down or not, but rumored still to hide in some dusty basement or salvage yard.

In November 2014 an interesting artifact did resurface. The head of *Progress*, which had been acquired by the David V. Nelson family, was sold by Leslie Hindman Auctioneers in Chicago below estimate for $5,000.[18] Unfortunately, there are no clear frontal images of the first *Diana* for direct comparison, but there are certainly similarities. While it is likely not the actual head of *Diana*, which had still been on display in 1909, it may well be a good copy.

Similarities may also be noted with sculptor Herbert Adams's 18-foot-tall *Goddess of Light*, which topped architect John Galen Howard's Electric Tower at the 1901 Pan-American Exposition in Buffalo—a structure itself inspired by the Giralda. The nude, winged female figure balanced on one foot and carried a torch in one upraised arm. The figure was purchased by the Humphrey Popcorn Company of Cleveland, Ohio, but was pulled to the ground and destroyed by a wrecking crew in July 1902, apparently due to the buyer's tardiness in removing it from the exhibition tower.[19]

•

Another unsolved puzzle is the disappearance of the second *Diana*'s drapery, the graceful swath that allowed the figure to turn into the wind. At some point, it simply vanished without record and without a trace. In a letter dated July 1924, Stanford White's son, Lawrence, wrote that the drapery had fallen off completely by that summer.[20] In December of that year, the *New York Times* reported that while the first *Diana* had but few draperies, the second wore nothing but a shimmering coating of gold foil.[21] This obviously was not true, at least not at the time of her installation and for a number of years following.

In 1925, when the figure came down, *American Architect* noted that the drapery had vanished "more than fifteen years before," when the bearings apparently became jammed and locked, so that *Diana*'s arrow always pointed into the northeast wind. "How this drapery became detached and where it was lodged is a mystery," they reported, "that has never been solved."[22] No newspaper anywhere in the country ever recorded such a newsworthy event at the time, particularly if, as later sources noted, the 6-foot-long piece of copper blew off in a windstorm.[23] Surely someone would have noticed, and some damage would have occurred wherever it might have landed.

Even more baffling were reports to the contrary. If indeed the drapery disappeared more than fifteen years before, around 1910 or earlier, why did articles dated 1911 specifically mention a "whirling, fluttery scarf-draped figure" that still served as a weather vane?[24] A 1916 advertisement in the *New York Evening World* featured a drawing of the Garden with a handsomely dressed gentleman gazing at a fully draped *Diana*.[25] In 1932 the *Philadelphia Enquirer* reported that the drapery had become unsafe after years of exposure and at some point was removed, but no other details were given.[26]

Diana was somewhat modified in 1905, but it had nothing to do with her drapery. A new copper arrow and string were fixed to her bow to replace the originals that had become so rusty that it was feared that they might fall. Without any rigging, a steeplejack climbed 30 feet up her leg, swung around her waist, grabbed on to her arm, and hoisted himself up the rest of the way. The 9-foot-long arrow weighing 25 pounds was hauled up after him and then carefully set into place.[27] Perhaps something similar happened to her drape—it was noticed in poor condition and quietly removed but oddly not commented upon at the time.

•

In December 1928 New York Life's new headquarters at 51 Madison Avenue, dubbed a "majestic cathedral of insurance" by the company and acknowledged as the most beautiful building in New York, was officially dedicated. President Calvin Coolidge pressed a button in the White House that unfurled an American flag in the New York Life dining room to mark the occasion, to the delight of a hundred executives, directors, and invited guests. As a symbol of his own proclaimed efforts to combine beauty with utility in the building as well as in business, President Darwin P. Kingsley was presented with a bronze reduction of Saint-Gaudens's *Diana* that was installed in a place of honor in his private office. After Kingsley retired as president in 1930, the *Diana* was placed in a paneled niche in the foyer, just outside the boardroom.[28]

Meanwhile, the full-sized second *Diana* still languished in a dark and dingy warehouse in Brooklyn. While Kingsley waited for New York University to raise the funds to rebuild the Madison Square Garden tower on its Bronx campus and install the *Diana*, he had also been putting out feelers once again to the Augustus Saint-Gaudens Memorial in New Hampshire, despite Homer Saint-Gaudens's long opposition to the figure's installation at the site. In January 1929, Kingsley received a letter from Charles Platt, noted architect and president of the memorial, finally and definitively declining to accept the donation. Platt wrote that there was neither a suitable site nor the funds available, and due to the informality of the grounds, the trustees intended to leave them exactly as they were during Saint-Gaudens's lifetime.[29] Aside from the enduring gossip surrounding the identity of the model, the *Diana*'s nudity also may have been rather less acceptable to the rural population of New Hampshire than to the citizens of New York City.[30]

As for NYU, the institution had other, more pressing construction projects that prevented it from allocating the now-estimated $365,000 needed to reassemble the Madison Square Garden tower. Although the university optimistically had the tower's carefully marked bricks and terra cotta deposited on campus within 50 yards of the spot where they hoped to erect it, the years passed, and the second *Diana* remained in storage.[31]

There were periodic inquiries as to what had become of the sculpture, but little other interest after the Wall Street crash in October 1929 and the spreading shadow of the Great Depression.[32] By the end of 1931, an impatient Kingsley made a final offer to NYU, pointing out that he had exhausted himself "in efforts to have her suitably placed and they have all come to nothing," while *Diana*'s storage was costing a great deal of money. The university conceded at last that it would not be able to raise the funds, but it passed on to Kingsley a tentative offer from the Pennsylvania Museum of Art to house the sculpture, at least "for the time being."[33]

Fiske Kimball, who was now director of the museum, was well aware of *Diana*'s plight from his days at NYU as consulting architect. Kimball offered that the museum would be happy to care for the figure if New York Life would pay for shipping expenses to its new $18 million building in Philadelphia's Fairmont Park. Leaping at the opportunity and not feeling "under the slightest obligation to NYU," Kingsley agreed to the terms in January 1932, provided the museum could place her appropriately. A spot in the U-shaped courtyard at the front of the building was likely, according to museum president Eli Kirk Price.[34] Henri Marceau, the museum's curator of fine arts, traveled to the Franklin Fireproof Warehouse in Brooklyn to inspect the *Diana* and report on her condition. All parties involved agreed to the arrangement, and on March 1, 1932, funding was secured from the Fairmount Park Art Association to cover repairs, including smoothing over the spots where the drapery had once been attached.[35]

DIANA GOES TO PHILADELPHIA

REMOVING DIANA ⊗ THE OLD MADISON SQUARE GARDEN
After looking down on the changing parade of life for more than 30
years from atop the old Madison Square Garden in New York, the
beautiful statue of Diana is to leave the city that had grown to love
her and take up her permanent abode in the Pennsylvania Museum
of Art at Philadelphia.

67. *Diana Goes to Philadelphia, Canton (OH) Repository* (Apr. 1, 1932). Newsbank / Readex and the American Antiquarian Society.

Kingsley hired a van to transport *Diana* to the Roman Bronze Works in Corona, Queens, long a subcontractor to Tiffany Studios, which had produced some of *Diana*'s bronze reductions. Damage to the abdomen and chest, more severe than originally thought, was repaired at a cost of $600 before the figure was trucked on to Philadelphia.[36]

Within the month, New Yorkers who had believed that *Diana* might go to Philadelphia on a temporary basis sadly learned that she had departed as an outright, irrevocable gift, and that there was no hope of reclaiming her.[37] Would Philadelphia welcome her warmly? Not entirely. The Rev. Mary "Joan of Arc" Hubbert Ellis, pastor of the Philadelphia Primitive Methodist Church, chairman of the Youth Protection Committee, and crusader against pornography and indecent shows, threatened a women's march to prevent the museum from installing the figure. "We are going after the whole situation and we mean business. . . . Of course, to do the right thing, we ought to go into the academy and the museum and clean them out," threatened Rev. Ellis. "They are just as bad as the burlesque theatres. But if we can't do that we can certainly do something to stop their putting such things out in the open, where children playing in the park have to see them."[38]

Diana slipped into town at dawn and was welcomed by museum staff, along with members of the Association against the Defamation of *Diana*, a group of civil and social leaders. Rev. Ellis suspended her campaign after a rebuff by the Woman's Christian Temperance Union, whose members had determined that art standards had evolved and that *Diana* posed no threat to innocent youth.[39] At a cost of $407.18, *Diana* was installed without incident on a large gilded-copper sphere set upon a pedestal on the museum's Great Stair Hall Balcony at the head of its grand staircase on April 29, 1932, and was unveiled to the public the following day.[40] Museum director Fiske Kimball happily reported that "no accession to the museum for many years has aroused the interest and admiration that this has."[41] Meanwhile Rev. Ellis's personal odd-job man was arrested on narcotics charges, and within weeks she herself was jailed for fraudulently soliciting funds for one of her nonexistent organizations.[42]

In 1967, when the fourth and last incarnation of Madison Square Garden was under construction on Eighth Avenue over the razed remnants of McKim, Mead & White's once-magnificent Pennsylvania Station, members of the Native New Yorkers Historical Association urged Mayor John Lindsay and the Art Commission to bring their goddess back home.

Mayor James Tate of Philadelphia replied to Lindsay's request, "Never. When no one wanted this poor little orphan girl, Philadelphia took her in, gave her a palatial home and created a beautiful image for her with a worldwide reputation." Added Tate, "Would you give Manhattan back to the Indians if they returned the $24 you paid for it?" Furthermore, when he proposed the move to *Diana* herself, her reported response was "New York was a great place to visit, but I wouldn't want to live there."

No, *Diana* would not leave her place of honor at the now renamed Philadelphia Museum of Art.[43] And in 2013–14, the *Diana* was regilded with 180 square feet of matted 23.4-karat red gold, funded by a grant from the Bank of America's Art Conservation Project and in accordance with

68. The second *Diana* installed on the Great Stair Hall Balcony. Philadelphia Museum of Art, Gift of the New York Life Insurance Company, 1932-30-1.

•

aesthetic preferences determined from correspondence between Augustus Saint-Gaudens and Stanford White.[44]

•

And what became of *Diana*'s most prominent models? Davida Johnson Clark—Augustus Saint-Gaudens's mistress and mother of his son Louis Paul Clark—continued to reside in the home Saint-Gaudens had purchased for her in the Noroton Heights section of Darien, Connecticut, where he made regular visits until he became too ill to travel.[45] After his death in 1907, she moved to Kearney, New Jersey, and then to Elizabeth, New Jersey, where she remained until her death at a hospital in Newark on September 15, 1910, of "post-operative intestinal paralysis."[46]

Julia "Dudie" Baird, the best known of *Diana*'s likely body models, appears to have tried performing on the stage before marrying salesman Charles Fite in 1897 and settling in a home in Brooklyn's suburbs.[47] In 1901 Saint-Gaudens wrote to her fondly, "Well, here's to you Dudie and to the day when we will meet again in N Y." He promised that the next time he went down to the city, he would "try to get some of the old chums together as of yore," signing with "My blessings and my affectionate regards."[48]

Dudie and her husband apparently separated by 1910, and little is known of her after that. But in 1949 a story made the rounds—true or not—of an old, battered woman stumbling into a Salvation Army kitchen one stormy night and begging for bread and soup. When the Salvation Army officer learned her name, he exclaimed in surprise, "Why, you are *Diana*." A crooked smile twisted across her "wretched" face as she replied, "I was *Diana*."[49]

The W. H. Mullins Company in Salem, Ohio, which cast the first and second *Dianas*, continued in the statuary business, manufacturing hundreds of examples of war heroes, mythological figures, animals, and birds in hammered or pressed copper, bronze, and zinc. No doubt tired of being blamed for the errors in casting the first *Diana*, the company put out the story that it was Mullins who received the commission for the statue from Stanford White and then hired Saint-Gaudens to create it. Supposedly Saint-Gaudens came to Salem to model the piece, but the "temperamental" sculptor threatened to abandon the project when *Diana*'s big toe fell off the plaster model. According to Mullins's fanciful account in an undated brochure, a quick-thinking company foreman met the crisis by reattaching the digit to Saint-Gaudens's satisfaction.[50]

As heroic statuary faded on the American scene after World War I, Mullins workers turned to the manufacture of metal boats, ceilings, elevator cabs, washing machine tubs, and automobile bodies with their associated parts. In 1939 the renamed Mullins Manufacturing Company merged with the Youngstown Pressed Steel Company, making virtually everything, including metal kitchen sinks, until finally closing its doors in the mid-1970s.[51]

•

Although gone for nearly a century, the memory of Stanford White's Madison Square Garden has survived not only in the story of his murder, but in numerous other towers that took inspiration from it or, by extension, from the Giralda in Seville. Among these were the 1892 Ferry Building in San Francisco designed by A. Page Brown, an alumnus of McKim, Mead & White; the 1899 Milwaukee Road Depot in Minneapolis; that 1901 Electric Tower by John Galen Howard as the centerpiece of the Pan-American Exposition in Buffalo; the 1904 Coney Island Dreamland's Beacon Tower by Kirby, Pettit & Green; the 1921 south tower of Chicago's Wrigley Building by Charles G. Beersman of Graham, Anderson, Probst & White, the successor to Daniel Burnham's firm; the 1925 Miami Freedom Tower built as headquarters for the *Miami News* by Schultze & Weaver; the 1926 Coral Gables Biltmore Hotel by Schultze & Weaver; the 1928 Cleveland Terminal Tower by Graham, Anderson, Probst & White; and the 1967 Country Club Plaza shopping complex in Kansas City, Missouri.[52]

•

As the *New York Times* summarized on the Madison Square Garden's closing in 1925, "there is probably no place in the country where more varied things have been seen or radically opposed thoughts uttered." The Garden celebrated "humor and athletic skill, and beauty and music, science and art, foible and fancy, demagogue and prophet. There was nothing like it in the life of the city,"[53] or, no doubt, in the life of the country. And from her post on the tower's top, *Diana* served as New York's tutelary deity, inspiring countless artists and poets, and no less those everyday souls who passed beneath her shadow.

Notes
·
Selected Bibliography
·
Index

Notes

Abbreviations

AAA	Archives of American Art, Smithsonian Institution
ASG	Augustus Saint-Gaudens
HSG	Homer Saint-Gaudens
LPB	Letter press book
MM&W	McKim, Mead & White
NYT	*New York Times*
Papers of ASG	Papers of Augustus Saint-Gaudens, Rauner Special Collections, Dartmouth College Library
SGNHS	Saint-Gaudens National Historical Park, Cornish, New Hampshire
SW	Stanford White
SW Correspondence	Stanford White Correspondence and Architectural Drawings, Avery Architectural and Fine Arts Library, Columbia University

Prologue

1. Robert Shackleton, *The Book of New York* (Philadelphia: Penn, 1917), 218.

2. "Mayor Grant and the Arcade," *NYT*, Nov. 27, 1889; "At Work on the Arcade," *NYT*, Jan. 28, 1891; "Madison Square Garden: An Account of the Passing of One of New York City's Architectural Landmarks," *American Architect* 128 (Dec. 20, 1925): 513.

3. "A Pyramid of Fire," *NYT*, Nov. 2, 1891; "Diana's Brow Ablaze," *Morning Advertiser* (New York), Nov. 2, 1891.

4. "The New Madison Square Garden," *New York Herald*, June 10, 1890; Frederic J. Haskin, "Madison Square Garden," *Watertown (NY) Daily News*, Feb. 6, 1911.

5. Fourth Avenue from Seventeenth Street to Thirty-First Street did not become known as Park Avenue South until 1959, although in 1888 Fourth Avenue had become Park Avenue from Thirty-Second Street north.

6. "Completion of the Tall Tower," *NYT*, Oct. 14, 1891. The tower itself was roughly 319 feet high, but the addition of a 4-foot base and the 18-foot *Diana* figure made the total height, to the brow of the *Diana*, 341 feet.

7. Lloyd Morris, *Incredible New York* (New York, Random House: 1951), 182. It would not be known as the "Great White Way" until after the turn of the century. Maxwell F. Marcuse, *This Was New York!* rev. and enlarged ed. (New York: LIM Press, 1969), 131.

8. "The Diana of the Tower," *NYT*, Nov. 8, 1891; "Diana Unveiled," *New York Herald*, Nov. 2, 1891; "Illuminating the Tower," *New York Sun*, Nov. 3, 1891.

9. Grace Mayer, *Once upon a City* (New York: Macmillan, 1958), 57; David Garrand Lowe, *Stanford White's New York* (New York: Watson-Guptill, 1999), 142.

10. "The New Madison-Square Garden Project," *NYT*, Mar. 27, 1888.

11. See Mark Twain (Samuel L. Clemens) and Charles Dudley Warner, *The Gilded Age: A Tale of To-Day* (Hartford: American Pub., 1873).

12. See "Completion of the Tall Tower," *NYT*, Oct. 14, 1891; "As If Seen from a Balloon," *New York Recorder*, Oct. 14, 1891; "Diana Unveiled," *New York Herald*, Nov. 2, 1891; "A Tower of Flaming Color," *New York World*, Nov. 3, 1891; "Golden Diana Stands Revealed," *New York Tribune*, Nov. 3, 1891; "Illuminating the Tower," *New York Sun*, Nov. 3, 1891; "Diana's a Daisy: She Was Taken to New York from Salem," *Salem (OH) Daily News*, Nov. 21, 1891; "The Week in Art," *Boston Evening Transcript*, May 21, 1892.

13. "The *Herald*'s Signal Lights This Evening," *New York Herald*, Nov. 3, 1891; "Election Returns to Flash in the Sky," *New York Herald*, Nov. 3, 1891; "At the Light," *New York Herald*, Nov. 4, 1891; "The *Herald*'s Light Flashed Out the News," *New York Herald*, Nov. 4, 1891.

14. "Madison Square Garden's Tower," *New York Sun*, Oct. 14, 1891; Charles De Kay, "The Madison Square Garden," *Harper's Weekly* 35 (July 18, 1891): 542.

15. Willa Cather, *My Mortal Enemy* (New York: Knopf, 1926), 21.

16. "The Diana of the Tower," *NYT*, Nov. 8, 1891. See also "A Huge Weathervane," *NYT*, Sept. 29, 1891; "Completion of the Tall Tower," *NYT*, Oct. 14, 1891; William A. Coffin, "The Tower of the Madison Square Garden," *Harper's Weekly* 35 (Oct. 24, 1891): 819; "The Madison Square Garden Weather Vane, the Huntress Diana," *Scientific American* 65 (Dec. 26, 1891): 407; "The Tower of Madison Square Garden," *Frank Leslie's Illustrated Newspaper* 74 (Mar. 31, 1892): 147.

17. Arthur Warren, "With Love and Gratitude the Nation Honors the Work of St. Gaudens," *Boston Sunday Herald*, May 30, 1897.

18. Royal Cortissoz, "The Metamorphosis of Diana," *Harper's Weekly* 37 (Nov. 25, 1893): 1124.

19. T. Dewing to SW, Feb. 14 [1895?], box 5:9, SW Correspondence.

20. A slangy mispronunciation of the French term *tout ensemble* or "all together."

21. As reported by his contemporaries in Anna De Koven, *A Musician and His Wife* (New York: Harper, 1926), 176.

Part One. On Madison Square

1. James D. McCabe Jr., *Lights and Shadows of New York Life; or, the Sights and Sensations of the Great City* (Philadelphia: National Publishing, 1872).

1. The "Red-Haired Trial"

1. Frederick L. Collins, *Glamorous Sinners* (New York: Ray Long & Richard Smith, 1932), 6. For descriptions of White by his contemporaries, see Edward Simmons, *From Seven to Seventy: Memories of a Painter and a Yankee* (New York: Harper, 1922), 238; H. Van Buren Magonigle, "A Half Century of Architecture, 3," *Pencil Points* 15 (Mar. 1934): 118; J. Monroe Hewlett, F. L. V. Hoppin, Albert Randolph Ross, and Philip Sawyer, "Stanford White as Those Trained in His Office Knew Him," *The Brickbuilder* 15 (Dec. 1906); Lacey Chanler and Margaret Chanler, *Roman Spring* (Boston: Little, Brown, 1934), 256–59. The standard biographical works on White are by Paul R. Baker and Charles C. Baldwin, with a more personal view by great-granddaughter Suzannah Lessard, while many others have dealt with his architectural work, including Leland M. Roth, Samuel G. White, Mosette Broderick, David Garrard Lowe, Richard Guy Wilson, and Lawrence Wodehouse, as listed in the selected bibliography.

2. Paul R. Baker, *Stanny: The Gilded Life of Stanford White* (New York: Free Press, 1989), 34–35.

3. Although biographers have described White's eyes as green or gray and his height as 6 feet 3 inches in his boot heels, his US passport application dated 1889 indicates he was 6 feet 1 inch tall, while his 1893 application states 6 feet ½ inch; both applications state blue eyes. According to Simmons, "he took short steps—trotting along the sidewalk like a busy little girl," *From Seven to Seventy*, 238.

4. Baker, *Stanny*, 132.

5. Philip Sawyer, *Edward Palmer York: Personal Reminiscences* (privately printed, 1951), 17–18; Albert Randolph Ross, in Hewlett et al., "Stanford White as Those Trained," 246.

6. "Richard White," Obituary, *New York Tribune*, Apr. 9, 1885; Charles C. Baldwin, *Stanford White* (1931; repr., New York: Da Capo Press, 1976), 24, 32; Baker, *Stanny*, 119; Richard Grant White to Alexina White, Wednesday [1870?], Richard Grant White Collection, New-York Historical Society; Suzannah Lessard, *The Architect of Desire: Beauty and Danger in the Stanford White Family* (New York: Dial Press, 1996), 76–77.

7. Mosette Broderick, *Triumvirate: McKim, Mead & White, Art, Architecture, Scandal, and Class in America's Gilded Age* (New York: Alfred A. Knopf, 2010), 65.

8. Michael MacDonald Mooney, *Evelyn Nesbit and Stanford White: Love and Death in the Gilded Age* (New York: William Morrow, 1976), 120.

9. Adeline Adams, *Daniel Chester French, Sculptor* (Boston: Houghton Mifflin, 1932), 41. See also *The Brickbuilder* 19 (Feb. 1910) for a series of tributes to McKim and details regarding his personality and working style.

10. William Mead's nickname "Dummy" has never been documented; Lawrence Wodehouse suggests it may have come from childhood or college days; *White of McKim, Mead and White* (New York: Garland, 1988), 19. Others attribute it to his whist playing, or perhaps his more silent partnership with the voluble redheads; Broderick, *Triumvirate*, xxii; Mary N. Woods, *From Craft to Profession: The Practice of Architecture in Nineteenth-Century America*

(Berkeley: Univ. of California Press, 1999), 120. For Mead, see "Story of Mead Family Told at Brattleboro," *Springfield (MA) Republican*, July 1, 1928; Sawyer, *Edward Palmer York*, 18; John Jay Chapman, "McKim, Mead and White," *Vanity Fair* 13 (Sept. 1919): 102; Lawrence G. White, *Sketches and Designs by Stanford White* (New York: Architectural Book Publishing, 1920), 17, 115; Broderick, *Triumvirate*, 517–19. See also C. H. Reilly, *McKim, Mead & White* (London: E. Benn, 1924), 12; Fiske Kimball, *American Architecture* (Indianapolis: Bobbs-Merrill, 1928), 161.

11. Charles Moore, *The Life and Times of Charles Follen McKim* (Boston: Houghton Mifflin, 1929), 56; Baldwin, *Stanford White*, 116.

12. Magonigle, "Half Century, 3," 118; Mooney, *Evelyn Nesbit*, 150; Bessie White to Prescott Hall Butler, June 5, 1884, SW Papers, New-York Historical Society, quoted in Baker, *Stanny*, 102.

13. Orrick Johns, "Stanford White's Genius Survives City's Change," *NYT*, Mar. 22, 1925.

14. MM&W journal entry, July 16, 1887, $500 commission, Madison Square Garden Co., MM&W Bill Book #3, MM&W Architectural Records and Drawings, Avery Architectural and Fine Arts Library, Columbia University.

15. Woods, *From Craft to Profession*, 67.

16. "A Wildly Varied Entertainment," *Brooklyn Eagle*, July 25, 1887.

17. "The Talk of New York," *NYT*, Feb. 20, 1887; "New Madison-Square Garden," *NYT*, June 24, 1887; "To Cost a Million," *NYT*, July 8, 1887; "Future Glory of Madison Square," *New York Herald*, July 8, 1887; "A Wildly Varied Entertainment," *Brooklyn Eagle*, July 25, 1887; "Diversion's New Temple," *New York Herald*, Oct. 30, 1887; "A Palace of Pleasure," *Harper's Weekly* 31 (Nov. 5, 1887): 807.

18. "A Chance for Architects," *NYT*, July 18, 1887.

19. "Out among the Builders," *Real Estate Record and Builders' Guide* 40 (Sept. 17, 1887): 1179; "A Palace of Pleasure," *Harper's Weekly* 31 (Nov. 5, 1887): 807.

20. Richard G. White to SW, June 14, 1887, box 27:10, SW Correspondence.

21. "Madison Square Garden Sold," *New York Tribune*, Dec. 15, 1886; "A Million in the Way," *New York Herald*, Dec. 16, 1886; *An Act to Incorporate the Madison Square Garden Company*, May 24, 1887, New York Life Archives.

22. "New Madison Square Garden," *NYT*, June 24, 1887; "A Big Amusement Scheme," *New York Tribune*, Mar. 10, 1887; "To Cost a Million," *NYT*, July 8, 1887; "Future Glory of Madison Square," *New York Herald*, July 8, 1887; "The New Madison Square Garden," *Real Estate Record and Builders' Guide* 40 (July 9, 1887): 923; Leland M. Roth, *McKim, Mead & White, Architects* (New York, Harper & Row, 1983), 158–59, 392n90; Baker, *Stanny*, 151.

23. Goldwin Goldsmith, "I Remember McKim, Mead & White," *Journal of the American Institute of Architects* 13 (Apr. 1950): 170.

24. Moore, *Life and Times of McKim*, 39; Lowe, *Stanford White's New York*, 97.

25. Baker, *Stanny*, 35. Other unsuccessful romances included Augustus Saint-Gaudens's sister-in-law Eugenie Homer, reel 38, frame 366, Papers of ASG; Broderick, *Triumvirate*, 73–74, also reports a failed romance with a neighbor, Anaïs Casey.

26. SW to ASG, May 8, 1880, quoted in Stanford White, *Stanford White: Letters to His Family*, ed. Claire Nicolas White (New York: Rizzoli, 1997), 105.

27. Saarinen Papers 2073:366, AAA, cited in Baker, *Stanny*, 94.

28. Lessard, *Architect of Desire*, 45.

29. Including her brother-in-law, Prescott Butler, who sent her a privately printed book of Valentine poetry, Saarinen Papers 2073:683–86l, AAA, cited in Baker, *Stanny*, 94, 418n7.

30. SW to Bessie Smith, [Sept.] 1883, "Letters from Stanford White's Wedding Tour, 1883–1884," Robert White Collection, quoted in Baker, *Stanny*, 97.

31. SW to Bessie Smith, n.d., White Family Papers, St. James, NY, quoted in Burke Wilkinson, *Uncommon Clay: The Life and Works of Augustus Saint Gaudens* (New York: Harcourt Brace Jovanovitch, 1985), 135.

32. Wilkinson, *Uncommon Clay*, 135.

33. Louise Hall Tharp, *Saint-Gaudens and the Gilded Era* (Boston: Little, Brown, 1969), 172.

34. A loan of some $450 made in 1883. SW to ASG, n.d., reel 14, frame 128, Papers of ASG.

35. Homer Saint-Gaudens, ed. *The Reminiscences of Augustus Saint-Gaudens* (New York: Century Co, 1913) 1:281; see also John Dryfhout, *The Work of Augustus Saint-Gaudens* (Hanover, NH: Univ. Press of New England, 1982), catalog no. 109.

36. Tharp, *Saint-Gaudens*, 183–84.

37. SW to Elihu Vedder, Jan. 6, 1885, in Regina Soria, *Elihu Vedder: American Visionary Artist in Rome (1836–1923)* (Rutherford, NJ: Fairleigh Dickinson Univ. Press, 1970), 180–81.

38. These were great-great-great-grandfather Matthias Nicoll and great-great-grandfather Edward Holland. Baldwin, *Stanford White*, 159.

39. Robert A. M. Stern, Thomas Mellins, and David Fishman, *New York 1880: Architecture and Urbanism in the Gilded Age* (New York: Monacelli Press, 1999), 705–6; Sarah Bradford Landau and Carl W. Condit, *Rise of the New York Skyscraper, 1865–1913* (New Haven: Yale Univ. Press, 1996), 43; Edwin G. Burrows and Mike Wallace, *Gotham: A History of New York City* (Oxford: Oxford Univ. Press, 1998), 668. The building later served as Stewart's warehouse, and after it was eventually abandoned it was taken over by the *New York Sun* and is now known as the Sun Building, although it houses the New York Department of Buildings.

40. Stern, Mellins, and Fishman, *New York, 1880*, 706; Eric Homberger, *The Historical Atlas of New York City: A Visual Celebration of Nearly 400 Years of New York City's History* (New York: St. Martin's Griffin, 1994), 102–3. The building was taken over by Wanamaker's, which ran it from 1896 to 1954, and in 1956 it was destroyed by fire and wrecking ball. Gayle, *Cast-Iron Architecture in New York* (New York: Dover), 1974), 161.

41. "Mrs. Stewart's Funeral," *NYT*, Oct. 29, 1886; "Mrs. Stewart's Millions," *NYT*, Nov. 2, 1886; "The Will of Mrs. Stewart," *New York Tribune*, Nov. 2, 1886. The family filed a series of lawsuits charging their distant cousin and Stewart's close companion/executor Judge Henry Hilton with fraud, deceit, and undue influence upon Cornelia Stewart. These lawsuits would drag on for almost three years until they were settled out of court, largely in favor of Judge Hilton, with Bessie White's mother receiving a reduced share of the residual estate in both

cash and properties. "Dissatisfied Stewart Heirs," *NYT*, July 24, 1887. See also "Judge Hilton's Answer," *NYT*, Oct. 26, 1887; "A. T. Stewart's Money," *NYT*, Mar. 14, 1888; "Dividing the Millions," *NYT*, Jan. 17, 1890; "To Have Hilton Set Aside," *New York Tribune*, July 26, 1887; "End of the Great Stewart Will Contest," *New York Herald*, Jan. 17, 1890.

42. Baker, *Stanny*, 138.

43. Lowe, *Stanford White's New York*, 9.

44. Elizabeth Drexel Lehr, *"King Lehr" and the Gilded Age* (Philadelphia: J. B. Lippincott, 1935), 202.

2. On Madison Square

1. "Open Only to Members," *NYT*, Mar. 15, 1886; Evander Berry Wall, *Neither Pest nor Puritan: The Memoires of E. Berry Wall* (New York: Dial Press, 1940), 103; Richard O'Connor, *The Scandalous Mr. Bennett* (Garden City, NY: Doubleday, 1962), 135, 139.

2. Designed by architect Henry Fernbach and opened March 1884. "Drama," *Life* 8 (Dec. 16, 1886): 386; "Paragraphs of the Playhouses," *New York Herald*, July 3, 1887; "Eden Musée Faces Bankruptcy Court," *NYT*, June 18, 1915; "Departed Glories of Twenty-Third Street," *NYT*, Feb. 10, 1924; T. Allston Brown, *A History of the New York Stage, from the First Performance in 1732 to 1901* (New York: Dodd, Mead, 1903), 52.

3. "A License Refused," *NYT*, Feb. 6, 1887; "Lenient to Koster & Bial," *NYT*, Feb. 22, 1887; "Sunday Law Enforcement," *NYT*, July 17, 1887; "Not a Severe Fine," *NYT*, July 27, 1887; "A Musical Problem," *NYT*, Aug. 31, 1887; "Not Guilty of Desecrating Sunday," *New York Tribune*, Dec. 29, 1887; "Justice Duffy Approves," *NYT*, Dec. 29, 1887.

4. "Koster & Bial's Leased," *NYT*, Aug. 1, 1887; Mary C. Henderson, *The City and the Theatre* (Clifton, NJ: James T. White, 1973), 147.

5. For contemporary descriptions of Madison Square see Henry Collins Brown, *Fifth Avenue Old and New, 1824–1924* (New York: Fifth Avenue Assoc., 1924), 73; John C. Van Dyke, *The New York: A Commentary on the Place and the People* (New York: Macmillan, 1909), 170, 172; Herbert A. Asbury, *The Gangs of New York* (Garden City, New York: Alfred A. Knopf, 1928), 133; Moses King, *King's Handbook of New York City* (Boston: Moses King, 1892), 152.

6. McCabe, *Lights and Shadows*, 128.

7. McCabe, *Lights and Shadows*, 203; *Appleton's Dictionary of New York and Its Environs* (New York: D. Appleton, 1880): 109; Marcus A. Benjamin, *Historical Sketch of Madison Square* (New York: Meriden Monographs #1, 1894): 11; "House of Refuge Destroyed," *New York Spectator*, May 23, 1839; Fifth Avenue Bank, *Fifth Avenue Events: A Brief Account of Some of the Most Interesting Events Which Have Occurred on the Avenue* (Boston: Walton Printing, 1916), 60–61. After the fire, a new House of Refuge was erected at Twenty-Third Street, and in 1854 its inhabitants were moved to Randall's Island. Benjamin, *Historical Sketch*, 10.

8. Miriam Berman, *Madison Square: The Park and Its Celebrated Landmarks* (Layton, UT: Gibbs Smith, 2001), 35.

9. "'Corporal' W. Thompson," Obituary, *New York Herald*, Mar. 14, 1872; Benjamin, *Historical Sketch*, 14; Berman, *Madison Square*, 35–36. Some tarried long enough so that a "jolly party was often forced to grope slowly homeward on that gloomy road" back to the city. Arthur Bartlett Maurice, *Fifth Avenue* (New York: Dodd, Mead, 1918), 60; New York City Department of Parks & Recreation, "Madison Square Park," NYC Parks website, accessed Jan. 22, 2008, http://www.nycgovparks.org/parks/madisonsquarepark/history.

10. Joseph Durso, *Madison Square Garden: 100 Years of History* (New York: Simon & Schuster, 1997), 16–17; James Trager, *The New York Chronology: The Ultimate Compendium of Events, People, and Anecdotes from the Dutch to the Present* (New York: HarperCollins, 2003), 90–91; Morris, *Incredible New York*, 26–27.

11. A. H. Saxon, *Enter Foot and Horse: A History of Hippodrama in England and France* (New Haven: Yale Univ. Press, 1968), 25; John McCormick, *Popular Theatres of Nineteenth-Century France* (London: Routledge, 1993), 29.

12. "A Successful Showman," *NYT*, Dec. 31, 1876.

13. "Franconi's Hippodrome," *New York Weekly Herald*, Mar. 12, 1853; "Magnificent Amusement," *Pittsburgh Republican*, Mar. 26, 1853; "Franconi's Hippodrome—Grand Dress Rehearsal," *New York Weekly Herald*, Apr. 30, 1853; Benjamin, *Historical Sketch*, 16; Kate Simon, *Fifth Avenue: A Very Social Story* (New York: Harcourt Brace Jovanovich, 1978), 55; Fifth Avenue Bank, *Fifth Avenue Events*, 70; "Hippodromes," *NYT*, May 23, 1853; "Franconi's Hippodrome," *New York Weekly Herald*, Sept. 10, 1853; "The Hippodrome," *NYT*, May 16, 1853; "Amusements," *NYT*, June 20, 1853.

14. "Serious Accident at the Hippodrome," *NYT*, June 27, 1853; "The Fatal Accident at the Hippodrome—Coroner's Inquest," *NYT*, July 7, 1853.

15. "Accident at the Hippodrome," *NYT*, July 4, 1853.

16. "The Accident at the Hippodrome," *Albany Evening Journal*, June 29, 1853.

17. "Where Is That Cattle Ordinance?" *NYT*, Aug. 20, 1852; "Cattle Show of the American Institute at Madison Cottage," *New York Daily Tribune*, Oct. 18, 1850; Stephen Jenkins, *The Old Boston Post Road* (New York, G. P. Putnam's Sons, 1913), 106–7; John Flavel Mines, *A Tour around New York* (New York: Harper Bros., 1893), 233–34.

18. Anita Leslie, *The Remarkable Mr. Jerome* (New York: Holt, 1954), 58.

19. "City Improvements," *New York Herald*, May 3, 1856; Henry Irving Dodge, "Forty Years on Twenty-Third Street," in *Valentine's Manual of Old New York*, ed. Henry Collins Brown (New York: Valentine's Manual Inc., 1924), 84.

20. "The Fifth-Avenue Hotel," *NYT*, Aug. 23, 1859; "The Last Novelty in American Hoteldom. Vertical Railway," *The Builder* 17 (Sept. 10, 1859): 607. Eno had no interest in running the establishment, so he leased it to Colonel Paran Stevens—widely known as the "Napoleon of popular hotels"—and his partner, Hiram Hitchcock. "Passing of the Fifth Avenue Hotel," *NYT*, July 7, 1907; Henry A. Gouge, *A New System of Ventilation* (New York: Van Nostrand, 1881), 33; Brown, *Fifth Avenue*, 65; King, *King's Handbook*, 202.

21. Dodge, "Forty Years," 86, 89; Simon, *Fifth Avenue*, 58.

22. Augustus Saint-Gaudens, "Reminiscences of an Idiot," [1905] typescript, Rauner ML-4, box 44:16, Augustus Saint-Gaudens Papers, Dartmouth College Library, 6 (hereafter cited as ASG, "Reminiscences of an Idiot").

23. William F. Mulhall, "The Golden Age of Booze," in *Valentine's Manual of Old New York*, ed. Henry Collins Brown (New York: Valentine's Manual Inc., 1923), 132.

24. Richard Harding Davis, "Stanford White," reprinted from *Collier's Weekly*, Aug. 4, 1905 (in 1906), 102; Chanler and Chanler, *Roman Spring*, 256; Collins, *Glamorous Sinners*, 7; Tharp, *Saint-Gaudens*, 136.

25. William Shepard Walsh, *A Handy Book of Curious Information* (Philadelphia: J. B. Lippincott, 1913), 334. It was preceded two years earlier by the first passenger elevator for public use, a rope-hoisted type installed by the Otis Brothers in the five-story china and glass emporium at Broadway and Broome Street for E. W. Haughwout & Company. Landau and Condit, *Rise of the New York Skyscraper*, 35; Gayle, *Cast-Iron Architecture*, 142; "Elevator Museum," accessed June 26, 2015, http://www.theelevatormuseum.org/timeline.php; "The Last Novelty in American Hoteldom," *The Builder* 17 (Sept. 10, 1859), 607; W. Sloane Kennedy, "The Vertical Railway," *Harper's New Monthly Magazine* 65, (Nov. 1882): 891–92; "The Fifth-Avenue Hotel," *New York Daily Tribune*, Aug. 2, 1859; Trager, *New York Chronology*, 122. Otis Tufts was no relation, however, to Elisha Otis of Yonkers, who invented the elevator safety brake as well as the steam engine drive and was founder of the Otis Elevator Company.

26. "Passing of the Fifth Avenue Hotel," *NYT*, July 7, 1907.

27. William O. Stoddard, *Lincoln's Third Secretary: The Memoirs of William O. Stoddard*, ed. with introduction by William O. Stoddard Jr. (New York: Exposition Press, 1955), 185; ASG, "Reminiscences of an Idiot," 19.

28. David M. Barnes, *The Draft Riots in New York, July, 1863* (New York: Baker and Goodwin, 1868), 35; "The Mob in New York," *NYT*, July 15, 1863; "Passing of the Fifth Avenue Hotel," *NYT*, July 7, 1907; Stoddard, *Lincoln's Third Secretary*, 185; Asbury, *Gangs of New York*, 128–49; Iver Bernstein, *The New York City Draft Riots* (New York: Oxford Univ. Press, 1990), 62.

29. H. Paul Jeffers, *Diamond Jim Brady: Prince of the Gilded Age* (New York: John Wiley, 2001), 298.

30. *Brooks Brothers, Centenary, 1818–1918* (New York: Brooks Brothers, 1918), 27; George T. Strong, *The Diary of George T. Strong*, vol. 3, ed. Alan Nevins and M. H. Thomas (New York: MacMillan, 1952), 573–79. For Saint-Gaudens's memories of these events, see ASG, "Reminiscences of an Idiot," 13; HSG, *Reminiscences of Augustus*, 1:14–15.

31. "Grant. Magnificent Reception," *New York Herald*, Nov. 21, 1865; "Reception of General Grant," *Harper's Weekly* 9 (Dec. 9, 1865), 774; Simon, *Fifth Avenue*, 59.

32. "Passing of the Fifth Avenue Hotel," *NYT*, July 7, 1907.

33. Benjamin, *Historical Sketch*, 40.

34. Jesse Lynch Williams, *New York Sketches* (New York: Charles Scribner's Sons, 1902), 47; Elizabeth Hawes, *New York, New York: How the Apartment Building Transformed the Life of the City* (New York: Alfred A. Knopf, 1993), 109.

35. Percy MacKaye, *Epoch: The Life of Steele MacKaye*, vol. 1 (New York: Boni & Liveright, 1927), plate 45, 343, 462; "The Madison-Square Theatre," *NYT*, Feb. 1, 1880.

36. "Cooled by Ice Air: The Talk of New York," *Brooklyn Eagle*, July 10, 1887; Wayne S. Turney, "A Glimpse of Theater History," accessed Apr. 28, 2009, http://www.wayneturney.20m .com/fitchclyde.htm; Lady Mary Anne Duffus Hardy, *Through Cities and Prairie Lands: Sketches of an American Tour* (New York: Chapman and Hall, 1881), 64–65; MacKaye, *Epoch*, 1:342; "The New Madison Square Theatre," *New York Tribune*, Feb. 2, 1880.

37. Marcuse, *This Was New York*, 336. The Albemarle was also one of the few hotels that openly refused to admit Jewish guests, perhaps under the powerful influence of A. T. Stewart's lawyer, Henry Hilton. As director of Stewart's Grand Union Hotel upstate in Saratoga Springs, Hilton organized the American Society for the Suppression of the Jews and in 1877 banned them from the racing resort's hotel, the largest in the world. The Albemarle relented a few years later and welcomed famed tragedienne Sarah Bernhardt on her first visit to the States in 1880, despite her "faultless nose of the best Hebrew type." "The Position of the New-York Hotels," *NYT*, June 20, 1877; "Burning Jewish Bosoms," *New York Herald*, July 24, 1879; "Mlle. Bernhardt Arrives," *NYT*, Oct. 28, 1880; Homberger, *Historical Atlas*, 166.

38. King, *King's Handbook*, 204; Marcuse, *This Was New York*, 337; M. H. Dunlop, *Gilded City: Scandal and Sensation in Turn-of-the-Century New York* (New York: Harper-Collins: 2001), 71; Dodge, "Forty Years," 98.

39. "Personal and General Notes," *New Orleans Daily Picayune*, May 2, 1882.

40. Marcuse, *This Was New York*, 337; Berman, *Madison Square*, 46; Jeffers, *Diamond Jim Brady*, 99; Mulhall, "Golden Age of Booze," 126.

41. "Bouguereau's Nymphs in Peril," *New York Herald*, Oct. 7, 1886.

42. Berman, *Madison Square*, 46. The painting was sold at auction in 1901 after Stokes's death and remained hidden in storage for twenty-five years. Robert Sterling Clark saw the painting in 1934 while inspecting the wine cellar at Manhattan Storage and remembered that he had enjoyed it at the Hoffman House during his student days. He purchased the painting in 1942, and it is now installed at the Sterling and Francine Clark Art Institute in Williamstown, Massachusetts. Other paintings in the bar, which featured both male and female nude figures, included Falero's *Vison of Faust*, a *Narcissus* by Correggio, *Boudoir of an Eastern Princess* by Etienne, an *Eve* in marble by Ball, and a bronze *Pan and Bacchante* by Schlessinger. "A Noted Bar Closed," *Charlotte Observer*, July 23, 1896; Benjamin, *Historical Sketch*, 40; King, *King's Handbook*, 206.

3. A Practical Education

1. Baker, *Stanny*, 17–18.

2. Royal Cortissoz, *John La Farge: A Memoir and a Study* (Boston: Houghton Mifflin, 1911), 117; Royal Cortissoz, *American Artists* (New York: Charles Scribner's Sons, 1923), 297.

3. Baker, *Stanny*, 17–18.

4. See Baker, *Stanny*, 408n2 for an argument as to the date.

5. SW to ASG, May 1878, in Baldwin, *Stanford White*, 59.

6. Lewis Mumford, *The Brown Decades* (1931; repr., New York: Dover, 1955), 116.

7. Mariana Griswold Van Rensselaer, *Henry Hobson Richardson, and His Works* (Boston: Houghton Mifflin, 1888), 128.

8. Baker, *Stanny*, 21.

9. Moore, *Life and Times of McKim*, 55; Alfred Hoyt Granger, *Charles Follen McKim: A Study of His Life and Work* (Boston: Houghton Mifflin, 1913), 104–5; Mooney, *Evelyn Nesbit*, 146; Michael George, "Biographical Notes on the Men of McKim, Mead & White," *Monograph of the Work of McKim, Mead & White, 1879–1915* (New York: Architectural Book Publishing, 1981), xxii.

10. Baker, *Stanny*, 20; Leland M. Roth, *The Architecture of McKim, Mead & White, 1870–1920: A Building List* (New York: Garland Publishing, 1978), xxi.

11. Baker, *Stanny*, 21.

12. Moore, *Life and Times of McKim*, 39; Baker, *Stanny*, 21; Francis S. Swales, "Master Draftsman, V: Francis H. Bacon," *Pencil Points* 5 (Aug. 1924): 102.

13. Glessner reel 643:477–78, Richardson Papers, AAA.

14. Moore, *Life and Times of McKim*, 46.

15. Worth (1794–1849) distinguished himself in the War of 1812 and then defeated the Seminole in Florida, taught at West Point, and died of cholera while commander of the newly conquered territories of Texas and New Mexico. The obelisk was installed in 1857, and Worth was then exhumed from his Brooklyn grave and reinterred. "William Jenkins Worth—Soldier," *Americana* 23 (1929): 276; Benjamin, *Historical Sketch*, 18; Donald M. Reynolds, *Monuments and Masterpieces: Histories and Views of Public Sculpture in New York City* (New York: Macmillan, 1988), 19–22.

16. Baker, *Stanny*, 133.

17. Charles Ranhofer, *The Epicurean* (New York: Charles Ranhofer, 1894), 100–101.

18. Berman, *Madison Square*, 52.

19. Mark Kurlansky, *The Big Oyster: History on the Half Shell* (New York: Ballantine Books, 2006), 107–8.

20. "A Chance for Architects," *NYT*, July 18, 1887.

21. Clayton Hamilton, "There Were Giants in Those Days," *The Players' Book* (New York: The Players, 1938), 42.

22. "Future Glory of Madison Square," *New York Herald*, July 8, 1887.

23. "A Palace of Pleasure," *Harper's Weekly* 31 (Nov. 5, 1887): 807–8.

24. George P. Lathrop, "Spanish Vistas," *Harper's Magazine* 65 (Aug. 1882): 373; Broderick, *Triumvirate*, 247–48.

25. After an etching by A. H. Haig, *American Architect and Building News* 18 (Dec. 26, 1885): 522.

26. "A Palace of Amusement: The Great Successor of the Madison Square Garden," *NYT*, Oct. 30, 1887.

4. Enter Augustus Saint-Gaudens

1. His father did not use a hyphen in his last name, and his brother spelled it St. Gaudens, perhaps to distinguish himself; Augustus Saint-Gaudens often did not use a hyphen, while his son did prefer it and published a number of biographical works spelled with the hyphen.

2. ASG, "Reminiscences of an Idiot," 56. While Saint-Gaudens recalled it as Beethoven's Seventh, that symphony does not have an andante movement, although the Fifth does.

3. James E. Fraser, typescript for biography of Augustus Saint-Gaudens, box 44:9, Papers of ASG.

4. SW to Alexina White, Nov. 28, 1878, White Family Papers, St. James, Long Island, NY, quoted in Wilkinson, *Uncommon Clay*, 82.

5. Firsthand observers variously described his eyes as either blue, hazel, or gray, although upon first meeting him, Augusta Saint-Gaudens described them as blue. Augusta Homer to her mother, n.d., box 27, Papers of ASG.

6. Kenyon Cox, *Artist and Public, and Other Essays on Art Subjects* (New York: Scribner's Sons, 1914), 183. Although he was redheaded as a child, Saint-Gaudens's hair later darkened and was described in firsthand accounts as ranging from dark brown to tawny brown to reddish brown, although his beard remained more clearly red. Janet Scudder, *Modeling My Life* (New York: Harcourt, Brace, 1925), 132.

7. Clarence King to John Hay, July 28, 1887, John Hay Library, quoted in Patricia O'Toole, *The Five of Hearts: An Intimate Portrait of Henry Adams and His Friends, 1880–1918* (New York: Simon & Schuster, 1990), 189.

8. ASG, "Reminiscences of an Idiot," 3, 42; Frances Grimes, "Memories of Saint-Gaudens's Studio in the 1900s," box 44:14, Papers of ASG, 7–8; Cox, *Artist and Public*, 183; Will H. Low, *Chronicle of Friendships* (New York: Charles Scribner's Sons, 1908), 217; Mrs. Daniel Chester French, *Memories of a Sculptor's Wife* (Boston: Houghton Mifflin, 1928), 187.

9. Maitland Armstrong, *Day Before Yesterday: Reminiscences of a Varied Life*, ed. Margaret Armstrong (New York: Charles Scribner's Sons, 1920), 260.

10. ASG, "Reminiscences of an Idiot," 3; HSG, *Reminiscences of Augustus*, 1:10.

11. ASG, "Reminiscences of an Idiot," 7; Wilkinson, *Uncommon Clay*, 9; Russell Lynes, "Saint-Gaudens, His Time, His Place," *AAA Journal* 25 (Oct. 1985): 4.

12. ASG, "Reminiscences of an Idiot," 4–5; HSG, *Reminiscences of Augustus*, 1:18–22.

13. ASG, "Reminiscences of an Idiot," 11–12; HSG, *Reminiscences of Augustus*, 1:38.

14. HSG, *Reminiscences of Augustus*, 1:40; Maitland Armstrong, "Saint-Gaudens: Recollections of His Friend Maitland Armstrong," *Scribner's Magazine* 61, no. 1 (Jan. 1917): 23.

15. ASG, "Reminiscences of an Idiot," 12, 18.

16. George F. Kunz, "Industrial Art: How It Is Advanced by Art in Education," *Proceedings of the 45th Annual Convocation of the University of the State of New York, October 17–19, 1908, Education Dept. Bulletin* 427 (Albany: Univ. of the State of New York, 1908): 94–95; Maggie MacMonnies Courant, interview in *New York Tribune*, Jan. 19, 1896, cited in Mary Smart, *A Flight with Fame: The Life and Art of Frederick MacMonnies* (Madison, CT: Sound View Press, 1996), 21–22.

17. ASG, "Reminiscences of an Idiot," 20A; HSG, *Reminiscences of Augustus*, 1:50–51.

18. According to Kunz, "Industrial Art," 94, it was a certain Mr. Leon Barre who made the suggestion.

19. Bailey Van Hook, *Angels of Art: Women and Art in American Society 1876–1914* (University Park: Pennsylvania State Univ. Press, 1994), 3.

20. Kathleen Adler, "'We'll Always Have Paris': Paris as Training Ground and Proving Ground," in *Americans in Paris, 1860–1900*, by Kathleen Adler, Erica E. Hirshler, and H. Barbara Weinberg (London: National Gallery, 2006), 11; see also Susan Waller, *The Invention of the Model: Artists and Models in Paris, 1830–1870* (Aldershot, England: Ashgate, 2006), 68–69.

21. ASG, "Reminiscences of an Idiot," 23; Van Hook, *Angels*, 224n23.

22. Warren, "With Love and Gratitude," May 30, 1897.

23. ASG, "Reminiscences of an Idiot," 23–24; Tharp, *Saint-Gaudens*, 31.

24. Supérieure des Beaux-Arts, Archives Nationale, Paris, cited in Kathryn Greenthal, *Augustus Saint-Gaudens, Master Sculptor* (New York: Metropolitan Museum of Art, 1985), 169n29. Following the reform of 1863, three attached ateliers were established at the École des Beaux-Arts for sculpture, three for painting, one for copperplate engraving, and one for engraving on semiprecious stones. For the École's complicated entrance requirements and competitions, see "Art Education in Paris," *New York Sun*, Dec. 20, 1891; Phillippe Grunchec, "Les Élèves américains peintres et sculpteurs," in *Le Voyage de Paris* (Château de Blérencourt, Musée National de la Coopération Franco-américaine, 1990); Albert Boime, *The Academy and French Painting in the Nineteenth Century* (London: Phaidon, 1971).

25. ASG, "Reminiscences of an Idiot," 29.

26. Casper Purdon Clarke, Director of the Metropolitan Museum of Art, interview, "Highest Art Appreciated Here," *NYT*, Apr. 5, 1908; ASG, "Reminiscences of an Idiot," 34–35C.

27. ASG, "Reminiscences of an Idiot," 35D.

28. HSG, *Reminiscences of Augustus*, 1:100; Tharp, *Saint-Gaudens*, 42.

29. ASG, "Reminiscences of an Idiot," 36.

30. ASG, "Reminiscences of an Idiot," 38.

31. He reputedly later saw it as "the necessary mistake of every American sculptor—the figure of an Indian." Low, *Chronicle*, 221.

32. ASG, "Reminiscences of an Idiot," 39B; Montgomery Gibbs to ASG, 1872, box 8:26, Papers of ASG.

33. The area where Saint-Gaudens had his studio had been touted as the healthiest spot in Rome but was later discovered to be a hotbed of fever. Letter from John Ruskin, May 12,

1872, *Fors Clavigera*, letter 18, *Works* 27:309, quoted in Arthur Severn, *The Professor: Arthur Severn's Memoir of John Ruskin*, ed. James S. Dearden (London: Allen & Unwin, 1967), 59.

34. ASG, "Reminiscences of an Idiot," 38, 38C, 40, 46–49.

35. There was one love affair in Rome with a model named Angelina, who likely posed in the nude for a figure of *Silence* commissioned by the New York City Grand Lodge of the Masonic Order. Saint-Gaudens hoped to elope to Paris with Angelina, but as he recalled later, "she wisely refused." ASG, "Reminiscences of an Idiot," 44; HSG, *Reminiscences of Augustus*, 1:133.

36. Wilkinson, *Uncommon Clay*, 66.

37. Tharp, *Saint-Gaudens*, 71–73.

38. ASG to Thomas Johnston Homer, Feb. 22, 1874, Papers of ASG.

39. ASG, "Reminiscences of an Idiot," 50–52; Chanler and Chanler, *Roman Spring*, 267; HSG, *Reminiscences of Augustus*, 1:157.

40. "Trinity Church," *Boston Daily Advertiser*, Feb. 10, 1877; "Description of the New Edifice," *NYT*, Feb. 10, 1877; see also Theodore E. Stebbins Jr., "Trinity Church at 125," in *The Makers of Trinity Church in the City of Boston*, ed. James F. O'Gorman (Amherst: Univ. of Massachusetts Press, 2004), 16–17.

41. Tharp, *Saint-Gaudens*, 103.

42. HSG, *Reminiscences of Augustus*, 1:166.

43. Louis Baury, "The Story of the Tile Club," *Bookman* 35 (June 1912): 381; Edward Strahan and F. Hopkinson Smith, *A Book of the Tile Club* (Boston: Houghton Mifflin, 1887); Ronald G. Pisano, "Decorative Age or Decorative Craze? The Art and Antics of the Tile Club (1877–1887)," in *The Tile Club and the Aesthetic Movement in America*, ed. R. G. Pisano (New York, Harry N. Abrams, 1999).

44. HSG, *Reminiscences of Augustus*, 1:162–63; ASG to SW, Mar. 1878, box 30:28, Papers of ASG.

45. SW to ASG, n.d. [May 1878?], box 30:28, Papers of ASG.

46. SW to John A. Dix, Feb. 12, 1879, reel 6, frame 96–98, Papers of ASG.

47. Baker, *Stanny*, 41; Broderick, *Triumvirate*, 39–41.

48. HSG, *Reminiscences of Augustus*, 1:160; Tharp, *Saint-Gaudens*, 125.

49. "Hades" in some versions. Moore, *Life and Times of McKim*, 44; Baker, *Stanny*, 75.

50. ASG, "Reminiscences of an Idiot," 61; Baker, *Stanny*, 51; Dryfhout, *Work*, 94; Moore, *Life and Times of McKim*, 45.

51. Wayne Craven, *Stanford White: Decorator in Opulence and Dealer in Antiquities* (New York: Columbia Univ. Press, 2005), 16.

52. C. Lewis Hind, *Augustus Saint-Gaudens* (New York: International Studio, 1908), xxvi; Margaret Innes Bouton, "The Early Works of Augustus Saint-Gaudens" (master's thesis, Radcliffe College, 1946), 102n44; Kenyon Cox, "Augustus Saint-Gaudens," *The Century* 35 (Nov. 1887): 28; Theodore Child, "Modern French Sculpture," *Harper's Magazine* 76 (Jan. 1888): 246; Louis Hourticq, *Art in France* (New York: Charles Scribner's Sons, 1911), 437.

53. HSG, *Reminiscences of Augustus*, 1:260–61.

54. SW to Alexina Mease White, Nov. 20, 1878, in White, *Stanford White: Letters*, 66.

55. Broderick, *Triumvirate*, 91.

56. ASG to SW, Mar. 1878, box 20:38, and SW to ASG, Apr. 1, 1880, box 22:14, Papers of ASG.

57. HSG, ed., "Intimate Letters of Stanford White: Correspondence with His Friend and Co-Worker Augustus Saint-Gaudens," *Architectural Record* 30 (Sept. 1911): 284ff; SW to ASG, Oct. 17, 1879, in HSG, *Reminiscences of Augustus*, 1:233; SW to ASG, Feb. 24, 1880, reel 14, frame 352–55, Papers of ASG.

58. "Editor's Chronicle," *Magazine of American History with Notes and Queries* 7 (Oct. 1881): 316; "Fine Arts," *New York Herald*, May 20, 1881.

59. ASG to Augusta Saint-Gaudens, quoted in Tharp, *Saint-Gaudens*, 146; SW to ASG, Feb. 24, 1879, in HSG, *Reminiscences of Augustus*, 1:231; SW to ASG, n.d., box 22:15, Papers of ASG.

60. ASG, "Reminiscences of an Idiot," 67–68; Marcuse, *This Was New York*, 235.

61. Glen Brown et al., *Augustus Saint-Gaudens: Biography, Exhibition of His Works, and Memorial Meeting* (Washington, DC: American Institute of Architects and the Corcoran Gallery of Art, Gibson Bros. Press, 1908), 70; Lorado Taft, *American Sculpture* (New York: Macmillan, 1917), 286; Wilkinson, *Uncommon Clay*, 377. Donatello's Saint George is now in the collection of the Bargello in Florence.

62. There is some question as to Louis's role in the carving of the reliefs. However, Augustus Saint-Gaudens writes, "I modeled reliefs on the Farragut," "Reminiscences of an Idiot," 66; and "I will see what I can do with the two low-reliefs," to John La Farge, Dec. 29, 1879, HSG, *Reminiscences of Augustus*, 1:267. Louis probably had a hand in them as well, and according to assistant Frances Grimes, Louis modeled the base, but no one knew it. Frances Grimes, "Interviews of Frances Grimes and Maxfield Parrish by Frank Spinny," tape 2, side A, AAA.

63. Taft, *American Sculpture*, 291; Richard Harding Davis, *Van Bibber and Others* (New York: Harper, 1892), 103. The New York Parks Department later subverted White's plan by planting sod around the monument to prevent the homeless from camping on the exedra and neglected the pebbled paths that should have led the visitor to a perfect view. Joyce K. Schiller, "The Artistic Collaboration of Augustus Saint-Gaudens and Stanford White" (PhD diss., Washington Univ., 1997), 148–55.

64. Ranhofer, *Epicurean*, 2:788.

65. "The Farragut Statue," *NYT*, May 25, 1881; "Farragut: The Admiral's Statue Unveiled," *New York Herald*, May 26, 1881.

5. Women, Horses, and a Curse?

1. Broderick, *Triumvirate*, 26.

2. In 1882 the hotel achieved national notoriety when a large table was booked by a group from the Armory Hall drinking establishment that included transvestites. Due to its fading reputation, the hotel was eventually abandoned by the New York Coaching Club,

went bankrupt, and closed in 1896, its shell torn down in 1906. "Bilking the Brunswick," *Washington (DC) Evening Critic*, Dec. 29, 1882; "M'Glory Indicted," *New York Evening World*, Dec. 3, 1891; Mark Caldwell, *New York Night: The Mystique and Its History* (New York: Scribner, 2005), 190; George Chauncey, *Gay New York: Gender, Urban Culture, and the Making of the Gay Male World, 1890–1940* (New York: Basic Books, 1994), 37; "Passing of Old New York Hotels," *NYT*, Sept. 28, 1902; "The Closing of the Brunswick," *New York Tribune*, June 24, 1896; James L. Ford, "Famous New York Hotels of the 'Seventies,'" in *Valentine's Manual of Old New York*, ed. Henry Collins Brown (New York: Valentine's Manual Inc., 1924), 169–70.

3. Reginald W. Rives, *The Coaching Club: A History* (New York: privately printed, 1935), 1; Benjamin, *Historical Sketch*, 46; McCabe, *Lights and Shadows*, 259.

4. The route ran up Fifth Avenue, then up the West Drive, curved around the north end of Central Park at 110th Street, then back down the East Drive, out of the park at Fifty-Ninth Street, and back down Fifth Avenue. "The Coaching Club Meet," *New York Herald*, May 26, 1887; Rives, *Coaching Club*, 91; "Ten Coaches on Parade," *NYT*, May 29, 1887; "Society Topics of the Week," *NYT*, May 29, 1887; "Whips and Wheels," *New York Herald*, May 29, 1887; Morris, *Incredible New York*, 149; Wall, *Neither Pest*, 92; Brown, *Fifth Avenue*, 57; Simon, *Fifth Avenue*, 67.

5. Berman, *Madison Square*, 13.

6. *New York Sun*, July 11, 1887.

7. "Popular Summer Concerts," *New York Herald*, Aug. 16, 1887; "Amusements," *NYT*, July 24, July 31, Aug. 16, Aug. 24, and Aug. 26, 1887.

8. "'Pinafore' at the Madison Square Garden," *New York Herald*, June 14, 1887; "Pinafore Revived," *New York Tribune*, June 14, 1887; "Theatres and Music," *Brooklyn Eagle*, June 19, 1887; "Amusements," *NYT*, June 14 and June 19, 1887.

9. "New-York City: The Fourth-Avenue and Harlem Railroads," *NYT*, Mar. 27, 1857; Brown, *Fifth Avenue*, 88; Trager, *New York Chronology*, 114; "Madison Square Garden," *American Architect* 128 (Dec. 20, 1925): 513; Baker, *Stanny*, 150.

10. Marcuse, *This Was New York*, 240; Frank Weitenkampf, *Manhattan Kaleidoscope* (New York: Charles Scribner's Sons, 1947): 267–68; "Madison Square Garden," *American Architect* 128 (Dec. 20, 1926): 512–13; Arthur Baer, "Madison Square Garden," *Saturday Evening Post*, Sept. 8, 1928, 114.

11. M. R. Werner, *Barnum* (New York: Harcourt, Brace, 1923), 311; Harvey W. Root, *The Unknown Barnum* (New York: Harper, 1927), 326.

12. For the Hippodrome, see "Mr. P. T. Barnum's Show," *NYT*, Oct. 21, 1873; P. T. Barnum, *The Life of Barnum, the World-Renowned Showman* (Chicago: P. Miller, 1890), 387, 391–92; Werner, *Barnum*, 312–13, 315; "Barnum's New Hippodrome," *New York Herald*, Feb. 9, 1874; "Mr. Barnum's New Hippodrome," *NYT*, Feb. 12, 1874; "Barnum's Roman Hippodrome," *NYT*, Apr. 25, 1874; "The Record of the Place," *NYT*, Apr. 22, 1880; "Amusements," *NYT*, Apr. 28, 1874; "Up in a Balloon," *New York Herald*, July 25, 1874; Marcuse, *This Was New York*, 240; Root, *Unknown Barnum*, 329.

13. Editorial, *NYT*, July 7 and July 8, 1874.

14. Andy Logan, "That Was New York: The Palace of Delight," *New Yorker* 41 (Feb. 27, 1965): 42.

15. "The Record of the Place," *NYT*, Apr. 22, 1880; Marc Elliot, *Down 42nd Street: Sex, Money, Culture, and Politics at the Crossroads of the World* (New York, Warner Books: 2001), 361; Durso, *Madison Square Garden*, 18.

16. "The Metropolitan Concert Hall, New York, NY," *American Architect and Building News* 6 (Dec. 20, 1879): 196; James L. Ford, "The Flash Age of New York," *Valentine's Manual of Old New York*, ed. Henry Collins Brown (New York: Valentine's Manual Inc., 1923), 22.

17. "Record of Amusements," *NYT*, May 30, 1875.

18. "Amusements," *New York Herald*, May 30 and June 5, 1875; "Opening of Gilmore's Concert Garden Last Night," *New York Morning Telegram*, May 30, 1875; "Local Miscellany: Moody and Sankey's Reception, Changes in the Hippodrome," *NYT*, Jan. 4, 1876; "Gilmore's Garden Transformed," *NYT*, Oct. 5, 1876.

19. Logan, "That Was New York," 44.

20. "Gilmore's Garden," *NYT*, Dec. 3, 1878.

21. "The Coney Island Improvements," *NYT*, May 6, 1877; "A Watering Place at Home: The Changes on Coney Island," *NYT*, Aug. 13, 1877; "Keeping Cool at Coney Island," *NYT*, Aug. 4, 1879; Stern, Mellins, and Fishman, *New York, 1880*, 947.

22. "Mr. Vanderbilt's Will," *NYT*, Jan. 9, 1877; "The Story of His Life," *NYT*, Dec. 9, 1885.

23. "Gilmore's Garden to Change Hands," *NYT*, Nov. 19, 1878; "Gilmore's Garden to Remain Open," *NYT*, Dec. 6, 1878; "Sports at Gilmore's Garden," *NYT*, Dec. 13, 1878; Durso, *Madison Square Garden*, 21, 23; "Skating at Gilmore's Garden," *NYT*, Jan. 1 and Jan. 20, 1879; "The Skating Rink at Gilmore's," *New York Herald*, Jan. 19, 1879; "Skating at Gilmore's Garden," *New York Herald*, Jan. 21, 1879.

24. "O'Leary against Hughes," *NYT*, Sept. 30, 1878; "O'Leary," *Springfield (MA) Republican*, Mar. 13, 1879; Walter Bernstein, "A Walking Fever Has Set In," *Virginia Quarterly Review* 56 (Autumn 1980): 701.

25. "A Six Days' Tramp Begins," *NYT*, Mar. 10, 1879; "The Champion in the Rear," *NYT*, Mar. 11, 1879; "The Hunt for O'Leary," *NYT*, Mar. 13, 1879.

26. "Terrible Scene at Gilmore's," *New York Herald*, Mar. 13, 1879; "Panic at Gilmore's Garden," *New York Tribune*, Mar. 13, 1879; "O'Leary Out of It," *Philadelphia Inquirer*, Mar. 13, 1879; "The Accident Last Spring," *New York Tribune*, Apr. 22, 1880; "Scenes Outside the Garden," *NYT*, Mar. 13, 1879; "O'Leary Out of the Race," *NYT*, Mar. 13, 1879.

27. "Nine Persons Seriously Injured," *NYT*, Mar. 13, 1879.

28. "Another Six-Day Tramp," *NYT*, Apr. 14, 1879.

29. "Future of Gilmore's Garden," *NYT*, Mar. 25, 1879; "Madison Square Garden to Be Converted into the New-York Arcade," *NYT*, June 27, 1879; "Gilmore's Garden in Demand," *NYT*, Aug. 7, 1879.

30. "Madison Square Garden," *New York Herald*, May 22, 1879; "Testing Electric Illumination," *NYT*, June 16, 1879; "Driving away Darkness," *New York Sun*, July 11, 1879; "A

Change in Gilmore's Garden," *NYT*, May 22, 1879; "Future of Gilmore's Garden," *NYT*, Mar. 25, 1879; "The Record of the Place," *NYT*, Apr. 22, 1880.

31. "Madison Square Garden," *New York Herald*, May 22, 1879; "A Change in Gilmore's Garden," *NYT*, May 22, 1879; "Sunday Music and Lager Beer," *NYT*, June 9, 1879; "Madison-Square Garden," *NYT*, June 1, 1879.

32. "Amusements," *New York Herald*, June 1, 1879; "The Madison Square Garden, Improving the Structure," *NYT*, Dec. 13, 1879; "The Record of the Place," *NYT*, Apr. 22, 1880.

33. "Dismantling the Garden," *NYT*, Apr. 24, 1880; "The Record of the Place," *NYT*, Apr. 22, 1880; "A Death Dance," *New York Herald*, Apr. 22, 1880; "The Madison Square Wreck," *New York Tribune*, Apr. 23, 1880; "The Disaster at the Fair," *New York Tribune*, Apr. 24, 1880; "The Tragedy at the Fair," *NYT*, Apr. 28, 1880; "Is Nobody to Blame?" *NYT*, Apr. 23, 1880; "A Fair That Was Fatal," *New York Tribune*, Apr. 22, 1880; "Madison Square Garden, a Fearful Accident," *Chicago Tribune*, Apr. 22, 1880.

34. The other victims included one of the fair organizers, Mrs. Anna B. Hegeman; her maid, Mary Ann Connolly; and one of the guests, Mrs. Annie Willets. "The Disaster at the Fair," *New York Sun*, Apr. 23, 1880; "Is Nobody to Blame?" *NYT*, Apr. 23, 1880; "A Fair That Was Fatal," *New York Tribune*, Apr. 22, 1880.

35. "Is Nobody to Blame?" *NYT*, Apr. 23, 1880; "The Madison Square Wreck," *New York Tribune*, Apr. 23, 1880. Although *The New Jerusalem* by Inness would be believed lost for more than a century, it had actually been recovered after the disaster and reworked by the artist into three smaller pieces, renamed and sold to three different collectors. Rachael Z. DeLue, *George Inness and the Science of Landscape* (Chicago: Univ. of Chicago Press, 2004), 274n1.

36. "The Madison Square Disaster," *NYT*, May 6, 1880; "The Madison Square Disaster: Admissions," *NYT*, May 7, 1880; "The Cause of the Disaster," *New York Tribune*, Apr. 22, 1880; "The Disaster at the Fair," *New York Sun*, Apr. 23, 1880; "The Madison Square Crash," *New York Herald*, May 13, 1880; "Blind to All Warnings," *NYT*, Apr. 29, 1880; "Trying to Fix the Blame," *NYT*, Apr. 30, 1880; "Protecting Dudley," *NYT*, Apr. 26, 1880; "Smith's Gaseous Theory: A Contractor's Explanation of the Garden Disaster," *NYT*, May 5, 1880; "The Disaster at the Fair: How Death Traps Are Built," *New York Tribune*, Apr. 30, 1880; "The Madison-Square Garden Roof," Letter to the Editor, *NYT*, May 2, 1880; "Defects of Madison-Square Garden," *NYT*, May 22, 1880; "The Madison-Square Garden," *NYT*, May 4, 1880; "The Responsibility," *NYT*, May 10, 1880; "Jury Speaks Its Mind," *NYT*, May 8, 1880.

37. "Another Six-Day Tramp," *NYT*, Apr. 14, 1879.

38. Editorial, *New York Sun*, Apr. 26, 1880.

39. "The Responsibility," *NYT*, May 10, 1880.

40. "A Death Dance," *New York Herald*, Apr. 22, 1880.

41. "The Garden Condemned," *NYT*, May 15, 1880; "Condemning Madison Square Garden," *New York Tribune*, May 17, 1880.

42. "The Madison-Square Garden: A Magnificent Place of Amusement to Be Erected on the Site," *NYT*, June 10, 1880; "P. T. Barnum's New Scheme," *New York Tribune*, June 10, 1880.

43. "P. T. Barnum's Museum Building Prospectus," *American Architect and Building News* 8 (Aug. 7, 1880): 61–62; "A Great Scheme Abandoned," *NYT*, Nov. 30, 1880.

44. "The Garden Condemned," *NYT*, May 15, 1880; "Condemning Madison Square Garden," *New York Tribune*, May 17. 1880.

45. "The Dakota," *NYT*, Oct. 22, 1884; Stern, Mellins, and Fishman, *New York, 1880*, 562; Christopher Gray, "Streetscapes: The Dakota; The Elusive Mystery of Its Name," *NYT*, Aug. 15, 1993. However, as clever as this jest may be, the name "Dakota" was selected by the building's owner, Edward Clark of the Singer Sewing Machine Co., long before the building was ever constructed, as the Indian carved on the facade testifies, for Clark proposed that streets on the West Side should be renamed after western American states.

46. "The Coming Horse Show," *NYT*, Aug. 30, 1883; "An Exhibition of Horses Promised," *NYT*, June 5, 1883; "Preparing for the Horse Show," *NYT*, Oct. 17, 1883; "The Horse Show," *New York Herald*, Oct. 19, 1883; "A Great Horse Show Promised," *NYT*, Oct. 2, 1883; "A Fine Horse Show Expected," *NYT*, Oct. 14, 1883; "Arrival of the Horses," *NYT*, Oct. 22, 1883; "The National Horse Show. Everything Ready," *New York Herald*, Oct. 21, 1883; "National Horse Show Formal Opening," *New York Herald*, Oct. 23, 1883; "Horses of Every Kind," *NYT*, Oct. 23, 1883; "Close of the Horse Show," *NYT*, Oct. 27, 1883; "Arranging a Horse Show," *New York Tribune*, June 5, 1883; "New York Horse Show. Reconstruction to Madison Square Garden Already Begun," *New York Herald*, Sept. 23, 1883; "The Horse Show," *New York Herald*, Oct. 22, 1883; "Prize Horses," *New York Herald*, Oct. 26, 1883; "National Horse Show," *New York Herald*, Oct. 25, 1883; "The National Horse Show," *NYT*, Sept. 15, 1883; "The Great Horse Show. A Brilliant Close of a Successful Season," *New York Herald*, Oct. 27, 1883; "The Horse Show," *New York Herald*, Oct. 23. 1883; "The Horse Show," *New York Herald*, Oct. 27, 1883; "Some Features of the Horse Show," *New York Tribune*, Oct. 26, 1883; Wall, *Neither Pest*, 93; Brown, *Fifth Avenue*, 71.

47. Lehr, *"King Lehr,"* 74; Brown, *Fifth Avenue*, 70–71; Wall, *Neither Pest*, 93.

48. "Firemen Who Were Not Needed," *NYT*, Mar. 14, 1884; "Saved from a Panic," *New York Herald*, Mar. 14, 1884; "Madison Square Garden: Changes Being Made to Secure Safety from Fire," *NYT*, Mar. 15, 1884; "Making the Big Garden Safer," *New York Tribune*, Mar. 15, 1884; "Madison Square Garden Exits," *New York Herald*, Mar. 15, 1884.

49. "Madison Square Garden to Go," *NYT*, Mar. 27, 1884.

50. "Madison Square Garden," *Harper's Weekly* 34 (Sept. 13, 1890): 718.

51. Logan, "That Was New York," 44.

52. "Before, During and After," *NYT*, July 18, 1882; "Capt. Williams Stops a Fight," *NYT*, May 13, 1884.

53. "Sullivan and Ryan Meet," *NYT*, Jan. 20, 1885; "Sparring to a Small House," *New York Tribune*, Nov. 25, 1884; "Sluggers under Arrest," *New York Tribune*, Nov. 19, 1884; Logan, "That Was New York," 44ff; Durso, *Madison Square Garden*, 59; Burrows and Wallace, *Gotham*, 1147, 1164.

54. "Leonard Jerome Dead," *New York Tribune*, Mar. 5, 1891; Jeffers, *Diamond Jim Brady*, 299; Leslie, *Remarkable Mr. Jerome*, 100, 103; "Mr. Leonard W. Jerome," *Harper's Weekly* 35

(Mar. 14, 1891): 192–93; "Leonard W. Jerome Dead," *NYT*, Mar. 5, 1891; Morris, *Incredible New York*, 27; Martin Gilbert, *Churchill and America* (New York: Simon & Schuster, 2005), 5; Simon, *Fifth Avenue*, 63.

55. Prior tenants included the Union League Club, the Turf Club in 1881, and the Madison Club in 1883. The University Club would occupy the site until 1899 and then be followed by the Manhattan Club. Leslie, *Remarkable Mr. Jerome*, 103; Benjamin, *Historical Sketch*, 32; Wodehouse, *White*, 51; Baker, *Stanny*, 119; Jeffers, *Diamond Jim Brady*, 298.

56. "The Talk of New York," *Brooklyn Eagle*, Feb. 20, 1887; De Kay, "Madison Square Garden," 542.

57. MacKaye, *Epoch*, 1:487.

58. Burrows and Wallace, *Gotham*, 1081; Richard Gilder to HSG, June 6, 1907, in HSG, *Reminiscences of Augustus*, 1:186–87.

59. "Low Prices Paid for White Pictures," *NYT*, Apr. 12, 1907; "White Sale Over: Brings $51,532," *NYT*, Apr. 13, 1907; "Stanford White Collection. Unusual Assemblage of Art Objects Now Shown at the Galleries," *NYT*, Nov. 26, 1907; "White Sale Closed: Last of Architect's Art Collection Sold," *NYT*, Dec. 11, 1907; Craven, *Stanford White*, 219–21. The auction included both old and contemporary paintings, Roman sculpture, furniture, oriental rugs, Flemish tapestries, a Louis XIV carved and painted ceiling, an Italian Renaissance fireplace, and a rhinoceros horn candelabra.

60. Dunlop, *Gilded City*, 155; Morris, *Incredible New York*, 45–46; McCabe, *Lights and Shadows*, 474; Kat Long, *The Forbidden Apple: A Century of Sex and Sin in New York City* (Brooklyn: Ig, 2009); Berman, *Madison Square*, 19; Edward Robb Ellis, *The Epic of New York City* (New York: Kodansha America, 1997), 363.

61. Allen Churchill, *Park Row* (New York: Rinehart, 1958), 217.

62. Asbury, *Gangs of New York*, 201.

63. "Murdered Man Was a Sport," *Rockford (IL) Republic*, June 27 1906; "Comstock Wants to Tell about White and Others," *NYT*, June 29, 1906; "Says She Knew Stanford White," *Philadelphia Inquirer*, July 5, 1906.

64. Philip Sawyer, in Hewlett et al., "Stanford White as Those Trained," *The Brickbuilder* 15 (Dec. 1906): 247.

Part Two. Building a Palace of Pleasure

1. "A Temple of the Muses," *New York Herald*, Mar. 24, 1889.

6. The Walls Come Down

1. Barnet Phillips, "The Construction of Great Buildings," *Harper's Weekly* 34 (Apr. 12, 1890): 282; "Tearing Down the Old Garden," *NYT*, Aug. 8, 1889; "Shutting Them Out," *Pittsburg Dispatch*, Aug. 8, 1889; "The Big Building Coming Down Rapidly," *New York Tribune*, Aug. 24, 1889.

2. Phillips, "Construction of Great Buildings," 282–83.

3. SW to W. Mead, July 31, 1889, box 22:24, SW Correspondence.

4. SW to W. Mead, Aug 3, 1889, box 22:24, SW Correspondence.

5. "A Palace of Amusement," *NYT*, Oct. 30, 1887; "A Palace of Pleasure," *Harper's Weekly* 31 (Nov. 5, 1887): 807–8; "Diversion's New Temple," *New York Herald*, Oct. 30, 1887.

6. "Description. Madison Square Garden," *Prospectus*, Mar. 24, 1888, 7, New York Life Archives; "No New Theatre in Madison Square," *New York Tribune*, Mar. 6, 1888.

7. "No New Theatre in Madison Square," *New York Tribune*, Mar. 6, 1888; "The Madison Square Garden Project," *Real Estate*, Mar. 10, 1888: 297.

8. Four hundred New Yorkers died in the storm that ran March 11–14. The best-known victim was former congressman and senator Roscoe Conkling, who struggled for three hours to walk from Wall Street to the New York Club on West Twenty-Fifth at Madison Square and died a month later from pneumonia. He would be memorialized by a bronze statue on the southeast corner of Madison Square Park by John Quincy Adams Ward in 1893. Another result of the blizzard would be the removal of aboveground telegraph and electrical wires, ordered below ground by the mayor and fought unsuccessfully by Western Union. Irving Werstein, *The Blizzard of '88* (New York: Thomas Y. Crowell, 1960), 70; "The Wires Come Down," *NYT*, Apr. 17, 1889.

9. "A Big Scheme in Jeopardy," *NYT*, Mar. 23, 1888.

10. "Objecting to the Tower," *NYT*, Mar. 27, 1888.

11. "Nothing Venture, Nothing Have," *NYT*, Apr. 15, 1888.

12. "Amusements," *New York Sun*, Sept. 7, 1888.

13. "A Palace of Amusement," *NYT*, Oct. 30, 1887.

14. ASG, "Reminiscences of an Idiot," 69–70.

15. Kenyon Cox to Jacob Dolson Cox, 1884, cited in H. Wayne Morgan, *Kenyon Cox: 1856–1919: A Life in American Art* (Kent, OH: Kent State Univ. Press, 1994), 114.

16. SW to Henry Adams, May 31, 1889, LPB 2:114–15, SW Correspondence.

17. "Description. Madison Square Garden," *Prospectus*, Mar. 24, 1888, 7, New York Life Archives.

18. HSG, *Augustus Saint-Gaudens, Adapted from a Lecture Given by His Son, Homer Saint-Gaudens* (Cornish, NH: Saint-Gaudens Memorial, 1927), 37; SW to Horace Bradley, Nov. 9, 1893, SW Correspondence.

19. "A Colossal Amphitheatre," *New York Herald*, Mar. 22, 1889; "To Build a Music Hall," *New York Tribune*, Mar. 15, 1889; "The Amusement Hall Project Supposed to Have Fallen Through," *New York Sun*, Mar. 16, 1889; "A Permanent Orchestra," *New York Sun*, Mar. 20, 1889; "No Palace on the Garden Site," *New York Sun*, Mar. 16, 1889.

20. "Not Abandoned, Mr. White Says," *New York Sun*, Mar. 17, 1889; "A Temple of the Muses," *New York Herald*, Mar. 24, 1889; "New Plans for the Madison Square Garden," *New York Sun*, Mar. 2, 1889.

21. "Out among the Builders," *Real Estate Record and Builders' Guide* 43 (Jan. 10, 1889): 76; "A New Madison Square Garden," *New York Tribune*, Mar. 23, 1889; "Financial Notice," *New York Sun*, Mar. 25, 1889; Logan, *That Was New York*, 58; Herbert Livingston Satterlee, *J. Pierpont Morgan: An Intimate Portrait* (New York: Macmillan, 1939), 260.

22. "The Plans Completed," *NYT*, Mar. 22, 1889.

23. "A Colossal Amphitheatre," *New York Herald*, Mar. 22, 1889; "Financial Notice," *New York Sun*, Mar. 25, 1889; "It Will Be a Mighty Pile," *New York Tribune*, Mar. 22, 1889; "A New Madison-Square Garden," *NYT*, May 5, 1889; "A Project That Still Lags," *NYT*, June 26, 1889; "Men & Things," *Real Estate Record and Builders' Guide* 43 (June 29, 1889): 908.

24. "Men & Things," *Real Estate Record and Builders' Guide* 43 (June 29, 1889): 908; "A Project That Still Lags, *NYT*, June 26, 1889; "A Real Estate Broker's Offer," *Real Estate Record and Builders' Guide* 44 (July 31, 1889); "An Offer of the Garden," *New York Herald*, July 31, 1889; "Out among the Builders," *Real Estate Record and Builders' Guide* 43 (Jan. 19, 1889): 77.

25. "Madison Square Stock All Sold," *New York Herald*, July 16, 1889.

26. "Pulling Down Madison Square Garden," *New York Tribune*, Aug. 8, 1889; "Changes in Madison Square Garden Plans," *New York Tribune*, Aug. 14, 1889.

27. "The Big Building Coming Down Rapidly," *New York Tribune*, Aug. 24, 1889; "Last of Madison Square Garden," *New York Herald*, Aug. 25, 1889; "Home News. New-York City," *New York Tribune*, Aug. 29, 1889.

7. Continental Influences

1. Newspaper clippings, MM&W Architectural Records Collection, PR 042, New-York Historical Society; Broderick, *Triumvirate*, 250.

2. Puddle iron, a form of wrought iron, has higher tensile strength due to increased carbon content. It was used as well for the internal structure of the Statue of Liberty, also designed by Eiffel's engineer, Maurice Koechlin.

3. Stuart Durant, *Palais des machines* (London: Phaidon, 1994), 21. Designed by French architect Ferdinand Dutert and engineer Victor Contamin, the palais was demolished in 1909. Detailed plans were published in English in "The Paris Exhibition," *Engineering* 43 (May 3, 1889): 453ff.

4. SW to ASG, April 6, 1889, LPB 2:18, SW Correspondence; Baker, *Stanny*, 124; Wilkinson, *Uncommon Clay*, 203.

5. HSG, *Reminiscences of Augustus*, 2:6.

6. According to studio assistant René Théophile de Quélin, it was not until Saint-Gaudens left the studio for three weeks to recover from a fit of anger that de Quélin encouraged MacMonnies to model some figures, including a copy of a Donatello relief that Saint-Gaudens later saw and appreciated. René de Quélin, "Early Days with

MacMonnies in St. Gaudens' Studio: A Personal Reminiscence," *Arts & Decoration* 16 (Apr. 1922): 425.

7. ASG, "Reminiscences of an Idiot," 66; HSG, *Reminiscences of Augustus*, 2:6, 15.

8. "Fred K. Macmonnies," *Chicago Daily Inter Ocean*, Sept. 1, 1895.

9. Smart, *Flight with Fame*, 22.

10. Smart, *Flight with Fame*, 65. For a brief period in 1885, MacMonnies returned to assist Saint-Gaudens in his studio in Cornish, New Hampshire, and then in New York, returning to Paris in 1886. Smart, *Flight with Fame*, 62–64.

11. Taft, *American Sculpture*, 336.

12. Alfred de Lostalot, "La Sculpture au salon de 1882," *Gazette des Beaux-Arts* 26 (Dec. 1882): 499, 507; Peter Fusco, "Jean-Alexandre-Joseph Falguière," in *The Romantics to Rodin: French Nineteenth-Century Sculpture from North American Collections*, ed. Peter Fusco and H. W. Janson (Los Angeles: Los Angeles County Museum of Art, 1980), 258–59.

13. See Fusco, "Jean-Alexandre-Joseph Falguière," fig. 130, 259; Paul Moreau-Vauthier, "Alexandre Falguière, sculpteur et peintre," *L'Art et les artistes* 24 (1932): 288, quoted in Jeanne L. Wasserman, *Diana in Late Nineteenth-Century Sculpture: A Theme in Variations* (Wellesley: Wellesley College Museum, 1989), np.

14. ASG to F. MacMonnies, Sept. 18, 1888, reel 3042, MacMonnies Family Papers, AAA, cited in Smart, *Flight with Fame*, 75.

15. "With Our Modern Dianas," *NYT*, Apr. 16, 1893.

16. Fairfax Downey, *Portrait of an Era as Drawn by C. D. Gibson: A Biography* (New York: Scribner's Sons, 1936), 30–32, 100; "C. D. Gibson and His Model," *Kansas City (MO) Times*, Jan. 28, 1895.

17. ASG to F. MacMonnies, Sept. 18, 1888, MacMonnies Family Papers, AAA, quoted in Smart, *Flight with Fame*, 77.

18. ASG to F. MacMonnies, Sept. 18, 1888, MacMonnies Family Papers, AAA, quoted in Smart, *Flight with Fame*, 75.

19. Smart, *Flight with Fame*, 34, 75–76; Tharp, *Saint-Gaudens*, 178.

20. Mary Fairchild MacMonnies Low, "Memoirs" (1938), 66, MacMonnies Family Papers, AAA, cited in Smart, *Flight with Fame*, 78.

21. ASG to F. MacMonnies, Apr. 21, 1889, reel 3042, MacMonnies Family Papers, AAA, in Smart, *Flight with Fame*, 79.

22. Smart, *Flight with Fame*, 99, 287; "First Citizen," *Brooklyn Eagle*, June 4, 1890.

23. ASG to F. MacMonnies, Feb. 1, 1891, reel 3042, MacMonnies Family Papers, AAA, quoted in Smart, *Flight with Fame*, 79.

24. Craven, *Stanford White*, 23, 29, 51.

25. Baker, *Stanny*, 309; Craven, *Stanford White*, 21.

26. Cortissoz, *American Artists*, 300; White, *Sketches and Designs*, 24–25.

27. "Washington Triumphal Arch," *NYT*, Apr. 28, 1889; "A Permanent Arch," *NYT*, May 4, 1889.

8. Laying Plans

1. "The New Madison-Square Garden," *NYT*, July 13, 1889.

2. Moore, *Life and Times of McKim*, 56.

3. W. Mead to SW, July 27, 1889, box 22:24, SW Correspondence.

4. Roth, *Architecture of McKim, Mead & White*, xxxi, xxxiv.

5. SW to W. Mead, July 31, 1889, box 22:24, SW Correspondence.

6. SW to W. Mead, Aug. 7, 1889, box 22:24, SW Correspondence.

7. SW to W. Mead, Aug. 13, 1889, box 22:24, SW Correspondence.

8. Madison Square Garden cross section, drawer 35, MM&W Architectural Records and Drawings, Avery Architectural and Fine Arts Library, Columbia University; SW to W. Mead, Aug. 13, 1889, box 22:24, SW Correspondence.

9. SW to W. Mead, Aug. 7, 1889, and SW to W. Mead, Aug. 15, 1889, box 22:24, SW Correspondence.

10. HSG, *Reminiscences of Augustus*, 1:373.

11. Reilly, *McKim, Mead & White*, 21. Quoting Browning, Wells wrote home from Florence, "Open my heart and you shall see graved inside of it 'Italy.'" C. Howard Walker, "Joseph Wells, Architect, 1853–1890," *Architectural Record* 66 (July 1929): 16.

12. Mrs. Villard was the daughter of William Lloyd Garrison, whose son married McKim's sister Lucy.

13. SW to Mrs. Harrison, Mar. 19, 1896, LPB 15:338, SW Correspondence.

14. Baldwin, *Stanford White*, 358. Evidence indicates that the Renaissance style is what the Bavarian-born Mr. Villard had actually requested. Roth, *McKim, Mead & White*, 86. Unfortunately for Villard, in trying to expand the railroad he had strained its finances and spent so much of his own fortune on the project that he was only able to take up residence there for several weeks before an angry mob, believing the huge structure to be his alone, forced him to vacate. Moore, *Life and Times of McKim*, 48; Reilly, *McKim, Mead & White*, 21; W. M. Kendall to R. Cortissoz, quoted in Walker, "Joseph Wells," 18.

15. The first revival was inspired by the German *Rundbogenstil* with its basis in the Romanesque, transplanted to the United States via England and particularly popular for federal buildings and commercial establishments. Landau and Condit, *Rise of the New York Skyscraper*, 11.

16. Mary Gay Humphreys, "Decorative Art in America," *Appleton's Annual Cylopaedia, 1884* (New York: Appleton, 1888), 244–45; William C. Shopsin and Mosette Broderick, *The Villard Houses: Life Story of a Landmark* (New York: Viking Press, 1980), 64.

17. Broderick suggests the *Diana* was directly inspired by the *Fortuna* on the Schloss Charlottenburg, but there is no direct evidence, and the figures are similar only in that they are nude females with one leg raised behind. *Triumvirate*, 263.

18. Martin Thomas, "How Exactly Does a Weather Vane Work?" *MadSci Network*, accessed July 12, 2014, http://www.madsci.org/posts/archives/1999-12/944415555.Eg.r.html.

19. Jean Lipman, *American Folk Art in Wood, Metal, and Stone* (New York: Pantheon Books, 1948): 49, 51, 58; William MacLeod, *Catalogue of the Corcoran Gallery of Art* (Washington, DC: Gibson Bros., 1876), 37. There were also a few *Fame* with trumpet weather vanes, which appear to be the work of at least three different New York makers ca. 1880–90: E. G. Washburne, J. L. Mott Ironworks, and J. W. Fiske. Jane Katcher, David A. Schorsch, and Ruth Wolfe, *Expressions of Innocence and Eloquence: Selections from the Jane Katcher Collection of Americana*, vol. 2 (New Haven: Yale Univ. Press, 2011), fig. 17.3, 274. There may also be an interesting comparison made to H. H. Richardson's 1870s Brattle Church in Boston and the Holy Beanblowers, those *Angels of Judgment* blowing their golden trumpets from the corners of the church's tower, carved by Italian craftsmen after designs by Bartholdi; see *Bacon's Dictionary of Boston* (Boston: Houghton Mifflin, 1886), 68.

20. ASG to SW, n.d., box 9, SW Papers, New-York Historical Society.

21. For details of the plan, see "Amended Plans for a Great Building," *New York Tribune*, Aug. 17, 1889; "On a Vast Scale," *NYT*, Aug. 17, 1889; "It Will Be a Mighty Pile," *New York Tribune*, Mar. 22, 1889; "A Temple of the Muses," *New York Herald*, Mar. 24, 1889; "A Building to Be Proud of," *New York Evening World*, Aug. 19, 1889; "A Colossal Amphitheatre," *New York Herald*, Mar. 22, 1889; "Theaters and Music," *Real Estate Record and Builders' Guide*, Aug. 4, 1889.

22. C. McKim to SW, Aug. 2, 1889, box 22:24, SW Correspondence; "Changes in Madison Square Garden Plans," *New York Tribune*, Aug. 14, 1889; "Tearing Down the Old Garden," *NYT*, Aug. 8, 1889; "On a Vast Scale," *NYT*, Aug. 17, 1889; "No More Madison Square Garden," *New York Herald*, Aug. 8, 1889.

23. "The New Madison Square Garden," *New York Tribune*, July 16, 1889; "A New Madison Square Garden," *New York Tribune*, Mar. 23, 1889; "To Be a Mammoth Building," *Pittsburg Dispatch*, July 18, 1889.

24. "Madison Square Garden. Plans Filed for a Fine Place," *New York Herald*, Sept. 27, 1889.

25. W. Mead to SW, Sept. 7, 1889, box 45:24, SW Correspondence.

26. SW to W. Mead, Aug. 13 and 15, 1889, box 45:22, SW Correspondence.

27. Louis De Coppet Berg, "Iron Construction in New York City, Past and Future," *Architectural Record* 2 (July 1892): 448; McKim, Mead & White, "An Architect's Service and Remuneration," n.d., New-York Historical Society, cited in Roth, *McKim, Mead & White*, 364.

28. Phillips, "Construction of Great Buildings," 282–83.

29. "Destroyed by Dynamite: Terrific Premature Blast on the West Side," *NYT*, Feb. 22, 1889.

30. Architect Richard M. Hunt designed the base, while Stanford White's friend F. Hopkinson "Hop" Smith laid the concrete foundation. "F. Hopkinson Smith, Author-Artist, Dies," *NYT*, Apr. 8, 1915; "Liberty's Place of Rest," *NYT*, Aug. 6, 1884; "The Statue Unveiled," *NYT*, Oct. 29, 1886; "David H. King, Jr., Dead," *NYT*, Apr. 21, 1916.

9. In the Office and Out

1. Magonigle, "Half Century, 3," 116, 117.

2. Moore, *Life and Times of McKim*, 43, 50, 52–54, 319–20. McKim was not reunited with his daughter until 1899.

3. J. Wells to C. Gilbert, July 30, 1884, Gilbert Papers, Manuscript Division, Library of Congress, quoted in Baker, *Stanny*, 103.

4. William Boring to C. Moore, 1927; W. McKim to Prescott Butler, July 13, 1893, both in McKim Papers, Manuscript Division, Library of Congress, cited in Woods, *From Craft to Profession*, 139.

5. Magonigle, "Half Century, 3," 116.

6. For the description of White's working style and office conditions, see Magonigle, "Half Century, 3," 117–18; Magonigle, "Half Century, 4," *Pencil Points* 15 (May 1934): 226; J. Monroe Hewlett, in Hewlett et al., "Stanford White as Those Trained," 245; Philip Sawyer, in Hewlett et al., "Stanford White as Those Trained," 247; F. L. V. Hoppin, in Hewlett et al., "Stanford White as Those Trained," 245–46; Simmons, *From Seven to Seventy*, 249; Albert Randolph Ross, in Hewlett et al., "Stanford White as Those Trained," 246.

7. C. Gilbert to Clarence Johnston, Aug. 24, 1892, Johnston Papers, Minnesota Historical Society.

8. SW to Mrs. Harrison, Mar. 19, 1896, LPB 15:338, SW Correspondence; Weitenkampf, *Manhattan Kaleidoscope*, 111.

9. See Baker, *Stanny*, 275–81; Broderick, *Triumvirate*, 90–91, 214, 275–76; Lessard, *Architect of Desire*, 205; Elizabeth Lee, "The Electrified Goddess: Augustus Saint-Gaudens, Stanford White and Diana at Madison Square Garden," *Nineteenth Century* 31 (Spring 2011): 18.

10. Broderick, *Triumvirate*, xviii.

11. Baker, *Stanny*, 280–81.

12. Broderick, *Triumvirate*, xvii; Lessard, *Architect of Desire*, 204.

13. Lessard, *Architect of Desire*, 205.

14. Frank Bruni, "Food, Sex and Silence," *NYT*, Apr. 22, 2017.

15. "A Bachelors' Home on 5th Avenue," *Real Estate Record and Builders' Guide* 46 (Sept. 6, 1890): 305; E. T. Littell, "Club Chambers and Apartment Hotels," *American Architect and Building News* 1 (Feb. 19, 1876): 59; "A Home for Bachelors," *NYT*, June 29, 1879.

16. Broderick, *Triumvirate*, 214.

17. Richard Grant White to Alexina White, Richard Grant White Papers, New-York Historical Society. Before his marriage, Stanford White lived with the senior Whites conveniently domiciled around the corner at 22 Washington Place.

18. Baker, *Stanny*, 86; Stern, Mellins, and Fishman, *New York, 1880*, 542.

19. ASG, "Reminiscences of an Idiot," 86ff. Saint-Gaudens eventually tired of having to clear his studio for the Sunday crowd, so the concerts were moved to rooms at the Art

Students League, where he had begun teaching life modeling in 1888. HSG, "The Reminiscences of Augustus Saint-Gaudens," *The Century* 78 (May–Oct. 1909): 228.

20. ASG to SW, Sept. 8, 1905, roll 505, frame 486, AAA, from MS 693, SW Papers, New-York Historical Society.

21. Ella Wheeler Wilcox, *New York Journal*, June 30, 1906. During the Thaw murder trial, Evelyn Nesbit recalled a conversation in which White warned her about Harry Thaw's use of morphine, telling her that there were lots of ways to take it, including smelling it up one's nose. When Nesbit related this conversation to Thaw, he laughed and said that White knew a lot more about it than he did. "Evelyn Tells Her Story," *NYT*, Feb. 8, 1907.

22. Magonigle, "Half Century, 4," 223; Low, *Chronicle*, 276; HSG, *Reminiscences of Augustus*, 1:306–11; Tharp, *Saint-Gaudens*, 164; see also Baker, *Stanny*, 87; for image see ASG to Joseph Wells, n.d., SW Papers, New-York Historical Society.

23. Royal Cortissoz, "In Memory of Stanford White," *New York Tribune*, Nov. 7, 1920; Cortissoz, *American Artists*, 301.

24. J. Wells to C. Gilbert, July 30, 1884, and Dec. 12, 1886, Gilbert Papers, quoted in Baker, *Stanny*, 104. Letters from Wells to White during 1880–81 were later destroyed by Lawrence Grant White. Broderick, *Triumvirate*, 275.

25. HSG, *Reminiscences of Augustus*, 1:283; Baldwin, *Stanford White*, 142, 356; Tharp, *Saint-Gaudens*, 204; SW to Mrs. Harrison, Mar. 19, 1896, LPB 15:338, SW Correspondence.

26. Richard O'Connor, *Hell's Kitchen: The Roaring Days of New York's Wild West Side* (Philadelphia: Lippincott, 1958), 86. Saint-Gaudens, Wells, and Babb were associated not only in New York but also in Cornish, New Hampshire, where Babb redesigned Saint-Gaudens's home and studio as well as a gristmill in town, while Wells designed a stone-arch bridge adjacent to Saint-Gaudens's property. HSG, *Reminiscences of Augustus*, 2:239–43; John Dryfhout, "The Cornish Colony," in *A Circle of Friends: Art Colonies of Cornish and Dublin* (Durham, NH: University Art Galleries, Univ. of New Hampshire, 1985), 33.

27. Glen Brown, "The Great Artist of the Age," *American Architect and Building News* 93 (Jan. 11, 1908).

28. SW to Paul K. Ames, Dec. 14, 1888, LPB 1:372a, SW Correspondence; Sewer Club Accounts, LPB 2:315, SW Correspondence. In the press, however, it was claimed that "sewer" referred to an old English drinking vessel, which each member was required to make for himself, and that the club was devoted primarily to drinking beer and talking about art. "Odd Clubs and Queer Clubman," *New York Herald*, Nov. 10, 1889. Accounts show that by November 1, 1888, White was paying part of Dewing's share and the shares of the other four, who were behind in their dues. Baker, *Stanny*, 132.

29. ASG to SW, Dec. 15, 1898, roll 505, frame 454, AAA, from MS 693, SW Papers, New-York Historical Society.

30. T. Dewing to SW, Feb. 14 [1895], box 5:9, SW Correspondence; ASG to SW, n.d., roll 505, frames 459–60, AAA, from MS 693, SW Papers, New-York Historical Society; ASG to

SW, Oct. 21, 1898, roll 505, frames 505–6, AAA, from MS 693, SW Papers, New-York Historical Society; ASG to SW, Apr. 26, 1894, box 20:42, Papers of ASG. In a letter to Homer Saint-Gaudens, Cortissoz noted that many readers of his extensively edited version of his father's autobiography would find the affair of the Sewer Club "repulsive." R. Cortissoz to HSG, Oct. 29, 1906, Papers of ASG.

31. Royal Cortissoz, "The Artistic Genius and Loveable Traits of Stanford White," *New York Tribune*, Nov. 7, 1920; Low, *Chronicle*, 277; ASG to J. Wells, n.d., roll 505, frame 508, AAA, from MS 693, SW Papers, New-York Historical Society.

32. SW to F. MacMonnies, May 30, 1890, listed on Ebay.com, accessed Jan. 2018.

33. Sawyer, *Edward Palmer York*, 22; Magonigle, "Half Century, 7," *Pencil Points* 15 (Nov. 1934): 563–64; David Gray, *Thomas Hastings, Architect* (Boston: Houghton Mifflin, 1933), 4, 5, 9, cited in Baker, *Stanny*, 277.

34. T. Hastings to ASG, Nov. 15, 1905, reel 11:82, Papers of ASG; Baker, *Stanny*, 277.

35. "A Notable Wedding," *New York Tribune*, Apr. 29, 1900; Baker, *Stanny*, 277.

36. Charles Rosenberg, "Sexuality, Class, and Role in Nineteenth-Century America," in *The American Man*, ed. Elizabeth H. Pleck and Joseph H. Pleck (Englewood Cliffs, NJ: Prentice-Hall, 1980), 230–32, cited in Chauncey, *Gay New York*, 83–85; E. Anthony Rotundo, *American Manhood: Transformations in Masculinity from the Revolution to the Modern Era* (New York: BasicBooks, 1993), 121; George Chauncey, "Gay New York: Urban Culture and the Making of the Gay Male World, 1890–1940" (PhD diss., Yale Univ., 1989), 20ff., cited in Timothy J. Gilfoyle, *City of Eros* (New York: W. W. Norton, 1992): 138.

37. An 1899 report cited in Ned Katz, *Gay American History: Lesbians and Gay Men in the USA*, rev. ed. (New York: Meridian, 1976), 46–47.

38. Chauncey, *Gay New York*, 33–34, 42, 50, 68, 216; "The Infamous Slide Closed by the Herald," *New York Herald*, Jan. 8, 1892; Caldwell, *New York Night*, 202; Luc Sante, *Low Life: Lures and Snares of Old New York* (New York: Farrar, Strauss and Giroux, 1991), 285; Long, *Forbidden Apple*, 23.

39. A. Garnier to Louis St. Gaudens, Nov. 1907, in HSG, *Reminiscences of Augustus*, 1:83–84.

40. HSG, *Reminiscences of Augustus*, 1:67–68; Tharp, *Saint-Gaudens*, 36.

41. See Doris Kearns Goodwin, *Team of Rivals* (New York: Simon & Schuster, 2005), 58, for a discussion of close male friendships and bed-sharing as a matter of routine in the nineteenth century, as well as a rebuttal by Larry Kramer, "Homo Sex in Colonial America," *Huffington Post*, accessed Aug. 13, 2012, http://www.huffingtonpost.com/larry-kramer/homo -sex-in-colonial-amerb205399.html.

42. Alexis L. Boylan, "Augustus Saint-Gaudens, Robert Louis Stevenson, and the Erotics of Illness," *American Art* 30 (Summer 2016): 20, 28.

43. French, *Memories*, 187.

44. Eve Kosofsky Sedgwick, *Between Men: English Literature and Male Homosocial Desire* (New York: Columbia Univ. Press, 1985), 123.

45. LPB 18:298, SW Papers, New-York Historical Society.

46. ASG to W. Low, Sept. 29, 1887, quoted in Low, *Chronicle*, 395; HSG, *Reminiscences of Augustus*, 1:384.

47. Saint-Gaudens spoke Italian, and perhaps the nickname came from the Italian *nove* for nine, as he was born in the ninth month.

10. The Walls Go Up

1. Woods, *From Craft to Profession*, 140, 141.

2. Phillips, "Construction of Great Buildings," 282.

3. W. Mead to SW, Sept. 17, 1889, box 22:24, SW Correspondence.

4. Phillips, "Construction of Great Buildings," 283.

5. "A Thirty-Five Years' Test of Materials: A Non-Technical Report of an Investigation Conducted upon the Razing of Madison Square Garden," *American Architect* 128 (Dec. 20, 1925): 519; see also Woods, *From Craft to Profession*, 155.

6. John Tauranac, *Elegant New York: The Builders and the Buildings 1885–1915* (New York: Abbeville Press, 1985), 42.

7. Baldwin, *Stanford White*, 202.

8. Broderick, *Triumvirate*, 251.

9. HSG, *The American Artist and His Times* (New York: Dodd, Mead, 1941), 144.

10. ASG to F. MacMonnies, Feb. 1, 1891, MacMonnies Family Papers, reel 3042, AAA, quoted in Smart, *Flight with Fame*, 81n26.

11. Lipman, *American Folk Art*, 49.

12. Leopold Eidlitz, "The Master Builder," *Real Estate Record and Builders' Guide* 7 (Feb. 21, 1891): 257; "Thirty-Five Years' Test," *American Architect* 128: 520; Phillips, "Construction of Great Buildings," 282; Mariana Griswold Van Rensselaer, "The Madison Square Garden," *The Century* 45, no. 25 (Mar. 1894): 742; "Technical Department: Skeleton Construction," *Architectural Record* 8 (Oct. 1897): 227; Frank W. Skinner, "The Steelwork of Madison Square Garden," *American Architect* 128 (Dec. 20, 1925): 537; Roth, *McKim, Mead & White*, 159.

13. "Technical Department: Skeleton Construction," *Architectural Record* 8 (Oct. 1897): 226–27.

14. Morris, *Incredible New York*, 198; Landau and Condit, *Rise of the New York Skyscraper*, 166.

15. William J. Fryer, "A Review of the Development of Structural Iron," in *A History of Real Estate, Building, and Architecture in New York City during the Last Quarter of a Century* (New York: The Real Estate Record Association, 1898), 465–68; "Thirty-Five Years' Test," *American Architect* 128: 520.

16. Skinner, "Steelwork of Madison Square Garden," 537.

17. "Technical Department: Skeleton Construction," *Architectural Record* 8 (Oct. 1897): 226–27; Landau and Condit, *Rise of the New York Skyscraper*, 39, 105.

18. Alan Burnham, "Forgotten Engineering: The Rise and Fall of the Phoenix Column," *Architectural Record* 125 (Apr. 1959): 223.

19. Fryer, "Review of the Development," 476–77; Landau and Condit, *Rise of the New York Skyscraper*, 56–7, 172.

20. Gayle, *Cast-Iron Architecture*, 98.

21. The exact circumstances of how Samuel Reeves, vice president and son of the Phoenix Company founder, came to patent the Phoenix column are unclear. See "The Engineering Contributions of Wendel Bollman," *Smithsonian Institution United States National Museum Bulletin* 240, Paper 36 (2010): 95. Most contemporary sources, like the *Annotated National Encyclopedia of American Bibliography* (New York: White, 1906), 281, declare Reeves to be the inventor.

22. Burnham, "Forgotten Engineering," 223; Landau and Condit, *Rise of the New York Skyscraper*, 56, 172.

23. Burnham, "Forgotten Engineering," 224. As noted by Burnham, it was the Phoenix Company's design for a 1,000-foot observation tower—intended for but never built at the Centennial Exposition in Philadelphia in 1876—that inspired Gustave Eiffel to design his own tower in Paris.

24. Phillips, "Construction of Great Buildings," 282.

25. Norman D. Anderson, *Ferris Wheels: An Illustrated History*, (Bowling Green, OH: Bowling Green State Univ.), 153.

26. The top chords of the trusses were connected by 12-inch, 32-pound I beams carrying 4-inch, 18-pound I beam purlins parallel to the trusses that supported the wood planking. For these and additional details on the trusses, see Skinner, "Steelwork of Madison Square Garden," 537–38; see also "Building Construction Details, No. XXXVII, The Madison Square Garden," *Engineering Record* 23 (Jan. 17, 1891): 111, and 23, no. 8 (Jan. 24, 1891): 124, for illustrations of the trusses.

27. "Truly a House Wonderful," *New York Sun*, Sept. 27, 1890.

28. "Would You Like to Catch Red-Hot Rivets All Day?" *NYT*, Oct. 6, 1901; J. B. Calvert, "Rivets," *Engineering and Technology*, http://mysite.du.edu/~jcalvert/tech/rivets.htm.

29. Phillips, "Construction of Great Buildings," 282; Skinner, "Steelwork of Madison Square Garden," 538.

30. King, *King's Handbook*, 542; Skinner, "Steelwork of Madison Square Garden," 539.

31. Skinner, "Steelwork of Madison Square Garden," 537; "Thirty-Five Years' Test," *American Architect* 128: 524.

32. These included Hammerstein's Theatre on Forty-Second Street, the New Olympic in Harlem, and Harrigan's Theatre on Thirty-Fifth Street, as well as what would become Carnegie Hall at Seventh Avenue and Fifty-Seventh Street.

33. "Theatres, Halls, and Audiences," *North American Review* 149 (Oct. 1889): 434.

34. "Chapter 534. An Act to Authorize the Construction of an Arcade over Certain Sidewalks in the City of New York," *Prospectus*, New York Life Archives; "Mayor Grant and the

Arcade," *NYT*, Nov. 27, 1889; "Can't Have the Sidewalk," *New York Sun*, Nov. 27, 1890; Saarinen Papers, box 10, folder 3:10, AAA.

35. "Progress at Madison Square Garden," *New York Tribune*, Jan. 18, 1890; "Thirty-Five Years' Test," *American Architect* 128: 519. However, the article erroneously reports the firm as "Welch, Glanzer & Maxwell."

36. "Making Rapid Progress," *NYT*, Dec. 16, 1889; Phillips, "Construction of Great Buildings," 283.

37. Joseph Wells daybook entry, Nov. 25, 1887, quoted in Baldwin, *Stanford White*, 364.

38. Walker, "Joseph Wells," 18; "Must Be Reconstructed: The Interior of the Plaza Hotel of Inferior Workmanship," *NYT*, Nov. 24, 1888; Joseph Wells Obituary, *Springfield (MA) Republican*, Feb. 5, 1890. For a fuller account of Wells's life, death, and career, see Broderick, *Triumvirate*, 57–58ff.

39. SW to Mrs. Harrison, LPB 15:338, SW Correspondence.

11. *Diana* Defrocked

1. SW to Henry Adams, Oct. 26, 1889, LPB 2: 245–46, SW Correspondence.

2. See John H. Dryfhout, "Diana," in *Metamorphoses in Nineteenth-Century Sculpture*, ed. Jeanne L. Wasserman (Cambridge: Fogg Art Museum, Harvard Univ., 1975), fig. 26. Her costume is also reminiscent of Edgar Degas's *Little Dancer, Fourteen Years Old*, shown at the 1881 Impressionists Exhibition, Paris, and of which there were also many drawings and studies.

3. All found in Saint-Gaudens Collection, SGNHS.

4. See Nikolaos Kaltsas, *Sculpture in the National Archaeological Museum, Athens* (Los Angeles: J. Paul Getty Museum, 2002), figs. 519, 520, 616; William L. Vance, *America's Rome* (New Haven: Yale Univ. Press, 1989), 1:258.

5. See photograph from Saint-Gaudens's now-destroyed student copybooks, box 63, Papers of ASG; see also HSG, *Reminiscences of Augustus*, 1:76.

6. Also known as *Artemis déese de la chase*, it was installed at the Louvre in 1798 and published in the *Musée François*, Livr. 15 and *Monum. Ant. Du Musée Napoléon*, Tom. 1, pl. 51.

7. Annick Daviss, Leo Lorenzi, and Jane Renoux, *Olympie: La Course des Femmes* (Paris: La Courtille, 1980), 27, cited in Allen Guttmann, *Women's Sports: A History* (New York: Columbia Univ. Press, 1991), 59, 60–62.

8. Including Antoine Coysevox's 1710 Rococo reworking of the *Artemis* as a lighthearted portrait of Princess Marie-Adélaïde of Savoy, wife of the Duke of Burgundy and mother of Louis XV, also on view at the Louvre.

9. HSG, *Reminiscences of Augustus*, 1:393.

10. Undated note in the Gotha Archives attributed to Baron Frederic-Melchior Grimm, the Duke of Saxe-Gotha's minister to France, editor of the Parisian *Correspondence litteraire*, and advisor to Houdon, cited in Guilhem Scherf, "Jean-Antoine Houdon," in *Cast in Bronze:*

French Sculpture from Renaissance to Revolution, ed. Geneviève Bresc-Bautier and Guilhem Scherf (Paris: Musée du Louvre Éditions, Somogy Art Publishers, 2009), 474.

11. Johann Joachim Winckelmann, *History of the Art of Antiquity,* trans. Harry Francis Mallgrave (Los Angeles: Getty Research Institute, 2006), 133.

12. Attributed to Jean Goujon in 1890 but now discounted. See H. Zerner, *L'Art de la Renaissance en France: L'invention du classicisme* (Paris: Flammarion, 1996), 360–61.

13. Including, in 1908, Edith Wharton and her lover, Morton Fullerton. Hermione Lee, *Edith Wharton* (New York: Alfred A. Knopf, 2007), 317.

14. See H. Harvard Arnason, *The Sculptures of Houdon* (New York: Oxford Univ. Press, 1975), 43, for a brief survey, including works of the period by Flamen, Coutou, and Desjardins.

15. Winckelmann, *History of the Art of Antiquity,* 133.

16. Anne L. Poulet, *Jean-Antoine Houdon: Sculptor of the Enlightenment* (Washington, DC: National Gallery of Art, 2003), 211.

17. Scherf, "Jean-Antoine Houdon," 47.

18. One such replica, set on a marble pedestal with a revolving top, was included in the collection of A. T. Stewart, Bessie White's great-uncle by marriage. Oliver Larkin, *Art and Life in America,* rev. ed. (New York: Holt, Rinehart & Winston, 1960), 295.

19. Vance, *America's Rome,* 1:258–60.

20. Undated sketchbook, ca. 1888, SGNHS.

21. US Bureau of the Census, *Twelfth Census of the United States,* 1900, roll T623–133, p. 22B; US Bureau of the Census, *Thirteenth Census of the US,* roll T624–887, p. 1A.

22. HSG, *Reminiscences of Augustus,* 1:221.

23. He would occasionally pour plaster over the actual fabric, incorporating it into the model. Greenthal, *Augustus Saint-Gaudens,* 51–52.

24. ASG to Abbot Henderson Thayer, Sept. 5, 1905, reel 13, frame 200, Papers of ASG; Tharp, *Saint-Gaudens,* 328; Cox, "Augustus Saint-Gaudens," 35.

25. Kenyon Cox, *Old Masters and New: Essays in Art Criticism* (New York: Duffield, 1908), 275.

26. Tharp, *Saint-Gaudens,* 165, 167.

27. HSG, *Reminiscences of Augustus,* 1:272–73.

28. F. MacMonnies to P. Bion, Bion Correspondence, Papers of ASG; "Damaged Beyond Repair," *New Haven Register,* Aug. 22, 1884; "A Cemetery Fire," *Hartford (CT) Courant,* Aug. 23, 1884; "The Morgan Mausoleum Ruined," *NYT,* Aug. 23, 1884; "Fine Arts. The Saint-Gaudens Angel Group Destroyed at the Morgan Tomb," *New York Herald,* Aug. 29, 1884; Tharp, *Saint-Gaudens,* 181.

29. Tharp, *Saint-Gaudens,* 179–82; Wilkinson, *Uncommon Clay,* 141–42. Davida's angelic form and distinctive tilt of the head were also reused in the *Angel with the Tablet* for the Ann Maria Smith Tomb in Newport, completed the following year. HSG, *Reminiscences of Augustus,* 1:350. The piece was later reworked with a smaller tablet as the memorial to Maria

Gouverneur Mitchell and installed at Saint Stephen's Episcopal Church in Philadelphia. Known as *The Angel of Purity*, it is now in the collection of the Philadelphia Museum of Art #2005–2–1. Curiously, brother Louis St. Gaudens signed his name to the piece and added the erroneously early date of 1880, perhaps in an attempt to deflect suspicion as to the identity of the model, although Saint-Gaudens would claim credit for the figure many years later. Dryfhout, *Work*, 234; HSG, *Reminiscences of Augustus*, 1:350.

30. Wilkinson, *Uncommon Clay*, 138.

31. Armstrong, *Day Before Yesterday*, 273; Armstrong, "Saint-Gaudens," 28.

32. Greenthal, *Augustus Saint-Gaudens*, 68.

33. The autographed copy of *Lamina*, published by J. B. Lippincott in 1885, remained in the family along with a drawing apparently by Low and with a great resemblance to an illustration on page 2 of the book. Wilkinson, *Uncommon Clay*, 143. Although she used the name Davida on government documents, her grandchildren always knew her as Albertina, according to Henry Duffy, curator, Saint-Gaudens National Historical Park, communication with author, Nov. 20, 2009.

34. Davida was buried in the Spring Grove Cemetery in Darien, Connecticut, next to a woman with a matching tombstone by the name of Maria Louisa Johnson (1822–1900), who had been born thirty-nine years earlier and was perhaps her mother or close friend. Henry Duffy, communication with author, Dec. 2009.

35. The use of "Johnson" as slang for a penis has been documented as early as 1863. John Ayto and John Simpson, eds., *Oxford Dictionary of Modern Slang* (New York: Oxford Univ. Press, 1997), 150.

36. David M. Lubin, cited in Stephen May, "Augustus Saint-Gaudens in the Metropolitan Museum of Art," *Antiques and Arts Weekly* (Aug. 11, 2009): 2.

37. Wodehouse, *White*, 207–8.

12. Baked Earth

1. After Barnum's death in 1891, James Anthony Bailey, who had been managing partner of the rival Great London Circus, took over ownership of the circus. In 1907, a year after Bailey's death, the Ringling Brothers purchased Barnum & Bailey but did not unite it with their own circus until 1918.

2. "Barnum Says He Will Build," *New York Herald*, Jan. 8, 1890; "Must Go to Brooklyn," *NYT*, Mar. 25, 1890; Philip B. Kunhardt Jr., Philip B. Kunhardt III, and Peter W. Kunhardt, *P. T. Barnum: America's Greatest Showman* (New York: Knopf, 1995), 342.

3. "Barnum Will Put Up Tents," *NYT*, Jan. 8, 1890; *Chillicothe (MO) Constitution*, Feb. 12, 1890.

4. Classified section, *Harper's Weekly* 34 (Jan. 18 and 25, 1890).

5. Blakely Hall, "New York's Big Garden," *Chicago Tribune*, June 29, 1890; "Tearing Down the Old Garden," *NYT*, Aug. 8, 1889.

6. "T. Henry French—His Hat," *New York Herald*, July 22, 1888; "T. Henry French's Nose," *NYT*, Oct. 14, 1889.

7. Moore, *Life and Times of McKim*, 328; Magonigle, "Half Century, 4," 224. Kendall joined McKim, Mead & White in 1882, was named partner in 1906, and became a senior partner in 1931. In later years, however, he denigrated Wells's design contributions to the firm. Walker, "Joseph Wells," 18; Shopsin and Broderick, *Villard Houses*, 42; Broderick, *Triumvirate*, 125–26.

8. Jay Shockley and Susan Tunick, "The Cooper Union Building and Architectural Terra Cotta," *Winterthur Portfolio* 39 (Winter 2004): 209–10.

9. James Taylor, "The History of Terra Cotta in New York City," *Architectural Record* 2 (July 1892): 138.

10. Taylor, "History of Terra Cotta," 141; "The Technical Department, Terra Cotta," *Architectural Record* 8 (June 1899): 128.

11. Taylor, "History of Terra Cotta," 144; Landau and Condit, *Rise of the New York Skyscraper*, 36.

12. Broderick, *Triumvirate*, 239.

13. "Thirty-Five Years' Test," *American Architect* 128: 519, reports that the terra cotta was furnished by the Atlantic Terra Cotta Company. However, Atlantic did not subsume the Perth Amboy Company until 1907. Corrado Parducci, interview with Dennis Barrie, Mar. 17, 1975, AAA; Susan Tunick, *Terra-Cotta Skyline: New York's Architectural Ornament* (New York: Princeton Architectural Press, 1997), 142; "The Technical Department," *Architectural Record* 8 (June 1899): 129–30.

14. "McKim, Mead & White, Early Work in Atlantic Terra Cotta," *Atlantic Terra Cotta Company* 9 (June 1927), quoted in Tunick, *Terra-Cotta Skyline*, 38, 56; James Taylor, "Terra Cotta—Some of Its Characteristics," *Architectural Record* 1 (July 1891): 64–65; Tunick, *Terra-Cotta Skyline*, 34–36; Parducci, interview with Dennis Barrie, Mar. 17, 1975, AAA.

15. W. Mead to SW, Aug. 2, 1889, box 22:24, SW Correspondence.

16. Including a portrait of founder Edwin Booth for the renovated Player's Club. Charles Merrill Mount, *John Singer Sargent: A Biography* (New York: W. W. Norton: 1955), 160–61.

17. Downey, *Portrait of an Era*, 97.

18. "Graceful Carmencita," n.d., Dance Clipping File, Lincoln Center, New York Public Library, quoted in Burke Doreen Bolger, "Carmencita," in *American Paintings in the Metropolitan Museum of Art*, vol. 3, ed. Kathleen Luhrs (New York: Metropolitan Museum in association with Princeton Univ. Press, 1994), 87–88; Mount, *John Singer Sargent*, 164, 168–73; "Carmencita Dances for the *Herald*," *New York Herald*, Apr. 20, 1890; *Town Topics* (New York), Apr. 3, 1890; Garnett McCoy, "Visits, Parties, and Cats in the Hall: The Tenth Street Studio B and Its Inmates in the Nineteenth Century," *Journal of the Archives of American Art* 6 (Jan. 1966): 8.

19. Ross, "Stanford White," 246.

20. Downey, *Portrait of an Era*, 98.

21. Baker, *Stanny*, 131.

22. SW to J. M. Montgomery, Mar. 31, 1890, LPB 3:56, SW Correspondence.

23. SW to ASG, Apr. 2, 1890, LPB 3:60, SW Correspondence.

24. "Madison Square Garden Almost Done," *New York Tribune*, Apr. 21, 1890; "Thirty-Five Years' Test," *American Architect* 128: 524.

25. "Thirty-Five Years' Test," *American Architect* 128: 520.

26. "A Great Amphitheatre," *New York Clipper*, June 14, 1890, 214. The opera house designed by architect Charles Garnier and dedicated in 1875 also displays strong horizontals, second-floor paired columns, a row of bull's-eye windows, and a lavender marble entrance hall.

27. De Kay, "Madison Square Garden," 542. The bronze eagle, designed by Saint-Gaudens but executed by brother Louis, became the emblem for the New York Life Insurance Company instead, and copies were installed on its office buildings in Kansas City, Omaha, and St. Paul around 1888–91. Art Inventories Catalog, Smithsonian American Art Museum, http://siris-artinventories.si.edu. It appears that the original design for the eagle and globe was then reworked by Philip Martiny and was installed on top of the McKim, Mead & White 1898 clock tower added to the New York Life Building on Broadway in lower Manhattan.

28. William H. Birkmire, *The Planning and Construction of American Theatres* (New York: John Wiley & Sons, 1906), 2; King, *King's Handbook*, 542; "Thirty-Five Years' Test," *American Architect* 128: 521.

29. "Thirty-Five Years' Test," *American Architect* 128: 520–21.

30. Russell Sturgis, "The Works of McKim, Mead & White," *Architectural Record*, *Great American Architects Series* 1 (May 1895): 15, 18; "The Madison Square Garden," *Real Estate Record and Builders' Guide* 45 (June 28, 1890): 915.

31. "The Madison Square Garden," *Real Estate Record and Builders' Guide* 45 (June 28, 1890), 915; Mooney, *Evelyn Nesbit*, 186; De Kay, "Madison Square Garden," 542.

32. Hoppin, "Stanford White," 246.

33. "Thirty-Five Years' Test," *American Architect* 128: 520; Logan, *That Was New York*, 60.

34. Mooney, *Evelyn Nesbit*, 186.

35. Saarinen Papers, box 10, folder 8:13, AAA.

36. Van Rensselaer, "Madison Square Garden," 743.

37. Van Rensselaer, "Madison Square Garden," 739.

38. Magonigle, "Half Century, 4," 224.

39. Van Rensselaer, "Madison Square Garden," 740–41.

40. Broderick, *Triumvirate*, 250; see correspondence between ASG and Van Rensselaer, box 19:43 and box 63:6, Papers of ASG; Wilkinson, *Uncommon Clay*, 195–96.

13. An Irksome Spring

1. "Madison Square Garden Almost Done," *New York Tribune*, Apr. 21, 1890.

2. Mount, *John Singer Sargent*, 181.

3. *Wheeling (WV) Register*, May 11, 1890; Mount, *John Singer Sargent*, 181.

4. "The New Madison Square Garden," *New York Clipper*, June 21, 1890; John Hollingshead, *Gaiety Chronicles* (Westminster: A. Constable, 1898), 43.

5. "City and Suburban News," *NYT*, Jan. 31, 1890.

6. "Musicians Make Protests," *NYT*, Apr. 4, 1890.

7. "The Strauss Orchestra Controversy," *Brooklyn Eagle*, Apr. 6, 1890.

8. Journal, 1888–94, McKim, Mead & White, MM&W Collection, cited in Baker, *Stanny*, 125, 151.

9. "Art Students to Begin Work," *New York Herald*, Sept. 30, 1889; William C. Brownell, "The Art-Schools of New York," *Scribner's Monthly* 16 (Oct. 1878): 775; "American Art Holds a Golden Jubilee," *NYT*, Jan. 25, 1925; "Artist Life," *Chicago Inter Ocean*, Mar. 13, 1877; John C. Van Dyke, "The Art Students League of New York," *Harper's New Monthly Magazine* 83 (Oct. 1891): 689–90; "Art Students League," *NYT*, Sept. 30, 1888; Downey, *Portrait of an Era*, 38–40. In 1888 tuition ranged from two dollars to twelve dollars a month, depending on the number of courses. "Art Study in New York," *New York Sun*, Dec. 16, 1888.

10. Louis Cox, "Louise Cox at the Art Students League: A Memoir," *Archives of American Art Journal* 27, no. 1 (1987): 17; Julie Graham, "American Women Artists' Groups: 1867–1930," *Woman's Art Journal* 1 (Spring–Summer 1980): 11; Brownell, "Art Schools," 776; Michael Landgren, *Years of Art: The Story of the Art Students League of New York* (New York: R. M. McBride, 1940), 46; Elizabeth Hollander, "Artists' Models in Nineteenth-Century America: A Study of Professional Identity," *Annals of Scholarship* 10, nos. 3–4 (1993): 286.

11. At a site on West Fifty-Seventh Street at Broadway, a block west of the new Carnegie Music Hall, would soon rise their five-story building in the French Renaissance style designed by Henry J. Hardenburgh of the "Dakota" fame.

12. Van Dyke, "Art Students League," 696; "The Fine Arts Society," *NYT*, Jan. 4, 1890; "An Elaborate Structure," *NYT*, Dec. 21, 1890.

13. Charles De Kay, "Girl Art Students," *NYT*, May 20, 1906. For an introduction to the rise of female art students post–Civil War, see Kirsten Swinth, *Painting Professionals: Women Artists & the Development of Modern American Art, 1870–1930* (Chapel Hill: Univ. of North Carolina Press, 2001), 1–23ff.

14. Jennie June, "Jennie June on Art Models in New York," *The Baltimore American*, Feb. 16, 1881; Kate Clark, "The Model: Scenes in Her Daily Life," *Duluth News-Tribune*, Apr. 23, 1899; Landgren, *Years of Art*, 81; "Our Girl Art Students," *New York Sun*, Mar. 3, 1889; "An Artist's Masked Model," *Omaha World-Herald*, June 22, 1890; "With the Art Students," *New York Sun*, May 26, 1895; "The Artist and His Model," *Wheeling (WV) Register*, Aug. 18, 1895.

15. HSG, *Reminiscences of Augustus*, 2:4, 9, 12, 16–18, 21, 26; "Art Fakirs Have a Show," *New York Herald*, Apr. 29, 1893.

16. Charlotte Adams, "Women as Models," *Chicago Daily Inter Ocean*, Nov. 6, 1887; "A Model's Gossip," *New York Sun*, Nov. 24, 1889; "Artist Life," *Chicago Inter Ocean*, Mar. 13, 1887.

17. "Like Trilby They Pose," *New York Sun*, Feb. 24, 1895; "Artists' Models," *Dallas Morning News*, Jan. 20, 1907; "New York's Girl Models," *New York Herald*, July 29, 1894.

18. June, "Jennie June on Art Models," 6; Charlotte Adams, "Artists' Models in New York," *The Century* 25 (Feb. 1883): 570–71; Katherine Pyle, "Some Types of Artists' Models," *The Cosmopolitan* 21 (May 1896): 123; "Nude Models," *New York Herald*, July 11, 1885; "A Model's Story," *Macon (GA) Telegraph*, July 28, 1891; "Posing as a Fine Art," *St. Louis Republic*, Apr. 8, 1894.

19. Alison Smith, "The Academy and the Professional Model in Nineteenth-Century Britain," in *Dictionary of Artists' Models*, ed. Jill Berk Jiminez (London: Fitzroy Dearborn, 2001), 28; Landgren, *Years of Art*, 52; Adams, "Artists' Models," 570, 577; Judith Fryer Davidow, *Women's Camera Work: Self/Body/Other in American Visual Culture* (Durham, NC: Duke Univ. Press, 1998), 55; "The Model and His and Her Ways," *Cleveland Plain Dealer*, Mar. 18, 1889; "An Artist's Masked Model," *Omaha World-Herald*, June 22, 1890.

20. As reported at the league's annual meeting. "The Art Students League," *NYT*, Apr. 17, 1890.

21. Sylvan Schendler, *Eakins* (Boston: Little, Brown, 1967): 42, 90–92.

22. "A Question of Nude Models," *New York Sun*, May 9, 1890.

23. "No More Mixed Classes," *NYT*, May 10, 1890; "Prudery in Art," *Albany Express*, May 9, 1890; "The Nude Apart," *New York Herald*, May 9, 1890; "A Question of Nude Models," *New York Sun*, May 9, 1890; "At Odds over Models," *New York Tribune*, May 9, 1890.

24. It was sculptor F. Edwin Elwell who had previously taught life modeling at the league. Whether he did use live models before a mixed class is not documented. However, Elwell achieved notoriety in 1905 when, as curator of sculpture at the Metropolitan Museum, he was forcibly ejected from the museum by police on the orders of board president J. P. Morgan for defying the museum's acting director and its board on a number of issues. After his removal, Elwell reported that he had received a supportive letter from Saint-Gaudens. "Squabble over Morgan Statue Ousts Curator," *NYT*, Aug. 25, 1905; "Museum Trustees Oust Curator Elwell," *NYT*, Oct. 17, 1905.

25. "Mr. St. Gaudens and Nude Models," *New York Tribune*, May 12, 1890; "News from New York. Members of the Students Art League Give Their Side of the Nude Model Case," *Chicago Herald*, May 11, 1890.

26. "Study Not the Nude Together," *New York Press*, May 9, 1890; "A Question of Nude Models," *New York Sun*, May 9, 1890; "Prudery in Art," *Albany Express*, May 9, 1890; "Nude Models Must Go," *New York Star*, May 10, 1890.

27. "Art Students Agitated," *New York Tribune*, May 8, 1890; "The Nude Apart," *New York Herald*, May 9, 1890; "A Question of Nude Models," *New York Sun*, May 9, 1890.

28. "A Question of Nude Models," *New York Sun*, May 9, 1890; "At Odds over Models," *New York Tribune*, May 9, 1890.

29. "He Didn't Pull the Life Class," *Philadelphia Record*, Jan. 14, 1888.

30. "Art Students League Raided by Comstock," *NYT*, Aug. 3, 1906; H. C. Broun, *Anthony Comstock* (New York: Boni, 1927), 217–19.

31. "No More Mixed Classes," *NYT*, May 10, 1890; "No Nude Models in Mixed Classes," *New York Tribune*, May 10, 1890.

32. "St. Gaudens Resigns," *New York Herald*, May 12, 1890; "Mr. St. Gaudens Has Not Resigned," *NYT*, May 15, 1890; "Art Notes," *NYT*, June 27, 1890. However, Saint-Gaudens did return to the league for the fall 1892 term in its new building. "The Art Students League, Its New and Elegant Quarters Thrown Open for Inspection," *NYT*, Oct. 16, 1892; "Seeking Arts' Elusive Touch," *New York Herald*, Oct. 12, 1890; Marcia Hyland Green, "Women Art Students in America: An Historical Study of Academic Art Instruction during the Nineteenth Century" (PhD diss., American Univ., 1990), 199.

33. "Labor's Big Battle," *New York Herald*, Apr. 30, 1890.

34. "Small Strikes in Process," Apr. 6, 1890, MM&W Newspaper Clippings, folder 1, New-York Historical Society.

35. "As Light as Day," *New York Morning Journal*, May 10, 1890.

36. Deshler Welch, "Entre Nous," *The Theatre* 9 (Apr. 19, 1890): 388.

37. "Did the Ballet Girls Smuggle," *New York Herald*, May 12, 1890; "Smuggled Costumes Seized," *Philadelphia Inquirer*, May 12, 1890; "Will the Girls Get Their Costumes," *New York Tribune*, May 13, 1890.

38. "Were the Costumes Smuggled?" *NYT*, May 12, 1890; "The Seized Ballet Costumes," *NYT*, May 14, 1890; "On with the Dance," *NYT*, May 23, 1890; Baldwin, *Stanford White*, 203.

39. "A Hard Nut for Immigration Experts," *New York Tribune*, Apr. 25, 1890.

40. "The Strauss Orchestra Controversy," *Brooklyn Eagle*, Apr. 6, 1890; "The Advent of Strauss," *NYT*, May 14, 1890.

41. "The Orchestra on Shore," *New York Tribune*, May 14, 1890.

42. "Trouble over the Garden Wall," *New York Tribune*, May 23, 1890; "Fighting the New Garden," *New York Herald*, May 23, 1890; "News Notes from Gotham," *Chicago Herald*, May 23, 1890.

43. "Theatre Owners Protest," *NYT*, May 23, 1890.

44. *New York Star*, Apr. 17, 1890.

45. "Plumbing in the Madison Square Garden, New York," *Engineering Record* 23 (Apr. 11, 1891): 315.

46. "Gossip of New York," *Philadelphia Inquirer*, May 25, 1890.

47. "A License for the Amphitheatre," *New York Tribune*, May 29, 1890; "A License Will Be Granted," *NYT*, May 29, 1890.

48. "Matthew S. Morgan," Obituary, *New York Herald*, June 3, 1890; "Matthew Somerville Morgan," Obituary, *New York Tribune*, June 3, 1890.

49. "The Hall's Acoustic Properties Good," *New York Tribune*, May 30, 1890.

50. "A Great Amphitheatre," *NYT*, June 8, 1890.

51. "Amusements," *NYT*, June 8, 1890.

52. "Theatrical Gossip," *NYT*, June 13, 1890.

14. Opening Night

1. Logan, "That Was New York," 60.

2. Chanler and Chanler, *Roman Spring*, 258.

3. Logan, "That Was New York," 60; Sturgis, "The Works of McKim, Mead & White," 16; "A Great Amphitheatre," *New York Clipper*, June 14, 1890.

4. For contemporary documentation of the Madison Square Garden opening, both structure and performance, see Alan Dale, "The New Madison Square Garden," *New York World*, June 17, 1890; "The Opening of Madison Square Garden," *New York Daily Tribune*, June 16, 1890; Hall, "New York's Big Garden"; "A Tremendous Crowd Attends," *New York Tribune*, June 17, 1890; "Strauss Opens the Great Amphitheatre," *New York Herald*, June 17, 1890; "Society at the Show," MM&W Newspaper Clippings, folder 1, New-York Historical Society; "A Great Amphitheatre," *New York Clipper*, June 14, 1890; "Truly a House Wonderful," *New York Sun*, Sept. 27, 1890; "Something New in Amusement: The True Significance of the Opening of the Madison Square Garden," *New York Herald*, June 22, 1890; "Opening the New Garden," *New York Sun*, June 17, 1890; "New York Is Gay Despite the Summer Heat," *Fort Wayne Daily*, June 29, 1890; "New Madison Square Garden," *Brooklyn Eagle*, June 8, 1890; "Strauss Opens the Great Amphitheatre," *New York Herald*, June 17, 1890; "The Big Garden Opened," *New York Daily Tribune*, June 17, 1890; "The New Madison Square Garden," *New York Clipper*, June 21, 1890; "Madison Square Garden," *Chicago Daily Tribune*, June 17, 1890; "To Open the Garden Gates," *New York Tribune*, June 15, 1890; "The Madison Square Garden," *Brooklyn Eagle*, June 17, 1890; "Something New," *New York Herald*, June 17, 1890; *Town Topics* (New York), May 18, 1893.

5. Marcuse, *This Was New York*, 241; Wilkinson, *Uncommon Clay*, 212.

6. Tauranac, *Elegant New York*, 42.

7. Hall, "New York's Big Garden."

8. "Madison Square Garden: An Account of the Passing of One of New York City's Architectural Landmarks," *American Architect* 128 (Dec. 20, 1925): 513. Other accounts alternatively place it at 330 feet long by 200 feet wide.

9. "The Madison Square Garden," *Real Estate Record and Builders' Guide* 45 (June 28, 1890): 914; Birkmire, *Planning and Construction*, 3, 207; "The Big Garden Opened," *New York Daily Tribune*, June 17, 1890.

10. Durso, *Madison Square Garden*, 78.

11. "He Couldn't Stand Splendor," *New York Sun*, June 18, 1890.

12. "Society at the Show," MM&W Newspaper Clippings, folder 1, New-York Historical Society; "Angry Ushers at the New Garden," *New York Sun*, June 17, 1890; Dale, "New Madison Square Garden"; "Object to the Jaundice Suits," *New York Herald*, June 18, 1890; "He Couldn't Stand Splendor," *New York Sun*, June 18, 1890; Baldwin, *Stanford White*, 204.

13. Logan, "That Was New York," 58.

14. Baker, *Stanny*, 153; Durso, *Madison Square Garden*, 77; Birkmire, *Planning and Construction*, 110.

15. Durso, *Madison Square Garden*, 84.

16. "A Brilliant Audience," *NYT*, June 17, 1890.

17. "Costumes for the Stage," *New York Sun*, July 13, 1890.

18. "A Peep behind the Scenes," *NYT*, June 29, 1890.

19. King, *King's Handbook*, 544.

20. "The Big Garden Opened," *New York Daily Tribune*, June 17, 1890; "The Madison Square Garden," *Brooklyn Eagle*, June 17, 1890.

21. "Truly a House Wonderful," *New York Sun*, Sept. 27, 1890.

22. "A Peep behind the Scenes," *NYT*, June 29, 1890.

23. Skinner, "Steelwork of Madison Square Garden," 538.

24. "A Peep behind the Scenes," *NYT*, June 29, 1890; "New York the City," *New York Herald*, Jan. 5, 1896; "The Madison Square Garden Roof," *Engineering Record* 23 (Jan. 17, 1891): 111; "Building Construction Details, the Madison Square Garden Moveable Skylight of 6 Sections," *Engineering Record* 23 (Jan. 24, 1891): 140; "Thirty-Five Years' Test," *American Architect* 128: 524.

25. "The Big Garden Opened," *New York Daily Tribune*, June 17, 1890.

26. Hall, "New York's Big Garden."

27. "Something New in Amusement," *New York Herald*, June 22, 1890.

28. "Editor's Easy Chair," *Harper's New Monthly Magazine* 81 (Oct. 1890): 797.

29. "Amusements," *NYT*, Aug. 26, 1890.

30. "A Peep behind the Scenes," *NYT*, June 29, 1890.

31. "Amusements," *NYT*, Aug. 3, 1890.

32. "Liquor with Music and Ballets," *New York Herald*, July 6, 1890; "A License for the Garden," *New York Tribune*, July 26, 1890; "Theatrical Gossip," *NYT*, June 26, 1890; "Editor's Easy Chair," *Harper's New Monthly Magazine* 81 (Oct. 1890): 797.

33. *Town Topics*, July 1890, quoted in Baldwin, *Stanford White*, 205.

34. "Theatrical Gossip," *NYT*, Sept. 10, 1890.

35. "Herr Strauss Says Farewell," *NYT*, Sept. 13, 1890.

36. "Truly a House Wonderful," *New York Sun*, Sept. 27, 1890.

37. "Amusements," *NYT*, Sept. 14, 1890; "Amusements," *New York Sun*, July 29, 1890; "Novelties at the Madison Square Garden," *New York Sun*, Sept. 17, 1890.

38. "Theatrical Gossip," *NYT*, Sept. 17, 1890.

39. "Madison Square Garden," *NYT*, Sept. 2, 1890; "Amusements," *NYT*, Sept. 14, 1890.

40. "Madison Square Garden," *NYT*, Sept. 21, 1890.

41. "Is It a New Departure," *Kansas City (MO) Times*, June 25, 1890.

15. More of the Pieces

1. For contemporary documentation of the Garden Theatre, see "The Garden Theatre: Private Inspection of a Handsome New Playhouse," *NYT*, Sept. 21, 1890; "The Garden Theatre," *NYT*, Sept. 28, 1890; "Madison Square Garden Theatre," *New York Herald*, Sept. 21,

1890; Van Rensselaer, "Madison Square Garden," 741; "The Garden Theatre," *New York Evening World*, Sept. 29, 1890; "Truly a House Wonderful," *New York Sun*, Sept. 27, 1890.

2. Saarinen Papers, box 10, folder 3:17, AAA.

3. Richard Wagner, *Art Life and Theories of Richard Wagner*, sel. and trans. Edward L. Burlingame (New York: Henry Holt, 1875), 282; Tauranac, *Elegant New York*, 42.

4. *Art Amateur*, Oct. 1, 1887, 107, cited in Craven, *Stanford White*, 109; see also Wayne Craven, *Gilded Mansions: Grand Architecture and High Society* (New York: W. W. Norton, 2009).

5. "The Garden Theatre," *NYT*, Sept. 21, 1890. Wall coverings may well have been manufactured by Paul Balin, the famed Parisian wallpaper designer whose faux-silk striped coverings White used on the walls of the 1881–83 Isaac Bell House in Newport, Rhode Island.

6. Van Rensselaer, "Madison Square Garden," 741.

7. J. H. Gest, "Sculptors of the World's Fair," *Engineering Magazine* 5 (July 1893): 442; "Philip Martiny," *Successful American* 6 (Aug. 1902): 522; ASG, "Reminiscences of an Idiot," 83–84; HSG, "Saint-Gaudens Established: The Reminiscences of Augustus Saint-Gaudens," *The Century* 78 (June 1909): 219; "Sculptor of M'Kinley Memorial," *Springfield (MA) Republican*, July 26, 1902; "A Sculptor Who Is a Captain of Industry," *NYT*, Mar. 27, 1904.

8. After *Regina e cortigiani a passeggio nei giardini di Versailles*, 1876, oil on canvas, private collection, illustrated in Tiziano Panconi, *Giovanni Boldini: L'opera complete* (Florence, Italy: Edifir, 2002), 166. Henry E. Hoyt (1837–1906) was described in 1890 as "the artist who has done more to advance scenic art of the present day than all his contemporaries combined" and was particularly associated with the Metropolitan Opera. John P. Ritter, "Scene Painting as a Fine Art," *The Cosmopolitan* 8 (Nov. 1889): 44.

9. Bessie White portrait, 1902, oil on canvas, private collection, Panconi, *Giovanni Boldini*, 429. White also had in his collection another of Boldini's views of Versailles, his 1876 *Noonday Promenade*, oil on cradled panel, now in a private collection.

10. "Society Topics of the Week," *NYT*, Oct. 5, 1890; "Madison Square Garden Theatre," *New York Herald*, Sept. 21, 1890; "Theater for the Elite," *Boston Daily Advertiser*, Sept. 12, 1890.

11. "They Will Not Strike," *New York Evening Telegram*, Oct. 18, 1890.

12. Van Rensselaer, "Madison Square Garden," 714.

13. "The Gleaner," *New York Evening World*, May 25, 1891.

14. For documentation of the 1890 horse show, see "Plans for the Horse Show," *New York Tribune*, Nov. 8, 1890; "Prizes for Fine Horses," *NYT*, Oct. 26, 1890; "Man's Best Friend," *New York Herald*, Nov. 9, 1890; "Society Topics of the Week," *NYT*, Oct. 26 and Nov. 2, 1890; "Our New York Letter by Broadbrim," *New Hampshire Sentinel*, Nov. 26, 1890; "Prize Horses in Ring and Stall," *New York Herald*, Nov. 11, 1890; "The Equine Four Hundred," *NYT*, Nov. 11, 1890; "The Great Horse Show Opens for Business," *New York Herald*, Nov. 10, 1890; "Crowds at the Big Show," *NYT*, Nov. 13, 1890; "The Finest Show in New York," *New York Sun*, Nov. 16, 1890; "The Horse Show Is Over," *NYT*, Nov. 16, 1890.

15. Downey, *Portrait of an Era*, 148.

16. Baer, "Madison Square Garden," 114.

17. "Costumes as They Are Worn," *NYT*, Nov. 16, 1890; "People at the Big Show," *NYT*, Nov. 15, 1890; "Our New York Letter by Broadbrim," *New Hampshire Sentinel*, Nov. 26, 1890; "John M. Lander Dead," *NYT*, Oct. 9, 1905.

18. "What We Are All Talking About," *New York Sun*, Nov. 16, 1890.

19. Roth, *McKim, Mead & White*, 102; "The Great Horse Show," *NYT*, Nov. 15, 1890; "Ready for the Horse Show," *New York Tribune*, Nov. 9, 1890.

20. "Plans for the Horse Show," *New York Tribune*, Nov. 8, 1890; "The Horse Show," *NYT*, Nov. 17, 1890; "The Finest Show in New York," *New York Sun*, Nov. 16, 1890; "People at the Big Show," *NYT*, Nov. 15, 1890.

21. "Many Canine Aristocrats," *NYT*, Feb. 24, 1891.

22. "A Beautiful Ballroom," *NYT*, Dec. 23, 1890; "In and About the City: The Ladies' Assembly," *NYT*, Jan. 9, 1891.

23. "New England Society Officers," *New York Tribune*, Dec. 16, 1890; "New Englanders Rejoice," *New York Tribune*, Dec. 23, 1890.

24. Van Rensselaer, "Madison Square Garden," 746; "Completion of the Tall Tower," *NYT*, Oct. 14, 1891; "A New Music Hall," *New York Sun*, Dec. 23, 1890; "The New Music Hall and Ball Room," *New York Tribune*, Dec. 23, 1890.

25. Van Rensselaer, "Madison Square Garden," 746; "Ladies First Assembly," *New York Sun*, Jan. 9, 1891; "The New Music Hall and Ball Room," *New York Tribune*, Dec. 23, 1890.

26. Under the management of Christopher Kiefer. *New York Tribune*, July 29, 1890.

27. Baker, *Stanny*, 156.

28. "The Ladies Assembly," *New York Tribune*, Jan. 9, 1891; "Ladies First Assembly," *New York Sun*, Jan. 9, 1891; "The Wit of Clara Belle," *Washington (DC) Evening Critic*, Feb. 9, 1890; "What It Costs to Give a Ball," *Springfield (MA) Republican*, Mar. 13, 1890; "Louis Sherry Dies; Famous Caterer," *NYT*, June 10, 1926; Baldwin, *Stanford White*, 207. The Assembly Ball was put on by the Matriarchs, a group of fifty women who paid the expenses and then each received twelve invitations to extend to others. It was a sister event to the Patriarchs' Ball, a social device invented by Ward McAllister in 1872 as a steppingstone for the newly rich to the best New York society. Each Patriarch could invite four ladies and five gentlemen, including himself and his family, and then submit the names of fifty distinguished others for review by McAllister and final vetting by Mrs. William Astor. The Patriarchs' event was preferred by the old guard, who were able to set the standards and bar those whose only recommendation was their money, while the younger crowd favored the Matriarchs' Assembly Ball.

29. Lehr, *"King Lehr,"* 86.

30. "A Beautiful Ballroom," *NYT*, Dec. 23, 1890; Van Rensselaer, "Madison Square Garden," 741, 746; "The New Music Hall and Ball Room," *New York Tribune*, Dec. 23, 1890; "A New Music Hall," *New York Sun*, Dec. 23, 1890; "New Englanders Dine While Ladies Look On," *New York Herald*, Dec. 23, 1890.

31. "A Beautiful Ballroom," *NYT*, Dec. 23, 1890.

32. "New Englanders Dine While Ladies Look On," *New York Herald*, Dec. 23, 1890.

33. "A Beautiful Ballroom," *NYT*, Dec. 23, 1890; "A New Music Hall," *New York Sun*, Dec. 23, 1890; "The True American Idea," *NYT*, Dec. 24, 1890; "In the Name of Reform," *New York Sun*, Dec. 24, 1890.

34. SW to T. Dewing, Jan. 5, 1891, and SW to Charles Barney, Jan. 5, 1891, LPB 3:412a, 413, 424, SW Correspondence; T. Dewing to SW, May 29, roll 505, frame 302–3, and T. Dewing to SW, Sept 11, roll 505, frame 289–90, AAA, copy of MS 693, SW Papers, New-York Historical Society; Baker, *Stanny*, 289; "Women Artists at Home," *New York Herald*, Nov. 4, 1894.

35. *Oxford English Dictionary*, 3rd ed., accessed Dec. 1, 2017, http://www.oed.com/view /Entry/260928?redirectedFrom=la+petite+mort#eid10651807.

36. Brander Matthews, *Vignettes of Manhattan* (New York: Harper, 1894), 92.

37. T. Dewing to SW, Sept. 11, roll 505, frame 289–90, AAA, copy of MS 693, SW Papers, New-York Historical Society; T. Dewing to SW, Feb. 14, 1895, box 5:9 SW Correspondence. See also Susan Hobbs, *The Art of Thomas Wilmer Dewing: Beauty Reconfigured* (Brooklyn: Brooklyn Museum, 1986), 10; Baker, *Stanny*, 132, 288–89.

38. SW to Charles Barney, Jan. 5, 1891, LPB 4:413, SW Correspondence; SW to James R. Ray, real estate agent, July 23, 1891, LPB 4:132, SW Correspondence. Sometime prior to October 1898, White and King would lease Studio 3 at the Holbein, which was used less but still used and shared into 1905. Baker, *Stanny*, 288–89.

39. "Madison Square Garden Arcade," *New York Herald*, June 10, 1888; "At Work on the Arcade," *NYT*, Jan. 28, 1891.

40. Saarinen Papers, box 10, folder 3:10, AAA.

41. "Saint Gaudens' Diana," *New York Tribune*, June 23, 1911.

42. Lowe, *Stanford White's New York*, 129; Paul R. Baker, "Stanford White and Italy," in *The Italian Presence in American Art 1860–1920*, ed. Irma B. Jaffe (New York: Fordham Univ. Press, 1992), 167; Tauranac, *Elegant New York*, 40.

43. Advertisement, *American Architect and Building News* 31 (May 2, 1891); Saarinen Papers, box 10, folder 3:10, AAA; Santiago Huerta, "La Mecánica de las bóvedas tabicadas en su contexto histórico: La Aportación de los Guastavino," in *Las Bóvedas de Guastavino en América*, ed. Santiago Huerta (Madrid: Instituto Juan de Herrera, 1999), 88; Janet Parks and Alan G. Neuman, *The Old World Builds the New: The Guastavino Company and the Technology of the Catalan Vault, 1885–1962* (New York: Avery Architectural and Fine Arts Library, Columbia Univ., 1996), 7–8.

44. Rafael Guastavino, *Essay on the Theory and History of Cohesive Construction Applied Especially to the Timbrel Vault*, 2nd ed. (Boston: Ticknor, 1893), 21.

45. Lisa J. Mroszczyk, "Rafael Guastavino and the Boston Public Library" (master's thesis, MIT, June 2004), 13; Parks and Neumann, *Old World*, 14–15.

46. McKim, Mead & White, Architects, to Purly & Philips, Architects, Jan. 22, 1892, Charles Follen McKim Papers, Boston Public Library.

47. Guastavino Fireproof Construction Co. Archive, Avery Architectural and Fine Arts Library, Columbia University; Parks and Neumann, *Old World*, 11; Peter Austin, "Rafael

Guastavino's Construction Business in the United States: Beginnings and Development," *APT Bulletin* 30, no. 4 (1999): 15; Mroszczyk, "Rafael Guastavino," 23.

48. Although a kind of cement made of lime mixed with volcanic ash was first used by the Romans, Portland cement was a stronger, more durable type developed first in Britain in the 1750s. The name "Portland" was said to have been assigned because it resembled in color a British stone by that name. It was shipped to the United States beginning in 1868, and then manufactured in the 1870s in the Lehigh Valley, Pennsylvania, using local limestone and clay, but it was soon made in upstate New York and elsewhere. American Cement Co., *History of the Portland Cement Industry in the United States* (Philadelphia: American Cement, 1895), 8, 12, 14ff.

49. Guastavino, *Essay on the Theory*, 117, 134–35; Austin, "Rafael Guastavino's Construction Business," 15.

50. Guastavino Fireproof Construction Co. Archive, Avery Architectural and Fine Arts Library, Columbia University; McKim, Mead & White account books, MM&W Architectural Records Collection, PR 042, New-York Historical Society; Guastavino advertisement, *American Architect and Building News* 32 (May 2, 1891).

51. "Los Triumfos de un Arquitecto Espanol," *Las Novedades*, May 14, 1891; Guastavino Fireproof Construction Company advertisement, *American Architect and Building News* 33 (Sept. 19, 1891).

52. John A. Ochsendorf, email to author, May 10, 2014. See also Saarinen Papers, series 2, box 10, folder 3, AAA.

53. "The Divine Sarah Again," *NYT*, Feb. 3, 1891; "Sarah Bernhardt's Effects," *NYT*, Feb. 6, 1891; "Theatrical Gossip," *NYT*, Feb. 20, 1891.

54. "The Madison Square Garden," *NYT*, Mar. 29, 1891.

55. "Ready for the Big Show," *NYT*, Mar. 25, 1891. The route continued to Fifty-Seventh Street, to Eighth Avenue, to Forty-Second Street, to Broadway, to Fourteenth, to Fourth Avenue, to the Bowery, to Grand, to Sullivan, to Canal, to Hudson, to Fifth Avenue, to Twenty-Seventh, and finally to the Garden.

56. "Many Canine Aristocrats," *NYT*, Feb. 24, 1891; "Cackling Fills the Garden," *NYT*, Feb. 5, 1891.

57. "Some Questions of Art: Diana of the Tower," *New York Sun*, Nov. 1, 1891.

Part Three. The Virgin and the Tower

1. Rupert Hughes, *The Real New York* (New York: SmartSet, 1904), 168.

16. On the Model Stand

1. J. Fraser, typescript, box 44:9, Papers of ASG.

2. Tharp, *Saint-Gaudens*, 225, 231.

3. "They Are Anxious to Pose," *Omaha World-Herald*, Sept. 1, 1895; "The Real 'Diana of the Garden,'" *New York Herald*, Dec. 5, 1897; "Live Topics about Town," *New York Sun*, May 17, 1909.

4. French, *Memories*, 212; "Artists' Models," *The Art Amateur* 33 (Sept. 1895): 70.

5. "An Artist to Wed His Model," *New Orleans Daily Picayune*, July 16, 1887; "Artists' Models," *The Art Amateur* 33 (Sept. 1895): 70; "Model's Life One of Hard Work; Low Pay," *Duluth News Tribune*, Mar. 12, 1922; Elizabeth Hollander, "On the Pedestal: Notes on Being an Artist's Model," *Raritan* 6 (Summer 1986): 29.

6. Adams, "Women as Models," Nov. 6, 1887; "The Life of a Model," *Philadelphia Inquirer*, Dec. 8, 1889; "Artist and Modiste Do Not Agree," *New York Herald*, June 21, 1891.

7. Hillary Bell, "Artists' Models," *Oregonian* (Portland OR), Oct. 10, 1886, and "The Nude in Art," *Oregonian*, Apr. 23, 1893; "The Model," *Colorado Springs Gazette*, Apr. 23, 1899; "For the Sake of Art," *St. Paul Globe*, Dec. 9, 1894.

8. N. C. White, introduction to *Thomas W. Dewing, A Loan Exhibition* (New York: Durlacher Brothers, 1963), quoted in Hobbs, *Art of Thomas Wilmer Dewing*, 153; "Evolution of the New York Artist's Model," *NYT*, Apr. 2, 1905.

9. "Harrison Fisher Discovered a New Type of Beauty," *NYT*, Jan. 22, 1911.

10. "Experiences of a Model," *Kansas City Times*, May 30, 1886.

11. "A Model's Gossip," *New York Sun*, Nov. 24, 1889; "Experiences of a Model," *Kansas City Times*, May 30, 1886; "The Real 'Diana of the Garden,'" *New York Herald*, Dec. 5, 1897; Gustav Kobbé, "The Artist and His Model," *The Cosmopolitan* 31 (June 1901): 122; Sadakichi Hartmann, "New Yorker kunstlermodelle," *New Yorker Staats-Zeitung*, Apr. 1, 1900, reprinted as "New York Artists' Models," in *Sadakichi Hartmann: Critical Modernist*, ed. Jane Calhoun (Berkeley: Univ. of California, 1991), 114.

12. "Models in Rebellion," *Dallas Morning News*, Jan. 27, 1895.

13. Pyle, "Some Types," 16; "Artists and the Models," *Omaha World-Herald*, June 2, 1890.

14. George Holme, "Artists' Models," *Munsey's Magazine* 10 (Feb. 1894): 527; Hartmann, "New York Artists' Models," 112; Pyle, "Some Types," 16. It would not be until 1898 and the formation of the Art Workers' Club for Women that a formal employment bureau served as intermediary between artists and models while also offering classes on the art of posing. David Slater, "The Fount of Inspiration," *Winterthur Portfolio* 39 (2005), 248.

15. William Merritt Chase, "How I Painted My Greatest Picture," *The Delineator* 72 (Dec. 1908): 969; Lilian Baynes, "An Artist's Model," *The Illustrated American*, Oct. 19, 1895, 501.

16. See Martha Banta, "Artists, Models, Real Things, and Recognizable Types," *Studies in the Literary Imagination* 16 (Fall 1983): 14–15.

17. Onoto Watanna and Sara Bosse, *Marion: The Story of an Artist's Model* (New York: W. J. Watt, 1916), 214.

18. Holme, "Artists' Models," 527.

19. "As to Girl Models," *St. Louis Republic*, Aug. 6, 1891.

20. Pegi Taylor, "A View from the Platform," in *Dictionary of Artists' Models*, ed. Jill Berk Jiminez (London: Fitzroy Dearborn, 2001), 2. See also Marie Lathers, "The Social Construction

and Deconstruction of the Female Model in Nineteenth-Century France," *Mosaic* 29 (June 1996): 41.

21. "Evolution of the New York Artist's Model," *NYT*, Apr. 2, 1905; "Temptations and Perils that Beset the Model," *St. Paul (MN) Appeal*, Aug. 8, 1906; Robert W. Chambers, *The Common Law* (New York: Appleton, 1911), 34–35; "Like Trilby They Pose," *New York Sun*, Feb. 24, 1895.

22. "The Real 'Diana of the Garden,'" *New York Herald*, Dec. 5, 1897; "New York's Girl Models," *New York Herald*, July 29, 1894; "An Artist to Wed His Model," *New Orleans Daily Picayune*, July 16, 1887; "Should Artists Marry?" *New York Herald*, Oct. 28, 1894; "Artists' Models," *Dallas Morning News*, Jan. 20, 1907.

23. "With the Art Students," *New York Sun*, May 26, 1895.

24. Holme, "Artists' Models," 531.

25. HSG, *Reminiscences of Augustus*, 1:68–69, 134, 147; ASG, "Reminiscences of an Idiot," 45; Dryfhout, *Work*, 51.

26. HSG, *Reminiscences of Augustus*, 1:128, 143; Dryfhout, *Work*, 66, fig. 40.

27. Account book, Papers of ASG, cited in Dryfhout, *Work*, 65; Bouton, "Early Works," 171. The fate of the *Venus* is unknown.

28. HSG, *Reminiscences of Augustus*, 1:130ff, 142; Bouton, "Early Works," 178–79; Royal Cortissoz, "Augustus Saint-Gaudens and Willard L. Metcalf, Two Notable Figures in American Art," *New York Herald Tribune*, Oct. 14, 1928.

29. HSG, "Saint-Gaudens the Master," *The Century* 78 (Aug. 1909): 615; Dryfhout, *Work*, 154; HSG, *Reminiscences of Augustus*, 2:363.

30. Winckelmann, *History of the Art of Antiquity*, 133.

31. HSG, ms. for *Reminiscences of Augustus Saint-Gaudens*, reel 50, frame 628, Papers of ASG.

32. The plaster head passed to Davida's son Louis Paul Clark, then to his son Louis John Clark, and then to his widow, June Clark Moore. Susan E. Menconi, *Uncommon Spirit: Sculpture in America, 1800–1940* (New York: Hirschl & Adler Galleries, 1989), 23; Dryfhout, *Work*, 154.

33. Another explanation was to prevent the bust of Davida from becoming part of his estate. William D. Fox to John Dryfhout, Feb. 27, 1979, SGNHS. The terra-cotta head is now in a private collection in Arkville, New York. Dryfhout, *Work*, 154.

34. Buckner Hollingsworth, *Augustus Saint-Gaudens* (New York: W. W. Norton, 1948), 61.

35. William Ordway Partridge, *The Angel of Clay* (New York: G. P. Putnam's Sons, 1900), 67.

36. Lionel Moses to HSG, Mar. 5, 1909, reel 24, frame 456-8, Papers of ASG, quoted in Dryfhout, "Diana," 201.

37. Margaret C. Adler, "Sacred Rites, Vengeful Goddesses, and Tall Tales," in *Wild Spaces, Open Seasons: Hunting and Fishing in American Art*, ed. Kevin Sharp (Norman: Univ. of Oklahoma Press, 2016), 23.

38. Low, *Chronicle*, 480; Frank Linstow White, "Figure of Diana," *Epoch* 10 (Dec. 11, 1891): 253, cited in Weitenkampf, *Manhattan Kaleidoscope*, 127.

39. "Artist and Modiste Do Not Agree," *New York Herald*, June 21, 1891.

40. Baker, *Stanny*, 280.

41. Baker, *Stanny*, 286.

42. Orson Lowell, "Three Important New York Exhibitions," *Brush & Pencil* 2 (May 1898): 89.

43. Bronze in the collection of the American Museum of Art, Smithsonian Institution, #1929.8.397. It was sold at the auction of the Stanford White collection in 1907 to Mrs. Edith Rogers Gellatly for $300, and after her death it was donated by her husband, John Gellatly, to the Smithsonian in 1929. The original plaster is lost, although a model in plaster "for the figure surmounting the tower of Madison Square Garden" was sold as item number 365 in the same auction. "Art Bargain Hunters Happy at White Sale," *New York Press*, Nov. 28, 1907; "Mrs. Gellatly Left $1,289,905, Bronze Diana by Saint Gaudens in Art Collection Worth $118,712," *NYT*, June 6, 1916.

17. The Tower Rises

1. Rosendale cement, from limestone with naturally occurring clay, was widely replaced in the early twentieth century by Portland cement with its greater strength for thicker mortar joints and lower production cost. "Rosendale Cement," *Architecture* 6 (July 15, 1902): 227; "Thirty-Five Years' Test," *American Architect* 128: 519–20; "Madison Square Garden," *Harper's Weekly* 34 (Sept. 13, 1890): 718.

2. Van Rensselaer, "Madison Square Garden," 745.

3. Simmons, *From Seven to Seventy*, 243.

4. "Thirty-Five Years' Test," *American Architect* 128: 520; Skinner, "Steelwork of Madison Square Garden," 537.

5. King, *King's Handbook*, 868; "Madison Square Garden," *American Architect* 128 (Dec. 20, 1925): 515; Roth, *McKim, Mead & White*, 161n3.

6. Van Dyke, *New New York*, 98; Landau and Condit, *Rise of the New York Skyscraper*, 120–22, 157, 161–63; "The Birth of the New York Skyscraper—A Romance of Architecture," *NYT*, May 21, 1905; Berg, "Iron Construction," 463. Aside from likely being the first skeleton-framed building, the 1889 Tower Building was also probably the first to successfully employ a system of diagonal wind-bracing, less necessary with the use of the wrought-iron Phoenix column in the 1890s. Landau and Condit, *Rise of the New York Skyscraper*, 57, 164–66.

7. Coffin, "Tower of the Madison Square Garden," 819; "Louisville's Awful Calamity," *NYT*, Mar. 29, 1890; Van Dyke, *New New York*, 100.

8. Landau and Condit, *Rise of the New York Skyscraper*, 157, 159–60.

9. "Madison Square Garden," *Harper's Weekly* 34 (Sept. 13, 1890): 718; Coffin, "Tower of the Madison Square Garden," 819; "The Tower of Madison Square Garden," *Frank Leslie's Illustrated Newspaper* 74 (Mar. 31, 1892): 147; "Completion of the Tower," *NYT*, Oct. 14, 1891.

10. "Thirty-Five Years' Test," *American Architect* 128: 519; Skinner, "Steelwork of Madison Square Garden," 537.

11. Aaron Betsky, *Building Sex: Men, Women, Architecture, and the Construction of Sexuality* (New York: William Morrow, 1995), x, xii, 28.

12. Armstrong, *Day Before Yesterday*, 340.

13. Emily Kies Folpe, *It Happened on Washington Square* (Baltimore: Johns Hopkins Univ. Press, 2002), 191–92; H. Langford Warren, "The Use and Abuse of Precedent," *Architectural Review* 2 (Apr. 3, 1893): 22; Roth, *McKim, Mead & White*, 103.

14. Warren, "Use and Abuse," 22; Baker, "Stanford White and Italy," 165.

15. "Heating and Ventilation of a Baltimore Church," *American Steam and Hot-Water Heating Practice* (New York: Engineering Record, 1895): 43; Folpe, *It Happened on Washington Square*, 193; Roth, *McKim, Mead & White*, 102.

16. "A Palace of Pleasure," *Harper's Weekly* 31 (Nov. 5, 1887): 807.

17. Van Dyke, *New New York*, 119.

18. Baer, "Madison Square Garden," 114; "The Garden Getting on Well," *New York Tribune*, May 13, 1896.

19. "The Garden Company's Finances," *New York Tribune*, May 13, 1891; "Concerts in the Garden," *NYT*, May 30, 1891; "Live Musical Topics," *NYT*, June 7, 1891.

20. Baker, *Stanny*, 199. The office space was a sublet from the Herter Brothers, whose premiere furniture-making and interior decorating firm had leased the Robert Leighton Stuart mansion in 1882 and was currently overseeing the mosaics for the Boston Public Library project. "City Real Estate," *NYT*, Nov. 19, 1882. In 1893 the Stuart house passed to the Presbyterian Church, and McKim, Mead & White moved their offices around the corner to the Mohawk Building at 160 Fifth Avenue.

21. "The Organization of an Architect's Office, No. VIII," *Engineering Record* 25 (Dec. 5, 1891): 4; Van Rensselaer, "Madison Square Garden," 739; Roth, *Architecture of McKim, Mead & White*, xxxv.

22. SW to ASG, Feb. 6, [1887], Papers of ASG.

23. Philip Sawyer, in Hewlett et al., "Stanford White as Those Trained," 247; Albert Randolph Ross, in Hewlett et al., "Stanford White as Those Trained," 246.

24. "A Tall Tower Nearly Finished," *New York Herald*, Oct. 9, 1891.

25. "The Gleaner," *New York Evening World*, June 2, 1891; De Kay, "Madison Square Garden," 542.

26. "More Victims of Electricity," *NYT*, June 7, 1891.

18. *Diana*, Doing and Making

1. ASG, "Reminiscences of an Idiot," 67.

2. "How Statues Are Made," *NYT*, Jan. 25, 1891; Frances Grimes, "A Sculptor's Life in the Early Twentieth Century," box 44:14, 2, Papers of ASG.

3. Saint-Gaudens's first use of Robert Treat Paine's labor-saving device for mechanical enlargement was not until the 1896 model for the *Sherman Monument*. Dryfhout, *Work*, 253.

4. For the mechanical side of sculpture-making, see Grimes, "Interviews of Frances Grimes," tape 3, side A, AAA; William Ordway Partridge, *The Technique of Sculpture* (Boston: Ginn, 1895), 52, 61–64, 79–80; "How Our Statues Are Made," *New York Evening World*, Oct. 17, 1889; "The Sculptor's Work," *Oregonian* (Portland OR), Sept. 30, 1894; Henry Flagg French to Benjamin Brown French, July 7, 1869, vol. 7, Benjamin Brown French Papers, Manuscript Division, Library of Congress; Malvina Hoffman, *Sculpture Inside and Out* (New York: W. W. Norton, 1939), 273–74.

5. Sculptor Oscar Lenz, one of Saint-Gaudens's pupils at the Art Students League, also claimed to have been given part of the modeling of *Diana*. "Oscar Lenz, Sculptor, Dies," *NYT*, June 26, 1912.

6. Daniel Chester French, quoted in J. Walker McSpadden, *Famous Sculptors of America* (New York: Dodd, Mead, 1925), 116; Simmons, *From Seven to Seventy*, 252.

7. HSG, *Augustus Saint-Gaudens, Adapted from a Lecture*, 50.

8. de Quélin, "Early Days," 425; HSG, *Reminiscences of Augustus*, 1:338, 341; Cox, *Artist and Public*, 185.

9. Partridge, *Technique of Sculpture*, 79. Paris became the capital of commercial plaster manufacture in the seventeenth century with the discovery of a deposit conveniently found in Montmartre and the development of means to refine it, hence "plaster of Paris."

10. Frances Grimes, "Reminiscences," 2, box 44:14, Papers of ASG. Although said to be from Nice and of declared French heritage (US Federal Census, 1910, Windsor, VT, p. 25A), Ardisson was born in Italy according to immigration records. National Archives, Immigration, Port of New York, series 10–16, copy M-237 (1860–97), cited in David Karel, ed. *Dictionnaire des artistes de lange française en Amérique du nord* (Quebec: Les presses de l'université Laval, 1992), 7.

11. "Assistants," *The Saint-Gaudens Memorial*, accessed Aug. 6, 2010, http://www.sgnhs.org/Augustus-Gaudens CD-HTML/Assistants/GrimesArdisson.htm.

12. Frances Grimes, "Reminiscences," 4, box 44:14, Papers of ASG; "Sculptor at Whitney Estate Commits Suicide," *NYT*, Aug. 20, 1926; "Galton Ardisson, Master Plaster Molder, Ends Life," *Springfield (MA) Republican*, Aug. 29, 1926.

13. Hoffman, *Sculpture*, 102.

14. HSG, *Reminiscences of Augustus*, 2:97–98; Grimes, "Interviews of Frances Grimes," tape 3, side A, AAA.

15. "The Use of Stamped Zinc: Architectural Ornaments," *Sheet-Metal Builder* 1 (1874): 120, and "In General," *Sheet-Metal Builder* 1 (1875): 120, 145, cited in Carol A. Grissom, *Zinc Sculpture in America, 1850–1950* (Newark: Univ. of Delaware Press, 2009), 87, 653; "William H. Mullins," *NYT*, Mar. 7, 1932.

16. Edward C. Rafferty, "A History of the Columbus Statue, Phillipsburg, N.J.," Dec. 1, 1993, accessed Sept. 15, 2010, http://vanderkrogt.net/statues/texts/phillipsburg.html.

17. Grissom, *Zinc Sculpture*, 62–63; "Great Is Diana," *Kalamazoo Gazette*, Nov. 3, 1892.

18. W. H. Mullins, "How the Statue Was Made," Letter to the Editor, *Charlotte (NC) Observer*, Dec. 16, 1894.

19. "Madison Square Garden Weather Vane," *Scientific American* 65 (Dec. 26, 1891): 407; H. M. Mullins, *Architectural Sheet Metal Work and Statuary*, 1896 catalogue, cited in Grissom, *Zinc Sculpture*, 654; A. D. Lemonte, ed. *A Story of People, the Story of Mullins, the Story of Your Job* (Salem, OH: Mullins Manufacturing Corp., 1947), 28, cited in Grissom, *Zinc Sculpture*, 62; Rafferty, "History of the Columbus Statue."

20. SW to Horace Bradley, Nov. 9, 1893, box 1:4, SW Correspondence; "Will Not Purchase the Statue," *NYT*, Jan. 8, 1892; Cortissoz, "Metamorphosis of Diana," 1124.

19. Oriental Fantasies

1. De Kay, "Madison Square Garden," 542.

2. "At the Top in New York," *Daily News*, Nov. 18, 1881.

3. Jamil M. Abun-Nasr, *A History of the Maghrib in the Islamic Period* (Cambridge Univ. Press, 1987), 95, 96; Roger Le Tourneau, *The Almohad Movement in North Africa in the Twelfth and Thirteenth Centuries* (Princeton, NJ: Princeton Univ. Press, 1969), 69. For documentation of the history and sources of Almohad architecture, specifically the Giralda, see Paul Lunde, "Ishbiliaya: Islamic Seville," *Saudi Aramco World* (Jan./Feb. 1993): 20–31; Paul Lunde, "The Giralda," *Saudi Aramco World* (Jan./Feb. 1994): 32–35; Ibn Sahib al-Sala, *al-Mann bil-Imamah* 2, no. 33, quoted in Lunde, "Giralda," 33; Abun-Nasr, *History of the Maghrib*, 95; Henri Basset and Henri Terrasse, *Sanctuaires et forteresses almohades* (Paris: Maisonneuve et Laronse, 2001), 106.

4. See the *Minaret of the Bride* at the Great Umayyad Mosque of Damascus and, even earlier, the pre-Islamic towers on which it may have been erected. Ross Burns, *Damascus, A History* (London: Routledge, 2005), 132, 148.

5. Exceeding the crumbling but once taller 283 BC lighthouse at Alexandria, built by Ptolemy and his Greek architect and well documented by Moorish scholars in the twelfth century.

6. Luis Martinez Montiel, *The Cathedral of Seville* (London: Scala Publishers, 1999), 12, 14.

7. Lunde, "Giralda," 32; Martinez Montiel, *Cathedral of Seville*, 12.

8. Martinez Montiel, *Cathedral of Seville*, 14.

9. It was specially built for the exposition on a hill named for the Spanish fortress the Trocadéro, which was taken by the French in 1823 during the storming of Cadiz when the French army sought to free the imprisoned Spanish King Ferdinand VII from his country's revolutionary forces. The hall, demolished for the 1937 Paris Exposition Internationale and replaced by the *Palais de Chaillot*, was also the design source for Carrère & Hastings's Ponce de Leon hotel in St. Augustine, Florida, completed in 1887.

10. Armstrong, *Day Before Yesterday*, 29.

11. SW to Alexina White, May 6, 1884, quoted in Baldwin, *Stanford White*, 167.

12. See Robert Koch, *Louis C. Tiffany, Rebel in Glass* (New York: Crown, 1964), 53.

13. Morris's designs, which stressed the importance of rich color, line, and flattened pattern as derived from nature, were sold as wallpaper by Morris & Company beginning in Boston in 1873. By the mid-1870s the firm had representatives for their growing line of wallpaper, fabric, and carpet in many American cities.

14. Craven, *Stanford White*, 12.

15. Mary W. Blanchard, "The Soldier and the Aesthete: Homosexuality and Popular Culture in Gilded Age America," *Journal of American Studies* 30 (Apr. 1996): 41–45. See "Seventh Armory Regiment Illustrated," *The Decorator and Furnisher* 6 (May 1885).

16. Augusta Saint-Gaudens to HSG, 1899, box 93:14, Papers of ASG; Tharp, *Saint-Gaudens*, 297.

17. Craven, *Stanford White*, 212.

18. See Van Rensselaer, *Henry Hobson Richardson*, 64–65; H. R. Hitchcock, *The Architecture of H. H. Richardson and His Time* (Cambridge: MIT Press, 1936; rev. ed. 1966), 139; Roth, *McKim, Mead & White*, 29; Warren, "Use and Abuse," 24.

19. Craven, *Stanford White*, 21. Broderick (*Triumvirate*, 247) questions whether he ever visited Spain, at least not prior to designing the tower.

20. Lathrop, "Spanish Vistas," 373. Author George P. Lathrop was also husband to Augusta Saint-Gaudens's beloved friend Rose.

21. Roth, *McKim, Mead & White*, 54.

22. Magonigle, "Half Century, 4," *Pencil Points* 15 (May 1934): 224; Skinner, "Steelwork of Madison Square Garden," 537–39.

23. "Thousands Hear Thomas," *NYT*, July 7, 1891.

24. "Open and Shut," *New York Sun*, Nov. 1, 1891.

25. "Some Questions of Art: The Tower of the Giralda," *New York Sun*, Nov. 15, 1891; *Tacoma (WA) Daily News*, Nov. 28, 1891.

26. "Some Questions of Art: The Tower of the Giralda," *New York Sun*, Nov. 15, 1891; Saarinen Papers, box 10, folder 3:11, AAA; Baker, *Stanny*, 157; Roth, *McKim, Mead & White*, 161.

27. Hughes, *Real New York*, 167.

28. Van Rensselaer, "Madison Square Garden," 745.

29. Hughes, *Real New York*, 168; Warren, "Use and Abuse," 21, 23.

30. De Kay, "Madison Square Garden," 542.

31. Martinez Montiel, *Cathedral of Seville*, 14.

32. "A Huge Weather Vane," *NYT*, Sept. 29, 1891; "A Pyramid of Fire," *NYT*, Nov. 2, 1891.

20. The Virgin Installed

1. "A Huge Weather Vane," *NYT*, Sept. 29, 1891; "Notes of the Stage," *New York Tribune*, Sept. 30, 1891.

2. SW to ASG, Sept. 9, 1891, LPB 4:234, SW Correspondence.

3. James W. Morrissey, *Noted Men and Women* (New York: Klebold Press, 1910), 182–84; "A Huge Weather Vane," *NYT*, Sept. 29, 1891.

4. "Raising a Greek Goddess," *New York World*, Oct. 1, 1891; "A Huge Weather Vane," *NYT*, Sept. 29, 1891.

5. "Madison Square Garden Weather Vane," *Scientific American* 65 (Dec. 26, 1891): 407; "Diana Returns to Us," *New York Sun*, Nov. 11, 1893.

6. SW to ASG, Oct. 3 [1891], LPB 4:263, SW Correspondence; "Time for Diana to Rise," *New York Sun*, Nov. 17, 1893.

7. According to Hoppin, builders and workmen responded cheerfully to White's directions and "impulses," whether they considered them vagaries or otherwise. Hoppin, "Stanford White," 246; J. B. Knight to SW, Feb. 9, 1892, box 1:8, SW Correspondence; "Removed from Her Perch," *New York Sun*, Sept. 13, 1892.

8. "Diana in Pajamas," *New York World*, Oct. 6, 1891.

9. "Completion of the Tall Tower," *NYT*, Oct. 14, 1891; "Is Diana Coming," *Chicago Herald*, Dec. 25, 1891.

10. "A Huge Weather Vane," *NYT*, Sept. 29, 1891.

11. "Madison Square Garden's Tower," *New York Sun*, Oct. 14, 1891; "As If Seen from a Balloon," *New York Recorder*, Oct. 14, 1891.

12. SW to ASG, Oct. 15, 1891, and SW to Frank du Mond, Oct. 15, 1891, LPB 4:312–314, SW Correspondence.

13. "Diana's Drapery Singed," *New York Sun*, Oct. 29, 1891.

14. "Diana Unveiled," *New York Herald*, Nov. 2, 1891.

15. "Now See Far-Reaching New York," *New York Herald*, Nov. 2, 1891; "Diana Is Now on View," *New York Sun*, Nov. 2, 1891.

16. "Diana Unveiled," *New York Herald*, Nov. 2, 1891; "Diana's a Daisy," *Salem (OH) Daily News*, Nov. 21, 1891; "Now See Far-Reaching New-York," *New York Daily Tribune*, Nov. 2, 1891.

17. While most newspaper accounts documented the lighting of the crescent at the base of the *Diana*, a story in the *New York Herald*, June 13, 1892, indicates that it was not illuminated until some seven months later. Perhaps they were out of regular service until that time.

18. "Diana Unveiled," *New York Herald*, Nov. 2, 1891; "Diana's a Daisy," *Salem (OH) Daily News*, Nov. 21, 1891.

19. "A Pyramid of Fire," *NYT*, Nov. 2, 1891; "Diana Unveiled," *New York Herald*, Nov. 2, 1891.

21. *Diana* Reigns

1. "Some Questions of Art: Diana of the Tower," *New York Sun*, Nov. 1, 1891.

2. "Diana's Brow Ablaze," *Morning Advertiser* (NY), Nov. 2, 1891; "Golden Diana Stands Revealed," *New York Tribune*, Nov. 3, 1891.

3. "Some Questions of Art: Diana of the Tower," *New York Sun*, Nov. 1, 1891.

4. Saarinen Papers, box 10, folder 3:14, AAA.

5. Edward Cary, "The Diana of the Tower," *The Century* 47 (Jan. 1894): 477.

6. "The Diana of the Tower," *NYT*, Nov. 8, 1891.

7. "Some Questions of Art: Diana of the Tower," *New York Sun*, Nov. 1, 1891; "That Statue of Diana," *New York Mercury*, Nov. 29, 1891; "Miss Liberty Catching First Glimpse of Diana," cartoon, *Harper's Weekly* 35 (1891): 834. There was also the rumor that every year she came down off her perch quite unnoticed to attend New York's French Ball. "World's Fair Doings," *Chicago Daily Inter Ocean*, Jan. 8, 1892.

8. *Chicago Sunday Tribune*, July 24, 1904.

9. "A Great Municipal Possession," *New York Daily Tribune*, Nov. 8, 1891.

10. "The Latest Work of Art," *Salt Lake Herald*, Nov. 8, 1891.

11. Cary, "Diana of the Tower," 477.

12. Thomas Lately, *Delmonico's, A Century of Splendor* (Boston: Houghton Mifflin, 1967), 231; "Diana at the Fair," *The Illustrated American* 12 (Oct. 1, 1892): 137.

13. Marceau to Phillip Rounsevelle, May 25, 1932. Rounsevelle had written to Marceau with the observation that many classical figures of Diana show the *chiton* drawn up over the left shoulder to hide the amputation of the left breast. Box 177:29, Fiske Kimball Records, Philadelphia Museum of Art.

14. *New York Mercury*, Nov. 22, 1891.

15. Anthony Comstock, *Traps for the Young* (New York: Funk & Wagnalls, 1883), 172; Anthony Comstock, *Morals Versus Art* (New York: J. S. Ogilivie, 1887), 10.

16. Comstock, *Traps for the Young*, 172; Comstock, *Morals Versus Art*, 10; Nixola Greeley-Smith, "Comstock Tells What Is Immoral and Why It Is So, Also When to Pull Down the Blinds on the Nude," *New York Evening World*, Mar. 29, 1913.

17. "Mr. Comstock's Work," *NYT*, Nov. 13, 1887; "Comstock Suppressing Fine Art," *New York Sun*, Nov. 12, 1887; "Comstock's Crusade on Art," *New York Sun*, Nov. 13, 1887; "Dr. De Costa Interviews Diana," *New York Herald*, June 20, 1892; Jennifer Hardin, "The Nude in the Era of the New Movement in American Art: Thomas Eakins, Kenyon Cox, and Augustus Saint-Gaudens" (PhD diss., Yale Univ., 2000), 99.

18. "Notes and Novelties," *The Collector* 3 (Dec. 1, 1891): 43; "That Diana Again," *The Collector* 3 (Apr. 15, 1892): 183; "Diana, New York's Goddess," *New York Sun*, Nov. 2, 1891. For a discussion of a sexualized context for Diana and male identity, see Lee, "Electrified Goddess," 15–20.

19. "Dr. De Costa Interviews Diana," *New York Herald*, June 20, 1892.

20. "Our Golden Diana," *New York Advertiser*, Nov. 12, 1893; "Will Outlast the Editors," *NYT*, Apr. 25, 1892.

21. "The Comstock Nuisance," *NYT*, Nov. 16, 1887.

22. "Philadelphia Gets 'Diana,' New York's Virgin," *Arts Magazine* 6 (Apr. 15, 1932): 17.

23. "A Huge Weather Vane," *NYT*, Sept. 29, 1891; "Completion of the Tall Tower," *NYT*, Oct. 14, 1891.

24. "As If Seen from a Balloon," *New York Recorder*, Oct. 14, 1891; "The Diana of the Tower," *NYT*, Nov. 8, 1891.

25. SW to ASG, Oct. 3, 1891, LPB 4:263, SW Correspondence.

26. W. Kendall to Lida Rose McCabe, Dec. 16, 1924, box 378:435, MM&W Architectural Records Collection, PR 042, New-York Historical Society.

27. "Some Questions of Art: Diana of the Tower," *New York Sun*, Nov. 1, 1891.

28. "Diana's a Daisy," *Salem (OH) Daily News*, Nov. 21, 1891.

29. "Diana Unveiled," *New York Herald*, Nov. 2, 1891.

30. "Notes and Novelties," *The Collector* 3 (Dec. 1, 1891): 43. See also *The Collector* (Nov. 15, 1891): 21–22; (Apr. 1, 1892): 171; and (Sept. 15, 1892): 290.

31. "Chicago Wants Diana," *New York Herald*, Aug. 21, 1892.

32. SW to H. Bradley, Nov. 9, 1893, box 1:4, SW Correspondence.

33. "The Tower of Madison Square Garden," *Frank Leslie's Illustrated Newspaper* 74 (Mar. 31, 1892): 147; "New York Is Soon to Be Separated from Diana," *Chicago Daily Inter Ocean*, Apr. 1, 1892.

34. Frederick Parsell Hill, *Charles F. McKim: The Man* (Francestown, NH: M. Jones, 1950), 27–28.

35. Baldwin, *Stanford White*, 211.

36. For documentation of *Diana*'s rumored move to the Chicago Columbian Exposition, see "Diana May Go to Chicago," *New York Herald*, Dec. 20, 1891; "Diana Will Not Go West," *New York Tribune*, Dec. 22, 1891; *New York Sun*, Dec. 23, 1891; "Note and Comment," *Springfield (MA) Republican*, Dec. 23, 1891.

37. "Is Diana Coming?" *Chicago Herald*, Dec. 25, 1891.

38. "Is Diana Coming?" *Chicago Herald*, Dec. 25, 1891. The Venetian *Fortuna* was created by Bernardo Falcone ca. 1680 and installed on the Dogana da Mar by 1682.

39. "Will Not Purchase the Statue," *NYT*, Jan. 8, 1892; "Does Not Care for Diana," *Chicago Daily Tribune*, Jan. 8, 1892.

40. *The Collector* 3 (Jan. 15, 1892): 87.

41. "Diana Goes to Chicago," *New York Sun*, Sept. 4, 1892.

42. "Diana of the St. Gaudens. Some Reflections of the Goddess on the Tower," *NYT*, Jan. 31, 1892.

43. LPB 3:29, 31, 33; 4:486, 490, 5:102, 126, 129, 455, SW Correspondence; June Hall McCash, *The Jekyll Island Cottage Colony* (Athens: Univ. of Georgia Press, 1998), 158.

44. ASG to SW, May 5, 1906, SW Papers, New-York Historical Society.

45. "We Will Have a New Diana," *New York World*, Mar. 18, 1892; "A New Diana for the Garden," *New York Evening Post*, Mar. 17, 1892; "Diana Going to Chicago," *NYT*, Mar. 18, 1892; "Diana to Be Taken Down," *New York Herald*, Mar. 18, 1892.

46. "Metropolis Day by Day. Will Have a New Diana," *New York World*, Mar. 18, 1892.

47. "Diana Too Big a Girl," *New York Sun*, Mar. 17, 1892; "Special Correspondence," *NYT*, Mar. 31, 1892.

48. HSG, *Reminiscences of Augustus*, 1:393; HSG, *Augustus Saint-Gaudens, Adapted from a Lecture*, 37.

49. J. Monroe Hewlett, in Hewlett et al., "Stanford White as Those Trained," 245; Warren, "With Love and Gratitude," May 30, 1897.

50. SW to F. MacMonnies, Feb. 25, 1892, MacMonnies Family Papers, quoted in Smart, *Flight with Fame*, 115.

22. Up under the Stars

1. "Up under the Clouds," *NYT*, May 27, 1892; "A Big Amusement Scheme," *New York Tribune*, Mar. 10, 1887; "Like Babylon's Hanging Gardens," *New York Herald*, May 15, 1891; "The Garden of the Garden," *New York Daily Tribune*, May 15, 1892.

2. James Traub, *The Devil's Playground: A Century of Pleasure and Profit in Times Square* (New York: Random House, 2004), 13. See also "Amusements: The Casino Promenade," *NYT*, July 8, 1883; "Amusements: The Casino Concerts," *NYT*, July 16, 1883; "The Stage," *Munsey's Magazine* 13 (June 1895): 306; "Our Theatres Next Week," *New York Evening World*, June 6, 1891, and June 20, 1891.

3. "In the Casino Roof Garden," *NYT*, May 13, 1889; "Talk of the Stage World. Mr. Aronson's Plans to Eclipse the Casino's Rivals," *New York Evening World*, July 8, 1891, and May 2, 1892; "Singing on the Roof," *New York Sun*, May 14, 1892; "A Cafe Chantant at the Casino," *NYT*, May 15, 1892; "News of the Theatres," *New York Sun*, May, 22, 1892; "The Casino's Roof Garden," *NYT*, May 26, 1892; "Rudolph Aronson's Company," *NYT*, May 30, 1892; "The Casino's Summer Garden on the Roof," *NYT*, July 4, 1893.

4. "Thirty-Five Years' Test," *American Architect* 128: 519.

5. "Thirty-Five Years' Test," *American Architect* 128: 520; Birkmire, *Planning and Construction*, 3–4; Roth, *McKim, Mead & White*, 159; "Like Babylon's Hanging Gardens," *New York Herald*, May 15, 1891; "The Garden of the Garden," *New York Daily Tribune*, May 15, 1892; "An Aerial Crush on the Roof Garden," *New York Herald*, May 31, 1892.

6. "Like Babylon's Hanging Gardens," *New York Herald*, May 15, 1891. However, it was soon discovered that when a large enough band played near the shaft, the foliage failed to prevent the sound from traveling down and disrupting the performance in the theater. "Gilmore on the Roof," *New York Herald*, June 7, 1892.

7. Goldsmith, "I Remember McKim, Mead & White," 170.

8. "New York to Have a Winter Circus," *New York Herald*, Mar. 20, 1892; "A Permanent Circus Here," *New York Sun*, Mar. 20, 1892; "Points about the New Circus," *New York Sun*, Mar. 21, 1892; Baker, *Stanny*, 162, 164–65; Baer, "Madison Square Garden," 114.

9. "The Actors Fund Fair," *NYT*, Apr. 10, 1892; "Beautifying the Garden," *NYT*, May 1, 1892; "Actresses Arrange for Their Great Fair," *New York Herald*, May 2, 1892; "A Village of Fairyland," *New York Daily Tribune*, May 2, 1892; "The First of the Fair," *New York Daily Tribune*, May 3, 1892; Baker, *Stanny*, 163.

10. SW to D. King, Mar. 10, 1892, LPB 5:215, and SW to William F. Wharton, Mar. 31, 1892, LPB 5:272, SW Correspondence; Baker, *Stanny*, 165.

11. Advertisement, *New York Sun*, May 15, 1892.

12. James Gordon, "Reclamation of Roofs," *Building Progress* 2 (Oct. 1911), 306.

13. "Our Theatres Next Week," *New York Evening World*, May 7, 1892; "Among the Player Folk," *New York Evening World*, May 18, 1892; "Like Babylon's Hanging Gardens," *New York Herald*, May 15, 1891; "The Garden of the Garden," *New York Daily Tribune*, May 15, 1892.

14. "Up under the Clouds," *NYT*, May 27, 1892; "Among the Player Folk," *New York Evening World*, May 18, 1892; "An Aerial Crush on the Roof Garden," *New York Herald*, May 31, 1892.

15. *New York Sun*, May 25, 1892.

16. "An Aerial Crush on the Roof Garden," *New York Herald*, May 31, 1892; "The Garden of the Garden," *New York Tribune*, May 15, 1892; "Amusements, a Great Crush," *New York Sun*, May 31, 1892; "The Stage," *Munsey's Magazine* (July 1892): 506; "Opening the Garden Roof," *New York Tribune*, May 31, 1892; "Amusements: The Madison Square Garden," *NYT*, May 31, 1892.

17. "Miss Yeamans Did Not Appear," *New York Herald*, June 21, 1892; "An Aerial Crush on the Roof Garden," *New York Herald*, May 31, 1892.

18. Loie Fuller, *Fifteen Years of a Dancer's Life* (Boston: Small, Maynard, 1913), 37–40; "The Two M'Caull Benefits," *New York Daily Tribune*, Jan. 19, 1892; "Theatrical Gossip," *NYT*, Feb. 11, 1892; "Miss Fuller's Skirt Dance," *New York Herald*, Feb. 25, 1892; "A Newfangled Dance," *Idaho Statesman*, Mar. 29, 1892; "Loie Fuller Goes to Court," *New York Herald*, May 27, 1892; "Merely Mechanical Movements by Which Effects Are Produced on the Stage Are Not Subjects for Copyright When They Convey No Ideas, Decides the Judge. Loie Fuller Loses Again," *New York Herald*, June 20, 1892.

19. "Another Crush on the Roof," *New York Herald*, June 1, 1892; "It Was Not Closed," *New York Herald*, June 2, 1892; "Says It Is Perfectly Safe," *New York Herald*, June 9, 1892; "Fire Escapes for the Garden," *New York Herald*, June 10, 1892; "A New Exit from the Roof Garden," *NYT*, June 3, 1892.

20. "A Lively Rushing Back and Forth," *New York Herald*, June 5, 1892.

21. "Gilmore on the Roof," *New York Herald*, June 7, 1892.

22. "Amusements: The Madison Square Garden," *NYT*, May 31 and June 14, 1892; "The Garden of the Garden," *New York Daily Tribune*, May 15, 1892; "Gay Summer Girls," *New York Herald*, June 26, 1892; "Madison Square Garden. To Be Complete after the Opening of the Roof Promenade," *NYT*, May 23, 1892; "Amusements," *NYT*, June 14, 1892.

23. "Like Babylon's Hanging Gardens," *New York Herald*, May 15, 1891.

24. "Shivering on the Roof," *New York Herald*, May 31, 1893.

25. "To Be an Attractive Resort," *NYT*, May 26, 1893.

26. "Successful First Night. Opening of the New Cafe Chantant at the Casino," *NYT*, June 5, 1892; *New York Evening World*, June 4, 1892; *New York Herald*, June 12, 1892; Robert H. Montgomery, "The Roof Gardens of New York," *Indoors and Out* 2 (Aug. 1906): 213–19; Theodore Osmundson, *Roof Gardens: History, Design, and Construction* (New York: W. W. Norton, 1999), 123; Hughes, *Real New York*, 266.

27. When Aronson applied for a patent on the idea, he was told that he had waited too long beyond the given two years of the garden's establishment. Paul Van Du Zee, "New York Roof Gardens," *Godey's Magazine* 129 (July–Dec. 1894): 203.

28. Gordon, "Reclamation of Roofs," 307.

23. A Home in the White City

1. "Diana off the Garden Tower," *New York Tribune*, Sept. 13, 1892; "Removed from Her Perch," *New York Sun*, Sept. 13, 1892.

2. See "Diana off the Garden Tower," *New York Tribune*, Sept. 13, 1892; "Removed from Her Perch," *New York Sun*, Sept. 13, 1892; "The Removal of Diana," *New York World*, Sept. 13, 1892.

3. LPB 6:99, 139, SW Correspondence.

4. "Diana off the Garden Tower," *New York Tribune*, Sept. 13, 1892.

5. Julian Ralph, *Harper's Chicago and the Fair* (New York: Harper & Bros., 1893), 235.

6. Thomas S. Hines, *Burnham of Chicago, Architect and Planner* (New York: Oxford Univ. Press, 1974), 75.

7. Henry Van Brunt, "Architecture at the World's Columbian Exhibition, Pt. I," *The Century* 44 (May 1892): 81–82; Mariana Griswold Van Rensselaer, "An Art Critic's Pen Picture," in *Rand, McNally & Co.'s A Week at the Fair: Illustrating the Exhibits and Wonders of the World's Columbian Exposition* (Chicago: Rand, McNally, 1893), 74; Charles Moore, "The Lessons of the Chicago World's Fair: An Interview with the Late Daniel H. Burnham," *Architectural Record* 33 (June 1913): 36, 38; Norm Bolotin and Christine Laing, *The World's Columbian Exposition* (Washington, DC: Preservation Press, 1992), 9; Hines, *Burnham*, 76.

8. Moore, *Life and Times of McKim*, 113.

9. Moore, "Lessons," 39; Erik Larson, *The Devil in the White City* (New York: Vintage Books, 2004), 84; Charles Moore, *The Life of Daniel H. Burnham, Architect, Planner of Cities* (Boston: Houghton Mifflin, 1921), 1:42–43; Hines, *Burnham*, 17. Burnham later became known for the saying, "Make no little plans, they have no magic to stir men's blood," which was commonly associated with the fair but apparently derived from a four-sentence statement attributed to a paper Burnham presented at a 1910 town planning conference in London. The

statement was reconstructed by Willis Polk, one of Burnham's partners, and used in a 1912 Christmas card after Burnham's death earlier that year. It was then published in his 1921 biography by Moore, *Life of Daniel H. Burnham*, 2:147; see "Make No Little Plans," *Journal of the American Institute of Architects*, Mar. 1957, 95–99, quoted in Suzy Platt, ed., *Respectfully Quoted* (New York: Dorset Press, 1992), 256.

10. Van Brunt, "Architecture," 88; Moore, *Life and Times of McKim*, 113, 117.

11. Moore, "Lessons," 42; Moore, *Life and Times of McKim*, 118; Burnham to ASG, Apr. 29, 1891, Augustus Saint-Gaudens Papers, MMC-1668, Library of Congress.

12. Burnham to ASG, June 22, 1891, Augustus Saint-Gaudens Papers, MMC-1668, Library of Congress; Moore, "Lessons," 41.

13. ASG, "Reminiscences of an Idiot," 114; Moore, "Lessons," 42; Moore, *Life of Daniel H. Burnham*, 1:47, 62, 117–18.

14. Armstrong, "Saint-Gaudens," 32.

15. Moore, "Lessons," 44.

16. George Perry Grimsley, *The Gypsum of Michigan and the Plaster Industry* (Lansing, MI: R. Smith Printing, 1904), 219; Ralph, *Harper's Chicago*, 136, 139, 147; Richard J. Murphy, *Authentic Visitors' Guide to the World's Columbian Exposition and Chicago* (Chicago: Union News, 1892), 12; Harper Barnes, *Standing on a Volcano* (St. Louis, MO: Missouri Historical Society Press, 2001), 120.

17. F. D. Millet, "The Designers of the Fair," *Harper's New Monthly Magazine* 85 (Nov. 1892): 878.

18. "Diana Too Big a Girl," *New York Sun*, Mar. 17, 1892; "Diana to Be Taken Down," *New York Herald*, Mar. 18, 1892; "Diana Going to Chicago," *NYT*, Mar. 18, 1892.

19. "Harmony in Fair Ranks," *NYT*, Aug. 21, 1892; "Chicago Wants Diana," *New York Herald*, Aug. 21, 1892.

20. Alfred Trumble, "Notes for the New Year," *The Collector* 3 (Jan. 1, 1892): 70.

21. Rossiter Johnson, *A History of the World's Columbian Exposition Held in Chicago in 1893* (New York: D. Appleton, 1897), 32.

22. Julian Ralph, "Our Exposition at Chicago," *Harper's New Monthly Magazine* 84 (Jan. 1892); "Diana off the Garden Tower," *New York Tribune*, Sept. 13, 1892.

23. *Boston Daily Globe*, Jan. 21, 1893.

24. Baker, *Stanny*, 179.

25. While designed and/or supervised by Martiny, the Chicago figures may have actually been executed by Martiny's assistant, Isidore Konti. Mary Jean Smith Madigan, introduction to *The Sculpture of Isidore Konti, 1862–1938* (Yonkers, NY: The Hudson River Museum, 1974).

26. Larkin G. Mead to C. McKim, Feb. 29, 1892, quoted in Moore, *Life and Times of McKim*, 119; "The World's Fair Decorations," *Boston Herald*, Nov. 13, 1892.

27. "Within the Magic City," *The Illustrated American* 13 (June 3, 1893): 649.

28. SW to F. MacMonnies, Feb. 25, 1892, MacMonnies Family Papers, quoted in Smart, *Flight with Fame*, 115.

29. ASG, "Reminiscences of an Idiot," 107; HSG, "Saint-Gaudens the Master," *The Century*, 617.

30. ASG to F. MacMonnies, Oct. 24, 1892, MacMonnies Family Papers, quoted in Smart, *Flight with Fame*, 120.

31. "Art Notes: *Diana*," *NYT*, Oct. 22, 1892; Draft of letter from ASG to P. Bion, Dec. 3, 1892, box 22:6, Papers of ASG. Interestingly, his dear friend Bion wrote in his will that Saint-Gaudens's letters in his possession be destroyed at Bion's death, which they were. HSG, *Reminiscences of Augustus*, 2:119.

32. "The Statue Too Nude for Chicago," *New York Sun*, Sept. 13, 1892; "Don't Want Diana," *Boston Daily Globe*, Sept. 13, 1892.

33. "In Church Circles," *Chicago Daily Inter Ocean*, Sept. 18, 1892.

34. Baldwin, *Stanford White*, 210.

35. "The Fine Arts," *Chicago Daily Tribune*, Sept. 18, 1892.

36. "The Bronze Diana," *Brownsville (TX) Daily Herald*, Sept. 22, 1892.

37. "A Raid on Diana," *Boston Daily Globe*, Sept. 14, 1892; "Diana Appreciated in Chicago," *New York World*, Sept. 15, 1892.

38. "Art, Drapery, and Morals," *New York Sun*, Sept. 18, 1892.

39. "The World's Fair," *New York Evening Post*, Sept. 17, 1892; "Diana Finds a Friend," *NYT*, Sept. 18, 1892.

40. SW to W. Mullins, Sept. 22, Sept. 27, Sept. 28, and Oct. 5, 1892, box 517:M–20. MM&W Architectural Records Collection, PR 042, New-York Historical Society.

41. William Cowper Brann, "Nude Art at Chicago," *The Iconoclast*, 202, reprinted in *Brann's Scrap-Book* (Upper Saddle River, NJ: Literature House/Gregg Press, 1970), 17.

42. "Art at the Chicago Fair," *New York Sun*, May 3, 1893; "The West Aghast," *Boston Herald*, May 3, 1893.

43. "For Artistic Street Decoration," *New York Herald*, July 11, 1892; "The Voyager in Marble," *NYT*, Oct. 13, 1892; Baker, *Stanny*, 175.

44. Barr Ferree, "Architecture," *Engineering Magazine* 5 (June 1893): 397.

45. Even White's planned European jaunt with his beloved Tommy Hastings in August 1892 had to be canceled due to the many obligations that had piled up. Baker, *Stanny*, 175–76.

46. Tharp, *Saint-Gaudens*, 318; Wilkinson, *Uncommon Clay*, 220.

47. ASG to Augusta Saint-Gaudens, undated, Papers of ASG, quoted in Tharp, *Saint-Gaudens*, 318.

48. Wilkinson, *Uncommon Clay*, 144–45, citing evidence in the Papers of ASG and Daniel H. Burnham Papers, Manuscript Division, Library of Congress. According to the 1900 US Federal Census, Mr. Clark's address was given as 452 Oxridge Rd., Darien, CT.

49. Frank D. Millet, "The World's Fair at Chicago, III," *Scribner's* 12 (Dec. 1892): 708; Moore, *Life of Daniel H. Burnham*, 1:50; "The Painting Machine at the World's Fair," *Scientific*

American 68 (Apr. 29, 1893); Tina Grant, "Binks Sames Corporation," *International Directory of Company Histories* 21 (Farmington Hills, MI: St. James Press, 1998), 63; *Western Electrician* 28 (May 11, 910): 135. According to Burnham and the *Scientific American* article, the compressor was invented by T. G. Turner of New York City, who had variously patented an electric light switch and a fire extinguisher. Perhaps accounts confused him with C. Y. Turner, who had been Millet's assistant on the project and was credited at the time with inventing "an apparatus for painting by machinery" that consisted of an electric motor that turned an air compressor, which was described as being in use in the agricultural building to spray paint the "interior of the roofs." "World's Fair Doings," *Chicago Daily Inter Ocean*, Nov. 12, 1892. To complicate matters, in 1897 *Railway and Locomotive Engineering* emphatically stated that the method of painting by spraying with air originated on the Southern Railway around 1882 and had been described in *Locomotive Engineering* seven or eight years before. Whet Moser, "The Contentious Historical Origins of Spray Paint," *Chicago Arts & Culture*, accessed July 20, 2012, http://www .chicagomag.com/Chicago-Magazine/The-312/November-2011/The-Contentious-Historical -Origins-Spray-Paint/. H. C. Bunner, the editor of *Puck*, is said to have been the first to use the term "White City" in an article in the October 1892 issue of *Scribner's Magazine*. The article was written in June 1892, but the issue was not available for sale until September 24, 1892.

50. De Koven, *Musician*, 185; Baker, *Stanny*, 179–80.

51. HSG, *Reminiscences of Augustus*, 2:74.

52. McKim to Burnham, Oct. 23, 1893, quoted in Moore, *Life and Times of McKim*, 127.

24. A Second *Diana*

1. *Morning Advertiser* (NY), as reported in *Chicago Inter Ocean*, Oct. 16, 1891.

2. Hartmann, "New York Artists' Models," 115; Holme, "Artists' Models," 527; Baynes, "Artist's Model," 497; "Artists' Models," *Chicago Daily Inter Ocean*, Feb. 23, 1895; "The Real Diana of the Garden," *New York Herald*, Dec. 5, 1897.

3. Baynes, "Artist's Model," 499; "Strike in a Studio," *St. Paul Globe*, Feb. 10, 1895; "Amusements," *Trenton (NJ) Evening Times*, Sept. 18, 1897.

4. Baynes, "Artist's Model," 499; for the sexual dynamic between middle-class men and working-class women, and a middle-class unease with the perceived heightened sexuality of the female working class in general, see April F. Masten, "Model into Artist: The Changing Face of Art Historical Biography," *Women's Studies* 21, no. 1 (1992): 19.

5. Baynes, "Artist's Model," 499.

6. "For the Sake of Art," *St. Paul Globe*, Dec. 9, 1894; Baynes, "Artist's Model," 499; "Models in Rebellion," *Dallas Morning News*, Jan. 27, 1895.

7. Pyle, "Some Types," 14. See also Eunice Lipton, "The Laundress in Late Nineteenth-Century French Culture," *Art History* 3 (Sept. 1980): 303.

8. "Strike in a Studio," *St. Paul Globe*, Feb. 10, 1895.

9. Baynes, "Artist's Model," 499, 501; "The Girl Art Student," *New York Sun*, Feb. 9, 1890.

10. "The Real Diana of the Garden," *New York Herald*, Dec. 5, 1897; "As to Girl Models," *St. Louis Republic*, Aug. 6, 1891; "For the Sake of Art," *St. Paul Globe*, Dec. 9, 1894; "Strike in a Studio," *St. Paul Globe*, Feb. 10, 1895.

11. "As to Girl Models," *St. Louis Republic*, Aug. 6, 1891; "Artists' Models," *New Haven Register*, Mar. 22, 1887.

12. "Model Charwoman at Hotel Plaza in New York," *Indianapolis Star*, Apr. 1, 1908; "Diana's Present Job," *Kansas City Star*, Apr. 2, 1908; "St. Gauden's Model," *San Jose Evening News*, Apr. 20, 1908; "Up and Down," *Missoula (MT) Missoulian*, May 1, 1908; "When the Models Pose Outdoors," *Cleveland Plain Dealer*, May 30, 1909; "Monuments: New York's No More," *Time* 90 (Sept. 1, 1967), http://content.time.com/time/magazine/article/0,9171,837251,00.html.

13. "Artist and Modiste Do Not Agree," *New York Herald*, June 21, 1891; "For the Sake of Art," *St. Paul Globe*, Dec. 9, 1894; "Letters," *Time* 90 (Sept. 22, 1967): 12.

14. Partridge, *Angel of Clay*, 67; "Some Artists' Models," *Washington Times*, Apr. 14, 1901.

15. "The Real Diana of the Garden," *New York Herald*, Dec. 5, 1897; "The Summer Girl at Home," *Fort Worth Morning Register*, Sept. 17, 1899; interview of Baird's friend Georgiana Carhart by Arnold T. Schwab, Feb. 9, 1956, in Arnold T. Schwab, *James Gibbons Huneker, Critic of the Seven Arts* (Stanford, CA: Stanford Univ. Press, 1963), 369n48. In a 1924 letter, William M. Kendall, a partner who had worked on the Madison Square Garden tower, states that Baird was the model. WMK to Lida Rose McCabe, Dec. 16, 1924, box 378:435, MM&W Architectural Records Collection, PR 042, New-York Historical Society.

16. "The Real Diana of the Garden," *New York Herald*, Dec. 5, 1897.

17. Kobbé, "Artist and His Model," 120.

18. Letter from Baird's grandniece Marcia Gaines to Barbara Dayer Gallati, June 25, 1993, cited in Barbara Dayer Gallati, "Beauty Unmasked: Ironic Meaning in Dewing's Art," cited in Hobbs, *Art of Thomas Wilmer Dewing*, 81n57; Pyle, "Some Types," 21; letter from Marcia Gaines to Susan A. Hobbs, June 29, 1993, and Hobbs interview with Katherine Stover Gaines, Feb. 2006, cited in Susan A. Hobbs, "Pretty Women: Charles Lang Freer and the Ideal of Feminine Beauty," *The Magazine Antiques* 170 (Nov. 1, 2006): 144. However, according to the 1880 federal census, her mother, Annie A. Baird, was the head of the household, and no father appeared in any later census. 1880 US Federal Census, New York, NY, Roll 888, Family History Film: 1254888, 491B; Wilkinson, *Uncommon Clay*, 214.

19. T. Dewing to C. Freer, Jan. 4, [1893], and July 2, 1898, Freer Papers, box 7, Freer Gallery of Art Archives, Washington, DC; Baynes, "Artist's Model," 499; "A Boston Model's Story," *Washington Post*, July 26, 1891.

20. SW to F. Millet, Jan. 24, 1894, LPB 8:497, SW Correspondence.

21. SW to Hugh Bolton Jones, Dec. 16, 1892, LPB 6:481–82, SW Correspondence. Unfortunately, White's financial situation at the time of his death required the sale of his collections at auction, and the paintings were not donated to the museum.

22. "The Real Diana of the Garden," *New York Herald*, Dec. 5, 1897. It is known that Saint-Gaudens had previously used plaster casts taken from the body of a model, and his account book shows that he paid $25 to have casts made of a model's legs for the 1874 figure of *Silence*. Bouton, "Early Works," 178.

23. W. M. Kendall to Lida Rose McCabe, Dec. 16, 1924, PR071, Box 378:435, MM&W Architectural Records Collection, PR 042, New-York Historical Society.

24. Watanna and Bosse, *Marion*, 151; "New York's Girl Models," *New York Herald*, July 29, 1894; "Scarcity of Perfect Models," *Chicago Daily Inter Ocean*, July 26, 1887.

25. Holme, "Artists' Models," 528; Bell, "Artists' Models"; "Scarcity of Perfect Models," *Chicago Daily Inter Ocean*, July 26, 1887; Kathryn Jarboe, "Picture People," *Munsey's* 18 (Nov. 1899): 205.

26. Clark, "Model," Apr. 23, 1899.

27. "In Quest of Diana," *New York Evening World*, Jan. 6, 1893.

28. "Actress to Become Model," *Boston Herald*, Nov. 29, 1896.

29. HSG to Arnold T. Schwab, Feb. 17, 1956, in Schwab, *James Gibbons Huneker*, 359n48.

30. HSG, *Reminiscences of Augustus*, 1:345; Wilkinson, *Uncommon Clay*, 111, 118, 195–96. Another claimant was film actress Vera Lewis. "Film Flickers," *Oregonian* (Portland OR), Sept. 23, 1917.

31. Hardin, "Nude," 299–300.

32. *Saginaw News*, Dec. 1, 1894 (from the *San Francisco Examiner*).

33. Jack Garridy, "Sexuality in the Lives of Florentine Renaissance Artists," 26, accessed July 12, 2012, http://www.williamapercy.com/wiki/index.php?title=Jack_Garridy. As a more contemporary example, in 1884 E. W. Kemble used a young boy to model for every character, including females, for his very popular illustration of Twain's *Huckleberry Finn*. E. W. Kemble, "Illustrating Huckleberry Finn," *The Colophon* 1, pt. 1 (1930).

34. ASG, "Reminiscences of an Idiot," 109A.

35. "Diana's Laurels Go to Annette: Goddess Suffers When Her Beauty Is Matched with Girl Swimmer's," *Cleveland Plain Dealer*, Dec. 8, 1910.

36. "New York's New Goddess," *Pittsburgh Press*, Jan. 5, 1893; Hardin, "Nude," 299.

37. Henry Duffy, email message to author, Feb. 23, 2011.

38. Alison Mairi Syme, *A Touch of Blossom: John Singer Sargent and the Queer Flora of Fin-de-siècle Art* (University Park: Penn State Press, 2010), 216; W. Graham Robertson, *Life Was Worth Living* (New York: Harper, 1931), 39–40. In the painting, Robertson was posed as Diana the Huntress, holding the leash of a large hound.

39. P. Bion to ASG, Sept. 6, 1892, box 22:7, Papers of ASG.

40. SW to ASG, indicating the mold is completed, Sept. 30, 1892, LPB 6:183, SW Correspondence.

41. "New York's New Goddess," *Pittsburgh Press*, Jan. 5, 1893.

42. SW to ASG, Dec. 20, 1892, LPB 7:11, SW Correspondence.

43. SW to ASG, Dec. 30, 1892, LPB 7:67, SW Correspondence; "New York's New Goddess," *Pittsburgh Press*, Jan. 5, 1893.

44. "St. Gaudens's Dummy Diana," *New York Evening World*, Jan. 4, 1893.

45. "To Test the New Diana's Height," *New York Herald*, Jan. 3, 1893.

46. "Bracelet for Diana's Arm," *New York Evening World*, Jan. 18, 1893; *Boston Daily Globe*, Jan. 6, 1893.

47. ASG to Winchester Donald, Mar. 21, 1893, quoted in HSG, *Reminiscences of Augustus*, 2:98.

48. SW to W. H. Mullins, June 26, 1893, LPB 7:343, SW Correspondence.

49. SW to J. T. Wagner, June 19, 1893, LPB 7:305, SW Correspondence.

50. H. Marceau to Rilla Jackman, June 5, 1946, box 177:29, Kimball Records, Philadelphia Museum of Art; "Diana Returns to Us," *New York Sun*, Nov. 11, 1893; "Gilding Diana," Philadelphia Museum of Art, accessed June 25, 2014, https://philamuseum.org/conservation/21.html.

51. The wheels were discovered during conservation at the Philadelphia Museum of Art in 2013 with the use of an internal borescope to reveal the figure's inner structure. "Gilding Diana: Investigation and Cleaning Tests," Philadelphia Museum of Art, accessed June 25, 2014, https://philamuseum.org/conservation/21.html.

52. SW to W. Mullins, Aug. 22, 1893, LPB 7:495, and Aug. 25, 1893, LPB 8:15, SW Correspondence; SW to W. Mullins, Miscellaneous file, box M–3, SW Papers, New-York Historical Society.

53. SW to ASG, Nov. 8, 1893, LPB 8:182, SW Correspondence.

54. "Personal and Political," *Boston Daily Advertiser*, Oct. 17, 1893.

55. Van Rensselaer, "Madison Square Garden," 747; Dryfhout, "Diana," 209; Thayer Tolles, "Augustus Saint-Gaudens, *Diana of the Tower*, ca. 1899–1907," in *American Dreams: American Art to 1950 in the Williams College Museum of Art*, ed. Nancy Mowll Mathews (New York: Hudson Hills Press in association with the Williams College Museum of Art, 2001), 104; see Richard Corson, *Fashions in Hair: The First Five Thousand Years* (New York: Hastings House 1965), 494; Jean Keyes, *A History of Women's Hairstyles, 1500–1965* (London: Methuen, 1967), 495.

56. "Our Golden Diana," *New York Advertiser*, Nov. 12, 1893.

57. "Some Notes on Sculpture," *The Magazine of Art* 15 (1892): xxiv.

58. "Our Golden Diana," *New York Advertiser*, Nov. 12, 1893.

59. In 1934, A. S. Vogan of Canton, Ohio, claimed credit for modeling *Diana*'s drapery and said that in 1893 he received a certificate of merit from the Metropolitan Museum of Art for his efforts. "A. S. Vogan Known as Sculptor, But He's Proud of Tomatoes, Too," *Canton Repository*, Mar. 25, 1934.

60. "Notes of New York," *Boston Evening Transcript*, Nov. 29, 1893.

61. P. Rounsevelle to H. Marceau, May 16, 1932, box 177:29, Kimball Records, Philadelphia Museum of Art.

62. "Diana Returns to Us," *New York Sun*, Nov. 11, 1893.

63. Cortissoz, "Metamorphosis of Diana," 1124.

64. "Diana Returns to Us," *New York Sun*, Nov. 11, 1893; "Diana Waits for a Calm," *New York Tribune*, Nov. 18, 1893; "Time for Diana to Rise," *New York Sun*, Nov. 17, 1893.

65. "Pistol Bullets in Delmonico's," *New York Herald*, Nov. 17, 1893; "Fusilade at Delmonico's," *New York Tribune*, Nov. 17, 1893.

66. "Diana the New," *New York Sun*, Nov. 18, 1893.

67. "Diana on Her Pinnacle," *New York Sun*, Nov. 19, 1893; "Diana," *New York Evening World*, Nov. 17, 1893.

68. "Diana on Her Pinnacle," *New York Sun*, Nov. 19, 1893.

69. "Diana," *New York Evening World*, Nov. 17, 1893.

70. "Diana the One-Legged," *New York Sun*, Nov. 26, 1893.

71. "The Chronicle of Arts," *New York Tribune*, Nov. 26, 1893; "Diana's Scarf Is Too Large," *New York Tribune*, Nov. 27, 1893.

72. Van Rensselaer, "Madison Square Garden," 747.

73. "Diana of the Tower," *New York Sun*, Oct. 20, 1894.

25. Within the Tower

1. SW to John Chanler, May 31, 1892, LPB 5:451, SW Correspondence.

2. Memo from Mr. Horton to SW, May 2, 1892, LPB 6:20, box 3:9, SW Correspondence.

3. Evelyn Nesbit, *Prodigal Days: The Untold Story of Evelyn Nesbit* (New York: Julian Messner, 1934), 34.

4. SW to H. E. Howland, Nov. 8 and Nov. 9, 1893, LPB 8:197, SW Correspondence.

5. SW to T. Dewing, Nov. 16, 1893, LPB 8:239, SW Correspondence.

6. "Completion of the Tall Tower," *NYT*, Oct. 14, 1891; "As If Seen from a Balloon," *New York Recorder*, Oct. 14, 1891; Coffin, "Tower of the Madison Square Garden," 819.

7. Baker, *Stanny*, 157; Nesbit, *Prodigal Days*, 31; "Living above the City," *Pittsburg Dispatch*, Sept. 13, 1891; "Cream of Current Chat," *Columbus (GA) Enquirer*, Nov. 18, 1891.

8. LPB 5:442, 499 and 6:10; box 2:8, SW Correspondence.

9. "Completion of the Tall Tower," *NYT*, Oct. 14, 1891; Gerald Langford, *The Richard Harding Davis Years* (New York: Holt, Rinehart & Winston, 1961), 153; De Koven, *Musician*, 176.

10. Chanler and Chanler, *Roman Spring*, 256.

11. SW to L. Sherry, Nov. 17, 1893, LPB 8:249, SW Correspondence; De Koven, *Musician*, 176.

12. SW to G. Lignane, Nov. 17, 1893, LPB 8:250, and Feb. 15, 1895, LPB 12:374, SW Correspondence; De Koven, *Musician*, 176.

13. Soria, *Elihu Vedder*, 209; Nesbit, *Prodigal Days*, 35; SW to ASG, Nov. 23, 1894, LPB 12:81, SW Correspondence; ASG to SW, May 23, 1894, box 20:42, Papers of ASG.

14. "Peter Cooper Hewitt," *Munsey's Magazine* 29 (Mar. 6, 1902): 892; *Biographical Directory of the State of New York* (New York: Biographical Directory, 1900), 391; Peter Pennoyer and Anne Walker Pennoyer, *The Architecture of Warren & Wetmore* (New York: W. W. Norton, 2006), 17; Baker, *Stanny*, 165, 277–78; Broderick, *Triumvirate*, 305; Lowe, *Stanford White's New York*, 146.

15. McKim to A. R. Ross, Oct. 24, 1893, quoted in Moore, *Life and Times of McKim*, 126.

16. Moore, *Life and Times of McKim*, 127.

17. "The Cold Storage Palace at the Columbian Fair and Its Destruction by Fire," *Scientific American* 69 (July 22, 1893): 52.

18. "The Horror at the Fair," *Chicago Daily Tribune*, July 11, 1893; "The Cold Storage Palace," *Scientific American* 69 (July 22, 1893): 53; "The Chicago Fire," *Harper's Weekly* 37 (July 22, 1893); "Fire in All Its Fury," *Chicago Daily Inter Ocean*, July 11, 1893; David Cowan, *Great Chicago Fires* (Chicago: Lake Claremont Press, 2001), 27–28; Andy Pearson, "Lessons Learned from the Cold Storage Fire at the Chicago World's Fair of 1893," *Report of the American Society of Heating, Refrigerating, and Air-Conditioning Engineers* (June 2009).

19. See "Fire Levels Fair Buildings," *New York Herald*, Jan. 9, 1894; "Great Fire at the Fair," *Idaho Statesman*, Jan. 9, 1894; "The White City in Flames," *NYT*, Jan. 9, 1894; "Vanished in Flame," *Chicago Daily Inter Ocean*, Jan. 9, 1894; "World's Fair Buildings Destroyed by Fire," *New York Sun*, Jan. 9, 1894; "The White City Burning," *New York Daily Tribune*, Jan. 9, 1894.

20. "The White City in Flames," *NYT*, Jan. 9, 1894.

21. "Again Fire Menaced," *Chicago Daily Inter Ocean*, Feb. 15, 1894; "Firebugs at the Fair," *Rockford (IL) Morning Star*, Feb. 15, 1894.

22. "Diana's Dome Gone," *Chicago Daily Inter Ocean*, Feb. 25, 1894; "Final Report of the General Manager of the World's Columbian Exposition, Sept. 1–Oct. 31, 1894," 96.

23. "Fire in Jackson Park," *Chicago Daily Inter Ocean*, Feb. 8, 1894; "Trying to Burn the Fair Buildings," *New York Daily Tribune*, Feb. 8, 1894; "World's Fair Incendiaries," *Chicago Daily Inter Ocean*, Feb. 9, 1894.

24. Lawrence White to Adolph Bregman, box 378:435, MM&W Architectural Records Collection, PR 042, New-York Historical Society; "Diana's Dome Gone," *Chicago Daily Inter Ocean*, Feb. 25, 1894; "Its Dome Is No More," *Chicago Daily Tribune*, Feb. 25, 1894; "Agricultural Building Dome Burned," *NYT*, Feb. 25, 1894.

25. De Koven, *Musician*, 177.

26. "Completion of the Tall Tower," *NYT*, Oct. 14, 1891; "Madison Square Garden's Tower," *New York Sun*, Oct. 14, 1891; "The Tower of Madison Square Garden," *Frank Leslie's Illustrated Newspaper* 74 (Mar. 31, 1892): 147; "Howard's Gossip," *Boston Daily Globe*, Nov. 2, 1891.

27. "Diana Unveiled," *New York Herald*, Nov. 2, 1891; "Flashing the Signal," *New York Herald*, Nov. 8, 1891; Coffin, "Tower of the Madison Square Garden," 819; Nesbit, *Prodigal Days*, 34.

Part Four. Epilogue

1. "Goddess Comes to Earth," *Cleveland Plain Dealer*, May 9, 1925.

26. *Diana* Redux

1. ASG to Robert E. Preston, Nov. 17, 1893, reel 5, Papers of ASG.

2. "Mr. St. Gaudens Talks about His Medal," *New York Tribune*, May 10, 1895; "St. Gaudens Revises His Medal," *NYT*, Mar. 28, 1894; Michael F. Moran, *Striking Change: The Great Artistic Collaboration of Theodore Roosevelt and Augustus Saint-Gaudens* (Atlanta: Whitman, 2008), 127; HSG, *Reminiscences of Augustus*, 2:67–72; Thayer Tolles, "A Bit of Artistic Realism: Augustus Saint-Gaudens's World Columbian Exposition Commemorative Presentation Medal," in *Coinage of the Americas Conference Proceedings*, vol. 2, *The Medal in America*, ed. A. Stahl, (New York: American Numismatic Society, 1997), 143, 154; "World's Fair Medal Finally Adopted," *NYT*, June 28, 1894; "The World's Fair Medal," *NYT*, Oct. 14, 1894; "That St. Gaudens Medal," *New York Herald*, Mar. 26, 1894; Dryfhout, *Work*, 185; "Art Appreciation in Boston," *New York Tribune*, Feb. 10, 1894; *American Architect and Building News* 53 (Feb. 17, 1894): 73–74. See also Frank H. Chase, *The Boston Public Library*, 4th ed. (Boston: Association Publications, 1921), 5; "Those Naked Library Boys," *Boston Herald*, Feb. 10, 1894; "St. Gaudens Shocks Boston," *Chicago Daily Inter Ocean*, Feb. 10, 1894; "Need of Clothing," *Boston Daily Globe*, Feb. 10, 1894; Douglass Shand-Tucci, *Boston Bohemia, 1881–1900*, vol. 1 (Amherst: Univ. of Massachusetts Press 1995), 209; "All Seeking Shocks," *Boston Daily Globe*, Apr. 15, 1894.

3. However, Saint-Gaudens's 1895 *Henry C. Nevins Tomb* in Mount Auburn Cemetery, Cambridge, displays two nude crouching cherubs, their nether parts hidden, while the unfinished post-1900 figures of *Art* and *Science* for the Boston Public Library piazza only reveal bare female bosoms.

4. "The Week in Art," *NYT*, Jan. 27, 1900; "Stained Glass Sells High," *New York Sun*, Nov. 28, 1907.

5. The bronze reduction was the gift of John Gellatly, although his wife was apparently the original buyer. "Mrs. Gellatly Left $1,289,905," *NYT*, June 6, 1916, Metropolitan Museum of Art, New York, #1929.8.397.

6. ASG to SW, May 23, 1894, box 20:42, Papers of ASG.

7. Lowe, *Stanford White's New York*, 132–33; Baker, *Stanny*, 126–27; Lessard, *Architect of Desire*, 63–64. In front of the exedra was placed a low wooden table set on two Ionic capitals that had come from the Madison Square Garden arcade. In addition, four cement casts from those on the Garden Theatre's proscenium arch were incorporated into the Orangerie, a shelter built into the hill behind the exedra to house gardening equipment. These were likely scavenged from the demolition by Lawrence Grant White in 1925. Lessard, *Architect of Desire*, 63.

8. Judith Fryer Davidson, "Jean-Antoine Houdon: Diana the Huntress," in *Art in the Frick Collection*, ed. Charles Ryskamp et al. (New York: Harry N. Abrams, 1996), 177; Wasserman, *Diana in Late-Nineteenth Century*.

9. Wasserman, *Diana in Late-Nineteenth Century*; Michael Edward Shapiro, *Bronze Casting and American Sculpture 1850–1900* (Newark: Univ. of Delaware Press, 1985), 104; E. Adina Gordon, "Augustus Saint-Gaudens: The Lure of Paris," in *Augustus Saint-Gaudens: A Master of America Sculpture*, ed. Musée des Augustins (Paris: Musée des Augustins, 1999), 95.

10. Edith Wharton and Ogden Codman Jr., *The Decoration of Houses*, (New York: W. W. Norton, 1978), 185, 187.

11. MacMonnies was also selling reproductions of his *Pan of Rohallion* and *Young Faun with Heron* by 1891. Gordon, "Augustus Saint-Gaudens," 95n64, 97; ASG to F. MacMonnies, Feb. 1, 1891, box 3042:146, AAA.

12. ASG to SW, May 14, 1894, box 20:42, Papers of ASG.

13. P. Bion to ASG, Oct. 26, 1893, box 22, Papers of ASG.

14. P. Bion to ASG, May 4, 1894; May 11, 1894; and May 23, 1894, box 22:8, Papers of ASG; Smart, *Flight with Fame*, 109n11.

15. P. Bion to ASG, Sept. 15, 1896, box 22:10, Papers of ASG; for the replacement bow, see Dryfhout, "Diana," fig. 37.

16. See Nichols House Museum, Boston, #T–59; Dryfhout, "Diana," fig. 38; *Augustus Saint-Gaudens: A Master of American Sculpture* (Paris: Musée des Augustins, 1999), fig. 22; Musée Rodin, Paris, #24; E. Adina Gordon, "The Sculpture of Frederick William MacMonnies: A Catalogue Raisonné," in Smart, *Flight with Fame*, 288.

17. P. Bion to ASG, Oct. 2, 1894, and Dec. 1, 1894, box 22:8, Papers of ASG; "Frank MacMonnies Dies in France at 56," *NYT*, Aug. 20, 1926.

18. ASG, "Reminiscences of an Idiot"; ASG to Augusta Saint-Gaudens, Dec. 24 [1894], box 28:4, Papers of ASG. No photograph of the piece exists, and it was never found at the Saint-Gaudens home in Cornish, New Hampshire. Dryfhout, "Diana," 209. However, there is a chance that it might be #T–59 in the collection of the Nichols House Museum, stamped 1894 with the E. Gruet foundry mark, or at least quite similar to it. The piece was not originally the property of Rose Nichols, Augusta Saint-Gaudens's niece but was donated to the museum ca. 1982 by Ethel (Polly) Thayer Starr, a Boston painter whose 1927 portrait of Miss Nichols hangs in the museum. Also similar is the small reduction in the collection of the Metropolitan Museum of Art, New York, #1985.353, donated by Lincoln Kirstein, cofounder of the New York City Ballet, who obtained the piece from Robert Schoelkopf. A third, quite similar piece appears in a photograph of Oscar de la Renta's private collection. *NYT Sunday Magazine*, Feb. 26, 2012. A newspaper article dated November 11, 1894, describes the studio of Caroline Peddle, a former student of Saint-Gaudens at the Art Students League, and mentions that "In one corner . . . is the original of the model from which Mr. St. Gaudens made his statue

of Diana," which may have more likely been one of the new reductions. "New York's Clever Women Sculptors," *New York Herald.*

19. "Casts and Images Made in Plaster," *New York Herald*, July 2, 1893. A bronze finish was commonly faked by applying a coat of thin shellac and then a layer of dull brown paint rubbed with a greenish bronze powder until the entire surface was evenly coated. "How to Bronze Plaster Casts," *New York Evening World*, May 19, 1893.

20. US copyright, SGNHS; Dryfhout, "Diana," 184.

21. Brooklyn Museum of Art #23.255.

22. Chesterwood National Trust for Historic Preservation, purchased at auction in the 1920s; in #1977.55 in the collection of the Currier Museum of Art, the sphere sits directly on a marble plinth.

23. ASG to Augusta Saint-Gaudens, Aug. 3, 1899, box 28:5, Papers of ASG; ASG to Doll & Richards, Nov. 28, 1899, box 5:3, Papers of ASG; "The Fine Arts," *Boston Evening Transcript*, Jan. 31, 1899.

24. Metropolitan Museum of Art, New York, #1908:37.

25. See Brooklyn Museum #23.255; Sheldon Museum of Art, Univ. of Nebraska #1985.N–676; Indianapolis Museum of Art #17.254, respectively.

26. "Reason St. Gaudens Has Left America," *San Francisco Call*, Mar. 20, 1898.

27. ASG, "Reminiscences of an Idiot," 109.

28. "The Week in the Art World," *NYT*, Mar. 5, 1898; "Reason St. Gaudens Has Left America," *San Francisco Call*, Mar. 20, 1898. See also HSG, *Reminiscences of Augustus*, 2:122.

29. P. Bion to ASG, Aug. 29, 1896, box 22:10, Papers of ASG; Tharp, *Saint-Gaudens*, 276–77.

30. Rose Standish Nichols, ed., "Familiar Letters of Augustus Saint-Gaudens," *Mc-Clure's* 31 (Oct. 1908), 604.

31. "The Week in the Art World," *NYT*, Mar. 5, 1898; ASG to Rose Nichols, Sept. 14, 1899, box 25:18, Papers of ASG; ASG to SW, Dec. 1, 1899, box 20:44, Papers of ASG.

32. ASG to Louis St. Gaudens, 1900, in HSG, *Reminiscences of Augustus*, 2:136.

33. William A. Coffin to HSG, in HSG, *Reminiscences of Augustus*, 2:137; ASG to C. McKim, Dec. 1897, cited in Tharp, *Saint-Gaudens*, 278; ASG to Rose Nichols, Sept. 12, 1898, box 28:4, Papers of ASG.

34. ASG to Augusta Saint-Gaudens, in HSG, *Reminiscences of Augustus*, 2:137.

35. ASG to Augusta Saint-Gaudens, July 1899, box 28:4, Papers of ASG. Davida, his longtime model and mistress, was in Paris for a time, bringing along their son, Novy, who was enrolled in a French school, but for whatever reason, perhaps homesickness, she did not care to stay. ASG to Louis St. Gaudens, n.d., box 24:5, Papers of ASG.

36. Tiffany & Co. to Augusta Saint-Gaudens, Oct. 30, 1899, box 19:27, Papers of ASG.

37. ASG to Augusta Saint-Gaudens, Aug. 3, 1899, box 28:5, Papers of ASG. For examples in collections, see SGNHS #1239; Cleveland Museum of Art #1946.354; Amon Carter Museum

of American Art #2001.2; National Gallery of Art #1975.12.1; Williams College #56.2; Smith College Museum of Art #1900:22–1; New-York Historical Society #1977.3.

38. See Smith College #SC 1900:22–1; Michele H. Bogart, "Augustus Saint-Gaudens, *Diana of the Tower*," in *The Quest for Unity: American Art between World's Fairs 1876–1893*, ed. Deborah Fenton Shepherd, David Hanks, and Kathleen Pyne (Detroit: Detroit Institute of Arts, 1983), 166–67. This rotating version was cast by the Aubry Brothers, by then associated with the Williams Foundry in West Hoboken, New Jersey.

39. The animal is not technically a griffin, which typically sports an eagle's head and talons along with its wings. For MacMonnies, see Gordon, "Sculpture of Frederick William MacMonnies," no. 41 & no. 42, 294–95; Gordon, "Augustus Saint-Gaudens," 96, 98. The *Running Cupid* was modeled by his assistant Janet Scudder.

40. Documented by a partial plaster model found in the studio of Louis St. Gaudens. Dryfhout, "Diana," 211–12; see National Gallery of Art #1975.12.1. One such example with inset bronze letters spelling out "Diana of the Tower" may have been presented as a gift to Augusta Saint-Gaudens's brother, Tom Homer (Dryfhout, "Diana," fig. 37, 209; now in a private collection).

41. As evidenced by EDS analysis conducted by the Metropolitan Museum in 1989. Laurette Dimmick, "Diana, 1893–94," in *American Sculpture in the Metropolitan Museum of Art*, vol. 1, ed. Thayer Tolles (New York: Metropolitan Museum of Art, 1999), 309n8; Dryfhout, "Diana," 183. According to Frances Grimes, Saint-Gaudens preferred a green patina rather than the ordinary brown bronze finish, at least on his larger pieces. Grimes, "Interviews of Frances Grimes," tape 3, side A, AAA.

42. ASG to SW, Dec. 1, 1899, box 20:44, Papers of ASG.

43. ASG to Doll & Richards, Nov. 28, [1899], and Doll & Richards to ASG, Jan. 9, 1900, box 5:39, Papers of ASG.

44. Tiffany & Co. to Augusta Saint-Gaudens, Oct 30, 1899, box 19:27, Papers of ASG; Tiffany & Co., New York, to Tiffany, Paris, Oct. 30, 1899, box 19:27, Papers of ASG. In September 1900, Tiffany's inventory included one large *Diana* and four small. Box 19:27, Papers of ASG. The exhibition at Tiffany's was said to include two of the original "experimental" models for the *Diana*. "The Week in Art," *NYT*, Jan. 27, 1900. For pricing, see Tiffany & Co. invoice, Feb. 18, 1901, box 19:27, Papers of ASG; for the marble base, see Tiffany & Co. to ASG, June 1, 1903, box 19:27, Papers of ASG; Dryfhout, "Diana," 186.

45. ASG to Doll & Richards, Nov. 14, 1899, box 40:41, Papers of ASG; ASG to Doll & Richards, Nov. 28, 1899, box 5:39, Papers of ASG.

46. ASG to Doll & Richards, Nov. 20 [1899], box 40:41, Papers of ASG.

47. ASG to Louis St. Gaudens, July 2, 1899, box 32:47, Papers of ASG; ASG to Jacob Schiff, Sept. 21, 1898, box 17:26, Papers of ASG; Currier Museum of Art #1977.55 was given to Philip Faulkner, former assistant Barry Faulkner's son, as a wedding gift in 1916 by Augusta Saint-Gaudens.

48. ASG to SW, Dec. 1, 1899, box 20:44, Papers of ASG.

49. ASG to Louis St. Gaudens, July 2, 1899, box 32, Papers of ASG.

50. Including one in 1902 to financier Payne Whitney and his bride Helen Hay, daughter of John Hay, to place in the main hall of the Fifth Avenue home White designed for them.

51. SW to ASG, Dec. 1, 1903, box 20:45, Papers of ASG; W. A. Swanberg, *Whitney Father, Whitney Heiress* (New York: Scribner, 1980), 204; ASG to SW, Nov. 30, 1903, and SW to ASG, Dec. 1, 1903, box 20:45, Papers of ASG.

52. ASG to Julia Baird, Dec. 24, 1901, ASG File, Players Club, quoted in Wilkinson, *Uncommon Clay*, 313.

53. ASG to SW, Sept. 27, 1900, quoted in Baldwin, *Stanford White*, 288; HSG, *Reminiscences of Augustus*, 2:246; ASG, "Reminiscences of an Idiot," 146; Fraser, typescript, Papers of ASG.

54. ASG to Louis St. Gaudens, Sept. 16 [1900?], box 32:47, Papers of ASG.

55. Dryfhout, "Diana," 183; ASG to G. Ardisson, Mar. 4, 1901, box 1:30 Papers of ASG; ASG to G. Ardisson, June 25, 1901, box 77, scrapbook 3, Papers of ASG. However, a few may still have been cast in France as late as 1903. Shapiro, *Bronze Casting*, 104, 106.

56. HSG, *Reminiscences of Augustus*, 2:359.

57. Henry Hering to Barry Faulkner, July 27, 1907, box 44:11, Papers of ASG.

58. Dryfhout, "Diana," 185–87.

59. Fusco, "Jean-Alexandre-Joseph Falguière," 259. See Falguière's *Head of Diana*, ca. 1882, #SC 1972:45, Smith College Museum of Art; Dryfhout, "Diana," 211; see also SGNHS #792; Carnegie Institute Museum of Art, #59.5.30.

60. SGNHS #902; Fogg Art Museum, Harvard Univ. #1961.168; Dryfhout, "Diana," 211, 213n43.

61. Dryfhout, "Diana," 186; Tiffany Studios to Augusta Saint-Gaudens, July 22, 1909, box 19:28, Papers of ASG.

62. Tiffany Studios to Augusta Saint-Gaudens, July 22, 1909, box 19:28, Papers of ASG. Augusta Saint-Gaudens continued to seek comparative bids from other firms, including Gorham in 1915. As costs and prices continued to rise, in 1917 the large *Diana* sold for $500 against a cost of $175, although she only cleared $175 after paying the now-30-percent commissions, with the small *Diana* selling for $275 against $125, clearing $77.50. See handwritten notes with prices dated October 1917, box 19:28, Papers of ASG; Roman Bronze Works to Augusta Saint-Gaudens, June 1, 1921, with costs for casting the head of Diana at $90, 35-inch Diana on tripod for $170, etc., box 44:1, Papers of ASG. See also Thayer Tolles, "The Puritan as Statuette," in *In Homage to Worthy Ancestors: The Puritan, the Pilgrim*, ed. Henry J. Duffy (Ossining, NY: Saint-Gaudens Memorial, 2011), 85–86; Christopher Gray, "Streetscapes: Tiffany Studios; In Queens, a Remembrance of a Luminous Legend," *NYT*, Dec. 27, 1987.

63. Gregory Schwarz, Feb. 8, 1995, SGNHS.

64. Sheila Gibson Stoodley, "A Monumental Show," *Art and Antiques* 2 (June 2009): 38; Dryfhout, "Diana," 211. After residing at the Museum of the City of New York from 1936 to 1970, the original 1894 cement cast (then in two pieces) was sold to collector Stephen

Goodyear in the mid-1970s, who then sold it to the Amon Carter Museum, Fort Worth, Texas, in 1981, along with White's 1927 bronze, which now decorates the Bass Performance Hall. The cement cast was carefully reconstructed and restored, and since March 2018 has been on display. Margaret Adler, "The Goddess in the Basement," *Panorama: Journal of the Association of Historians of American Art* 4 (Spring 2018), https://editions.lib.umn.edu/panorama /article/the-goddess-in-the-basement/.

65. F. E. Osterkamp to Edward Robinson, Dec. 1, 1927, and June 6, 1928, memo dated June 7, 1928, Metropolitan Museum of Art Archives; "Augustus Saint-Gaudens and Willard Metcalf," *New York Herald*, Oct. 14, 1928.

66. Likely at the Deprato Foundry, Pietrasanta, Italy. Dryfhout, *Work*, 207.

67. Henry Duffy, email messages to author, Feb. 23, 2011, and Aug. 9, 2018.

68. In 1979 White's cement cast was used again for a series of bronzes cast by the Madison Square Garden Corporation in honor of their centennial celebration. A limited edition of six was cast at the Bedi-Makky Art Foundry in Brooklyn under the auspices of art dealer Peter Davidson, with one installed at the fourth incarnation of Madison Square Garden and another installed at Brookgreen Gardens, South Carolina, in 1991, while the remaining three were sold into private collections. Peter H. Davidson, "Saint-Gaudens and the Huntress," *Sculpture Review* 40, no. 32 (1991): 37. According to the records of the Princeton Art Museum, a series of six was cast from the White cement in 1987 and one was given as a gift to the museum in 1990. In June 2016, one of the three in private collections was donated to the Society of the Four Arts Philip Hulitar Sculpture Garden, Palm Beach, Florida. *Palm Beach Daily News*, June 12, 2016. Editions continued to be made in the 1970s and in 1985 for the Conner Rosencranz Gallery by Christine Roussel, Inc., New York, one of which was installed at the Cornish Colony Museum in Windsor, Vermont, until its closure in 2011.

27. A Murder at the Garden

1. See, in particular, Collins, *Glamorous Sinners*; Langford, *Richard Harding Davis Years*; Mooney, *Evelyn Nesbit*; Paula Uruburu, *American Eve: Evelyn Nesbit, Stanford White, the Birth of the "It" Girl* (New York: Riverhead Books, 2008); Simon Baatz, *The Girl on the Velvet Swing: Sex, Murder, and Madness at the Dawn of the Twentieth Century* (New York: Mulholland, 2018); and Mary Cummings, *Saving Sin City: William Travers Jerome, Stanford White, and the Original Crime of the Century* (New York: Pegasus Books, 2018). See also accounts by Nesbit, *Prodigal Days*; and Harry Thaw, *The Traitor* (Philadelphia: Dorrance, 1926). For fiction, see E. L. Doctorow, *Ragtime* (New York: Random House, 1975); the 1981 musical version; and the 1955 film *The Girl in the Red Velvet Swing*.

2. Nesbit, *Prodigal Days*, 13.

3. "Evelyn Tells Her Story," *NYT*, Feb. 8, 1907; Nesbit, *Prodigal Days*, 5, 12–13; "New Type of Beauty," *Biloxi (MS) Daily Herald*, June 23, 1901.

4. Nesbit, *Prodigal Days*, 2–3, 17.

5. "Evelyn Tells Her Story," *NYT*, Feb. 8, 1907; Evelyn Nesbit, *The Story of My Life* (London: John Long Ltd., 1914), in Deborah Paul, ed., *Tragic Beauty: The Lost 1914 Memoirs of Evelyn Nesbit* (Raleigh, NC: Lulu, 2006), 36; Nesbit, *Prodigal Days*, 28.

6. Nesbit, *Story of My Life*, in Paul, *Tragic Beauty*, 38; Nesbit, *Prodigal Days*, 35, 90.

7. Nesbit, *Prodigal Days*, 41; "Evelyn Tells Her Story," *NYT*, Feb. 8, 1907.

8. Mooney, *Evelyn Nesbit*, 52; Phyllis Leslie Abramson, *Sob Sister Journalism* (Westport, CT: Greenwood Press, 1990), 68.

9. Nesbit, *Prodigal Days*, 34, 42.

10. Nesbit, *Story of My Life*, in Paul, *Tragic Beauty*, 48, 103; Nesbit, *Prodigal Days*, 5–7.

11. "Theatrical Folk Tell Relations of White and Thaw," *New York Daily Tribune*, June 27, 1906.

12. According to Nesbit (*Prodigal Days*, 194), Thaw injected cocaine as a sexual stimulant.

13. Nesbit, *Prodigal Days*, 140.

14. Nesbit, *Prodigal Days*, 170. In truth, Truxton Beale, the former minister to Persia and Turkey, had shot the editor of a San Francisco newspaper in 1902 after he published an unflattering item about Beale's fiancée-to-be. Beale was acquitted on the grounds of self-defense after he claimed he thought Marriott was about to draw a gun. "Editor Marriott's Shooters Acquitted," *San Jose (CA) Evening News*, Jan. 7, 1903. See also Hendrik Hartok, "Lawyering, Husbands' Rights, and 'the Unwritten Law' in Nineteenth-Century America," *Journal of American History* 84 (June 1970): 67–96.

15. Nesbit, *Prodigal Days*, 173; Thaw, *Traitor*, 141; "Jerome Checks Thaw Defense," *NYT*, Feb. 12, 1907.

16. Paula Uruburu, *American Eve*, 277.

17. Thaw reportedly asked if Smith knew Truxton Beale and was familiar with the incident. "Thaw's Talk with Smith," *NYT*, Mar. 13, 1907.

18. "Emotional Insanity the Thaw Defense," *NYT*, June 29, 1906; Nesbit, *Prodigal Days*, 173–74; Thaw, *Traitor*, 143–45; "Thaw Was Insane the Defense Pleads," *NYT*, Feb 5, 1907.

19. Thaw, *Traitor*, 145; "Three Bullets Found," *New York Daily Tribune*, June 27, 1906; "Thaw Was Insane the Defense Pleads," *NYT*, Feb. 5, 1907; "Thaw Kills Stanford White," *New York Daily Tribune*, June 26, 1906; "Thaw Murders Stanford White," *NYT*, June 26, 1906; Nesbit, *Prodigal Days*, 174; Baker, *Stanny*, 373. According to some sources, he was shot first in the shoulder, then beneath the left eye, and finally in the mouth. Baatz, *Girl on the Velvet Swing*, 111.

20. "Thaw Kills Stanford White," *New York Daily Tribune*, June 26, 1906; "Thaw Was Insane the Defense Pleads," *NYT*, Feb. 5, 1907.

21. "Emotional Insanity the Thaw Defense," *NYT*, June 29, 1906; *New York Daily Tribune*, June 29, 1906; "Says White Swore He Would Kill Thaw," *NYT*, Feb. 7, 1907; Nesbit, *Prodigal Days*, 175; "Thaw Was Insane the Defense Pleads," *NYT*, Feb 5, 1907.

22. "Emotional Insanity," *New York Sun*, June 29, 1906.

23. "White Funeral Party Eluded the Curious," *NYT*, June 29, 1906.

24. These were executed by John La Farge. John La Farge to SW, Dec. 29, 1892, SW Papers, New-York Historical Society; St. James Episcopal Church website, accessed Mar. 7, 2013, http://stjamesstjames.org/history.html.

25. Cox, *Artist and Public*, 79; Baker, *Stanny*, 376.

26. "Widow Alone Tearless at White's Funeral," *New York Sun*, June 28, 1906.

27. *New Orleans Daily Picayune*, July 28, 1906.

28. Collins, *Glamorous Sinners*, 177.

29. "Thaw Talked Like Sane Man," *NYT*, Mar. 13, 1907; "Crisis Is Reached in Thaw Trial," *NYT*, Mar. 14, 1907; Cait Murphy, *Scoundrels in Law: The Trials of Howe & Hummel* (New York: Harper, 2010), 253.

30. ASG, Letter to the Editor, *Collier's Weekly*, Aug. 6, 1906, reprinted in *American Institute of Architects Quarterly Bulletin* 7 (July 1906): 102.

31. ASG to A. Garnier, July 6, 1906, in HSG, ed., "Intimate Letters of Stanford White: Correspondence with His Friend and Co-Worker Augustus Saint-Gaudens," *Architectural Record* 30 (Oct. 1911): 406.

32. Baker, *Stanny*, 280.

33. "Thaw Indictment In," *New York Daily Tribune*, June 28, 1906.

34. "Evelyn Thaw Recounts More of White's Brutality," *Wilkes-Barre Times*, Feb. 19, 1907; "Says She Knew Stanford White," *Philadelphia Inquirer*, July 5, 1906; "Stanford White's 'Den' a Real Den of Orgies," *Salt Lake Evening Telegram*, July 2, 1906. However, a signed letter from Stanford White to MacMonnies, dated July 6, 1895, requests that "Mac" have "one 18 year old smooth skinned firm breasted pretty little model 'in tap' for me," indicating an interest in slightly older girls. Lot 197, auction Feb. 28, 2017, *Invaluable* website, accessed Feb. 19, 2017, http://www.invaluable.com.

35. "Murdered Man Was a Sport," *Rockford (IL) Republic*, June 27, 1906.

36. "Harry Thaw Indicted for Murder in First Degree," *Denver Post*, June 28, 1906.

37. "Murdered Man Was a Sport," *Rockford (IL) Republic*, June 27, 1906; "Modern Sybaris," *Grand Forks (ND) Herald*, June 30, 1906.

38. "Stanford White, Voluptuary and Pervert, Dies the Death of a Dog," *Vanity Fair*, July 13, 1906, 3. As William Randolph Hearst, known for his contribution to "yellow" sensational journalism in the 1890s, was a major buyer at the postmortem auction of White's collection of art, antiques, and architectural elements, Paul A. Becera (oral communication, Mar. 27, 2018) wonders if there might have been a connection with this treatment in the press as an attempt to lower sales prices.

39. See headlines like "Anthony Comstock to Stamp Out Immorality among Wealthy Perverts Like White," *Riverside (CA) Independent Enterprise*, June 29, 1906; "War Declared in Gotham on White's Class," *Duluth News-Tribune*, June 29, 1906; and "Thaw's Crime May Purge City of Sin," *Olympia (WA) Daily Recorder*, June 30, 1906. For a discussion of the appeal of very young girls, child prostitutes, nude photography, and Stanford White's involvement, see Dunlop, *Gilded City*, 153ff.

40. Nesbit, *Prodigal Days*, 5.

41. "Guest of White at Dinner," *Anaconda (MT) Standard*, Jan. 28, 1908; Lessard, *Architect of Desire*, 291.

42. Nesbit, *Prodigal Days*, 4–5; Mooney, *Evelyn Nesbit*, 77.

43. Nesbit, *Prodigal Days*, xii.

44. Paul, *Tragic Beauty*, 118–19; "Evelyn Tells Her Story," *NYT*, Feb. 8, 1907; "Thaw Must Wait Turn," *New York Daily Tribune*, July 1, 1906.

45. Paul, *Tragic Beauty*, 124–25, 143; Nesbit, *Prodigal Days*, 7.

46. "Thaw Kills Stanford White," *New York Daily Tribune*, June 26, 1906; "Emotional Insanity the Thaw Defense," *NYT*, June 29, 1906; "Thaw Was Insane the Defense Pleads," *NYT*, Feb 5, 1907.

47. Nesbit, *Prodigal Days*, 108–9, 113, 192–93; Uruburu, *American Eve*, 223; "Evelyn Tells Her Story," *NYT*, Feb. 8, 1907; Collins, *Glamorous Sinners*, 150–51; Mooney, *Evelyn Nesbit*, 87; Paul, *Tragic Beauty*, 143.

48. Actor Arthur Pelham claimed he was hired by White the summer of 1904 to show him Paris "as it should be seen." "San Josean to Be in Thaw Trial," *San Jose Mercury News*, Aug. 11, 1906.

49. "With Deliberate Aim Shot Him Down," *Denver Post*, June 27, 1906; "Theatrical Folk Tell Relations of White and Thaw," *New York Daily Tribune*, June 27, 1906.

50. "Whipping of Boy Starts Hunt for Harry K. Thaw," *NYT*, Jan. 10, 1917; "Two Boys Accuse Thaw," *NYT*, Jan. 14, 1917.

51. Citing box 8:13, SW Correspondence, Baker points out that some of the volumes may have been inherited from his father, *Stanny*, 375–76, 455n17. Thaw insisted that workmen in buildings near White's Twenty-Fourth Street apartment would hear young girls scream, which he reported to Anthony Comstock. "Comstock a Thaw Witness," *Kansas City Star*, Jan. 22, 1908.

52. "Nesbit Defends Mother, Blames Mrs. Harry Thaw," *NYT*, Jan. 29, 1907; Uruburu, *American Eve*, 244–45n370, 386; "Howard Nesbit a Suicide," *NYT*, Dec. 27, 1928.

53. While in Paris, Nesbit's hair began to fall out, and the doctors suggested she shave her head. As her hair slowly grew back, Nesbit noticed that without her wig she bore a striking resemblance to her younger brother. Douglas O. Linder, "Testimony of Evelyn Nesbit Thaw, Harry Thaw Trial 1907, direct examination by Delphin Delmas," *Famous Trials*, accessed Mar. 2016, http://famous-trials.com/thaw/426-transcript.

28. The Tower Falls

1. Tex [Charles L. J.] Rickard, "Tex Rickard Gives Rules for Making a Big Fortune," *Omaha World-Herald*, Feb. 14, 1924.

2. Haskin, "Madison Square Garden."

3. "Real Estate," *New York Daily Tribune*, Apr. 6, 1897. Under a reorganization plan, the primary stockholders were asked to pay an assessment of $2.50 a share and surrender

three-quarters of their stock. Second mortgage bondholders were asked to surrender their lien, to take preferred stock for their bonds, to pay an assessment or contribution equal to 40 percent of their holdings, and to accept for the said assessment an income bond whose interest was only payable when earned. "Madison Square Garden; Plan of Reorganization Submitted," *NYT*, July 26, 1897.

4. At this point the tax bill stood at $35,000, the interest on the first mortgage bonds at $62,500, and the interest on the second mortgage at $45,000. Needed maintenance and repairs would cost $15,000, and insurance was $8,000, while the operating expenses ran $52,000 a year. "A Crisis for the Garden," *New York Daily Tribune*, Apr. 22, 1900.

5. "Garden as Postal Centre," *New York Daily Tribune*, Feb. 19, 1900; "Our New Up-Town Post Office," *NYT*, Apr. 13, 1900.

6. "Madison Square Garden for Sale," *NYT*, Nov. 12, 1908; "The Garden Is Up for Sale," *New York Sun*, Nov. 12, 1908; "Madison Square Garden," *NYT*, Nov. 13, 1908; "We Need an Amphitheatre," *NYT*, Apr. 11, 1911.

7. "The Garden Is Up for Sale," *New York Sun*, Nov. 12, 1908; "Madison Square Garden," *NYT*, Nov. 13, 1908; "Noted Hall to Go, High Pile to Come," *Cleveland Plain Dealer*, Dec. 29, 1909.

8. "Morgan Tries Again to Sell the Garden," *NYT*, Jan. 26, 1911. Of the figure, $2.65 million was the appraised value of the land and the buildings only $500,000.

9. "Madison Sq. Garden Sold for $3,400,000," *NYT*, Apr. 9, 1911; "Madison Sq. Garden Surely Sold Now," *NYT*, June 9, 1911; "Admits Syndicate Has Garden Option," *NYT*, Apr. 17, 1911; "Garden Goes in February," *New York Sun*, Aug. 8, 1911.

10. "The Old Garden to Go," *New York Daily People*, June 9, 1911; "Admits Syndicate Has Garden Option," *NYT*, Apr. 17, 1911; "Madison Sq. Garden Surely Sold Now," *NYT*, June 9, 1911; "Garden Goes in February," *New York Sun*, Aug. 8, 1911; "50-Acre Building for New York City," *NYT*, June 25, 1911.

11. "May Let the Garden Stand," *NYT*, Jan. 16, 1912; "Motion Pictures in Madison Garden," *NYT*, May 23, 1911; "The Garden Roof Ready," *NYT*, May 27, 1912.

12. New York Life sued for $2,358,504, which included interest and back taxes; there was also a second mortgage of $650,000, said to be held by the estate of the late J. P. Morgan. "Madison Sq. Garden on Financial Shoal," *NYT*, June 16, 1916; "Fate of Madison Square Garden in the Balance," *NYT*, Nov. 19, 1916; "Madison Sq. Garden Sold for $2,000,000," *NYT*, Dec. 9, 1916; "Syndicate Buys Garden," *NYT*, Jan. 3, 1917; "Brisk Boxing Year Ahead," *NYT*, Jan. 28, 1917.

13. The license was lost primarily due to a technicality in the garden's lease as well as management's failure to remit the state tax on four bouts. "Boxing Licenses Revoked," *NYT*, Mar. 12, 1917; "New York to See Notable Fights," *NYT*, Sept. 14, 1919.

14. "Boxing Bill Passed in Assembly 91–46," *NYT*, Apr. 25, 1920; "Walker Boxing Bill Signed by Governor," *NYT*, May 25, 1920.

15. "'Tex' Rickard Gets Madison Sq. Garden," *NYT*, July 13, 1920.

16. "Boxing Fans for Dempsey," *NYT*, Jan. 26, 1919.

17. "'Tex' Rickard Gets Madison Sq. Garden," *NYT*, July 13, 1920.

18. "Fat Women and Men Join Squad to Lose Excess," *Cleveland Plain Dealer*, Oct. 19, 1921.

19. "Garden to Be Made into Gym," *Salt Lake Telegram*, Jan. 31, 1921; "Going Up for Exercise," *Ogden (UT) Standard-Examiner*, Feb. 4, 1921.

20. "Garden Nearly Ready," *NYT*, Sept. 14, 1920.

21. "Boxing at Garden Pays $186,918 Tax," *NYT*, Mar. 28, 1921.

22. "The New Swimmin' Hole," *Lexington (KY) Herald*, Aug. 23, 1921; "Largest Swimming Pool," *Trenton (NJ) Evening News*, Sept. 25, 1921; "Broadway's Diving Champ," *Rockford (IL) Morning Star*, July 7, 1921; "[Illegible] the Ocean," *New York Tribune*, July 10, 1921; "One Thousand Policemen Will Protect Reserved Sections of Big Arena," *Richmond (VA) Times-Dispatch*, June 12, 1921.

23. "'Tex' Rickard on a Girl's Charge," *NYT*, Jan. 23, 1922; "Child Accuser of Rickard on Grill 5 Hours," *New York Tribune*, Feb. 4, 1922; "Tex Rickard Again Indicted on New Charges by Girls," *New York Evening World*, Feb. 23, 1922; "Gasko Girl, 12, Supports Story against Rickard," *New York Tribune*, Mar. 23, 1922; "State Rests Case against Rickard," *NYT*, Mar. 24, 1922; "Jury Acquits Rickard in 1 Hr. 37 Min," *New York Tribune*, Mar. 29, 1922; "Rickard Not Guilty," *NYT*, Mar. 29, 1922; "Rickard's Accusers Escape," *NYT*, June 26, 1922.

24. "Garden Hears Last Roar of Gay Crowds," *NYT*, May 6, 1925.

25. "Plan High Building to Replace Garden," *NYT*, Apr. 19, 1924; "28-Story Building to Replace Garden," *NYT*, May 17, 1924.

26. James Fraser quoted in McSpadden, *Famous Sculptors*, 302.

27. Cass Gilbert to Clarence Johnson, Aug. 24, 1882, Johnston Papers, Minnesota Historical Society, quoted in Geoffrey Blodgett, *Cass Gilbert: The Early Years* (St. Paul, MN: Minnesota Historical Society Press, 2001), 53.

28. Baker, *Stanny*, 88.

29. "Rickard to Build Garden on 8th Ave," *NYT*, June 18, 1924; "Rickard Enlarges New Garden Site," *NYT*, June 20, 1924.

30. "Plan High Building to Replace Garden," *NYT*, Apr. 19, 1924; Gilbert, "New York Life Insurance Building," memorandum, Jan. 23, 1924, New York Life Insurance Correspondence, 7, New-York Historical Society, quoted in Mary Beth Betts, "Cass Gilbert: Twelve Projects," in *Inventing the Skyline: The Architecture of Cass Gilbert*, ed. Margaret Heilbrun (New York: Columbia Univ. Press, 2000), 147; "Count of Ten Near for the 'Garden,'" *NYT*, Apr. 27, 1924; "May Scrap the 'Garden,'" *San Diego Union*, May 17, 1924.

31. Lawrence White to Darwin Kingsley, Feb. 11, 1925, box 378:435, MM&W Architectural Records Collection, PR 042, New-York Historical Society.

32. "Says Dallas Has Chance to Get $22,000 Statue of Diana from New York," *Dallas Morning News*, Apr. 15, 1925; "Diana and Her Tower Find a Home at Last within N.Y. University," *NYT*, Apr. 28, 1925; "Use Statue for Aerial," *Cleveland Plain Dealer*, June 8, 1924; W. M. Kendall to HSG, Sept. 17, 1924, reel 5:528, box 5:36, Papers of ASG; "University Heights

Approved for Diana," *NYT*, Feb. 4, 1925; "Diana May Crown the Manhattan Bridge," *NYT*, Mar. 18, 1925; "Wants Diana at Coney," *NYT*, Mar. 31, 1925; "Diana Newest Eight," *Seattle Daily Times*, May 12, 1925; "Dealers Seeking Diana Franchise," *Pittsburgh Press*, June 14, 1925; "City May Get Diana, Now atop the Garden," *NYT*, Dec. 5, 1924; "Urges a New Site for Garden Diana," *NYT*, Dec. 12, 1924; Vladimir Dekanel, "Diana of the Tower," unpublished manuscript, 7, New York Life Insurance, SGNHS.

33. HSG to Lawrence White, Sept. 9, 1924, and Feb. 27, 1925, Papers of ASG, with copies at SGNHS; HSG to Lawrence White, June 20, 1928, roll 505, AAA, from MS 693, SW Papers, New-York Historical Society; "Would Destroy Statue of Diana," *NYT*, Mar. 15, 1925.

34. "Would Destroy Statue of Diana," *NYT*, Mar. 15, 1925; HSG to Ida Metz Reed, Sept. 9, 1924, and HSG to George B. Upham, Sept. 15, 1924, box 5:36, Papers of ASG.

35. "Diana's Fate Now a Matter of Days," *NYT*, Feb. 8, 1925; E. E. Brown to D. P. Kingsley, Apr. 23, 1925, quoted in Elmer Ellsworth Brown, "Report of the Chancellor, New York University, 1924–1925," 29, SGNHS. In 1973, NYU sold the campus to the City University of New York, which renamed the campus the Bronx Community College.

36. D. P. Kingsley to E. E. Brown, Apr. 27, 1925, box 378:435, McKim, Mead & White Architectural Records, New-York Historical Society.

37. "Art Exhibitions of the Week," *NYT*, Feb. 22, 1925; "Favor Heights for Diana," *NYT*, Feb. 16, 1925.

38. "Diana May Adorn University Heights," *NYT*, Feb. 3, 1925; "Diana and Her Tower Find a Home at Last within N.Y. University," *NYT*, Apr. 28, 1925; "Elihu Root to Head Group Saving Diana," *NYT*, Apr. 29, 1925; C. Gilbert to A. L. Aiken, Apr. 10, 1925, New York Life Insurance Letter book, 3/8/1924–3/30/1926, 198, New-York Historical Society, quoted in Betts, "Cass Gilbert," 149; "Diana Finds a Home," *NYU Alumnus*, June 1925, 29; "N.Y.U. Acquires Site for Diana's Tower," *NYT*, July 26, 1925.

39. D. P. Kingsley to E. E. Brown, Apr. 27, 1925, quoted in Brown, "Report of the Chancellor," 30–31; Dekanel, "Diana of the Tower," 8.

40. "New Rickard Arena Work Is Under Way," *NYT*, Jan. 10, 1925; "New Garden Dims All Indoor Arenas," *NYT*, Nov. 22, 1925; "Bike Races Tonight Open New Garden," *NYT*, Nov. 28, 1925; "Garden Is Opened in Blaze of Color," *NYT*, Dec. 16, 1925.

41. "Circus Quits Garden to 'Auld Lang Syne,'" *NYT*, May 3, 1925.

42. "Garden Hears Last Roar of Gay Crowds," *NYT*, May 6, 1925.

43. "Diana Sees Last Bout from Her High Tower," *NYT*, May 6, 1925. See also Damon Runyon, "Madison Square Passes as Fistic Arena: A Reporter's Last Report," *San Diego Union*, May 6, 1925.

44. Damon Runyon, "'Boo' Is Garden Swan Song," *Detroit Times*, May 6, 1925; "Terris Gets Verdict in 12-Round Battle," *NYT*, May 6, 1925; "Passes Madison Square," *Seattle Daily Times*, May 6, 1925.

45. "Madison Square Garden, Land Mark of New York, Is Passing," *Riverside (CA) Daily Press*, May 5, 1925; "Diana Comes Down from Her Tower," *NYT*, May 7, 1925; "Diana

Removed from Garden Top," *Springfield (MA) Republican*, May 7, 1925; Skinner, "Steelwork of Madison Square Garden," 538.

46. Nesbit, *Prodigal Days*, 33–34; Pauline Kiernan, *Filthy Shakespeare* (New York: Gotham, 2006), 192; "Madison Square Garden, Land Mark of New York, Is Passing," *Riverside (CA) Daily Press*, May 5, 1925.

47. "Diana Comes Down from Her Tower," *NYT*, May 7, 1925; "Diana Removed from Garden Top," *Springfield (MA) Republican*, May 7, 1925; Joslin Construction Co. to Lawrence White, May 5, 1925, MS 693, SW Papers, New-York Historical Society; Dekanel, "Diana of the Tower," 9; "Madison Square Garden," *American Architect* 128 (Dec. 20, 1925): 514.

48. "Diana Comes Down from Her Tower," *NYT*, May 7, 1925; "Diana Removed from Garden Top," *Springfield (MA) Republican*, May 7, 1925.

49. "Diana Comes Down from Her Tower," *NYT*, May 7, 1925; Dekanel, "Diana of the Tower," 12; "Rebuild Garden in Philadelphia," *Canton (OH) Evening Repository*, May 17, 1925.

50. "Diana Removed from Garden Top," *Springfield (MA) Republican*, May 7, 1925; "Nude Man Tried to Play Diana; No, Police Decide," *Omaha World-Herald*, May 7, 1925.

51. A light, portable derrick commonly used to carry weights up to 6 tons, with a boom ca. 30 feet long that was secured to the base of an A-frame and typically operated by hand-powered winch. *Material Handling Cyclopedia* (New York: Simmons-Boardman, 1921), 227.

52. For more technical details of the demolition, see Skinner, "Steelwork of Madison Square Garden," 538–41.

53. "Thirty-Five Years' Test," *American Architect* 128: 524; "Pigeons Will Be Homeless When Diana and Garden Go," *NYT*, Feb. 23, 1925; "Plight of Pigeons Bestirs New Friends," *Springfield (MA) Republican*, Mar. 2, 1925; "Protection for Animals," *NYT*, Jan. 30, 1898.

54. Skinner, "Steelwork of Madison Square Garden," 542; "Prison Guards Keep Eyes on Steeplejack," *Miami Herald Record*, May 9, 1921.

55. Robert T. Small, "Foreign Capitals and Other Cities Contribute Gossip," *Oregonian* (Portland OR), Dec. 6, 1925; "Thirty-Five Years' Test," *American Architect* 128: 519.

56. "Thirty-Five Years' Test," *American Architect* 128: 524; Skinner, "Steelwork of Madison Square Garden," 542.

57. "Lay Stone for New Insurance Building," *NYT*, June 18, 1927.

29. The Last of the Story

1. "Fire at World's Fair," *New York Herald*, July 6, 1894; Smart, *Flight with Fame*, 143.

2. Margot Gayle, "Montgomery Ward & Company and Three Statues on Chicago's Skyline," *Chicago History* 11 (Summer 1982): 106. Mrs. Howard Chudacoff of the Chicago Historical Society wrote to John Dryfhout, curator at the Saint-Gaudens National Historical Park, April 8, 1968, that "We have no record of what happened to the Diana," SGNHS.

3. "With the Art Students," *New York Sun*, May 26, 1895; Mullins Manufacturing Company advertising brochure (Salem, OH: n.d. [post-1932]), 27, SGNHS.

4. Gayle, "Montgomery Ward," 106; unsigned ms., SGNHS; Dryfhout, *Work*, 194.

5. Gayle, "Montgomery Ward," 106; unsigned ms., SGNHS.

6. Letter from F. W. Jameson, Montgomery Ward & Co., 1937, and G.S.C. Newsletter, 1959, quoted in Gayle, "Montgomery Ward," 106; John Dryfhout to Alfred Life, June 28, 1969, SGNHS. There is also a story that *Diana* adorned a tower on the Marshall Field Building, but this is likely a matter of confusion with Montgomery Ward. See Cortissoz, "Augustus Saint-Gaudens and Willard L. Metcalf."

7. Gayle, "Montgomery Ward," 108; "Climbs Montgomery Ward Tower in Spite of Wind," *Rockford (IL) Republic*, Feb. 14, 1913; "Steeplejack Falls 100 Feet from Stack to Death," *Washington Times*, Apr. 19, 1916.

8. Gayle, "Montgomery Ward," 108; "Artistic Weather Vane for Chicago," *NYT*, Oct. 9, 1900; unsigned ms., SGNHS. An interesting comparison and striking similarities also may be noted between Rhind's draped female relief figures for Grant's Tomb in New York and those on the base of Saint-Gaudens's *Farragut Monument*.

9. Metropolitan Museum of Art, *Catalogue of a Memorial Exhibition of the Works of Augustus Saint-Gaudens* (New York: 1908; 2nd issue, Boston: D. B. Updike, Merrymount Press, n.d.), 37.

10. Box 22:14, Papers of ASG.

11. "The Augustus Saint-Gaudens Memorial Exhibition," *Bulletin of the Art Institute of Chicago* 3 (Oct. 1909): 18.

12. Mullins Manufacturing Company advertising brochure, 27, SGNHS.

13. Grissom, *Zinc Sculpture*, 63; "Old Mullins Plant's Statue of Diana 'Stood' atop Madison Square Garden," *Youngstown (OH) Vindicator*, Aug. 17, 1980.

14. Gayle, "Montgomery Ward," 108.

15. In 1929 a second, bronze, nonmovable, clothed version of the *Progress* figure, perhaps by sculptor-architect Joseph Conradi, was installed on top of the four-story pyramidal tower addition to the Ward Administrative Building on West Chicago Avenue. Named *The Spirit of Progress*, this figure was 2 feet shorter, carried a torch, and differed somewhat in the position of arms and legs. Gayle, "Montgomery Ward," 110. For comparative photographs, see Gregory H. Jenkins, "J. Massey Rhind. Progress. A Second Look," *Chicago Sculpture in the Loop*, accessed Nov. 5, 2014, http://chicagosculptureintheloop.blogspot.com, Feb. 17, 18, 19, 2010; "Madison Square Garden," *American Architect* 128 (Dec. 20, 1925): 513.

16. *Chicago Tribune*, July 20, 1947.

17. "Madison Square Garden," *American Architect* 128 (Dec. 20, 1925): 516.

18. "The Ultimate Chicago Souvenir: The Head of Montgomery Ward," Leslie Hindman Auctioneers, accessed Dec. 1, 2014, https://www.lesliehindman.com/head-of-montgomery-ward/.

19. "The Pan-American 'Goddess of Light,'" *Inland and American Printer* 27 (July 1901): 519; "News from 1902," *Pan-American Exposition at Buffalo in 1901*, accessed Dec. 10, 2014, http://panam1901.org/thisday/1902newsjuly.htm.

20. L. G. White to R. Cortissoz, July 14, 1924, box 376:435, SW Papers, New-York Historical Society.

21. "Diana's Thirty-Year Reign Soon to End," *NYT*, Dec. 28, 1924.

22. "Diana of Madison Square Garden," *American Architect* 127 (June 3, 1925): 515.

23. "Philadelphia Gets 'Diana,' New York's Virgin," *Arts Magazine* 6 (Apr. 15, 1932): 17.

24. "Monuments: New York's No More," *Time* 90 (Sept. 1, 1967); Haskin, "Madison Square Garden."

25. Advertisement for Monroe Clothes, *New York Evening World*, Nov. 24, 1916.

26. "St. Gaudens's Diana to Take Up Abode in City of Penn," *NYT*, Mar. 25, 1932.

27. "Put New Arrow on Diana's Bow," *New York World*, Apr. 21, 1905. However, according to the *New York Tribune*, gale winds drove the steeplejack back, and 14-foot rigging was to be installed to complete the job. "Plans Call on Diana, Steeple Jack Will Give Arrow to Woman in High Life," Apr. 22, 1905.

28. "Huge Home Opened by New York Life," *NYT*, Dec. 13, 1928; Dekanel, "Diana of the Tower," 11–12; "D. P. Kingsley Dies," *NYT*, Oct. 7, 1932. However, Kingsley remained as chairman of the board of New York Life until his death in 1932.

29. C. Platt to D. P. Kingsley, Jan. 24, 1929, SGNHS.

30. The town of Cornish, however, had grown significantly as an artists' colony and in sophistication since the first arrival of Saint-Gaudens in 1885. Its various residents included Thomas and Maria Oakley Dewing, George de Forest Brush, Louis and Anetta St. Gaudens, Frederic MacMonnies, James Earle Fraser, Kenyon Cox, Henry and Lucia Fairchild Fuller, Paul Manship, Daniel Chester French, Frederic Remington, and Maxfield Parrish, along with a variety of architects, writers, musicians, and composers. See Alma M. Gilbert and Judith B. Tankard, *A Place of Beauty: The Artists and Gardens of the Cornish Colony* (Berkeley, CA: Ten Speed Press, 2000).

31. Lawrence White to S. George Webb, Mar. 27, 1925, box 378:435, McKim, Mead & White Architectural Records, New-York Historical Society; Brown, "Report of the Chancellor," 24–25, 28.

32. "Who Wants 'Diana' by Saint Gaudens? It's Going Begging," *Chicago Evening Post*, Oct. 22, 1929; Dekanel, "Diana of the Tower," 12.

33. D. P. Kingsley to E. E. Brown, Dec. 16, 1931, box 177:27, Kimball Records, Philadelphia Museum of Art. Further correspondence in the collection between NYU and Kingsley includes Harold O. Voorhis, Assistant to the Chancellor, NYU, to Kingsley, Jan. 25, 1932; Kimball to Brown, Dec. 23, 1931; Kingsley to Voorhis, Jan. 28, 1932; Kimball to Kingsley, Jan. 27, 1932; Kingsley to Kimball, June 14, 1932; Kimball to Kingsley, June 17, 1932. See also Dekanel, "Diana of the Tower," 12; Brown, "Report of the Chancellor," 27–28.

34. "Old Garden's Diana Is Lost to New York," *NYT*, Mar. 25, 1932.

35. Minutes of the Fairmont Park Art Association Board, Feb. 25, 1932, box 177:27, Kimball Records, Philadelphia Museum of Art. See also a comment (livius drusus, 2013-06-29) reporting a response from Philadelphia Museum of Art's senior curator of American Art,

Kathy Foster, on the article "Saint-Gaudens' Diana to be Regilded," *The History Blog*, accessed June 17, 2014, http://www.thehistoryblog.com/archives/25809.

36. Ricardo Bertelli to Henri Marceau, Mar. 7, 1932, Marceau to Bertelli, Mar. 17 and Mar. 23, 1932, box 177:27, Kimball Records, Philadelphia Museum of Art; "Old Garden's Diana Is Lost to New York," *NYT*, Mar. 25, 1932; "Statue of Diana Arrives in Philadelphia," *New York Sun*, Apr. 22, 1932. Roman Bronze Works was established in 1897 by Ricardo Bertelli, and the company had moved from Manhattan to Tiffany's factory in Corona, Queens, in 1927.

37. "Old Garden's Diana Is Lost to New York," *NYT*, Mar. 25, 1932. Perhaps in response and to reemphasize its cultural heritage, in December 1932 the Metropolitan Museum moved its half-size *Diana* from a room at the extreme south end of the building to a much more conspicuous location in an arch over the main stairway. "Museum Acquires Famous Sculpture," *NYT*, Dec. 10, 1932.

38. "Philadelphia Pastor Would Banish Diana," *NYT*, Mar. 27, 1932; "Art: Lady Higher Up," *Time* 19 (Apr. 4, 1932), accessed Aug. 2001, http://content.time.com/time/magazine/article/0,9171,743477,00.html; "Diana Enters Philadelphia," *Philadelphia Record*, Apr. 22, 1932.

39. "Diana Enters Philadelphia," *Philadelphia Record*, Apr. 22, 1932; "Rumpus over Nude Diana," *Indiana (PA) Evening Gazette*, Mar. 30, 1932; "Women Will March in Protest Against Nude Diana," *Seattle Daily-Times*, Mar. 31, 1932.

40. F. Kimball to Miss Driscoll, Fairmont Park Association, Jan. 4, 1933, box 177:29, Kimball Records, Philadelphia Museum of Art; "Diana Is Unveiled in Art Museum," *Philadelphia Ledger*, Apr. 29, 1932; "Bad Diana; Philadelphia Gets Naughty Statue Despite Preacher," *Pittsburg Press*, May 1, 1932. The copper sphere was manufactured by Biddle-Gaumer Company, Philadelphia. E. H. Pedersen to C. L. Sherman, May 13, 1932, box 177:29, Kimball Records, Philadelphia Museum of Art.

41. F. Kimball to D. P. Kingsley, June 13, 1932, box 177:29, Kimball Records, Philadelphia Museum of Art.

42. "Crusader's Aide Is Held as Addict," *Trenton (NJ) Times-Advertiser*, Apr. 3, 1932; "Woman Vice Crusader Jailed in Philadelphia," *Boston Daily Globe*, May 25, 1932.

43. "Lindsay Courts Diana, but Philadelphia Says No," *NYT*, Aug. 22, 1967; "Monuments: New York's No More," *Time* 90 (Sept. 1, 1967).

44. David W. Dunlap, "A Gilded Goddess Would Rather Be in Philadelphia," *NYT*, Jan. 22, 2014; Cynthia Haveson Veloric, "Golden Girl: The Regilding of Saint-Gaudens' Diana," *Antique Fine Art* 13 (Autumn 2014): 126–29; "Gilding Diana," Philadelphia Museum of Art, accessed June 25, 2014, https://www.philamuseum.org/conservation/21.html. Cynthia Haveson Veloric, "Preservation Diary: The Regilding of Saint-Gaudens' Diana," *Nineteenth Century* 37 (Spring 2017): 38–41.

45. Grimes, "Interviews of Frances Grimes," tape 3, side B, AAA.

46. US Federal Census records, 1910; "Fairfield County Cemeteries," *USGenWeb Project* website, accessed Feb. 27, 2012, http://www.ctgenweb.org/county/cofairfield/pages/cemetery/cm_darien/springgrove.htm. As for Louis Clark, after his mother's death and

his burning of stacks of letters and papers relating to Saint-Gaudens, he moved to Los Angeles, where he worked as a machinist in the shipyards, married Alida Frances Provan, and had three sons. Around 1930 the family moved to San Diego, where Louis worked as a porter at a hospital. He died in that city in 1958. US Federal Census records 1900, 1920, 1930; California Death Index 1940–1997.

47. *Trenton (NJ) Evening Times*, Sept. 18, 1897; "The Drama," *NYT*, Nov. 21, 1897; "Theatrical Gossip," *NYT*, Dec. 16, 1897; US Federal Census records, 1900, Brooklyn Ward 22, Kings, New York, roll: 1059, 18B.

48. ASG to Julia Baird, Dec. 24, 1901, ASG File, Players Club, quoted in Wilkinson, *Uncommon Clay*, 313.

49. Stanley Irving Stuber and Thomas Curtis Clark, *Treasury of the Christian Faith* (New York: Association Press, 1949), 650.

50. Mullins Manufacturing Company advertising brochure.

51. Grissom, *Zinc Sculpture*, 652–53; "Old Mullins Plant's Statue of Diana 'Stood' atop Madison Square Garden," *Youngstown (OH) Vindicator*, Aug. 17, 1980; Stephen Pierson, "Davida Johnson Clark," in *Dictionary of Artists' Models*, ed. Jill Berk Jiminez (London: Fitzroy Dearborn, 2001), 119; Rafferty, "History of the Columbus Statue."

52. See Landau and Condit, *Rise of the New York Skyscraper*, 193; see Richard L. Kagan, *The Spanish Craze: America's Fascination with the Hispanic World, 1779–1939* (Lincoln: Univ of Nebraska Press, 2019).

53. "Garden Hears Last Roar of Gay Crowds," *NYT*, May 6, 1925.

Selected Bibliography

Baatz, Simon. *The Girl on the Velvet Swing: Sex, Murder, and Madness at the Dawn of the Twentieth Century.* New York: Mulholland Books, 2018.

Baker, Paul R. *Stanny: The Gilded Life of Stanford White.* New York: Free Press, 1989.

Baldwin, Charles C. *Stanford White.* First published 1931. Reprinted with a new introduction by Paul Goldberger. New York: Da Capo Press, 1976.

Berman, Miriam. *Madison Square: The Park and Its Celebrated Landmarks.* Layton, UT: Gibbs Smith, 2001.

Bolotin, Norm, and Christine Laing. *The World's Columbian Exposition.* Washington, DC: Preservation Press, 1992.

Bouton, Margaret Innes. "The Early Works of Augustus Saint-Gaudens." Master's thesis, Radcliffe College, 1946.

Broderick, Mosette. *Triumvirate: McKim, Mead & White, Art, Architecture, Scandal, and Class in America's Gilded Age.* New York: Alfred A. Knopf, 2010.

Burns, Sarah. *Inventing the Modern Artist: Art and Culture in Gilded Age America.* New Haven: Yale Univ. Press, 1996.

Chauncey, George. *Gay New York: Gender, Urban Culture, and the Making of the Gay Male World, 1890–1940.* New York: Basic Books, 1994.

Cortissoz, Royal. "The Metamorphosis of Diana." *Harper's Weekly* 37, (Nov. 25, 1893): 1124.

Crane, Esther. *The Gilded Age in New York, 1870–1910.* New York: Black Dog & Leventhal, 2016.

Craven, Wayne. *Stanford White: Decorator in Opulence and Dealer in Antiquities.* New York: Columbia Univ. Press, 2005.

Cummings, Mary. *Saving Sin City: William Travers Jerome, Stanford White, and the Original Crime of the Century.* New York: Pegasus Books, 2018.

Dimmick, Laurette. "Diana, 1893–94." In *American Sculpture in the Metropolitan Museum of Art*, vol. 1, edited by Thayer Tolles, 309. New York: Metropolitan Museum of Art, 1999.

Dryfhout, John H. "Diana." In *Metamorphoses in Nineteenth-Century Sculpture*, edited by Jeanne L. Wasserman, 201–17. Cambridge: Fogg Art Museum, Harvard Univ., 1975.

———. *The Work of Augustus Saint-Gaudens*. Hanover, NH: Univ. Press of New England, 1982.

Dunlop, M. H. *Gilded City: Scandal and Sensation in Turn-of-the-Century New York*. New York: Harper-Collins, 2001.

Greenthal, Kathryn. *Augustus Saint-Gaudens, Master Sculptor*. New York: Metropolitan Museum of Art, 1985.

Grimes, Frances. "A Sculptor's Life in the Early Twentieth Century," Rauner Special Collections, Dartmouth College Library, ASG Papers, box 44:14.

Hardin, Jennifer. "The Nude in the Era of the New Movement in American Art: Thomas Eakins, Kenyon Cox, and Augustus Saint-Gaudens." PhD dissertation, Yale Univ., 2000.

Landau, Sarah Bradford, and Carl W. Condit. *Rise of the New York Skyscraper, 1865–1913*. New Haven: Yale Univ. Press, 1996.

Lee, Elizabeth, "The Electrified Goddess: Augustus Saint-Gaudens, Stanford White and Diana at Madison Square Garden," *Nineteenth Century* 31, no. 1 (Spring 2011): 13–24.

Lessard, Suzannah. *The Architect of Desire: Beauty and Danger in the Stanford White Family*. New York: Dial Press, 1996.

Lowe, David Garrard. *Stanford White's New York*. New York: Watson-Guptill, 1999.

Magonigle, H. Van Buren. "A Half Century of Architecture, 2–7," *Pencil Points* 15 (Jan., Mar., May, July, Sept., Nov. 1934), 9–12ff.

Millet, Frank D., "The Decoration of the Exposition," in Frank D. Millet et al, *Some Artists at the Fair*. New York: Charles Scribner's Sons, 1893, 1–42.

Mooney, Michael MacDonald. *Evelyn Nesbit and Stanford White: Love and Death in the Gilded Age*. New York: William Morrow, 1976.

Moore, Charles. *The Life and Times of Charles Follen McKim*. Boston: Houghton Mifflin, 1929.

———. *The Life of Daniel H. Burnham, Architect, Planner of Cities*, 2 vols. Boston: Houghton Mifflin, 1921.

Musée des Augustins. *Augustus Saint-Gaudens: A Master of American Sculpture*. Paris: Musée des Augustins, 1999.

Nichols, Rose Standish, ed. "Familiar Letters of Augustus Saint-Gaudens." *McClure's Magazine* 31 (Oct. 1908): 603–16, and 32 (Nov. 1908): 1–16.

Ochsendorf, John Allen. *Guastavino Vaulting: The Art of Structural Tile*. New York: Princeton Architectural Press, 2010.

Osmundson, Theodore. *Roof Gardens: History, Design, and Construction*. New York: W. W. Norton, 1999.

Roth, Leland M. *The Architecture of McKim, Mead & White 1870–1920: A Building List*. New York: Garland Publishing, 1978.

———. *McKim, Mead & White, Architects*. New York: Harper & Row, 1983.

Saarinen, Aline. Aline and Eero Sarinen Papers, 1906–77, Archives of American Art, Smithsonian Institution.

Saint-Gaudens, Augustus. Augustus Saint-Gaudens Papers, 1891–1920. MMC–1668, Library of Congress, Washington, DC.

———. Papers of Augustus Saint-Gaudens. Rauner Special Collections, Dartmouth College Library.

———. "Reminiscences of an Idiot" [1905] typescript, Rauner ML-4, 44:16, Augustus Saint-Gaudens Papers, Rauner Special Collections, Dartmouth College Library.

Saint-Gaudens, Homer. *The American Artist and His Times*. New York: Dodd, Mead, 1941.

———. *Augustus Saint-Gaudens, Adapted from a Lecture Given by His Son, Homer Saint-Gaudens*. Cornish, NH: Saint-Gaudens Memorial, 1927.

———. "Augustus Saint-Gaudens Established: The Reminiscences of Augustus Saint-Gaudens," *The Century* 78 (June 1909): 212–28.

———. "Saint-Gaudens the Master: The Reminiscences of Augustus Saint-Gaudens," *The Century* 78 (Aug. 1909): 611–26.

Saint-Gaudens, Homer, ed. "Intimate Letters of Stanford White: Correspondence with His Friend and Co-Worker Augustus Saint-Gaudens," *Architectural Record* 30, no. 2–4 (Aug., Sept., Oct., 1911), 106–16ff.

———. *The Reminiscences of Augustus Saint-Gaudens*. 2 vols. New York: Century, 1913.

Schiller, Joyce K. "The Artistic Collaboration of Augustus Saint-Gaudens and Stanford White." PhD dissertation, Washington Univ., 1997.

Smart, Mary. *A Flight with Fame: The Life and Art of Frederick MacMonnies*. Madison, CT: Sound View Press, 1996.

Tharp, Louise Hall. *Saint-Gaudens and the Gilded Era*. Boston: Little, Brown, 1969.

Tolles, Thayer. "Augustus Saint-Gaudens, *Diana of the Tower*, ca. 1899–1907." In *American Dreams: American Art to 1950 in the Williams College Museum of Art*, edited by Nancy Mowll Mathews, 102–5. New York: Hudson Hills Press in association with the Williams College Museum of Art, 2001.

Tunick, Susan. *Terra-Cotta Skyline: New York's Architectural Ornament*. New York: Princeton Architectural Press, 1997.

Uruburu, Paula. *American Eve: Evelyn Nesbit, Stanford White, the Birth of the "It" Girl*. New York: Riverhead Books, 2008.

Van Rensselaer, Mrs. Schuyler [Mariana Griswold]. "The Madison Square Garden," *The Century* 45, no. 25 (Mar. 1894): 732–47.

Wasserman, Jeanne L. *Diana in Late Nineteenth-Century Sculpture: A Theme in Variations*. Wellesley: Wellesley College Museum, 1989.

Wasserman, Jeanne L., ed. *Metamorphoses in Nineteenth-Century Sculpture*. Cambridge: Fogg Art Museum, Harvard Univ., 1975.

White, Samuel G., and Elizabeth White. *McKim, Mead & White: The Masterworks*. New York: Random House, 2003.

White, Stanford. *Stanford White: Letters to His Family*. Edited by Claire Nicolas White. New York: Rizzoli, 1997.

Wilson, Richard Guy. *McKim, Mead & White, Architects*. New York: Rizzoli, 1983.

Wodehouse, Lawrence. *White of McKim, Mead and White*. New York: Garland Publishing, 1988.

Index

Page numbers appearing in italics refer to illustrations.

Abbey, Edward Austin, 124, 151, 268
Abu Ya'qub al-Mansur, 222
Abu Ya'qub Yusuf, 221–22
Académie des Beaux-Arts, 43
Académie Nationale de Musique-Théâtre
　de l'Opéra, 153, 378n26
accidents: Barnum's Roman Hippodrome,
　71; explosives, 112; Gilmore's Garden
　building collapse, 74–76; MSG I col-
　lapse, 77–81, 361nn34–35. *See also* fires
　and fire safety
Actors Fund Fair, 248
Adams, Edward Dean, 22
Adams, Herbert, 334
Adams Memorial (Saint-Gaudens), 8, 136
Adler, Margaret, 202
advertising: built-up Phoenix, 130; *Diana*
　as, 239; Franconi's Hippodrome, 33;
　Guastavino's firm, 191; MSG II, 147–48,
　187, 207, 249–50, 334–35; MSG II tower
　apartments, 282; Saint-Gaudens's
　reproductions, 299
Aesthetics Movement, 225
African Americans, 37
Agostini, Joseph, 22
Ahmad ibn Basu, 221–22
air conditioning and heating, 38–39, 134
Albermarle Hotel, 39, 66, 353n37

alcohol, selling of, 167–68, 177
Ali al-Ghumari, 222
Alien Contract Labor Law, 166
Allen, Louise, 174
Allen, Ray, 174
Almohad Empire, 220–22
American Architect, 69, 333, 334
American Architect and Building News, 49,
　191, 226
American Art Association, 84–85
American Colonial style, 106
American Museum of Art, 390n43
"Americans" (hockey team), 324
American Safe Deposit Building, 148
American Society for the Suppression of
　the Jews, 353n37
American style, 5
Amon Carter Museum of American Art,
　304, 413n64
Angelina (model), 357n35
Angel of Purity (Saint-Gaudens), 375n29
Angel with a Tablet (Saint-Gaudens),
　375n29
Apollo Belvedere (Saint-Gaudens), 200
archery, 137
Architect of Desire (Lessard), 117–18
architectural education and training, 43,
　111. *See also specific school*

431

Ardisson, Gaétan, 214, 215, 300, 392n10

Armory Hall, 123

Army, Navy, and Civilian Boxing Board of Control, 318–19

Aronson, Rudolph, 246, 250–51, 253, 400n27

Arthur, Chester A., 225

artistic freedom, 238–41. *See also* nudes and nudity; obscenity/obscenity laws

art reductions and reproductions: as an industry, 293; Falguière's works, 99; MacMonnies's works, 101–2, *102*, 293, 294, 410n11; Saint-Gaudens's works, 291–304, 323, 325, 335, 337, 409n5, 410n18

Arts and Crafts Movement, 224–25, 394n13

Art Students League, 158–64, *161*, 198, 199, 392n5, 410n18

Art Workers' Club for Women, 388n14

Assembly Ball, 186, 385n28

Association against the Defamation of *Diana*, 338

Aster, John Jacob, 95

Aster, Mrs. John Jacob, 187

Astor, Mrs. William, 385n28

Astor, William Waldorf, 22

Atalanta (Greek mythology), 128

athletics: archery, 137; baseball, 31; bicycle racing, 91; boxing, 21, 83, 192, 318–20, 324–25; ice hockey, 324; walking, 74–76; women and, 91, 100, 137

Atlanta Terra Cotta Company, 377n13

Aubry Brothers, 296, 300, 301, 412n38

Avery Architectural and Fine Arts Library (Columbia University), 117

Avet, Louis, 52, 123

Babb, George Fletcher, 120–21, 370n26

bachelor homes, 118–20, 123, 282

Badger Babb Club, 120

Bailey, James Anthony, 147, 376n1

Baird, Julia "Dudie," 268–72, 340, 404n18

Baker, Paul R., 15, 116–17

Baldwin, C. C., 22

Balin, Paul, 384n5

ballet, 157–58, 165–66, 168, 174–75, 176–77

Bank of America, 338–39

Barnum, Phineas T., 70–73, 80–81, 147, 219

Barnum & Bailey Circus, 91, 95, 134, 147, 192, 376n1

Barnum Museum Company, 80–81

Barnum's American Museum, 70

Barnum's Roman Hippodrome, 70–73, *71*, 80

baseball, 31

Beale, Truxton, 415n14

Beaux-Arts style, 5, 19, 228

Becera, Paul A., 416n38

Beckwith, J. Carroll, 195, 286, 307

Bedi-Makky Art Foundry, 414n68

Belmont, August, II, 66

Benedick, 118–20, 123

Benedict, Helen Ripley, 122

Bennett, James Gordon, Jr., 27–28, 66, 74

Berbers, 220–22

Bernhardt, Sarah, 191–92, 225, 226, 353n37

Biard, Pierre I., 107–8

bicycle racing, 91

Biddle-Gaumer Company, 424n40

Bierstadt, Albert, 77, 78, 79

Bigelow, Kennard & Co., 296

Bigelow, William, 45

Biltmore House, 151

Binks, Joseph, 265

Bion, Paul, 261, 294, 402n31

bisexuality, 117–18

blizzards, 90, 364n8

Boldini, Giovanni, 181–82, 384n9

Bollman, Wendel, 130

Boston Daily Globe, 274

Boston Herald, 260–61, 271

Boston Public Library, 18, 113, 120, 190, 291, 296, 391n20, 409n3

Boucicault, Dion, 133–34

Bouguereau, William, 39

Bowdoin, George S., 22

Bowery, 123

boxing, 21, 83, 192, 318–20, 324–25

Boylan, Alexis L., 124

Braem, Henry M., 149

Brattle Square Church (Boston), 44–45, 368n19

Breese, James, 283

bricks: amount of, 6, 96, 128–30, 134, 205; collapse of, 78–79, 89; dismantling of, 317, 323; as filler, 151; Hudson River, 129; patterns, 210, 222, 227; reuse of, 89; Roman, 134, 148–49; safety and, 167, 247; substitutes for, 148–49, 227; as support, 188, 206

Broderick, Mosette, 117

bronze d'art, 293

Brook club, 46

Brookgreen Gardens, 414n68

Brooklyn Eagle, 20

Brooklyn Museum, 304

Brooks and Denton, 250

Brown, Elmer Ellsworth, 326

Browne, Grant Hugh, 318

Bruni, Frank, 118

building and construction, 126–35; acoustics, 168, 398n6; architectural terra cotta, 149; built-up Phoenix, 129–30, 373n21, 390n6; cast iron, 129–30; cooling and heating, 38–39, 134; demolition of MSG I, 89–90, 95–96, 108, 112; demolition of MSG II, 324, 325–26,

327–28, *128*; diagonal wind-bracing, 206, 390n6; Guastavino Tile Arch System, 189–91; ironwork, 36, 97–98, 129–30, 131–32, 153, 365n2; plumbing systems, 167; Portland cement, 191, 387n48, 390n1; puddle iron, 97, 365n2; riveting, 130, 131–32, 217, 233, 275, 323, 332; rolled wrought iron, 129–30; Rosendale cement mortar, 205, 390n1; skeleton steel framing, 206, 390n6; strikes, 165; timbrel vaulting, 189–91; truss systems, 130–33, 373n26; ventilation systems, 184–85, 208; weather, building for, 206; wrought-iron beams, 36, 97–98, 129, 132, 153. *See also* bricks; elevators; fires and fire safety; lighting; terra cotta

built-up Phoenix, 129–30, 373n21, 390n6

Burnham, Daniel Hudson, 243, 257, 258–59, 283, 400n9, 402n49

Burnham, Franklin P., 284

Burns Restaurant & Hotel, 314–15

Butler, Prescott Hall, 23

Byrne & Tucker, 167

Café de Paris (roof garden), 252–53

Café Martin, 47

Cameron, Mose, 326

cannabis, 119

Capri, Ugo da, *204*

Carmencita, 150, 151, 157, 188

Carnegie, Andrew, 22, 94

Carnegie Hall, 373n32

Carrara marble, 145

Carrère & Hastings, 121

Carrier-Belleuse, Albert-Ernest, 293

Carter, Robert, *312*

Cartwright, Alexander J., 31

Casino Theatre (New York), 174, 226, 246, 247, 249–50, 250–51, 252

Casino Theatre (Newport, RI), 27–28, 179–80, 181, 187

cast iron, 129–30

Cellini, Benvento, 138

Century, 237, 238

Century Association Clubhouse, 46, 115–16, *116*, 120, 135, 147, 151, 313

Chase, William Merritt, 9, 58, 159, 197, 199, 264

Cherry Blossom Grove (roof garden), 252–53

Chicago: great fire, 149; Haymarket riot, 165; sculptures, 8, 92

Chicago Art Institute, 329, 331, *332*

Chicago Daily Inter Ocean, 286–87

Chicago Daily Tribune, 262

Chicago Herald, 262

Chicago Tribune, 176, 286–87, 332–33

Chicago World's Fair (Columbian Exposition): Cold Storage Warehouse fire, 283–87, 329–30; commemorative medal for, 291, 296; *Diana* and, 9, 243–45, 254–66, 283–87, 329–30, 332; popularity of art reductions, 293

"Choosing the National Flower" (ballet), 157, 174

Christine Roussel, Inc., 414n68

Church, Frederick, 159

Churchill, Randolph, 83

Churchill, Winston, 83

Circe Drinking (Capri), *204*

Cirque des Champs-Élysées, 32

Civil War, 36–38

Clark, Davida Johnson, *143*, 143–46; birth of, 143; child with Saint-Gaudens, 9, 125, 158, 272n47, 339, 389nn32–33, 411n35, 424n46; death of, 339–40,

376n34, 424n46; in France, 411n35; home of, 265, 339–40; as model for *Angel with the Tablet*, 375n29; as model for *Diana*, 143, 158, 200–202, *201*, 271, 339–40, 389n32; name of, 145–46, 265, 376n33, 376n35; as Saint-Gaudens's mistress, 9–10, 125, 158, 198, 200, 264–65, 339–40

Clark, Edward, 362n45

Clark, Kate, 271

Clark, Louis John (Davida's grandson), 389nn32–33

Clark, Louis Paul "Novy" (Davida's son), 9, 125, 158, 272n47, 339, 389nn32–33, 411n35, 424n46

Clark, Robert Sterling, 353n42

Cleopatra (play), 191–92

Cleveland Museum of Art, 304

Codman, Ogden, Jr., 293

Cold Storage Palace (Chicago World's Fair), 283–87, 329–30

Cole, Thomas, 77

Coleman, Samuel, 224

Collas machine, 293

Collector, 242, 244, 259

Collier's Weekly, 240, 311

Colonie club, 46

Colored Orphan Society, 37

Columbia Hall, 123

Columbian celebration (New York), 264

Columbian Exposition. *See* Chicago World's Fair

Columbia University, 117, 264

Comstock, Anthony, 164, 238–41, 243, 262, 270, 276, 417n51

Concert Club, 119

concert halls, 28, 72–73, 133, 373n32

Coney Island, 73

Conkling, Roscoe, 364n8

Connelly, Mary Ann, 361n34

Conner Rosencranz Gallery, 414n68

Conradi, Joseph, 422n15

Constantinople (Istanbul), 48, 224

Contamin, Victor, 365n3

Cook, Daniel, 120

cooling and heating, 38–39, 134

Cooper, Peter, 129

copyright, 295, 301, 323, 411n19

Cornelius Vanderbilt II mansion, 144

Cornish, NH, 300–302, 303, 322–23, 335, 366n10, 370n26, 423n30. *See also* Saint-Gaudens National Historical Park

Cornish Colony Museum (Windsor, VT), 414n68

Cortissoz, Royal, *117*, 277

Coup, W. C., 70, 72

Cox, Kenyon, 144, 159–60, 164, 268, 286

Crane, Walter, 272

Cressonois, Paul, 157–58, 174

Crocker, Charles, 22

Curtis, F. S., 80

Dakota apartment building, 81, 362n45

Daly, Lillie, 267–68

Darling, Alfred P., 22

David (Donatello), 272

David (Mercié), 145

David (Michelangelo), 145

Davida. *See* Clark, Davida Johnson

Davidson, Peter, 414n68

Dazien & Co., 166

Decoration of Houses (Wharton), 293

De Costa, Benjamin Franklin, 239–41

Degas, Edgar, 374n2

De Kay, Charles, 228

Delano, Sara, 23

De la Renta, Oscar, 410n18

Della Robbia, Andrea, 62

Delmonico, Charles C., 46–47

Delmonico, Giovanni (John), 47

Delmonico, Pietro (Peter), 47

Delmonico's restaurant, 46–47, 65, 81, 186, 278

Del Varga, Perino, 229

Democratic Party, 7, 20, 39, 172–73

Depew, Chauncy M., 173

De Quélin, René Théophile, 365n6

De Vargas, Luis, 229

Dewing, Thomas Wilmer: on *Diana*, 243; friendships of, 9, 119; homes of, 119; models for, 197, 204, 268, 269; Sewer Club and, 121, 187, 370n28; studio of, 187–88; works of, 120, 204, 269

diagonal wind-bracing, 206, 390n6

Diana (MacMonnies), 98–103, *102*, 137, 293, 294, 365n6

Diana of the Crosswinds (first sculpture): costs of, 218; critiques of, 8, 216, 234, 237–45, 262–64; defects and modifications, 9, 218, 238, 241, 254–55, 267, 335, 340; description of, 8–9; fires and, 235, 284–87, 329–30; illumination of, 8, 49, 232–33, 234, 235, 236, 395n17; inauthenticity of pose, 238; inspiration for, 9, 98–103, 136–46, 367n17, 374n2; installation of, 230–36, *233*; "interview" with, 244; locations of, 329–41, 422n6; models for, 9–10, 158–59, 162–63, 195–204, 339–40, 392n5; name of, 8; plans for, 104–12, 128; poem about, 255; preliminary sketches, *108*; removal to Chicago World's Fair, 9, 243–45, 254–66, 283–87, 329–30, 332; sculpting process, 9, 212–18, 392n3, 392n9; size and proportion of, 241–43, 245, 260; unveiling of, 8–10, 229, 235–36; weather vane positioning, 107

Diana of the Crosswinds (second sculpture): copyright of, 295, 301, 323, 411n19; costs of, 275, 277; critiques of, 276, 277, 280; dismantling of, 324, 326–28, 334; inspiration for, 277; installation of, 277–80; models for, 267–72, 291, 340, 405n26, 405n38; new location for, 322–39, *339*; reductions and reproductions of, 99, 291–304, 323; repair and upkeep, 321; sculpting process, 267–80, 405n26; size and proportion of, 276, 277, 278, 280; value of (1925), 322

Diana of the Tower (Saint-Gaudens), 296, 297, *298*, 301, 302, 329

Diana Smiling (Saint-Gaudens), *142*

Diana the Huntress (Houdon), *139*, 139–40, 293, 301

Dictionary of Greek and Roman Antiquities, 136

Dictionnaire des antiquités, 136–37

discrimination, 353n37

Dodworth dance studio, 47

dog shows, 73, 74, 91, 192

Doll & Richards Fine Arts, 296, 299

Donatello, 62, 64, 272, 365n6

Draft Riots, 36

drug use, 119, 308–9, 370n21

Dryfhout, John, 202

Drysdale, Charles, 326–27

Dubois, Paul, 293

Dudley, Henry J., 80

Dundee, "Italian" Johnny, 325

Dutert, Ferdinand, 365n3

École des Beaux-Arts (Paris): ateliers established for, 99, 356n24; Hastings and, 121; Hunt and, 19; MacMonnies and, 99, 145; McKim and, 17, 44, 60; neoclassical style of, 61; prizes awarded by, 99; Richardson and, 43; Saint-Gaudens and, 54–55, 142, 200

École Gratuite de Dessin (Paris), 54, 200

Édifices de Rome Moderne (Letarouilly), 113

Edison, Thomas, 84, 98

Edward VII (king), 35

Eickemeyer, Rudolf, 308

Eiffel, Gustav, 206

Eiffel Tower, 91, 97, 365n2, 373n23

elevators: cost of, 35; effects of invention of, 129; Eiffel Tower, 97; fire safety and, 251–52; hydraulic, 97; MSG II tower, 7, 90, 111, 112, 167, 209; piston-driven, 97; rope-hoisted, 352n25; screw, 35–36, 352n25; steam-powered, 112, 167, 223; tourist pay-to-ride, 7, 90, 97, 111, 209, 249

Ellis, Mary "Joan of Arc" Hubbert, 337–38

Elwell, F. Edwin, 380n24

Engineering Record, 167

Enniskillen Dragoons, 157

Eno, Amos F., 34–35, 351n20

equestrian events, 21, 32–33, 66–67, 74, 81–83, 182–85, *183*, 192

Espinosa, Leon, 157–58

Evening World, 274, 280

Eve Tempted (Powers), 141

explosives, 112

Fairchild, Mary, 100–101

"fairie," defined, 122–23

Fairmont Park Association, 336–37

Faith (Giralda Tower, Seville), 49, *93*, 93–94, 106, 223, 228–29

Falguière, Jean-Alexandre-Joseph, 99, 107, 137, 293, 301

Fame (Biard), 107–8

Fame (Mercié), 107–8, 368n19

F. & D. Company, 318

Farragut Monument (Saint-Gaudens), 60–65, *65*; casting of, 63, 294; collaboration with White, 8; commission for, 59; copyright for, 301; dedication of, 64; homeless and, 358n63; Louis Saint-Gaudens's role, 61, 63, 92, 200, 358n62; nudity and, 200; reception of, 64–65, 145; Rhind's work and, 422n8; studio for, 59, 92, 98

Federated Trades, 158

Fellowes, Cornelius, 22

female models: for *Diana* (first sculpture), 9–10, 158–59, 162–63, 195–204, 339–40, 392n5; for *Diana* (second sculpture), 267–72, 291, 340, 405n26, 405n38; as employment, 160, 197, 388n14; White's preferences for, 63, 307–8, 312–13, 315, 416n34, 417n51. *See also* Baird, Julia "Dudie"; Clark, Davida Johnson; Nesbit, Florence Mary "Evelyn"

Festspielhaus (Germany), 180

Field, Benjamin H., 67

Field Columbian Museum, 329–30

Fifth Avenue Hotel, 34–37, 38, 39, 351n20

"Fight of the Century" (1910), 319–20

figure drawing, 158–64, 195–204, 238–39, 291

fires and fire safety: arson, 286–87; Barnum's American Museum fire, 70; Barnum's Roman Hippodrome fires, 70; Chicago World's Fair building fires, 284–87; *Diana* sculpture (first) and, 235, 284–87, 329–30; elevators and, 251–52; Franconi's Hippodrome fire, 33; Hoffman House fire, 41; near MSG, 210–11; MSG II Amphitheatre and, 167, 171; New York House of Refuge fire, 30; roof garden fire escapes, 251–52;

safety regulations and, 82, 167, 171; Saint-Gaudens studio fires, 304

Fisher, Harrison, 197

Fisk, James, Jr., 39–40

Fite, Charles, 340

Fitzpatrick, Nellie, 268

Flatiron Building, 317

Florodora (musical), 313

Flying Mercury (Giambologna), 108, *109*

Fogg Art Museum (Harvard), 304

Fortuna statues, 106, 243, 367n17

Fountain of Diana (sculpture), 138, 375n12

four-in-hand driving, 66–67

Franconi's Hippodrome, 32–33

Frank, Nathaniel, 118

Franklin Fireproof Warehouse, 326, 336

Frawley Law, 318

Frederick Keppel Gallery, 296

freedom of expression, 238–41. *See also* nudes and nudity; obscenity/obscenity laws

French, Daniel Chester, 164, 166–67, 249, 258, 283, 302–3

French, Mrs. Daniel Chester, 124

French, T. Henry, 148, 170

French Gothic style, 106

Fuller, Loie, 250–51

Gambrill, Charles, 43, 44

Gambrill & Richardson, 43–45, 66–67, 358n2

Garden, M. G., 330

Garden Athletic Club, 318

Garnier, Alfred, 123–24, 312

Garnier, Charles, 378n26

Garrison, William Lloyd, 17

Gayle, Margot, 329–30, 332

Gay White Way, 4

Gellatly, Edith Rogers, 390n43

Gellatly, John, 390n43

Giambologna, 108, *109*

Gibbs, Montgomery, 56

Gibson, Charles Dana, 100, 159, 268, 307

Gilbert, Bradford, 207

Gilbert, Cass, 321–22, 324, 326

"Gilded Age," origin of term, 6

Gilmore, Patrick Sarsfield, 72–73, 250, 252

Gilmore's Garden, 72–76

Giralda bell tower (Spain), 3, 49, *93*, 93–94, 106, 219–29, *221*, 334

Goddess of Light (Adams), 334

Goelet, Harriet Louise Warren (Mrs. Robert), 283

Goelet, Mrs. Ogden, 181

Goelet, Robert, 283

Goelets, the, 19

Goodyear, Stephen, 413n64

Gorham, 413n62

Goujon, Jean, 375n12

Grand Central Depot, 70

Grand Central Station, 147

Grant, Hugh J., 134, 172

Grant, Ulysses S., 37

Great London Circus, 376n1

Great Roman Hippodrome, 70–73, *71*, 80

Great White Way, 317, 346n7

Greek Sculpture (von Mach), 137

Greek Slave (Powers), 141

Green-Wood Cemetery, 92

Grimes, Frances, 358n62, 412n41

Gruet, Adolphe, 63, 294

Gruet, Edmund-Paul, 294

Guastavino Fireproof Construction Company, 190–91

Guastavino Tile Arch System, 189–91

Guastavino Vaulting (Ochsendorf), 191

Gulliver, W. C., 22

Hahnemann Homeopathic-Hospital Fair, 77–81

Hammerstein, Oscar, 166–68

Hammerstein's Paradise Roof Garden, 252–53

Hammerstein's Theatre, 373n32

Hardenbergh, Henry, 81

Hardin, Jennifer, 271

Harlem Railroad Company, 21, 69–70, 80

Harmonie club, 46

Harper's Magazine, 226

Harper's New Monthly, 176

Harper's Weekly: article about MSG project, 126; *Diana* sculpture (first), 234; *Diana* sculpture (second), 276; MSG II as investment, 148; MSG II tower, 208, 219, 228; publishing of MSG II plans, 21; representation of Giralda tower in, 49

Harrigan's Theatre, 373n32

Hastings, Thomas "Tommy," 116, 121–22, 124, 402n45

Hay, Helen, 413n50

Hay, John, 413n50

Hayes, Rutherford B., 18

Haymarket Square riot, 165

Head of an Infant (Velasquez), 226

Hearst, William Randolph, 416n38

heating and cooling, 38–39, 134

Hegeman, Anna B., 361n34

Henderson, W. J., 255

Henry C. Nevins Tomb (Saint-Gaudens), 409n3

Hercules Iron Works, 284

Herter Brothers, 391n20

Hewitt, Peter Cooper, 283

Hiawatha (Saint-Gaudens), 55–56, 143, 200

Higinbotham, Harlow N., 262

Hill, David B., 172

Hilton, Henry, 349n41, 353n37

Hippodrome (P. T. Barnum's), 70–73, 71, 80

Hippotheatron, 70

Hitchcock, Hiram, 22, 90, 91, 351n20

Hoffman, John T., 39

Hoffman House, 39–41, 40, 66, 353n42

Holbein Studio Building, 187

Homer, Augusta. See Saint-Gaudens, Augusta "Gussie" Homer

Homer, Eugenie (Genie), 62, 348n25

Homer, Winslow, 56, 58, 119

homosexuality, 60, 116–17, 122–23, 124, 315

Hooper, Marian "Clover," 92

Hoppin, Francis, 242, 395n7

Horn, John, 30–31

horses. See equestrian events

Hosmer, Harriet, 53–54

Hotel Brunswick, 66–67, 89, 358n2

Hotel Imperial, 120, 148, 187

Hotel Plaza, 268

Houdon, Jean-Antoine, 139, 139–40, 301, 393

Howard, John Galen, 334

Howe, Seth B., 32

Howells, William Dean, 18, 171–72

Hoyt, Henry E., 181, 384n8

Hudson River Railroads, 70

Hultgren, Albertina. See Clark, Davida Johnson

Humphrey Popcorn Company, 334

Humphries, Joe, 325

Hunt, Richard Morris, 19, 105, 151, 207, 257, 258, 264

H. Wunderlich & Co., 296, 301

Hyde, James T., 22

ice hockey, 324

Indianapolis Museum of Art, 304

Inness, George, 77, 159, 361n35

ironwork, 36, 97–98, 129–30, 131–32, 153, 365n2

Iselin, Adrien, 22, 67

Istanbul (Constantinople), 48, 224

Italian Renaissance style, 5, 18, 105–6, 108, 116, 138, 189, 223, 367nn14–15

Jay, William, 66

Jeffries, James J., 320

Jerome, Jennie, 83

Jerome, Leonard, 66, 83–84

Johnson, Davida. See Clark, Davida Johnson

Johnson, Eastman, 77

Johnson, John Arthur "Jack," 319–20

Johnson, Maria Louisa, 376n34

Jones, Edith, 34

Joslin Construction Company, 324

Jouffroy, François, 54, 99, 107

Judson Memorial Church, 148, 207

Jugged Club, 120

Kane, DeLancey Astor, 66

Keats, John, 145–46, 376n33

Kendall, William Mitchell, 148, 149, 377n7

Kertbeny, Karl-Maria, 122

KIFE, 119

Kimball, Fiske, 324, 326, 336, 338

King, David H., Jr., 104, 111–12, 126–27, 134, 156, 188, 209, 235

King, Van Rensselaer, 235

King Model Houses, 127

Kingsley, Darwin P., 322, 323, 326, 328, 335–37

Kirstein, Lincoln, 410n18

Kittredge, Clark & Co., 215–16

Knickerbocker Athletic Club, 74, 313
Knickerbocker Base Ball and Social Club, 31
Knight, J. B., 254–55
Knoedler Gallery, 239
Knowles, John H., 64
Koechlin, Maurice, 365n2
Konti, Isidore, 401n25
Koster & Bial's Music Hall, 28, 150
Krafft-Ebing, Richard von, 122
Kurtz Studio, 234–35

labor movement, 165–66
La Farge, John, 42, 58, 77, 106, 113, 119, 144, 264, 283
Lamb, Thomas W., 324
Lambs club, 46
Lamina (Keats), 145–46, 376n33
Lander, John, 184
landscape architecture, 37, 256–57
Lanier, Charles, 22
Lathrop, Francis, 49, 58, 120
Lathrop, George, 226
L. C. Tiffany & Associated Artists, 224–25
Le Brethon, Jules, 52–53, 123
Le France, Bertie, 74
Lenz, Oscar, 392n5
Leslie Hindman Auctioneers, 333
Lessard, Suzannah, 117–18
Letarouilly, Paul, 113
licenses and permits, 134, 167–68, 177, 188, 318–19, 418n13
life drawing. *See* figure drawing
lighting: anecdotes about, 210–11;
    Barnum's Roman Hippodrome, 73;
    Chicago World's Fair, 265; of *Diana*, 8,
    49, 232–33, 234, 235, 236, 395n17; fires,

41; Franconi's Hippodrome, 33; Gay
    White Way, 4; Gilmore's Garden, 76;
    MacKaye's Lyceum Theatre, 84; MSG
    II, 76, 77, 81, 91, 110, 165, 171, 173, 175,
    179, 210–11, 248, 325; in Paris, 97, 98;
    Washington Square Arch, 103; White's
    tower apartment, 282, 325
Lincoln, Abraham, 36, 37, 301
Lindsay, John, 338
liquor laws, 167–68, 177
Little Dancer, Fourteen Years Old (Degas), 374n2
long-distance walking, 74–76
Lord & Taylor, 74
Lorme-Aubry bronze foundry, 296
Louis XVI style, 3, 181, 187
Louvre Museum, 140
Lovelace, Francis, 30
Lovely Lane First Methodist Church, 207, 208
Low, Will, 145–46, 376n33
Lyceum Theatre, 84

Mach, Edmund von, 137
MacKaye, Steele, 38, 84
MacMonnies, Frederick William: Chi-
    cago World's Fair and, 258, 261, 265,
    329; *Diana* sculpture, 98–103, *102*, 137,
    293, 294, 365n6; education, 99, 145;
    Falguière and, 99, 137; inspirations of,
    298; *Pan of Rohallion* sculpture, 410n11;
    reductions and reproductions of
    artwork, 101–2, *102*, 293, 294, 410n11;
    Running Cupid with His Bow sculp-
    ture, 298; Saint-Gaudens and, 98–103,
    145, 261, 265, 366n10; Saint Paul the
    Apostle Catholic Church, 101; social
    life of, 283; *Standing Cupid* sculpture,

298; Washington Square Arch, 103; *Young Faun with Heron* sculpture, 410n11

MacMonnies, Mary Fairchild., 100–101, 265

Madison Club, 363n55

Madison Cottage, 32, 34

Madison Square Garden I (1879–90), 66–85, *77*; building collapse, 77–81, 361nn34–35; commissioning of, 19–22, 28; demolition of, 89–90, 95–96, 108, 112; Gilmore's Garden, 72–76; opening of, 76; purpose of, 69, 76–77, *77*; repairs and improvements, 76–82; safety issues, 82

Madison Square Garden II (1890–1925): arcade for, 134, 188–91, *189*, *190*; building costs, 5, 20, 90–91, 94–95, 104, 108, 127, 134, 150, 209, 248, 316; commissioning of, 19–22, 47–49, 90–91; construction of, 110, 126–35, *131*, *133*, 147–56, 165, 169, 188–91; construction schedule, 147, 157, 165; critiques of, 20, 47, 155–56, 168, 187, 252; demolition of, 324, 325–26, 327–28, *328*; early events at, 3; effects on neighborhood, 238–39; entrances, *152*, *155*; excavation for, 112; last performances at, 324–25; legacy of, 305, 341; location of, 4–5, 192; management of, 147, 170, 171, 177, 209, 316; opening and dedication, 3, 5–7, 9–10, 157–58, 165–68, 169–78; operating costs, 209, 316–17; ownership of, 21; plans for, *48*, 49, 90–95, 104–12, *110*, 126, 190–91; popularity of, 192; purpose of, 20, 21, 94, 177, 192, 305, 319–21; roof garden, 4, 110, 151, 153–54, *154*, 246–53, *251*, 318, 320; sale of, 316, 317–21, 418n8; site purchase cost, 21–22; size of, 3;

style of, 3, 153–54, 169, 189; swimming pool, 320; ticket sales (opening), 170; ticket sales (post-opening), 177; views from, 7; White's murder at, 9–10, 305–15

Madison Square Garden II Amphitheatre: acoustics, 168, 398n6; building costs, 209; construction of, 129–30, *133*, 134, 151, 154, 157, 165, 167, 169; critiques of, 168, 170, 175–76, 177–78; fire and, 167, 171; future of, 317; inspiration for, 28; opening of, 169–78; planning for, 20, 109, 111, 127; purpose of, 177, 192; safety of, 167, 171

Madison Square Garden II Concert & Assembly Hall, 185–87

Madison Square Garden II Theatre, 3, 170, 179–82, *180*, 191–92, 226, 231–32, 249, 317

Madison Square Garden II Tower: apartments in, 6, 10, 249, 281–82, 308, 325; building costs, 6, 90–91, 127, 219; construction of, 205–11, 219–22, 227; critiques of, 205, 207, 208, 219, 227–29, 237–45; dedication of, 5–7, 9, 237–38; demolition of, 324, 327–28, *328*; elevator in, 7, 90, 111, 112, 167, 209, 235; height of, 4; hidden stairways in, 320; inspirations for, 44–45, 49, 91, *93*, 93–94, 128, 219–29, *221*; lights from, 210–11; opening of, 5–7; plans for, 49, 90–94, 127, 128, *208*, 219–22; proposed removal of, from plans, 127; tower symbolism, 207–9. *See also Diana of the Crosswinds* (first sculpture); *Diana of the Crosswinds* (second sculpture)

Madison Square Garden III (1925–68), 321–22, 324

Madison Square Garden IV (1968–), 338

Madison Square Garden Company:
amphitheater acoustics and, 168,
398n6; ballet costume scandal, 165–66;
board members, 6, 21–22, 90–91, 134,
158, 209, 317; building committee,
90–91, 127; centennial celebration,
414n68; Anthony Comstock and, 243;
Diana installation, 231; expenses,
418n4; founding of, 21–22, 67, 82–84;
mayor's office and, 134; MSG II
prospectus, 90, 94–95, 127; opening
night, 169; profits and losses, 133–34,
185, 209, 248, 316–17, 320; purchases
original MSG site, 21–22; reorganization of, 316, 417n3; shareholders,
21–22, 90–91, 94–95, 104, 147–48, 158,
316–18, 417n3; stock split, 90; taxes,
316, 418n4, 418n12; White's membership in, 158
Madison Square Garden Corporation,
414n68
Madison Square Park, 2, 4, 27–41; city
planning and, 31, 32; Civil War and,
36–38; as desirable place to live, 33–34,
67–68, 83–84; land owners, 30–32,
69–70; opening of, 32; as social center
of the city, 36–38
Madison Square Presbyterian Church, 34
Madison Square Theatre, 38–39
Majestic (roof garden), 252–53
male friendships, 124, 371n41
male models, 160, 162, 199, 200, 271–72,
291, 392n5, 405n33, 405n38
Mamzelle Champagne (musical), 306, 309,
310
Mandolin Orchestra, 250
Manhattan Beach, 73
Manhattan Club, 363n55
Mannerist sculptors, 138, 202
Mansfield, Richard, 231–32

Marble Palace, 52
Marceau, Henri, 238, 336, 396n13
Marshall Field & Company, 265, 422n6
Martiny, Philip, 181, 260–61, 378n27,
401n25
Matriarchs, the, 385n28
Matt Morgan Art Pottery, 168
Maynard, George, 58
McAllister, Ward, 385n28
McCord, Frank R., 254
McDonnell, Charles E., 126
McKim, Annie Bigelow (first wife), 23, 60,
61, 113
McKim, Charles Follen: apprenticeships,
43–45, 120; architectural skills of, 44;
architectural styles preferred, 17;
birth of, 17; daughter of, 23, 60, 113,
369n2; death of White, 311; education of, 17, 43–45, 60; health of, 113;
homes of, 119; lends money to Saint-
Gaudens, 99; marriage and divorce
of Annie, 23, 60, 61, 113; marriage to
Julia, 113–14, 121; memberships of,
115; nicknames of, 23, 44, 60; personality of, 17–18, 43–44, 113, 114; resignation of, 45; sexuality of, 60, 116, 124;
social life of, 118–25, 283; stillborn
child of, 114; travels of, 44, 60–61,
258–59. *See also specific commission*
McKim, James Miller (father), 17
McKim, Julia Amory Appleton (second
wife), 113–14, 121
McKim, Mead & White: architectural
style of, 5, 18, 19, 228; client profile, 17,
19; draftsman, 114–15, 210; employees,
105–6, 111, 114, 115–18, *117*, 147, 210,
321, 377n7; formality at, 114; founding
of, 45; growth of, 114; legacy of, 5; location of, 15, 113, 209–10, 391n20; as MSG
II shareholder, 158; office atmosphere

of, 18–19; social life outside of, 113–25, 150–51, 369n19; success of, 17–18, 103, 114. *See also specific commission, partner, or employee*

McKim, Sarah Speakman (mother), 17

Mead, Larkin Goldsmith (father), 18

Mead, Larkin, Jr. (brother), 18, 260

Mead, Mary Jane Noyes (mother), 18

Mead, Olga Kilyeni (wife), 119

Mead, William Rutherford, *117*; apprenticeships of, 120; death of White, 311; homes of, 119; joins McKim's firm, 45; marriage of, 119; nicknames of, 18, 347n10; personality of, 18; Saint-Gaudens cartoon of, 18; sexuality of, 116; social life of, 118–25, 283. *See also specific commission*

Mercié, Marius-Jean-Antonin, 107–8, 145, 293

Mercury (sculpture), 108, *109*

Metamorphoses (Ovid), 137–38

Metropolitan Club, 46, 313

Metropolitan Museum of Art: Saint-Gaudens exhibition, 331; sculptures at, *102*, *109*, *201*, *295*, 406n59, 410n18, 412n41, 424n37; trustees and employees, 118, 303, 380n24; White and, 270

Metropolitan Opera, 168

Michelangelo, 145

Middle Eastern style, 190

Mildeberger, Margaret, 31

Millet, Francis, 58, 124, 259, 264, 265, 286, 402n49

Mills, Darius Ogden, 22

Mitchell, Maria Gouveneur, 375n29

models/modeling, 158–64, 195–204; background experience of, 162–63, 195–96; demand for, 162; detachment and, 160; hiring, 197–98; ideal qualities and characteristics, 196–97,

271–72; identity of, 162–63; income, 162, 197–98, 269; intelligence of, 197; male vs. female nudes, 160; physical strength required, 196–97; reputation of, 198; respect for, 197; studio romances, 198–99; typical day, 195–96, 198–200. *See also* Baird, Julia "Dudie"; Clark, Davida Johnson; female models; figure drawing; male models; Nesbit, Florence Mary "Evelyn"; nudes and nudity

Montgomery Ward & Company, 330–34, *331*, *333*, 422n6, 422n15

Moody, Dwight D., 73

Moore, June Clark, 389n32

Morals versus Art (Comstock), 238–39

Morel, Bartholomé, 229

Morgan, Edwin D., 143–44, 145

Morgan, J. Pierpont: Chicago World's Fair and, 264; Metropolitan Museum of Art and, 380n24; MSG II board and, 6, 21–22, 94–95, 317; MSG II opening, 170, 185; revivals sponsored by, 73; sale of MSG II, 317

Morgan, Matthew Sommerville, 168

Morgan Tomb Project, 143–44, 145

Morning Courier (New York), 16

morphine, 370n21

Morris, William, 224, 394n13

Morrissey, James, 171, 209, 231–32

Morton, Levi P., 173

Mullins, John F., 325

Mullins, William H., 215–18, 255, 274–75. *See also* W. H. Mullins Company

murals, 58, 120, 286

murders, 9–10, 39, 305–15, 323, 341, 370n21

Museum of the City of New York, 413n64

musicians, artists vs. laborers, 166

Music Mutual Protective Union, 158

National Academy of Art, 84–85, 198

National Academy of Design, 53, 84, 159, 323

National Gallery of Art, 304

National Horse Show Association of America, 21, 81, 82, 169, 184

National Sculpture Society, 323

Native New Yorkers Historical Association, 338

Nelson, David V., 333

Nesbit, Florence Mary "Evelyn," 9–10, 287, 306–15, 370n21, 417n53

Nesbit, Howard, 315

New-England Society of New-York, 185

New Jerusalem, The (Inness), 361n35

New Madison Square Garden Corporation, 324

New Mexico, 24, 106

New Olympic Theatre, 373n32

Newport, RI, 27–28, 60, 179–80, 181, 187, 375n29

Newport Casino, 27–28

New York Advertiser, 276

New York and Harlem Railroad Company, 21, 69–70, 80

New York and New Haven Line, 69–70

New York Board of Fire Commissioners, 167

New York Bureau of Buildings, 167

New York City Common Council, 32, 34, 37

New York Club, 46

New York Coaching Club, 66–67, 83, 358n2

New York Daily Tribune, 176, 238

New York Department of Buildings, 80

New-York Enquirer, 16

New York Evening World, 334

New York Excise Board, 177

New York Grand Lodge of the Masonic Order, 200

New York Herald: *Diana* sculpture (first), 242, 243; *Diana* sculpture (second), 270; election results, 7; *Farragut Monument*, 65; MSG II Concert & Assembly Hall, 187; MSG II opening, 176; MSG II roof garden, *251*, 252

New York Herald Building, 264

New York House of Refuge of the Society for the Reformation of Juvenile Delinquents, 30

New York Ladies Walking Club, 74

New York Life Insurance Company, 318–19, 321–28, 378n27, 418n12

New York Mercury, 238

New York Parks Department, 358n63

New York Record, 234

New York Society for the Suppression of Vice, 164, 238–39, 262

New York State Capitol, 60

New York Sun: *Diana* sculpture (first), *199*, 234, 241, 243, 262, 263–64, 329; *Diana* sculpture (second), 280; MSG II opening, 175, 177; on public safety, 80; Sun Building, 349n39; tower dedication, 237

New York Times: Barnum's Roman Hippodrome, 71, 73; on beam riveting, 131–32; *Diana* sculpture (first), 8, 234, 237, 240–41, 244, 286–87, 334; fire at Chicago World's Fair building, 286; Franconi's Hippodrome, 33; on gay lives, 118; Gilmore's Garden, 75–76; MSG I collapse, 80; MSG I safety, 82; MSG II closing, 341; MSG II commission, 47; MSG II Concert & Assembly Hall, 187; MSG II horse shows, 185; MSG II opening, 176, 177; MSG II planning, 20, 90–91; MSG II stockholder split, 90; MSG II tower lights, 210; owners of, 83; Saint-Gaudens's *Farragut Monument*, 65; White's murder, 314

New York University (NYU), 323–24, 326, 335–36

New York World, 216

Niblo's Garden, 158

Nicholas, H. I., 22

Nichols House Museum, 410n18

North Africa, 220–23

North Carolina, 151

Novedades, Las (New York), 191

Noyes, John H., 18

nudes and nudity: awards for artwork depicting, 54; *Diana* and, 8, 100, 137–42, 204, 234–35, 238–41, 261–64, 269–70, 336; figure drawing, 158–64, 195–204, 238–39, 291; male, 55, 160, 200, 263–64, 272, 291, 409n3; Saint-Gaudens's first sculpting attempts at, 200. *See also* models/modeling

Nymph of Fontainebleu (Cellini), 138

Nymphs and Satyr (Bouguereau), 39, 41, 353n42

obscenity/obscenity laws, 164, 238–41, 243, 261–64, 262, 270, 276, 337–38

Ochsendorf, John A., 191

Oelrichs, Herman, 22, 26, 90, 134

Olmstead, Frederick Law, 42–43, 256–57

"Oriental style," 219–29

Osborn, Francis P., 22

Osterkamp-Mead, 302–3

Otis, Elisha, 352n25

Otis Elevator Company, 97, 352n25

Ovid, 137–38

Paine, Robert Treat, 392n3

painters and paintings: Art Students League and, 159; Europe as inspiration, 53; Hoffman House and, 39–41, 40, 42, 353n42; MSG I building collapse and, 77–78; sculpting vs., 212; Tile Club, 58–59; White and, 42. *See also* figure drawing; *specific artist or painting*

Palais des Machines, 97–98, 132, 365n3

Palais du Trocadéro, 223–24, 393n9

Palmer, Erastus D., 141

Palmer, Mrs. Potter, 262

Pan-American Exposition (Buffalo), 334

Pan of Rohallion (MacMonnies), 410n11

pansexuality, 123

parades, 37, 67, 71, 192, 264

Paris Exposition Universelle International, 53, 97–98, 101, 105, 107, 132, 137, 223–24

Paris Hippodrome, 147

Parmigianino, 202, 204

Patriarchs' Ball, 47, 385n28

"Peace and War" (ballet), 157

Pearsal, T. W., 22

Peddle, Caroline, 410n18

pedestrian races, 74–76

Pelzer, Alfons, 216

Pelzer, Hubert, 216

Pennsylvania Museum of Art. *See* Philadelphia Museum of Art

permits and licenses, 134, 167–68, 177, 188, 318–19, 418n13

Perth Amboy Terra Cotta Company, 149, 377n13

Peters, Solomon, 30

Philadelphia, 336–38

Philadelphia Enquirer, 335

Philadelphia Museum of Art (Pennsylvania Museum of Art), 336–39, 339

Philadelphia Times, 170

Phoenix Iron Company, 130, 373n21, 373n23, 390n6

Piccirilli brothers, 202

Pilat, Ignaz, 37

plaster of Paris, 214, 259, 274, 392n9

Platt, Charles, 335–36

Players' Club, 46, 264, 283, 313

Plaza Hotel, 135

pleasure gardens, 72–73

plumbing systems, 167

Poitiers, Diane de, 138

Portland cement, 191, 387n48, 390n1

Post, George B., 19, 144, 149, 207, 257, 258, 259, 285–86

Post & McCord, 129, 231, 274

Post Building, 149

Powers, Hiram, 141

Pratt truss, 131

Pre-Raphaelite Brotherhood, 224

Presentation of the Virgin in the Temple (La Farge), 113

Price, Eli Kirk, 336

Princeton Art Museum, 414n68

Produce Exchange, 149

Progress Lighting the Way for Commerce (sculpture), 330–31, *331, 333–334*, 422n15

prostitution, 85, 122–23

Psyche of Naples (Saint-Gaudens), 200

Psychopathia Sexualis (Krafft-Ebing), 122

public banquets, 185–86

puddle iron, 97, 365n2

Puritan (Saint-Gaudens), 8, 92

Quartet Club, 119

Queen Anne style, 106

railroads, *69*, 69–70, 130, 131

Raimondi, Marcatonio, 229

Ranhofer, Charles, 46

rape, 308, 311, 321

Reclining Nude Figure of a Girl (Dewing), 269

Reeves, Samuel, 373n21

Remington, Frederic, 159

Reminiscences of Augustus Saint-Gaudens (Saint-Gaudens), 124

Renaissance Revival style, 5, 18, 105–6, *116*, 367nn14–15

Renwood, Minnie, 250, 251

reproductions. *See* art reductions and reproductions

Republican Party, 7, 37, 39, 173

Rhind, John Massey, 330, 331, 422n8

Richardson, Henry Hobson, 43, 44–45, 58, 91–92, 226, 368n19

Richardsonian Romanesque style, 44

riche, 19, 27

Rickard, George Lewis "Tex," *319*, 319–22, 324, 325, 326

"Riddle of Man-Manly Love" (Ulrichs), 122

Rinehart, Henry, 53–54

Ringling Brothers, 318, 324, 376n1

riots, 36, 165

Robert Louis Stevenson (Saint-Gaudens), 300

Robert R. Randall Monument (Staten Island), 92

Robertson, W. Graham, 272, 405n38

Rock Creek Cemetery, 92

Rodman, Mlle., 174

rolled wrought iron, 129–30

Roman Bronze Works, 301, 337, 424n36

Romanesque style, 106, 367n15

Roman Hippodrome (P. T. Barnum's), 70–73, *71*, 80

Romano, Giulio, 229

Roosevelt, Franklin D., 23

Roosevelt, James, 23

Roosevelt, J. Roosevelt, 66

Roosevelt, Teddy, 34, 47

Rosendale cement, 205, 390n1

round-arched style, 106, 367n15

Rounsevelle, Phillip, 396n13

Royal Meteorological Society, 206

Ruiz, Hernán, 222

Rundbogenstil style, 106, 367n15

Running Cupid with His Bow (MacMonnies), 298

Ruskin, John, 224

Russell, Lillian, 192, 274

Ryder, Albert Pinkham, 119

Saarinen, Aline, 116

Sailors' Snug Harbor (Staten Island), 92

Saint Gaudens, Andrew (brother), 52, 55

Saint-Gaudens, Augusta "Gussie" Homer
   (wife): as artist, 56; children of, 63;
   death of, 301–2; health of, 56, 57, 144; as
   inspiration for *Diana*, 9, 101; marriage
   to Augustus, 56–57, 59; personality of,
   56; physical characteristics of, 51, 56,
   57; reproduction rights of, 301; travels
   of, 101

Saint-Gaudens, Augustus, 50–65; apprenticeships of, 52–53, 123; arrest of, 56;
   artistic goals, 53–54; awards received,
   54; bas-reliefs, 24; birth and childhood
   of, 51–53; copyright of works, 295, 301,
   323, 411n19; death of, 300–301; death
   of White, 311–12; early commissions
   of, 8, 55–56, 57, 58; early romances of,
   56, 357n35; education of, 52–56, 84, 142,
   200; on Edward VII (king), 35; emigration of to US, 52; exhibitions of work,
   299, 331, 332; finances of, 57, 99, 145,
   294; in France, 53–55, 59, 60–64, 98–103,
   123, 137–38, 200, 296–97, 300; health of,
   56, 297, 300–301, 311; homes of, 119, 158,
   231, 265, 370n26; hyphenation of name,
   355n1; inspirations of, 8, 64, 93–94;
   in Italy, 9, 55–56, 61–63, 84, 138–41,
   143, 200, 298, 356n33, 357n35; mistress
   of (*see* Clark, Davida Johnson); in
   New Mexico, 24, 106; nicknames,
   63, 161; obscenity laws and, 163–64;
   personality of, 24, 50–51, 56, 213–14;
   physical characteristics of, 50–51, *51*,
   355nn5–6; reductions and reproductions of artwork, 291–304, 323, 325, 335,
   337, 409n5, 410n18; relationship with
   White, 10, 50–51, 57–59, 63; reputation
   of, 296; sexuality of, 10, 116–18, 121,
   122–25; social life of, 9, 116–25, 283;
   studio (Cornish, NH), 300–302, *303*,
   304, 322–23, 366n10, 370n26; studio
   (New York), 24, 50, 57, 62, 64, 91–92, 98,
   119, 144–45, 159, 195–96, 212–18, 267–80,
   365n6; studio (Paris), 54–55, 59, 60–61,
   296–97; studio (Rome), 9, 55–56, 57,
   356n33; writings of, 124. *See also specific
   commission*

Saint Gaudens, Bernard (father), 51–52,
   53, 84

Saint-Gaudens, Homer (son), 124, 127, 144,
   202, 271, 297, 304, 322–23

Saint-Gaudens, Louis (brother). *See* St.
   Gaudens, Louis (brother)

Saint Gaudens, Mary McGinness
   (mother), 51–52

Saint-Gaudens National Historical
   Park (Cornish, NH), 272, 322–23, 335;
   artwork at, *51, 57, 142, 143, 161, 217, 275,
   279, 302, 303, 304*

Saint George (Donatello), 64

Saint Paul the Apostle Catholic Church,
   101

Saint Stephen Episcopal Church, 375n29

Salon de la Société Nationale des Artistes Français, 98

Salt Lake Herald, 238

Samuel French & Son, 148

Sankey, Ira D., 73

Santa Maria de la Sede (Spain), 49

Sargent, John Singer, 9, 124, 150, 157, 226, 272

Satan's Circus, 5

Schermerhorn, William C., 28

Schmidt, Richard E., 330

Schoelkopf, Robert, 410n18

sculpting process, 9, 212–18, 267–80, 293, 392n3, 392n9, 405n26. *See also* art reductions and reproductions; female models; male models; models/ modeling

Seagrist, Francis W., Jr., 95–96

Seidl, Anton, 177–78

Seventh Regimental Armory, 224, 225

Seville, Spain. *See* Giralda bell tower (Spain)

Sewer Club, 121, 187, 370n28

sexuality, 116–25; bisexuality, 117–18; "fairie" defined, 122–23; homosexuality, 60, 116–17, 122–23, 315; male friendships, 124, 371n41; McKim's, 60, 116, 124; Mead's, 116; pansexuality, 123; *Psychopathia Sexualis* (Krafft-Ebing), 122; Saint-Gaudens's, 10, 116–18, 121, 122–25; Thaw's, 313–15; Wells's, 116, 119, 121, 122; White's, 10, 116–18, 119, 121–25, 267, 313–15

Shaw Memorial (Saint-Gaudens), 91–92, 195

Sherman, William Tecumseh, 173, 176

Sherman Monument (Saint-Gaudens), 98, 296, 301, 392n3

Sherry's restaurant, 186, 282

Shirlaw, Walter, 286

Shook, Sheridan, 72–73

Silence (Saint-Gaudens), 200

skeleton steel framing, 206, 390n6

skyscrapers, 36, 207, 317, 318, 330

Smith, Al, 319

Smith, Ann Maria, 375n29

Smith, James Clinch, 310

Smith, John Lawrence, 23

Smith, Sarah Nicoll Clinch, 23

Smith & Prodgers construction, 80

Smithsonian American Art Museum, 291

smuggling, 165–66

Society of American Artists, 84–85

Society of the Four Arts Philip Hulitar Sculpture Garden, 414n68

Spanish style, 3, 49, 93, 93–94, 106, 189–90, 219–29, 221, 393n9

Spirit of Progress (Conradi), 422n15

Springfield, MA, 8, 92

stamped statuary, 215–16

Standing Cupid (MacMonnies), 298

Standing Lincoln (Saint-Gaudens), 8, 92

Starr, Ethel (Polly) Thayer, 410n18

Staten Island, 92

Statue of Liberty, 206, 237

steel skeleton framing, 206, 390n6

Sterling and Francine Clark Art Institute, 353n42

Stevens, Paran, 351n20

Stevenson, Robert Louis, 124

Stewart, A. T. (Alexander Turney), 25–26, 52, 186, 349n39, 349n41, 353n37, 375n18

Stewart, Cornelia Mitchell Clinch, 25, 349n41

Stewart, David, 92

St. Gaudens, Louis (brother): *Angel of Purity* project, 375n29; as apprentice to Augustus, 56, 297, 299; birth of, 52; Boston Public Library project, 120;

bronze eagle, 378n27; club member-
ships, 120, 121; *Diana* sculpture (first),
213; *Diana* sculpture (second), 273, 297,
301; *Farragut Monument*, 61, 63, 92, 200,
358n62; in France, 61, 63; homes of, 119,
120, 423n30; in Italy, 56; namesake, 125
Stillman, James, 22
Stoddard, William O., 36
Stokes, Edward S. "Ned," 39–40, 353n42
Stokes, James, 67
Story, William Wetmore, 53–54, 55–56
Strauss, Eduard, 158, 166, 173–74, 175,
176–78
strikes, 165
Stuart, Robert Leighton, 391n20
Sturgis, Russell, 120
Sullivan, John L., 21, 83, 219
Sun Building, 349n39
supper parties, 47

Tate, James, 338
Tenderloin district, 121, 123
Terrace Garden, 252–53
terra cotta: "architectural," 149; cost of,
150; critiques of, 156, 176; Davida head
made from, 202, 389n33; as decorative
skin, 155–56; dismantling of, 323; history of ornamental, 148–49; Pompeian,
149, 247; as protective sheathing, 206,
327; tiles, 153, 190–91; White's study
of, 105
Terris, Sid, 325
"Tex's Rangers" (hockey team), 324
Thaw, Harry Kendall, 306–7, 308–15,
370n21
Thierry (friend), 124
Thompson, Alfred, 157
Thompson, William, 31, 32
Thorne, Charles H., 330

Thorne, George R., 330
Tiffany, Louis Comfort, 9, 19, 106, 224–25,
264
Tiffany & Co., 52, 53, 95, 299, 301
Tiffany Studios, 337
Tile Club, 58–59
Tileston, William M., 74, 79
timbrel vaulting, 189–91
Times Square, 73
Tipaldi Brothers, 250
"To *Diana* off the Tower" (Henderson), 255
Town Topics (gossip paper), 177, 313
Traps for the Young (Comstock), 238–39
Trinity Church (Boston), 6, 8, 34, 45, 58,
59, 226
Trinity Church (New York), 34
Triumvirate (Broderick), 117
Trumble, Alfred, 242, 259
truss systems, 130–33, 373n26
Tuckerman, Lucius, 118
Tufts, Otis, 35–36, 352n25
Turf Club, 363n55
Turner, C. Y., 402n49
Turner, T. G., 402n49
Twain, Mark, 6
Twatchman, John, 58

Ulrichs, Karl Heinrich, 122
Union Depot, 69, 69–70
University Club, 84, 363n55
Uruburu, Paula, 315
US Congress Immigration Investigating
Committee, 166
US Postal Service, 316
US Treasury Department, 165–66

Velasquez, 226
van der Bent, Teunis, 111

Vanderbilt, Cornelius, 21, 70, 73–74, 81, 181, 219

Vanderbilt, George B., 151

Vanderbilt, William Henry "Billy," 73–74, 76, 80–81

"Vanderbilt Row," 27

Vanity Fair, 313

Van Rensselaer, Mariana Griswold, 156, 205, 228, 271

vaulting, 189–91

Vázquez, Juan Bautista, 229

Vedder, Elihu, 58, 77

ventilation systems, 184–85, 208

Venus de' Medici (Saint-Gaudens), 200

Victory Monument (Saint-Gaudens), 301

Villard Houses, 18, 106

Vogan, A. S., 406n59

Wagner, Richard, 181

Walker Bill, 319

walking competitions, 74–76

Walthausen, John, 273, 274–75, 291

Wanamaker's store, 349n40

Ward, John Quincy Adams, 90, 242

Ware, William R., 18–19

Warren, Whitney, 283

Washington Square Arch, 5, 103, 248

W. A. Underwood, 247

weather, building for, 206

weather vanes, history and positioning of, 107

Weir, J. Alden, 58, 286

Welch, Gloninger & Maxwell, 134

Wells, Joseph Morrill: death of, 134–35, 147; as draftsman, 105–6, 111, 114, 115, 120, 121, 147, 149, 370n26, 377n7; nicknames, 105; sexuality of, 116, 119, 121, 122

Westminster Kennel Bench Show of Dogs, 73, 74, 91

Weston, Edward Payson, 74

Wharton, Edith, 293

Wharton, Teddy, 34

Wharton, William F., 22

Wheeler, Candace, 224

White, Alexina Black Mease (mother), 16, 89

White, Elizabeth "Bessie" Smith (wife): death of Stanford, 311; as hostess, 281; inheritance of, 25–26, 158, 186–87; marriage of, 23–24, 48, 120, 145, 224; portrait of, 182, 384n9; travels of, 151; Washington Square Arch and, 103

White, Lawrence Grant (son), 89, 117, 122, 309, 322–23, 326, 334, 409n7

White, Richard Grant (father), 16, 42, 63

White, Richard Grant (son), 25

White, Richard Mansfield (brother), 16

White, Stanford: apprenticeships, 43–45, 66; architectural skills of, 17, 44; architectural styles preferred, 17; art collection of, 25, 84–85, 149, 226, 291, 300, 326, 404n21, 416n38; birth of, 15, 16; cartoon depiction of, *312*; in Constantinople (Istanbul), 48, 224; creative ability of, 42; death of, 9–10, 84–85, 291, 305–15, 323, 326, 341, 370n21, 404n21; deceased children, 25; drug use and, 119–20, 370n21; early romances of, 23, 348n25; education of, 15–16, 42–43; finances of, 85, 326, 404n21; in Florida, 25; in France, 60–63, 97–103, 104–5, 111, 223–24; health of, 151, 244–45, 248, 264, 310–11; hideaways of, 10, 38, 119, 187–88, 281, 287, 307, 325; homes of, 23, 25, 119, 248–49, 291–93; in Italy, 62, 102, 111; joins McKim's firm, 45; in London,

62–63, 90, 102; marriage of, 23–26, 48, 120, 145, 224; memberships of, 115; MSG board membership, 158; Nesbit and, 9–10, 287, 305–15, 370n21; in New Mexico, 24, 106; nicknames, 14, 16, 63, 115, 121; in North Carolina, 151; papers of, 117; personality of, 13–15, 18–19, 24, 42, 113, 114–15, 120; physical character-istics of, 13–15, *14*, 347n3; privacy of, 249; relationship with Saint-Gaudens, 10, 50–51, 57–59, 63; sexuality of, 10, 116–18, 119, 121–25, 267, 313–15; social life of, 9–10, 34–36, 45–46, 118–25, 282–83, 287; in Spain, 226–27; theater and, 38; travels (unspecified), 89–90, 95, 108, 113, 145, 255; use of color, 26, 171–72; wardrobe of, 26; work style, 18–19, 22–23, 113, 114–15, 120, 151; writ-ings about, 15, 116–18. *See also specific commission*

White Captive (Palmer), 141

White Cross Society, 239–41

Whitney, Payne, 413n50

W. H. Mullins Company, 215–18, 230, 231, 255, 262–63, 274–76, 330–33, 340–41

Wildey, Netta, 268

Willard, Walter, 120

Willets, Annie, 361n34

Williams, Jesse, 174

Williams Foundry, 412n38

Winckelmann, Johann, 140, 201, 203

wind bracing, 206, 390n6

Wolfe, John, 39

Woman's Christian Temperance Union, 238, 262, 338

women: as artists, 199; athletics and, 91, 100, 137; as female art students, 159–64. *See also* female models

Woodward, James E., 21

Woodward, James T., 22

Work, Frank, 67

World's Columbian Exposition. *See* Chi-cago World's Fair

Worth, William Jenkins, 45–46, 354n15

wrought-iron beams, 36, 97–98, 129, 132, 153

Young Faun with Heron (MacMonnies), 410n11

Youngstown Pressed Steel Company, 341

Youth Protection Committee, 337–38

Suzanne Hinman holds a PhD in American art history and has been a curator, professor, museum director, and art model. She frequently speaks on Gilded Age art and architecture and has published scholarly articles on American art as well as presented papers at national conferences.

Her interest in American art and architecture stems from her academic background, with a BA in art history from UCLA, an MA in anthropology from UC Berkeley, and a PhD in art history from the University of New Mexico. After ten years of teaching at UNM and in the California State University system, she opened a gallery in Santa Fe, then later became director of galleries at the Savannah College of Art and Design, the world's largest art school. Her interest in the artists and architects of the American Gilded Age shifted to New York City and the Cornish Art Colony in New Hampshire when she became associate director of the Hood Museum of Art at Dartmouth College. The author continues to reside near Cornish as an independent scholar.